THE ESSENTIAL HISTORY OF RUGBY UNION

ENGLAND

FOREWORD BY BILL BEAUMONT

IAN MALIN AND JOHN GRIFFITHS

WH S

First published in 2003
by Headline Book Publishing
for WHSmith, Greenbridge Road, Swindon SN3 3LD

10 9 8 7 6 5 4 3 2 1

ISBN 0 7553 1271 6

Design by designsection, Frome, Somerset
Editor Julian Flanders
Designers Craig Stevens and Kathie Wilson
Photographs supplied by Colorsport pages 4, 75-6, 82, 84-7, 89, 90, 92, 93-4, 97, 99-100, 102, 107, 109, 111-12, 116, 119, 124, 126, 130, 133, 135, 138, 142, 144, 147, 149, 150-51, 153, 155, 157-59, 163-64, 166, 168-69, 174, 177 & 184; EMPICS pages 27, 31, 43, 45, 50, 53, 57, 60, 61t & b, 63-4, 66, 71, 74, 78, 80, 88, 98, 105, 114, 118, 173, 176, 178, 183, 185 (both), 236, 259, 274, 286, 288, 294, 300, 311, 316 & 321;
John Griffiths pages 8, 17-20, 22, 26, 34, 36, 40, 72, 192, 194 (all), 200 & 209;
Twickenham Museum and Library pages 9, 11, 38, 41, 46 & 55
The P.G. Wodehouse poem 'The Great Day' on page 35
is reproduced courtesy of Random House/A.P. Watt

The authors would like to thank the staff at the Twickenham Museum and Library for their help in researching this book. The reference works of Barry Bowker, Terry Godwin, Rev Frank Marshall, Raymond Maule and Owen Owen have proved invaluable in the compilation of the statistics. Thanks also to Tim Auty for assistance with the collation of the older photographs

Printed and bound in Great Britain by Clays Ltd, St Ives PLC, Bungay, Suffolk

HEADLINE BOOK PUBLISHING
A division of Hodder Headline
338 Euston Road
London NW1 3BH

www.headline.co.uk
www.hodderheadline.com

Contents

Foreword
By Bill Beaumont

Like any other supporter of England I will always remember the first time I saw a live international. It was the Calcutta Cup match at Murrayfield in 1964 and I went on that Edinburgh trip with the school. For a 12-year-old boy it was all fantastically exciting. The players I remember were Malcolm Phillips, who was later to be a colleague on the International Board, and the Liverpool fly-half Tom Brophy, while Scotland had a couple of outstanding half-backs in Hastie and Chisholm and a very effective back-row forward in Jim Telfer. I never thought then that I would be returning to Murrayfield 16 years later for a game that was to be the defining moment in my rugby life, the Grand Slam win in 1980. In 1964 my big ambition was to be goalkeeper for Blackburn Rovers.

Until then, my sightings of the England rugby union team had been confined, like most people's, to occasional flickering images on a black and white television screen. Television managed to capture Richard Sharp, one of the great English fly-halves, in action and I recall his contribution to England's championship win in 1963 and the Calcutta Cup match a couple of years later when Andy Hancock scored a try from inside his own 25, when it seemed half of Scotland was left trailing in his wake.

Reading this history of the England team I'm reminded that in the era I grew up, the 1960s and 70s, the team often went through flat periods punctuated by the occasional highs. In 1980 we carried a lot of baggage in to the championship. England had not won a Grand Slam for 23 years and I just remember the overwhelming feeling of relief that we had exorcised our demons at last. We knew we had the best team in Europe at the time but sometimes being the best on paper and the best on the pitch are two different things. I remember 15 March 1980 as if it was yesterday, those early tries by John Carleton and Mike Slemen, and the silky running skills of Clive Woodward are still vivid memories. It's funny, although the Grand Slam is a holy grail in rugby and so difficult to achieve, there was no tangible reward. In my day there was not even a trophy for winning the Five Nations. For me the equivalent of a medal is the shirt I wore that day. Alan Tomes, the Scotland lock, asked me to swap it in the tunnel afterwards but I just couldn't part with it. I still have it at home and I still wouldn't be without it.

But my life changed after that day. From being just another captain of a team in a minority sport, I became a recognised public figure, spoken of in the same sentence as people like George Best. That took some getting used to. Of course, Will Carling a decade later became a celebrity sportsman in quite another league from me. Carling's team were a great side and, although their achievements flattered them a bit, as Wales and France were declining forces, he led them to three Grand Slams. The only question-mark against them was that they fell short against the southern hemisphere's best teams.

In the 21st century Clive Woodward has constructed a team that can compete with the best in the world. Comparing it with the teams I led is impossible as the game has changed beyond recognition. But what is beyond dispute is that two players in the first England team I featured in, David Duckham and John Pullin, would have been great in any era. I also suspect that Clive Woodward, my old colleague in that 1980 side, would have made sure that Prince Obolensky would have lasted more than one season. The Prince and Jason Robinson together in the same England side would have kept any opposition defence on their toes.

Bill Beaumont

Chapter One: 1871-99
Eminent Victorians

On 22 March 2003 England entertained Scotland at Twickenham. A crowd of 75,000 watched the home side chalk up a 21st successive victory at a ground that had become something of a fortress and a live terrestrial television audience of almost five million viewers saw Martin Johnson's team retain the Calcutta Cup with an emphatic 40-9 victory.

England's fully professionalised squad had prepared with a set of specialised coaches at a swish country club set in 123 acres of Surrey countryside and with its own private rugby pitch and many of them – Johnson, Jonny Wilkinson, Lawrence Dallaglio and Jason Robinson – were recognised international sporting superstars. Every move each of the 20 England players who took to the field made against Scotland that day would be filmed for computer analysis. The elite modern-day players, with their six-figure salaries, live in enclosed worlds of strict dieting, training and conditioning. They are worlds apart from the traditional image of beer-drinking rugby hearties.

How different to 132 years earlier when England and Scotland met for the first time in rugby union's first international. On 27 March 1871, just a few hours before the commune of Paris was proclaimed, two 20-a-side teams met at Raeburn Place, the home of Edinburgh Academicals. A year earlier two association football teams had also met in a Scotland-England international but England's FA had insisted on picking the sides. It seems the only qualification for the Scotland team had been a passing interest in whisky and the incensed Scots insisted that the first rugby international should be on their terms. England's players, 14 from London and three each from Manchester and Liverpool, therefore travelled north in third-class railway carriages, on bare-board seats, and arrived bleary-eyed at around dawn of the Monday morning of the match.

Everything, it appeared, was loaded against the English. The Raeburn Place pitch was small by English standards, some 120 yards long by 55 yards wide, and the umpire H.H. Almond, later a celebrated headmaster of Loretto School, was soon involved in rugby union's first controversy.

The Rugby Football Union, founded two months earlier, had adopted en bloc most of the laws of Rugby School; the Scots used laws adapted since 1868 in what was called the *Green Book*. Both Scottish tries in their win, by one goal and a try to a goal, were disputed, particularly one where their half-back Arthur was judged to have knocked the ball on, but not 'deliberately'. The Rugby Football Union later changed the law to omit the word 'deliberately'. During the match the England captain, the Blackheath forward Frederick Stokes, argued about the merits of the knocked-on try with Mr Almond. Almond, though, stood his ground and the first ever official of an international rugby union match was later to write in a famous dictum: 'When an umpire is in doubt, I think he is justified in deciding against the side which makes the most noise. They are probably in the wrong.' The referee was always right, then, and not for the last time a much-fancied England team was sent packing 't'ae think again'.

The England XX, 1871: Standing: J. E. Bentley, A.S. Gibson, F. Tobin, D.P. Turner, F. Stokes (captain), J.H. Clayton, R.R. Osborne, H.J.C. Turner. Middle row: J.H. Luscombe, R.H. Birkett, J.F. Green. Sitting: A.StG. Hamersley, W. MacLaren, C.W. Sherrard, A. Lyon, C.A. Crompton. Front: A. Davenport, A.G. Guillemard, J.M. Dugdale, B.H. Burns.

For the record, England's first international try was scored by Reginald Birkett, the father of John Birkett, the Harlequin who would later lead England five times just before the First World War. Some 4,000 supporters had watched the match on a crisp, sunny afternoon and international rugby union had begun. But, as the controversy showed, the laws urgently needed to be standardised and already there was disquiet about the dangers in this code of football. In the previous autumn correspondence had begun in

The Times after a surgeon had noted the growing amount of cases of young men being treated for broken bones after games of rugger. The debate led to the setting up of the Rugby Football Union to codify the laws of this game that had originated at Rugby School 47 years earlier. The injuries were mainly the result of 'hacking' or kicking the ball on the ground, rather than today when thumping tackles are the chief concern.

Scots Return

But whatever the ill-feeling from that first international, it was not too sour to prevent the Scottish clubs from later that year accepting an invitation to a return fixture at Kennington Oval. England's first four matches were all to be against Scotland, two won and one drawn until, looking across the Irish Sea for new opponents, they found another international team with which to grapple.

When Ireland visited the Oval on 15 February 1875 England won emphatically by a goal, a drop goal and a try to nil. But the dice were loaded as much in the favour of England as they had been for Scotland four years earlier. The day was enveloped in a London fog and it was a miserable

England meet Scotland in 1872. England's home matches took place at the Oval until 1879.

international baptism for the Irish. The pitch was a quagmire and the visiting team was made up of players from North and South unions who had never seen each other before, let alone worked out tactics to neutralise the threat from the men in white.

A New Fixture

Across the Irish Sea, the physicality of the new game had great appeal and it developed quickly. But, just as the Scots had their *Green Book*, the laws the Irish were developing were still in their experimental stages. At Trinity College in 1868 the early Irish laws had been passed and the versions of rugby known as Jesuit Rules or Catholic College Rules were developed at the Jesuit colleges of Belvedere and Clongowes Wood.

The heavy Oval defeat did not deter the Irish from offering England a return fixture the following year at Leinster Cricket Ground at Rathmines. Ireland were led for the first time by an Ulsterman, Dick Bell, and for the first time they wore the shamrock as a crest, on their white jerseys. To add to the confusion for the spectators of this new game, England also wore white. A heavy frost in the week leading up to the fixture on 13 December had put the match in doubt but a late thaw enabled the game to be played. Thousands turned up but, oddly, with admission only one shilling and nothing for ladies, the gate receipts amounted to a modest £22 and 9 shillings. There were either a lot of women in the crowd or many of the paying customers had refused to part with their money before they witnessed this new spectacle.

Ireland, with 12 survivors from the Oval defeat, were beaten by a goal and a try to nil, but England (who fielded another pair of brothers, the Grahams, forwards from the Wimbledon Hornets club) were met with some powerful tackling. Such an improvement in the opposition ensured the new fixture was now well and truly established. And, there was another odd postscript to the match. In the days before fixture secretaries, someone had got their wires crossed because England's first trip to Ireland was on the same day as the Varsity match. The first 15-a-side game between Oxford and Cambridge was creating a little bit of history in England and depriving the visitors of a large chunk of their talented players.

It was to be another six years, though, before Ireland prevented England's winning run. At Lansdowne Road in 1882 the teams each scored two tries in their drawn encounter, but controversy again reared its head. The Irish back Robert McLean appeared to have kicked the winning goal but the umpire Dr Nugent disallowed the kick. The Irish writer Jacques McCarthy was livid:

'Without any possibility of contradiction, Ireland won by a goal and a try to two tries but the official result was a draw. McLean kicked a goal for Ireland off a try by Taylor but Nugent decided it was no goal.' McCarthy even slyly remarked that one of England's scorers, Blackheath's Wilfred Bolton, was really Irish.

Ireland were worthy opponents by now, but it was the England-Scotland encounter that was to become the leading international rugby fixture of this bewhiskered Victorian era.

The Calcutta Cup

The England-Scotland fixture has become known as the Calcutta Cup match and again Rugby School was at the forefront of its inception. A group of old boys from the school were resident in the Indian city and tried to set up a rugby club there. The locals were not, however, too keen on this rumbustious new game, especially as the grounds in India tended to be rock-hard and the early missionaries could not convert them to its charms. The Calcutta club had some early fixtures with the 3rd Buffs but when that regiment left in 1876 the fixtures dried up. The club, though, had money in the bank which its founder and captain G.A.J. Rothney rather unselfishly persuaded the members to spend on a trophy which celebrated the workmanship of Indian craftsmen and would keep alive the memories of doomed attempts to spread the rugby gospel in Calcutta.

This trophy was presented to the Rugby Football Union and in 1878 the RFU announced the annual challenge between the English and Scots who would play for the cup. It is of beaten silver, stands 18 inches high, has snakes for handles and a miniature elephant on its lid. And those Indian craftsmen did not need raw materials. They took the rupees from the club and melted them down. The Calcutta Cup has taken a battering at the hands of players over the years and England, when the cup is in their possession, insist on keeping it in the museum at Twickenham.

In 1879 England and Scotland played their first international for the Calcutta Cup at Raeburn Place. For the fourth time in only eight years the sides drew the

Since 1878 the Calcutta Cup has been fought for by England and Scotland.

match, the Scots scoring a drop goal, the English a try which was converted by Frederick Stokes's brother, Lennard. Penalties could not be kicked at goal until 1892 and in those days a drop goal was worth as much as a converted try. In a strong, chilly March wind a crowd of 8,000 turned out to watch what was fast becoming a close rivalry and the appeal of international rugby was slowly growing.

The game and its laws were evolving fast to keep up with this spectator appeal. Though a players' rather than fans' game, even the early rugby law-makers and administrators realised they needed to spread its appeal. With the Oxford-Cambridge game being reduced from 20-a-side to 15-a-side, the Rugby Football Union decided in 1877 to follow suit. On 5 February against Ireland at the Oval, England fielded its first XV. Instead of 13 or 14 forwards, there were nine or ten. England, led by Liverpool's Edward Kewley, adapted to the new 15-man game quickly, selecting a more lightweight, mobile pack. They scored four tries, two of them converted, without reply.

'Monkey' to the Fore

Kewley was one of England's early Victorian pioneers and northern clubs such as Liverpool had become an important crucible for emerging talent. England now had innovative, dashing sportsmen with talent to burn. In 1877 that first 15-a-side international saw England score their first try through a three-quarter, Albert 'Monkey' Hornby, an Old Harrovian who played for Preston Grasshoppers. Hornby, playing his first international a week before his 30th birthday, may have been something of a late developer but he was a natural sportsman, becoming the first man to captain England at rugby and cricket. 'Monkey' was also top banana at boxing, shooting and riding; the epitome of the Victorian Corinthian sportsman. Typically, he refused to play in the 1883 international against Scotland because it coincided with his plans to go shooting that weekend. He was never selected again. But this snub didn't prevent him from becoming an RFU member and, apparently, a very strict referee.

A year after Hornby's debut there was another notable first appearance in the Scotland fixture by Richmond's Edward Temple Gurdon. It was a scoreless draw but this seemed to suit the Old Haileyburian. Temple Gurdon, who went on to establish a long-standing record of 16 caps, developed a speciality of 'working' the ball with his feet and keeping it in the scrum. Opponents would break off the scrum, often probably in sheer boredom, and Temple Gurdon, a sort of early version of Dean Richards, would emerge with it and hack it on past a bemused defence.

England's pioneers were looking for new frontiers to cross and, inevitably, Wales were soon to join Scotland and Ireland in competition and 'Triple Crown' entered the sporting lexicon. Wales had given a good account of themselves against English county opposition and they were awarded an international fixture on a chill day in February 1881. This was the first international at Blackheath, but the only one staged at Richardson's Field, which was soon sold off. The teams had changed at the, aptly named, Princess of Wales pub on Blackheath and walked the half mile to the ground. The game, however, was an unmitigated disaster for the new rugby nation. England, led by Lennard Stokes on his own club ground, won by seven goals, a drop goal and six tries to nil. Blackheath forward George Burton was equally at home, running in four tries. Amazingly, that would remain an international record for a forward for 97 years.

In Wales there was an outcry over the humiliation. The Wales team had been chosen by Richard Mullock and became known in Wales, disparagingly, as 'Mullock's Private Army' and there were claims that it was unrepresentative of the real growing strength of Welsh rugby. It was led by the Australian-born James Bevan, who played in four Varsity matches, and 10 of the Wales side never played for the country again. The traumatic defeat, quite the most overwhelming international reverse in the infant international era, caused the clubs to come together and led to the formation of the Welsh Rugby Union the following month.

Wales were to wait 22 months for a return fixture in Swansea, the first home international for the fledgling nation. Once again they were overpowered by the England team led by Edward Temple Gurdon and containing an Australian back, the Oxford student Gregory Wade, who ran in three tries on his debut. After helping to win all eight of his adopted nation's matches Wade, a barrister and politician, returned home to become premier of New South Wales. His British and Irish opponents were just relieved to see the back of him.

A Passing Game

England were now developing a distinctive style of play, a passing game instigated by the Oxford forward Harry Vassall. Rugby was no longer about ferocious forward rushes. A newspaper report of 1887 summed it up: 'If one comes on to the field before play has commenced, the men waiting for the game are not taking drop-kick practice, or dribbling the ball, as was their wont before the rage for passing came in, but are now seen playing at catch-ball and slinging the ball from hand to hand, not high in the air, but at about the level of the hands from the ground.'

England discovered that it was easier to control this awkward-shaped oval ball when it was in the hand. Rugby union began to look more like the modern game. Heeling from the scrum had been made legal and Vassall realised that this quick ball could be exploited. He encouraged the tactic and made his half-backs, who played to the right and left of the scrum, pass the ball off the ground to their three-quarters in one sweeping movement. Nobody in this era was more adept at exploiting the new time and space than Vassall's university friend Wade and Vassall had used his growing influence to persuade the selectors to pick Wade for the Wales game. For the first time England were playing with three three-quarters instead of two.

Vassall wrote of Wade: 'He was prodigiously strong, very fast, a first-rate swerver and he had the shove-off you did not forget in a hurry.' When Wade died in 1922 one obituary declared that he was 'the best three-quarter we ever had in England.' In the 1880s, though, Wade had a rival in the Blackheath three-quarter Wilfred 'Baby' Bolton. Both scored fine tries in another handsome 1883 defeat of the Irish at Whalley Range in Manchester, which had staged its first international game in 1880.

The Irish, once again, were finding the going tough when they left their own shores. The accounts at the Irish AGM were said to be unintelligible and as a result no travelling expenses were allowed for the journey across the Irish Sea. If that wasn't enough to sour the players' mood as they crossed the water, the crossing was so rough that one of the Irish players, Robert Hughes, had to be carried off the boat to the team's hotel. He only played for a few minutes and a 14-strong team were no match for England.

The First Triple Crown

A month later at Raeburn Place, England beat Scotland by two tries to one. England had become the first holders of the mythical Triple Crown and the first holders of what eventually evolved into the Six Nations Championship. They repeated the feat the following year and did not lose a match until 1887 when Ireland finally beat them with a rousing display in Dublin. England's first golden era had ended and the Irish were ecstatic. They were now taking the game seriously. One of their forwards, John Macauley, even got married in order to obtain leave to play. One Irish journalist said that Macauley's action was 'truly heroic and his wife fully endorses the enthusiasm'. For England, the honeymoon was over as the home countries married skill and steel to provide real opposition.

Controversy was still never too far away. In 1884 England had left Whalley Range for the new home at Rectory Field and 8,000 spectators watched the Calcutta Cup match on a cold, sunny March day. The Scottish forwards outplayed the home pack but still lost the match when England scored a disputed try through the Oxford forward Richard Kindersley. The Scots claimed that there had been a knock-on by their side moments earlier and a scrum should have been awarded as these were the days before the advantage law. A dispute delayed play for 10 minutes and, after much scratching of heads, the try was awarded and Bolton converted.

The fallout from the dispute lasted for years; the Rugby Football Union cancelled the fixture the following year and the Scots did not recognise the result until 1886. The Scots finally, and reluctantly, accepted the result, but did not accept the RFU's right to lay down the law. Matters were coming to a head. When a committee, the International Board, was set up to discuss disputes and policies, the miffed Rugby Football Union refused to attend.

50 Greatest Players

LENNARD STOKES Full-back/Three-quarter

Club: Blackheath

Debut: v Ireland, 15 February 1875

No. of Caps: 12 **No. of Points:** 17 conversions and 2 drop goals (before scoring by points was introduced)

The first England rugby superstar was the Blackheath utility back Lennard Stokes. His international career began in 1875 when 20-a-side was the order of the day and by the time it ended six years later, teams of 15 had become firmly established. Stokes was a household name in either formation.

He used his acceleration and dodging powers to good effect in attack and was described as the longest drop-kicker in the Home Unions. Before scoring by points was introduced in the late 1880s, matches were decided on the majority of goals (converted tries or drop goals) scored. Stokes's match-winning potential was so great that in his 12-match career the national side lost only once and his 17 conversions stood for more than a century as the England career record until overtaken by Jonathan Webb.

Arthur Guillemard, an early historian of the English game, described Stokes as the outstanding back of the late 19th century: 'It is not too much to say that at this post his equal, either in science or play, has never been seen from the date of the foundation of the Union,' he wrote in 1892.

Stokes was appointed captain in 1880 and in his five matches in charge never led a losing side. 'He enjoyed a wonderful hold on his men,' continued Guillemard, who confirmed that his admirable play and a great reputation 'naturally made him the idol of the ring'.

A similar boycott the following year saw Scotland, Ireland and Wales lose patience. They refused to play the senior rugby nation until a four-nation board was established. England, perversely, still selected a squad but there was no one to play them. Their power off the field, as well as on, was no longer absolute.

Self-imposed Exile

In self-imposed exile, England looked for challenges beyond the home nations. In 1888 a trailblazing British team left for Australia to play 16 matches – a tour marred by the death of the captain, Lancashire and Swinton's Bob Seddon, who drowned while sculling on the Hunter River. Seddon had only played three times for England. Just a year later a visiting New Zealand Maori side were entertained at Blackheath. England won 7-0, but even this game was marked by controversy when three Maori players walked off in disgust at the awarding of a disputed try.

England eventually ended a three-year sulk, the IB was established and a fixture against Wales was played in Dewsbury on 15 February 1890. England's dominance of the 1880s was over. They fielded eight new caps, but it was a famous day for Wales who won by a try to nil. It was the first victory of the Welsh over their great rivals and the first to exercise the minds of those new members of the International Board. Ironically, the game was won by a player based in Dewsbury, the former Cardiff half-back Bill Stadden. Two minutes after the break Stadden feigned to throw the ball into the line-out. The English forwards backed off and Stadden bounced the ball and went through unopposed to score the only try.

The afternoon in Dewsbury was dreadful, with a swirling wind and snow and mud underfoot. A Welsh critic noted that those bigger English forwards were outplayed by the more thick-set Welsh pack and that the Welsh backs, particularly the outstanding full-back Billy Bancroft, were more adaptable in the atrocious conditions The game, though, had another unhappy postscript. Stadden was made a scapegoat for the controversy and was never picked again by Wales. He committed suicide in Dewsbury at the age of 45 in 1906.

England's domination may have ended as the game entered the final decade of the 19th century but the remainder of 1890 was successful. The Scots were beaten at Raeburn Place by a goal and a try to nil and, under the new scoring system adopted by Scotland, this translated to 6-0; a pretty decisive result against the fearsome foot rushes of the Scots. A fortnight later Ireland were beaten 3-0 at Blackheath. The popularity of the game was spreading – a crowd of 12,000 saw the match at Rectory Field – and rugby union was no longer a game entrenched in the middle-class bastions of

Great Matches

INTERNATIONAL CHAMPIONSHIP Raeburn Place, Edinburgh, 5 March 1892
Attendance: 12,000

Scotland 0 **England 5**

This was the last great hurrah for English rugby before the 1895 formation of the Northern Union (later the Rugby League) robbed the national side of its greatest assets: northern-bred, raw-boned, tough-as-teak forwards and wily, elusive backs. The northern industrial towns supplied this side with 13 players, including its entire back division.

England had won the Triple Crown twice before, in 1883 and 1884, but the class of '92 created a unique record for the International Championship, winning its three games without conceding a score. Wales had been beaten 17-0 at Blackheath and Ireland 7-0 in Manchester before England travelled to Edinburgh seeking only their third win on Scottish soil in 21 years.

A dour, hard-fought game was resolved just before half time when William Bromet of Tadcaster went over beneath the posts and Heckmondwike's Dicky Lockwood converted. Identifying players must have been a major problem for the press. Some reporters attributed the English try to the giant Sammy Woods and even the identity of the conversion-taker varies from report to report.

The England team pose for the camera.

Scotland: H.J. Stevenson; P.R. Clauss, W. Neilson, G.T. Campbell; C.E. Orr (captain), D.G. Anderson, G.T. Neilson, F.W.J. Goodhue, R.G. MacMillan, J.E. Orr, M.C. McEwan, J.N. Millar, J.D. Boswell, W.R. Gibson, W.A. McDonald

England: T. Coop; R.E. Lockwood, F.H.R. Alderson (captain), J.W. Dyson; A. Briggs, H. Varley, S.M.J. Woods, T. Kent, W. Yiend, E. Bullough, F. Evershed, H. Bradshaw, W.E. Bromet, W. Nichol, J.T. Toothill

Scorers: Try Bromet **Conversion** Lockwood

Referee: R.G. Warren (Ireland)

Oxbridge and the London and Home Counties clubs. The team that won in Edinburgh in 1990 contained five of the successful northern pack including the new captain John Hickson of Bradford. Unfortunately, Hickson would be a central figure in the latest and most damaging crisis to beset the game in England.

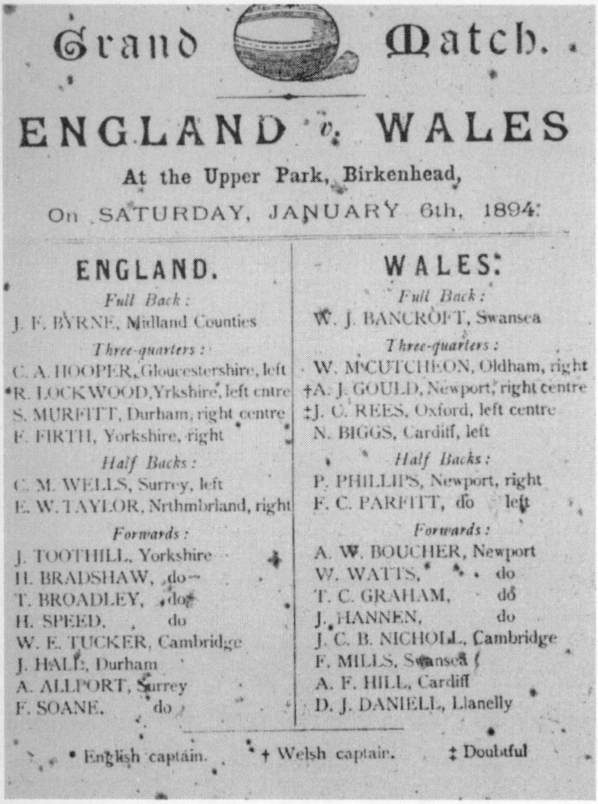

Grand Match.

ENGLAND v. WALES

At the Upper Park, Birkenhead,

On SATURDAY, JANUARY 6th, 1894.

ENGLAND.	WALES.
Full Back:	*Full Back:*
J. F. BYRNE, Midland Counties	W. J. BANCROFT, Swansea
Three-quarters:	*Three-quarters:*
C. A. HOOPER, Gloucestershire, left	W. McCUTCHEON, Oldham, right
*R. LOCKWOOD, Yrkshire, left centre	†A. J. GOULD, Newport, right centre
S. MURFITT, Durham, right centre	‡J. C. REES, Oxford, left centre
F. FIRTH, Yorkshire, right	N. BIGGS, Cardiff, left
Half Backs:	*Half Backs:*
C. M. WELLS, Surrey, left	P. PHILLIPS, Newport, right
E. W. TAYLOR, Nrthmbrland, right	F. C. PARFITT, do left
Forwards:	*Forwards:*
J. TOOTHILL, Yorkshire	A. W. BOUCHER, Newport
H. BRADSHAW, do	W. WATTS, do
T. BROADLEY, do	T. C. GRAHAM, do
H. SPEED, do	J. HANNEN, do
W. E. TUCKER, Cambridge	J. C. B. NICHOLL, Cambridge
J. HALL, Durham	F. MILLS, Swansea
A. ALLPORT, Surrey	A. F. HILL, Cardiff
F. SOANE, do	D. J. DANIELL, Llanelly

* English captain. † Welsh captain. ‡ Doubtful

The programme for England's match against Wales at Birkenhead in 1894.

'Broken Time' Payments

The northern forwards were hard men who took their rugby seriously. Their lives were far removed from the privileged youth of characters like 'Monkey' Hornby. The working men of the north claimed they could no longer play the game without some form of payment and many northern clubs were in favour of compensating players for lost wages – the so-called 'broken time' payments. The northern clubs met with resistance from a Rugby Football Union full of characters such as G. Rowland Hill and the Reverend Frank Marshall who believed profoundly in the amateur principle. The topic of veiled professionalism was debated at a meeting of the Rugby Football Union on 20 September 1893 at London's Westminster Palace Hotel. A proposal was made by two delegates from Yorkshire 'that players be allowed compensation for bona fide loss of time'.

In opposition was the trenchant Rowland Hill, honorary secretary of the RFU who was supported by the vice-president Seymour Whalley of Lancashire. These two gentlemen proposed an amendment 'that this meeting, believing that the above principle is contrary to the true interest of the game and its spirit, declines to sanction the same.' The amendment was carried by 282 votes to 136. And the Rugby Football Union was not finished. It tightened up its strict rules on amateurism and laid down the law to its northern upstarts. A new by-law thundered: 'Only clubs composed entirely of amateurs shall be eligible for membership (of the RFU) and its headquarters shall be in London where all general meetings shall be held.' When laws banning any form of professionalism were passed at a general meeting in September 1895, 22 clubs in Yorkshire and Lancashire withdrew from the RFU and at a hotel in Huddersfield set up a Northern Union.

A New Rugby Code

A new code of rugby emerged and a century of mistrust and recrimination followed. The northerners viewed the Rugby Football Union as a bastion of snobbishness and hypocrisy, while the supporters of Rowland Hill saw their stance as necessary in preserving a unique and classless game played for pleasure. The truth lies somewhere between the two stances. But what is beyond dispute is that for the next 100 years many players were lost to rugby league with the Rugby Football Union unreasonably preventing a union player from even having a trial with a league club. And what happened in the short term was that the new pure whiter than white amateur team of England were weakened by the loss of many northern players. The wall between the two codes only really collapsed when rugby union was thrown open in 1995.

England's amateur guardians would have been excused a satisfied smile had they watched the first international following the split. At Rectory Field on 4 January 1896 England thrashed Wales 25-0. The new-look England were led by Ernest William 'Little Billy' Taylor, another all-round sportsman who became a golf professional and played cricket for Northumberland. Wales were hampered by the early loss of Owen Badger, the Llanelli three-quarter, who broke his collarbone tackling his opposite number Jim Valentine. Against 14 men England were rampant, running in seven tries.

These were ominous times, though. Later in the year Valentine, who was killed by lightning in 1904, joined rugby league. England, meanwhile, lost their next four internationals, the final defeat a 13-9 reverse in Dublin in front of a crowd of 15,000. They were also to lose the last three matches of the century; the 1899 game against Wales in Swansea a particularly humiliating 26-3 defeat. It was a disaster that was to herald the start of a golden era in Welsh rugby as 11 years passed before England were to

Jim Valentine, one of many talented Union players lost to the newly formed Northern Union.

win the fixture again. The last game of the century was a 5-0 loss to the Scots at Rectory Field. *The Times* refered to the northern players in the England pack, such as the brothers James and Joseph Davidson, two builders from the Aspatria club, as 'delinquents'.

And so the century ended in a whitewash for England. The crisis over 'broken time' payments had taken its toll and English rugby did not have a home to call its own. But the Victorian era had seen English teams make a massive contribution to the development of rugby football. Pioneers like Harry Vassall, Gregory Wade and Edward Temple Gurdon altered the game on the hoof and helped turn it from a new pastime for the middle-classes into an international sport played and watched by thousands and into something that at least resembles rugby union as it is played in the 21st century.

50 Greatest Players

EDWARD TEMPLE GURDON Forward

Clubs: Cambridge University, Richmond

Debut: v Scotland, 4 March 1878

No. of Caps: 16 **No. of Points:** 1 try (before scoring by points was introduced)

In every decade of the game's history there has been a forward who has stood out for his outstanding technique. The man who lorded it over his opponents in the early years of international rugby was Temple Gurdon.

He was well versed in the game at his school Haileybury, before going up to Cambridge where he won his Blue. His college refused him leave to play for England in 1877, but he finally made his debut in the 1878 match against Scotland. 'In every respect he was one of the best forwards that ever represented England,' wrote a critic. Gurdon was a muscular forward who used his weight and strength effectively and was 'usually to be found in the very heart of the scrummage'. A deadly tackler, he was particularly adept at dribbling, a long-since defunct skill but an important attacking ploy in the early years of the game.

All told, he played 16 times for England in a career that spanned nine seasons, a record that 'evidenced his sterling worth' and which stood until the early 20th century. Only once, moreover, was he on the losing side. He was also England's first successful captain, leading an unbeaten side on nine occasions including back-to-back Triple Crowns in 1883 and 1884, when 'he set his players an excellent example'.

Chapter Two: 1899-1914
Under a Long White Cloud

The aftermath of the northern clubs' split from the Rugby Football Union lingered on into the new century. When the split took place in 1893 there were 481 clubs in the union. By 1903 this number had almost halved to 244 and the effects of the split seriously damaged the national side, whatever the mandarins of amateurism thought. Meanwhile, the game in Wales was thriving. Thanks to the growth of clubs in South Wales rugby union fast became a game that helped forge a national identity. The century began with a 13-3 victory over the English at Gloucester, a January day that marked the beginning of a marvellous run of six Triple Crowns before the First World War.

The Boer War was at its height but there was still an appetite in Britain for watching sport. In 1905, over 110,000 spectators watched football's FA Cup final at Crystal Palace and later that year, at the same London ground, England's rugby team would play the New Zealand tourists – opponents who would revolutionise the sport of rugby union. Dave Gallaher's All Blacks won 15-0, scoring five tries without reply, in a game that helped strip England of any illusions that it dominated the 15-man version of football. The game was watched by 45,000 spectators, many of whom hung from trees or from any vantage point they could find.

The *Manchester Guardian* takes up the story in a match report under the headline 'England Routed'. 'The numbers were not comparable for the people who gathered there for the Association Cup final but no such press of people has ever looked on a rugby football match in England before... it was interesting to compare the physiques of the two teams as they came out to be photographed. Apart from a few giants, Casey who weighs 15 stones and can run a good 100 yards and Sullivan, a pocket Hercules, the size of the men in the two teams was not conspicuously different, but in muscular development the vast superiority of the New Zealanders is apparent to the least observant spectator.'

England, led by a new captain, the Nottingham forward Vincent Cartwright, were swamped on a heavy pitch, the *Guardian*'s correspondent noting the visitors' superiority: 'Their strength is in the individual dash of separate members, quickness on the ball and the avoidance of the English habit of invariably passing to the wings without a first effort to make ground and draw the opposition. At the same time they were a team of rare coherence playing a team that had less acquaintance with each other even than English teams usually have. The score of fifteen points to nothing does not fully express the extent of the beating.'

England were, indeed, in some disarray. Earlier that year they had suffered a whitewash at the hands of Wales, Ireland and Scotland and their captain, the Richmond forward Frank Stout, had been summarily dropped. The elevation of Cartwright was expected to change England's fortunes against this unknown team from the other side of the globe. In reality, it stopped the progress of England's international side in its tracks. The New Zealanders, better drilled and better skilled, had made the white-shirted English side look green. The only silver lining was the huge gate profits of £1,039 13s 11d.

A World Game

The All Blacks emerged at a time when the game was expanding across the world map. In 1900 France won the gold medal in Paris as the sport appeared for the first time in the Olympic Games, and Japan and the United States had also taken up the game. The All Blacks, though, brought the game to a new level. Gallaher and his vice-captain Billy Stead were great thinkers about the game, even writing a book together, *The Complete Rugby Footballer*. They brought an intelligence to the game which, allied to the physical nature of the tourists' play, made them an unstoppable force.

They arrived in Britain with a host of prearranged moves, such as an innovation at the line-out which they would split into two, the ball being thrown in to allow the blind-side wing forward to run through the gap and take the ball to the opposition. This use of the line-out as an attacking platform was unheard of in England where it was considered merely a throw-in to restart the match. In 32 games, the All Blacks were defeated only once, by Wales in Cardiff. By the end of 1905, those two sides had well and truly displaced England as the leading sides in the world.

The drubbing, though, had healthy long-term effects on the game. Dave Gallaher's side, the so-called 'Originals', captured the public's imagination and helped revive the game in England. All they needed now was a hero to rally around – and they got one. For the match against Scotland at Richmond earlier in 1905 England had chosen a new half-back in Adrian Dura Stoop; he was to become one of the most influential players in England's history.

Stoop and his Harlequins club-mate Ronnie Poulton-Palmer helped transform England's fortunes in these pre-First World War days. They both learned the game as pupils at Rugby School. One was to live for over half a century after winning his first cap and one of the most famous club grounds in England is named after him; the other was to die tragically young and is now largely forgotten.

Footballing Genius

Stoop, the son of a Dutch father and a Scottish mother, was born in 1883 and was at Rugby School in 1900 when a plaque commemorating William Webb Ellis was placed in the Doctor's Wall. He was noticed by Harlequins when their A-team visited the school and went on to captain the club from 1906 until the outbreak of the First World War. Stoop was eulogised in the newspapers of the day. One Sunday wrote in 1910: 'There is no finality to his genius' and a report of the Quins' game against Old Merchant Taylors was pretty typical: 'On the run of play the Taylors had every bit as much of the play as the Harlequins. It was just Stoop's extra genius that turned the scale. Stoop carried too many guns for John Raphael, the Taylors' full-back. When it came to tactics Raphael was left with too much to do by his colleagues in defence. Nothing better could have been seen than the quick intelligence which Stoop exercised as he feinted to attack on the left and then got in the punt to get the try. He again drew Raphael and left Lambert with a start for the last try.'

Another report from this era sums up the dominance of Stoop and Harlequins on the thinking of the day. 'The so-called boom in rugby football in the London district is due to a great degree, as is generally admitted, to the example and success of Harlequins. The paramount difficulty which immediately faced the would-be imitator of the Harlequins was the novelty of their methods. To play the game as they played it involved the unlearning of certain old shibboleths, the assimilation of certain ideas of startling newness. People talk scornfully of hand-ball winning at what should be football till one begins to wonder if passing is a patent invention of Mr Adrian Stoop.'

These reporters were not merely flattering a sporting celebrity. Stoop established back play and a framework for the modern game. He saw what the All Blacks could do in 1905 at a time when backs were not used in fixed positions. In 1905 England played with five three-quarters. When Stoop started his England career the two half-backs alternated as scrum-halves in much the same way as centres do today, depending on which side of the field the game was being played. Stoop recognised the wisdom of playing a specialist scrum-half inside a fly-half. This fly-half position he made his own.

In an article on coaching Stoop was later to write: 'The scrum-half should concentrate on speed first and accuracy next. His pass must never

50 Greatest Players

ADRIAN STOOP Fly-half

Clubs: Oxford University, Harlequins

Debut: v Scotland, 18 March 1905

No. of Caps: 15 **No. of Points:** 6

Adrian Stoop's name became synonymous with Twickenham when his club, Harlequins, decamped there when the new ground opened in 1909. Stoop, one of the great thinkers on back play, was already an England Test half-back at the time, but it was the exciting brand of open rugby that he brought to the club scene that transformed Harlequins into a leading London club and proved the catalyst for a sea-change in the fortunes of the England side.

Stoop was installed as fly-half and captain for England's first Twickenham international, against Wales in January 1910, and ignited the national side with the same attacking principles that had served Harlequins so well. England never looked back, went on to beat Wales 11-6 and finished the season as winners of the International Championship for the first time since 1892. Stoop was hero-worshipped from Land's End to Hadrian's Wall. His unorthodoxy catapulted England out of a lengthy spell in rugby's doldrums and launched a long period of English dominance in the International Championship, though he was to retire from the international scene in 1912.

Stoop lived until 1957, playing his last game in Eastbourne just months before the outbreak of the Second World War at the age of 55. The newspapers were respectful to the last. One kindly report noted: 'Veteran A.D. Stoop captained the Harlequins and if the speed of former days has gone, the old resource and judgment are still there for youth to see and admire.' Stoop became an RFU selector and president and a member of the International Board. He also became a referee, taking charge of the first Mobbs Memorial match between the East Midlands and the Barbarians in 1921.

travel behind his partner or more than chest-high. He must tell his forwards where the ball is in a loose scrum and as soon as the ball is out should shout "out left" or "out right" to help them to break quickly.' Stoop maintained that the test of the fly-half is the amount of room he gives his wing on the touchline. He latched on to the idea that a quick pass across the field can take the ball well clear of roaming wing-forwards. His theories were simple and effective and, allied to his perfect control of passes, his speed off the mark and intuitive thinking, he changed the face of the English game.

Stoop was also a radical thinker. In the 1910 match against Wales, the first at Twickenham, he stunned the Grand Slam champions. From the kick-off Stoop fielded the ball. The tradition would have been to kick for touch and the Welsh team drifted across field. Stoop, though, wrongfooted them by setting off infield and then switched play to the opposite wing, leaving the Welsh and probably most of the English team, bemused. The ball was transferred quickly to Poulton who cross kicked for Berry. Gent, Solomon and Birkett then combined before the burly wing Frederick Chapman darted over for the first try at Twickenham before a Welsh hand had touched the ball. The game was 75 seconds old. The crowd were stunned and Stoop's ingenuity laid the foundations for an 11-6 win, the first over the Welsh in the century. And, in a few seconds of genius, Adrian Stoop signalled a new dawn for England.

Twist to the Tale

There was a twist to this Twickenham tale, though. Bert Solomon, who scored England's second try, was from Cornwall and very highly rated. But the centre played only one game for England. The Redruth player had travelled to London on the milk-train but after the match shocked his new team-mates by announcing: 'That's it, I've finished.' He ignored all further invitations from Twickenham because it was said that he felt out of place among the haughty public-school types in the England dressing-room. This legend of Cornish rugby was later offered 400 gold sovereigns to play rugby league. He refused and stayed in his Redruth butcher's shop.

Ronnie Poulton's impact on the game was not as profound as Stoop's but in this period he earned himself a reputation as England's greatest player. Poulton scored five tries for Oxford on his Varsity match debut as newspapers tagged him a 'genius'. Later he changed his name to Poulton-Palmer – a condition of his inheritance of part of the Huntley-Palmer biscuit fortune. As the spectre of war began casting its shadow over Europe Ronnie Poulton-Palmer had everything. He enlisted in the 4th Royal Berkshire Regiment for service in France. On 5 May 1915 he was killed by a sniper's bullet in a trench in Belgium.

Stoop helped England regroup after the 1905 debacle and after defeats by Wales and Ireland in 1906, he was chosen at scrum-half in a new partnership with Plymouth's James Peters against Scotland at Inverleith. The pair helped inspire a first win against the Scots for four years and the first victory against any side for two years. Stoop's quick service created tries for the wings John

Great Matches

INTERNATIONAL CHAMPIONSHIP **Twickenham, 15 January 1910**
Attendance: 25,000

England 11 **Wales 6**

The RFU's new headquarters at Twickenham, having been purchased in 1907-08, was finally ready to stage major matches by the autumn of 1909, and what a start there was to this first international at the ground.

Wales kicked off deep into the English 25 where Adrian Stoop, the home side's captain, immediately showed his predilection for attacking rugby by shunning the safe option of a kick to touch and instead launching an ambitious handling movement. Less than a minute later his initiative culminated in a try in the right corner scored by Fred Chapman. After Chapman had kicked a penalty, Wales scrambled a try, but former Welsh triallist Dai Gent made a telling break from a loose scrum and Solomon, England's fiery tempered centre, ran in a try which Chapman converted. The Durham winger had scored the first try, penalty and conversion in international rugby at Twickenham.

England had not beaten Wales since 1898 and the early 1900s had been a golden period of Welsh dominance. Yet the new ground, the early score and Stoop's insouciance at fly-half had somehow galvanised the men in white to lift their game. A stout English defence kept the Welsh in check for the rest of the match and they ran out deserved winners as well as going on to claim their first championship title since 1892.

An illustrated celebration of Fred Chapman's first-minute try.

England: W.R. Johnston; F.E. Chapman, J.G.G. Birkett, B. Solomon, R.W. Poulton; A.D. Stoop (captain), D.R. Gent; H.J.S. Morton, W.A. Johns, L. Haigh, D.F. Smith, E.L. Chambers, H. Berry, L.E. Barrington-Ward, C.H. Pillman
Scorers: Tries Chapman, Solomon **Conversion** Chapman **Penalty Goal** Chapman

Wales: J. Bancroft; R.A. Gibbs, J.P. Jones, W.J. Trew (captain), P.L. Hopkin; R. Jones, R.M. Owen; B. Gronow, J. Pugsley, C.M. Pritchard, D.J. Thomas, T.H. Evans, H. Jarman, J. Webb, I. Morgan
Scorers: Tries Gibbs, Webb

Referee: J.D. Dallas (Scotland)

Raphael and Tom Simpson. Peters, born in Salford of West Indian parents, became the first black player to play for England. 'A delightful running show was provided by Peters,' wrote the *Manchester Guardian.* He went on to play six internationals before a dockyard accident cost him three fingers. He later played rugby league for Barrow after being banned by the RFU for organising league matches in that same Royal Navy dockyard.

Stoop and Peters, one the gifted pukka epitome of the establishment, the other the outsider but every bit a pioneer himself, could have been England's most famous half-back combination. Sadly they were only in harness twice, both scoring tries in the first England international against France at Parc des Princes on 22 March 1906. England won 35-8 with a convincing forward display in the swirling wind. England scored nine tries, four of them from the Gloucester wing Arthur Hudson, who had only been selected for the side at the last minute. Stoop's new ideas were bearing fruit at last.

New Tourists – the Springboks

If Dave Gallaher's Originals had awakened England to the potential of an organised and innovative game, there were new visitors who would help the country that discovered rugby union to snap out of its turn-of-the-century complacency. With the Boer War still a recent memory, the South Africans visited in 1906 and the new tourists proved almost as successful as the All Blacks had been a year before. They beat Ireland and Wales before coming to Crystal Palace where another impressive crowd of around 40,000 saw Cartwright's team hold the Springboks to a 3-3 draw. It was a foul day made for the bigger South African pack but a second-half try by the wing Frederick Brooks, the first player to be capped by the Bedford club, saved the day for England and their drenched supporters. Oddly, Brooks had played for Rhodesia in the Currie Cup earlier. Even stranger, he never played for England again.

The selectorial process in England was often bizarre. Arnold Alcock, a Gloucester GP, played for Guy's Hospital at the time of his England call-up. He was an average forward and surprised to be elevated into the national team. Lancelot Slocock, meanwhile, had expected to be selected. It would appear a clerical error had mixed the two. Liverpool's Slocock would receive his call-up to the side a month later for the visit of France to Richmond. Alcock would never play for England again and Slocock, a second lieutenant in the King's Liverpool Regiment, was killed in action in 1916.

France, those first Olympic champions, came to England for the first time for an international on 5 January 1907 at the Athletic Ground. In a report

50 Greatest Players

CHARLES PILLMAN Forward

Club: Blackheath

Debut: v Wales, 15 January 1910

No. of Caps: 18 **No. of Points:** 26

The player credited with developing the distinctive feature of the wing-forward or flanker role in English rugby was the Blackheath forward, Charles Pillman. He packed on the side of the scrum where he could quickly detach himself and used his pace to attack and disrupt the opposing fly-half. So successful was his technique that the selectors nominated him to perform his specialist duties against Wales in 1910 in the first international staged at Twickenham.

Aged 20, Pillman enjoyed a dream debut, playing an important part in a great victory. England defeated Wales for the first time since 1898 and the tall, slim youngster's effective winging operations helped England go on and win the International Championship title for the first time in 18 years. Pillman showed a remarkable ability to read a game, often lending a helping hand to his colleagues in attacks, and was quite simply the 'find' of the year.

He was the star player for the 1910 Lions in South Africa where his versatility led to his playing fly-half in the Port Elizabeth Test match. He created the two tries of the Lions's 8-3 victory and was the tourists' leading scorer for the visit.

Back home 'Cherry' Pillman was the anchor of the England packs that laid the foundations of four championship titles including two Grand Slams in the seasons leading up to the outbreak of the First World War. His legacy was that by the 1920s every international side adopted England's example and fielded a winger in the Pillman mould.

in *The Times*, the writer looks into a crystal ball: 'Within the space of a very few years an international championship, organised on even broader lines than is now the case, will be the accomplished thing. Pure amateurism will, of course, be the essence of that competition and in such a competition France, in a very short time, is likely to play an honourable part.' Not yet, though. The first French team to play England were crushed 41-13, a huge margin at the time. A crowd of around 6,000 saw the visitors, weighing an average of a stone lighter, run off their feet by an England team captained by Blackheath's forward Basil Hill. Douglas Lambert, the strapping new wing from Harlequins, scored five of England's nine tries. Lancelot Slocock, making his debut, also scored. Again this happy tale for England has an unhappy postscript. Lambert, who scored 22 points against the French in 1911, was killed in action in October 1915.

Despite the morale-boosting victory, 1907 was to prove a miserable season. England retained the pack that had dismantled France for the trip to Swansea a week later but they were totally unprepared for the onslaught of the Welsh side who ran up a 22-0 victory. Only 12,000 supporters turned up at St Helens, to watch Wales run in six tries without reply. England with a new captain, John Green, left out Stoop and six other players for the game in Dublin where Ireland won 17-9 and at Rectory Field a month later Scotland won 8-3. Peters scored a consolation in the final minute, the only try the Scots conceded in the season.

50 Greatest Players

RONALD POULTON Wing/Centre

Clubs: Oxford University, Harlequins, Liverpool

Debut: v France, 30 January 1909

No. of Caps: 17 **No. of Points:** 28

The star three-quarter of the England side in the seasons before the Great War was Ronnie Poulton (later Poulton-Palmer). He made his name as a wing of rare pace at Oxford and his characteristic swerve brought him five tries in the 1909 Varsity match, an individual record for the long-running series that still stands. The England fly-half W.J.A. Davies wrote: 'His easy grace and charm of manner, his versatility on the football field, that characteristic run are vivid impressions of probably the greatest figure that ever played rugby football.'

He later settled at Harlequins, becoming a household name in club rugby circles for his attacking contributions to the exciting back division that Adrian Stoop assembled at Twickenham. Poulton followed Stoop into the England side, appearing intermittently as a wing and centre before attracting rave notices in the Calcutta Cup win at Twickenham in 1911. Thereafter he became a regular fixture in the national side.

His most memorable try for England opened the scoring against the 1913 Springboks. Owen Owen elegantly described Poulton's corkscrewing runs that day: 'A pass reached Poulton [who] set off on a swerving run. The defence was beaten and the runner's eccentric course carried him like a leaf swept by the wind across to the right-hand corner.' Poulton captained England to the back-to-back Grand Slam in 1914 and set an England International Championship record that still survives by scoring four tries against France in the last match before the First World War. He was killed in action, aged 25, in 1915. Men of all ages mourned the passing of a rugby genius.

50 Greatest Players

NORMAN WODEHOUSE Forward

Clubs: United Services, Royal Navy

Debut: v France, 3 March 1910

No. of Caps: 14 **No. of Points:** 6

Like many of the international players in the seasons leading up to the Great War, Norman Wodehouse caught the attention of the national selectors through his consistent performances for a gifted United Services side based in Portsmouth.

After impressing with his high work rate at the heart of the scrums and mauls, he was blooded in France in 1910 but injury forced him to withdraw from the side that beat Scotland to win the first ever Five Nations title. He was ever present in the side that finished with two home wins in 1911, contributing a try to the Calcutta Cup victory, and his emergence as an inspiring leader of the Navy's pack led to his promotion as captain of the England side that beat France in the last match of the 1912 season to claim a share of the championship spoils.

His finest year followed in 1913 when he became the first man to lead England to the Grand Slam. E.H.D. Sewell, one the leading contemporary critics, rated the Navy man high on his list of England's outstanding captains: 'One of the soundest of scrummagers and quite the best leader of his day,' he wrote. 'A magnificent player in all phases.' In a distinguished naval career that saw him advance to vice-admiral, Wodehouse served during the First World War with distinction and was recalled from the reserve list for active service in 1940. He was lost at sea in 1941 whilst commanding a convoy.

England continued to be inconsistent and change their personnel, but in this pre-First World War era a significant move off the field was to change the face of English international rugby. The Australians visited for the first time in 1909 and while they could hardly match the New Zealanders as a box-office draw, the first international against England was also the last at Blackheath. The game was won 9-3 with England's only try scored on his debut by the Northampton winger Edgar Mobbs. He later died at Passchendaele in 1915, but is immortalised in an annual game between the East Midlands and the Barbarians.

Blackheath, Richmond and Leicester, which hosted the 1909 visit of France, were no longer big enough to house the England rugby team. The Rugby Football Union wanted a new home of its own and found it in the south-west London suburb of Twickenham, a thoroughly urbanised area with a well-watered plain where market gardening was carried out. In 1907 ten and a quarter acres were bought by Rugby Football Union committee member Billy Williams for £5,572, 2s 6d. The following year, work began on a new stadium – known affectionately as 'Billy Williams' Cabbage Patch' – that would facilitate 24,000 standing and 6,000 seated spectators.

Showpiece Ground

Twickenham became the showpiece ground and the move there coincided with England's on-the-field revival almost from the first blast of the referee's whistle in that 1910 game against Wales. Four more international victories were won there before the touring South Africans arrived in 1913. In front of 30,000 spectators, and despite a fantastic double-swerve run and try by Ronnie Poulton, the Springboks broke the unbeaten record with a 9-3 win.

The new home of English rugby would continue to inspire the men in white. In the last two seasons before the Great War, England racked up eight successive victories to end the 1914 season with back-to-back Grand Slams. Poulton was an unstoppable force and the new loose-forward Charles 'Cherry' Pillman was the star of a dominant pack.

The game was given a royal seal of approval with the visit to Twickenham of the Prince of Wales who saw Scotland defeated in 1913 and King George V who watched the victory over Ireland a year later. The narrow 16-15 victory

England v Scotland, March 1913. England's F.E. Oakeley (centre) tries to break down the wing, with support from team-mates Cherry Pillman (right), Ronald Poulton-Palmer (far right) and Sidney Smart (left).

50 Greatest Players

CYRIL LOWE Wing

Clubs: Cambridge University, RAF, Blackheath

Debut: v South Africa, 4 January 1913

No. of Caps: 25 **No. of Points:** 58

The smallest international player of his generation, 'Kid' Lowe occupied the England right-wing berth for ten seasons before retiring in 1923. He never missed an international and but for the Great War, which robbed him of five seasons of international rugby, would almost certainly have played nearly 50 Tests – a phenomenal record considering that the only regular opponents of the day were the European nations.

Lowe was the deadliest finisher England had seen. His eight tries in the 1914 campaign have never been surpassed in the history of the International Championship while his 18 tries stood as the overall England career record for 67 years and helped the side to four Grand Slams, two before the First World War and two after, when he ran with the same pace and determination he had displayed as a young Cambridge undergraduate. Against Ireland at Twickenham in 1921, moreover, he showed that he wasn't just a runner in of tries. Finding his way to the try-line blocked, he swivelled towards the posts and promptly dropped a left-footed goal that was described as the 'most delightful' score of the match.

over Scotland at Inverleith was to be the last in Britain for some time. The rugby historian Owen Owen reflected: 'Few among the spectators could have imagined that in six months' time, sport would be thrust out of the mind for five full years and that no less than 11 of the men who played in this splendid last encounter would fall in the war.'

Significantly, one of the tries that day was scored by Ronnie Poulton who in England's final game of that triumphant 1914 season was to cross the French line four times in a 39-13 win at Stade Colombes. The next time Poulton crossed the Channel it was to a conflict of a more serious kind and Twickenham was to fall silent for six years.

Poulton and Adrian Stoop were England's two giants of this era but Dave Gallaher's Originals were the real guiding lights of the world game. On one muddy Edwardian afternoon in south London, the New Zealanders had demonstrated the true potential of the game.

Chapter Three: 1915-39
A Baron and a Prince

If the Twickenham of the 21st century is unrecognisable as the modest stadium that hosted those early games before the Great War there are echoes of the past in all sorts of corners of the ground. Two glass-fronted restaurants in the East Stand, Wakefield's and Obolensky's, are a reminder of the two England players from between the wars who are imprinted on the memories of anyone who saw them play. There are parallels between the pair with Adrian Stoop and Ronnie Poulton-Palmer. Wavell Wakefield, later Baron and then Lord Wakefield of Kendal, was to become a pillar of the game, captain of England, Rugby Football Union president, member of the International Board and Tory MP, dying in 1983 at the age of 85. Alexander, or Prince, Obolensky was, like Poulton-Palmer, to die tragically in a war.

History shows that Wakefield was England's most successful captain until the days of Will Carling and that the 1920s were the most successful era in English rugby history. But after the traumas of the First World War all the Home International sides had to rebuild and it was not until January 1920 that Twickenham hosted an international, the visit of France.

Wakefield, the Harlequins forward, was in the pack that day. Between then and his last game in 1927, also against the French, he helped revolutionise the art of forward play. Just as Stoop had taken the ideas of Dave Gallaher and established the tactics of roles behind the scrum, Wakefield dismantled the traditional British thinking about the pack by ending the idea that forwards were just there to win set-piece ball. He developed play in the loose, particularly concentrating on the role of the open-side flanker as a player who would put pressure on the opposition fly-half. Wakefield devised defensive systems for the forwards. With Stoop he is the single most important figure in the English game in establishing modern rugby union as a sport of specific roles for specific positions. This pair of Corinthians created the template from which 20th century rugby was forged.

Some of England's players survived in the 1920s. The most famous survivor was the Blackheath wing Cyril Lowe, a pocket battleship of a player, quick, with a scissor-sharp tackle. Lowe had scored eight tries in the championship-winning last season before the war and scored 18 tries between 1913 and 1923. He may have been prolific but there were many who thought Lowe would have scored more tries had he seen the ball more often. In this respect he is often compared with Rory Underwood who was eventually to break Lowe's try-scoring record over 70 years later.

Jeeves and... Lowe?

P.G. Wodehouse, the century's greatest comic writer and a contemporary of Lowe's at Dulwich College, was one of England's critics who thought Lowe was at best underused. Wodehouse penned a droll poem, 'The Great Day', which recounts the day he watched England play and someone actually gave Lowe a pass. In the last verse Lowe receives the ball from his three-quarters:

50 Greatest Players

WAVELL WAKEFIELD Forward

Clubs: Cambridge University, RAF, Leicester, Harlequins

Debut: v Wales, 17 January 1920

No. of Caps: 31 **No. of Points:** 18

The dominant personality of English rugby during its Golden Era in the early 1920s was Wavell Wakefield. Although a forward of immense physical strength and all-round ability, it was his tremendous pace that brought him six Test tries during a career that produced 31 caps – the then record number of caps for an Englishman.

But it was Wakefield's ability to think about the game that underpinned England's three Grand Slam wins of 1921, 1923 and 1924. He brought his analytical mind to the mechanics of forward play at a time when 'first up, first down' was the scrummaging norm in Britain. This simply meant that front rows were invariably formed by the first three forwards arriving at the scene. As England's pack leader in 1923, Wakefield set about developing fixed positions in the scrum, with specialist props, hookers, second rows and loose forwards performing their respective duties at the set-piece. His pack played with such cohesion that England swept all before them on the way to a Grand Slam, and the next season Wakefield's methods again brought dividends as England won back-to-back Grand Slams for the first time.

After retirement, Wakefield went on to make a valued contribution to the RFU as a thoughtful administrator.

There was sweat upon his forehead,
And his stare was simply horrid,
He stood and goggled feebly at the ball.
It was plain he suffered badly,
For the crowd now cheering madly,
Saw him shudder, start to run, then limply fall.
Then a doctor who was handy,
Fanned his face and gave him brandy;
And at last, though his recovery was slow,
He regained his health and reason
By the middle of next season.
But the shock came very near to killing Lowe.

Wodehouse's tacit criticism of England's play in the early 1920s doesn't quite tally with the facts. What was true was that, although they scored plenty of tries in this period, their success was forged on the anvil of their forward power and the head blacksmith was Wavell Wakefield.

After Wakefield had led them to their third Grand Slam in four years in 1924, a *Manchester Guardian* report of the final win of the season, a 19-0 victory over the Scots at Twickenham, sums up England's superiority at the time. 'The English forwards were the stronger, especially in the loose, where they were untiring and remorseless. Rarely did the Scottish eight get away in these fierce rushes by which they have sometimes snatched a victory against superior backs. Wakefield, Voyce and Cove-Smith have the faculty of always being there. Wakefield is one of the great forwards of football. He is like the rhinoceros, whom the big-game hunters dread because of the fearful speed which it combines with immense bulk. On Saturday Cove-Smith was not far behind him and figured largely in contests of legitimate ferocity. Having been at one time in the grip of a Scotsman who screwed his neck with his right arm while pulling pieces of his shirt with his left, he resumed with the utmost nonchalance. It was a great game.'

Ronald Cove-Smith, the Old Merchant Taylors' lock, and the Gloucester flanker Tom Voyce were two of Wakefield's key forwards of the time. Voyce, with his wavy ginger hair, is regarded as one of the finest back-row forwards of any era and clubs like Gloucester were emerging as important breeding grounds of the sport. In England rugby union was expanding from the pre-war game played largely at public schools and universities. Grammar schools were taking up the sport and in towns like Gloucester, Northampton and Bristol it was overtaking soccer as the major spectator sport.

England's success and the building of Twickenham had helped increase public interest in the sport. After the darkness of the First World War the public were hungry for sporting spectacles. At that Twickenham game against Scotland in 1924, a newspaper wrote: 'Yesterday's rugby crowd was probably a record for the game. It must have numbered about 45,000 people while the 15,000 seats available could have been sold three times over. A big rugby match where rival national feelings are well aroused could attract a crowd of 100,000 and equal the records of the Association Cup final, if the accommodation were adequate.'

In 1921 England duly recorded their first Grand Slam of the era. It was settled at Stade Colombes with a 10-6 victory over the French. Cyril Lowe must have received at least one pass because he scored the deciding try. Indeed Lowe scored in three of the four wins that year.

France, though, were becoming a difficult team to beat after their uncertain start in the competition. The French were now picking their teams not from university students or the fashionable Parisian club Stade Francais but from

50 Greatest Players

W.J.A. 'DAVE' DAVIES Fly-half

Clubs: United Services, Royal Navy

Debut: v South Africa, 4 January 1913

No. of Caps: 22 **No. of Points:** 24

English rugby was blessed during the 1920s by a guiding genius of a fly-half. That the player was a Welshman by birth was largely ignored: W.J.A. 'Dave' Davies was the most-loved back in English rugby at the time.

He made his name through stylish performances for the Navy and United Services sides. While Davies had all the running and passing skills of his predecessor Adrian Stoop, it was the long-raking tactical kicking and accurate left-footed drop-kicking that set him apart as England's finest exponent of the fly-half's arts.

Davies featured in four England Grand Slam sides, captaining the successful teams of 1921 and 1923, and was never on a losing England side in the International Championship. England's only defeats during his career span were against Wales in 1920 and 1922, when Davies was absent through injury. The key to this success was Davies's half-back partnership with his naval colleague Cecil Kershaw – they were known in rugby circles as Dave and K. While stationed in Portsmouth the two regularly trained together and developed a strong understanding of each other's play.

their rugby heartlands in the south. Clubs like Toulouse, Perpignan, Bayonne and Dax were producing tough forwards and the French pack gave Wakefield's eight a thorough examination before a crowd of around 40,000 in Paris. Marshall Foch, the commander of the allies during the war, watched the match and unveiled a memorial to all the French players who had died in combat.

England were now captained by 'Dave' Davies who had taken over from Stoop as the fly-half and pivot of the side. Davies had broken his leg in the 1919-20 season but he went on to lead England to another championship in 1923. In his three years as captain England never lost, their worst result a draw against the French in 1922. England were so dependent on Davies that their next game after that victory in Paris, when their skipper was not available, resulted in a 28-6 trouncing at the hands of Wales in Cardiff. For the first time in the championship the players wore numbers on their backs, but the Arms Park mudbath soon obscured the innovation. Wales seemed happy with the conditions, running in eight tries to two. It was England's

50 Greatest Players

CECIL KERSHAW Scrum-half

Clubs: United Services, Royal Navy

Debut: v Wales, 17 January 1920

No. of Caps: 16 **No. of Points:** 6

'Dave' Davies's scrum-half partner for club and country was Cecil Kershaw. The pair guided England to two Grand Slams and were regarded by rugby historians as the game's greatest halves until the advent of Gareth Edwards and Barry John nearly 50 years later.

Kershaw was the epitome of the attacking scrum-half. He linked cleverly with the back row and posed all manner of problems for defences. His partner once wrote: 'I doubt whether he ever kicked the ball more than a dozen times in our four seasons together in the England side.' Arguably his finest hour was at Twickenham in 1920 when England needed to defeat Scotland to earn a share in the Five Nations title. Kershaw stole the ball from a Scottish heel and raced 25 yards, swerving outside the full-back, to score a delightful solo try that sealed England's victory.

Apart from his qualities as an attacker, he possessed the all-round skills demanded of his position. In particular he had a fast and accurate service. In his youth he had become an accomplished fencer and no doubt the strong forearms required to make a success of that sport stood him in good stead on the rugby field. Certainly his record made impressive reading: in 16 successive England Tests between 1920 and 1923 he was on the losing side only twice, against Wales in difficult conditions in 1920 and 1923.

heaviest defeat in Wales since 1907. England's captain, the Blackheath back-row forward Len 'Bruno' Brown, never played again.

England must have feared the worst when they crossed the Irish Sea a month later but normal service was resumed once Davies was back at fly-half. The rout was quickly forgotten with a 12-3 victory in Dublin and after the draw against the French in front of 40,000 spectators, who included King George V, England strung together nine successive victories, only interrupted by an All Blacks win at Twickenham in January 1925.

Another Classic

This was another classic match between the two best sides in the world at the time. At the end of an unbeaten tour New Zealand, the so-called 'Invincibles', met England, the Grand Slam champions. The All Blacks won 17-11 but played with 14 men for all but eight minutes after their forward Cyril Brownlie earned an unwelcome footnote in history by becoming the first player to be sent off at Twickenham. A crowd of 60,000 included the

Maurice Brownlie scores for the All Blacks against England at Twickenham in 1925.

50 Greatest Players

RONALD COVE-SMITH Forward

Clubs: Cambridge University, King's College Hospital, Old Merchant Taylors'

Debut: v Scotland, 19 March 1921

No. of Caps: 29 **No. of Points:** 3

A studious player who was a firm believer in Wavell Wakefield's philosophy that forwards should pack down in fixed positions in the scrummage, Ronald Cove-Smith became the expert second row lock of the triumphant England sides that largely dominated the Five Nations Championship in the 1920s.

He was a skilful all-round forward renowned for his immense strength. 'Cove had the power to wheel a scrum towards the touchline, denying the opposing scrum-half the chance to link easily with his backs,' wrote a critic shortly after he had appeared in his third England Grand Slam outfit, in 1924.

He also had impeccable leadership credentials. He had captained a successful side at Merchant Taylors' School and led the first Cambridge side to appear in a Twickenham Varsity match, in 1921. Then, in the absence of Wavell Wakefield, he led the 1924 British/Irish Lions to South Africa and finally skippered England in 1928, when he guided a largely experimental side to victory over Australia and on to its fourth Grand Slam in seven years. He returned as leader in 1929 but lost his place after the defeat against Ireland at Twickenham. At the time, only Wakefield held more England caps.

Prince of Wales and the incident was something of a sensation at the time. The sending-off – for kicking – seemed to disturb England more than the All Blacks, however, and a brilliant late try by England's debutant stand-off Harold Kittermaster came too late against a side who won with an awesome display of forward power in front of a dead-eyed kicker in Mark Nicholls.

England's era of domination was over and those key forwards Wakefield, Voyce and Cove-Smith past their best. Wakefield's final game as captain in 1926 was something of an anticlimax. Scotland's 17-9 win at Twickenham was their first on English soil for 17 years and gave the Scots the championship. It was also England's first defeat at Twickenham by northern hemisphere opposition. By now England's supporters and press had expected victories at Twickenham and a sour mood followed the Scottish defeat. The *Manchester Guardian* report, headlined 'Full-back's Expensive Mistakes', pointed the finger of blame at the young Cumbrian full-back Tom Holliday. The correspondent opines: 'The expectation would have been fulfilled had one Englishman not made two bad and inexcusable blunders. Young backs

50 Greatest Players

TOM VOYCE Flanker

Club: Gloucester

Debut: v Ireland, 14 February 1920

No. of Caps: 27 **No. of Points:** 15

A key element in Wavell Wakefield's theory of specialist scrum positions was the dynamic play of the Gloucester flanker, Tom Voyce. He had pace, safe hands and an uncanny sense of position and was an ever present in the Grand Slam wins of 1921, 1923 and 1924. The slim, sinewy Gloucester man was one of the first England schoolboy internationals to graduate with honours at senior level. As a youngster he was capped for the England Schools as a fly-half, but after the war he converted to the back row and became regarded as the foremost flanker in the country.

A photograph of Voyce scoring the decisive try at Inverleith against Scotland in 1923 sums up perfectly his qualities of strength and determination. He is seen straining every sinew to break a despairing Scottish tackle after showing what the rugby correspondent of *The Times* described as 'a rare sense of anticipation... to score a fine try'.

Instantly recognisable with his mop of gingery, wavy hair, Voyce was one of the most popular men of his era and was devoted to rugby all his life. He served his beloved Gloucester as a player and administrator until his death in 1980 and after serving as president of the RFU in 1960-61 was awarded the OBE for his services to the game.

are told, or ought to be, that they must not wait for the ball to bounce but Holliday committed that fault twice in less than 10 minutes and each time Scotland scored a try.'

A scapegoat had been found and poor Holliday, who froze in front of 50,000 spectators, including the King, never played for England again. Voyce, however, in his last appearance for England had a fonder memory as he scored one of the memorable tries of that period after the Scots had run up a 14-point lead. The rugby historian J.B.G. Thomas described it: 'A good forward rush with Voyce, Periton and Wakefield in the van ended in the formation of a set scrummage 15 yards out from the Scottish goalline and near to the right-hand touchline. Scotland won the strike and the English back row headed by Voyce half-tackled Waddell and the ball went loose. It was driven through but the Scottish loose forward John Paterson got back to assist full-back Dan Drysdale. As they gathered the ball jointly, Voyce rushed into them and with a tremendous feat of strength tore the ball out of their grasp, parted them and then stormed over the line like a Goliath on one knee with the two defenders hanging on to him.'

The process of rebuilding began. Wakefield, who carried on as a player, was a hard act to follow as captain. Although the new skipper, Bristol's swift-running centre Len Corbett, made a perfect start with England's only try in a narrow win over Wales and followed it by leading the side to a victory over the Irish, there were defeats in Edinburgh and Paris. Corbett lasted only a season, the French defeat being difficult to take as it was the 17th time the sides had met and the first time France had won. Even Wakefield, in his final

Wakefield in the line-out in England's 11-0 defeat of France at Twickenham in 1926.

game, struggled against the solid French pack, although a broken rib hardly helped. France scored the only points of the match, a try by their wing Edmond Vellat, and thoroughly enjoyed their day in the Parisian sun.

Fire Brigade Called

It was a minor blip, though. England, now led by Ronnie Cove-Smith, won the 1928 Grand Slam even though the four victories were hardly in the thrilling style of the Wakefield era. A fortnight after the touring New South Wales Waratahs were dispatched at Twickenham by 18-11 in January, England beat Wales 10-8 in Swansea, Ireland 7-6 at Lansdowne Road, France 18-8 at Twickenham and Scotland 6-0 at Twickenham. The fire brigade had had to pump water off the Swansea pitch which was still a muddy morass and, by all accounts, England were desperately lucky to emerge from the mud smelling of roses. The Welsh pack outplayed them only to be let down by their poor back play. The Harlequins fly-half Colin Laird and the Blackheath wing William Taylor scored the decisive tries.

In the previous season Laird had become England's youngest-ever player, scoring another try on his debut, also against Wales, at 18 years 134 days old. England were fielding a new back division that included the Cambridge University centre Carl Aarvold, later to captain the side. England saved their best rugby for the French game when the sun shone after a bleak period of weather and the Richmond wing Godfrey Palmer scored two tries, one of them spectacular, along with another brace by Waterloo back-row forward Harold 'Joe' Periton. Periton, an Irishman, was to take over the captaincy midway through the next season when the brilliant Scottish wing Ian Smith scored two tries in a 12-6 win over the English at Murrayfield in front of 80,000. Scotland won the championship on one of their greatest days. The decade ended with an experimental England side avoiding a wooden spoon with a 16-6 win in Paris with Aarvold scoring two tries. The 1920s were over and, following a golden era for Welsh rugby, England's four Grand Slams made them the most successful of the northern hemisphere sides.

50 Greatest Players

CARL AARVOLD Centre/Wing

Clubs: Cambridge University, West Hartlepool, Blackheath

Debut: v Australia, 7 January 1928

No. of Caps: 16 **No. of Points:** 12

As an undergraduate, the tall and powerful Carl Aarvold displayed the positional sense and uncanny judgement that became the hallmarks of his play. He played in four winning Cambridge Varsity sides to create a record that has never been surpassed.

Only 20 when he won his national spurs in 1928, the Twickenham crowds warmed to his graceful, long-raking strides in the centre of a dynamic three-quarter line. Aarvold's jinking run set up one of the four tries in the 18-11 defeat of the Australians and his unselfish distribution in the championship matches was a considerable asset during a Grand Slam season in which backs scored 75 per cent of England's tries.

Towards the end of his career Aarvold moved to the wing for England, but he was less of a force taking a pass for a try than he was as a try-maker in the centre. He captained the side in seven successive Tests between 1931 and 1933, leading England to a share of the championship in 1932.

The 1930s, though, were to be a fallow period for England. There were isolated successes such as the Triple Crown wins of 1934 and 1937 and the 1936 victory over the All Blacks, quite the most dramatic and unexpected triumph in their history, but the 1928 Grand Slam was to be England's last for 29 years. The 1930s were also a bleak time for the International Championship. France were suspended in 1931 with the home unions complaining that the French clubs were paying their players. The French, improving all the time in the 1920s, were not allowed to play again until after the war. In their last game at Stade Colombes on Easter Monday, 1931, they had plenty to prove and won 14-13 with a late drop goal. For the first time since 1907 England finished the season without a win.

Carl Aarvold's side were then beaten 7-0 by the South Africans. England half-backs Wilf Sobey and Roger Spong were a dynamic pairing but the England team selection for a game against a huge Springbok pack verged on the bizarre with three hookers making up the front row. Bennie Osler's tourists were dour and efficient, but they won all their internationals on their trip and clearly a gap was opening up between northern and southern hemisphere rugby.

England went two years without a win and soon overhauled their team yet again. Bernard Gadney, a strong scrum-half from Leicester with a long pass,

England's Peter Cranmer (second right) outstrips Ireland's David Lane (right) in the 14-3 victory at Twickenham in February 1935.

became one of the most influential of England's players in this pre-war era. Gadney picked up the reins of captaincy from the Blackheath wing Tony Novis in 1934 and captained the British Lions on their 1936 tour to Argentina. And after another modest season in 1935 Gadney was still in charge when England faced the touring All Blacks in 1936. Jack Manchester's New Zealanders may have lacked the ruthlessness of the 1905 Originals and the 1924 Invincibles but they were expected to be much too powerful for the home nations.

The Prince

It was a punishing tour of 28 matches and injuries took their toll but Scotland and Ireland were beaten before the All Blacks travelled to Cardiff four days before Christmas and were narrowly beaten by Claude Davey's Wales. England fielded a side that contained two highly rated new wings in Sale's Hal Sever and, more intriguingly, a young Russian prince, the Oxford University student Alexander Obolensky. The son of prince Sergei Alexandrovich, aide-de-camp of the governor general of Moscow, Alexander was born in St Petersburg during the Great War, and came to England when his family fled the Russian Revolution. Alexander went to Trent College where today awards that carry his name are given to outstanding pupils. Obolensky had played in the scoreless Varsity match of 1935 and was considered to be an outstanding if erratic rugby player. His selection against the All Blacks was a risk but it helped England to what still might be viewed as their most famous victory.

There is *Movietone News* coverage of the 13-0 win over the All Blacks on 4 January 1936 which is perhaps why Obolensky's fame transcended the sport. He became England's first rugby union celebrity, scoring two spectacular first-half tries with Sever adding a third. But it was the manner of the scoring, like Adrian Stoop who instigated the first try at Twickenham 26 years earlier, that marked Obolensky out as a glorious one-off. It was England's first victory over the New Zealanders and 70,000 witnessed it live. The *Manchester Guardian* wrote: 'Obolensky scored one of the most brilliant tries ever seen in an international match and another almost as good, and he would have scored third, fourth and fifth tries but for grand tackling by Ball. He showed great speed and backed this up with a keen eye for unexpected holes in defence.'

England's selectors, though, got it right for once in choosing a pack to give their rampant new wings enough ball. The All Blacks weighed in at around 12st 10lb per man, but England's second row, the marine Charlie Webb and

Allan Clarke, were the heaviest pairing that had ever been fielded, weighing a combined 33 stones. Players like the props Ray Longland and Douglas Kendrew were experienced hard men. They provided possession in spades. After 28 minutes and from a scrum the ball was whipped down the line for Obolensky to beat his busy marker Nelson Ball. He turned inside Ball and then outside to beat the covering defence, squeezing in between the touchline and the covering full-back Gilbert for the first try.

Twickenham Stunned

Ten minutes later the prince was to top this with something even more regal. The English backs moved the ball to the right and the centre Peter Cranmer slipped his marker with a side-step on halfway. He pounded through the gap and found the fly-half Peter Candler to his left. Candler headed in a straight line towards the New Zealand 25, passing outside to Obolensky who instead of tearing down the right checked in full stride to wrong-foot the defence and set off on a diagonal run. His long stride took him clear and he dived over. The brilliant display of the unorthodox stunned Twickenham and the rout was completed when Sever sprinted 35 yards for another memorable try.

England's Alex Obolensky holds off Scotland's Kenneth Fyfe in the 9-8 victory in March 1936.

Oddly, this touch of genius was never to be repeated. England's next match a fortnight later against Wales in Swansea was the antithesis of the glorious open rugby at Twickenham. It finished in a pointless draw and the rest of the season petered out, a narrow defeat by Ireland and a narrow win over Scotland.

Obolensky rose without trace, playing one season for England, never scoring a try in the International Championship. He died in the service of his adopted country while flying a Spitfire in 1940. It is this early tragic death that accounts for Obolensky's fame because, in reality, that fame only lasted 80 minutes. Hal Sever, for instance, is not remembered even though he had a more prolific try-scoring career for England. Sever's try against Ireland in

50 Greatest Players

ALEX OBOLENSKY Wing

Club: Oxford University

Debut: v New Zealand, 4 January 1936

No. of Caps: 4 **No. of Points:** 6

He set no special records for England. Indeed he only appeared four times in the white jersey. Yet his deeds against the All Blacks on a cold January day made him a household name.

The player was Alex Obolensky, an exiled Russian prince who was studying at Oxford University. His two tries against New Zealand on his debut made 'Obo' an overnight star. He was an electric runner who used his acceleration to deceive opponents, but it was his love of the unorthodox that marked him out from the run of the mill wings of the day. His second try against the All Blacks, in particular, was a classic. Receiving the ball far out on his right wing, he ghosted through the New Zealand defence to finish off scoring wide out to the left of the posts.

Captured on film by *Movietone News*, it was probably the first famous try to be seen by a wide audience. Vivian Jenkins, the Welsh full-back at the time, recalled spending several hours at an Oxford Street cinema just to see the two or three minutes of newsreel between feature films (Wales were due to play England a fortnight later).

Obolensky's fame has never waned, though he never again set the rugby world alight. He kept his place for the three championship matches in 1936 – a scoreless draw with Wales, defeat in Dublin and a one-point win against Scotland back at Twickenham. But he never again appeared in a cap match and was killed tragically young in a flying accident early in the Second World War.

1937 is considered one of the greatest Twickenham has ever witnessed. Obolensky's feats, though, gave the game a massive shot in the arm at a time when England were struggling to match the consistency of the 1920s. Ironically, he wasn't around the following year when the Triple Crown and championship was won by a side now captained by the St Mary's Hospital full-back Harold 'Tuppy' Owen-Smith.

Wales were beaten 4-3 at Twickenham with a drop goal from Sever just pipping a try by Wilf Wooller. Ray Longland was still the cornerstone of the pack in a dreary match. Sever's late brilliant try beat Ireland 9-8 before Sever again showed his worth with one of two tries in another breathless victory at Murrayfield by 6-3 over the Scots, 'Jimmy' Unwin, the first player to be capped from Rosslyn Park, scoring a try on his debut. Peter Cranmer took over the captaincy the following season but Scotland won the Triple Crown after a 21-16 win at Twickenham. Unwin again scored a try against the Scots but did not survive the cull in the last season before the Second World War. Wales were beaten 3-0 on a boggy Twickenham pitch but England lost 5-0 to Ireland before a dominant England pack helped set up a 9-6 victory at Murrayfield over the Scots. Scotland scored two tries in England's 200th international match but were beaten by three penalties by the Waterloo

Great Matches

TOUR MATCH **Twickenham, 4 January 1936**
Attendance: 73,000

England 13 **New Zealand 0**

'A remarkable match, with a still more remarkable result,' reported *The Times* after the All Blacks were beaten on English soil for the first time. The Prince of Wales and 73,000 spectators witnessed a victory that was ascribed to the solidity of a heavy pack ably assisted by a close-marking midfield back division with a fine turn of speed in attack.

But the match will forever be inextricably linked to the name of a Russian prince, Alex Obolensky, whose two first-half tries put paid to any hopes New Zealand might have entertained regarding victory. First he turned his marker inside out and outstripped the defence with a straight run of 40 metres along the right wing to open the scoring after 20 minutes. Then, on the stroke of half-time, his turn of pace took him on an unorthodox cross-field run. He not only rounded the All Blacks through sheer pace, but in so doing lost his own support players. Having veered in sharply from the right, he finished off by turning in from the left wing to score a wonderful solo try that was greeted with a loud and enthusiastic fervour rarely witnessed at Twickenham.

Peter Cranmer dropped a goal from 30 yards early in the second half and New Zealand's rout was complete when he sent Hal Sever sprinting 35 yards for the final try.

England: H.G. Owen-Smith; A. Obolensky, P. Cranmer, R.A. Gerrard, H. Sever; P.L. Candler, B.C. Gadney (captain); D.A. Kendrew, E.S. Nicholson, R.J. Longland, C.S.H. Webb, A.J. Clarke, W.H. Weston, P.E. Dunkley, E.A. Hamilton-Hill
Scorers: Tries Obolensky 2, Sever **Drop Goal** Cranmer

New Zealand: G.D.M. Gilbert; N.A. Mitchell, C.J. Oliver, N. Ball; T.H.C. Caughey, E.W.T. Tindill, M.M.N. Corner; A. Lambourn, W.E. Hadley, J. Hore, S.T. Reid, R.R. King, J.E. Manchester (captain), A. Mahoney, H.F. McLean

Referee: J.W. Faull (Wales)

centre Jack Heaton, an injustice that might have rankled with the Scots had not the Second World War intervened to ensure that the result was quickly consigned to history. Heaton's international career had not quite ended but a month after the win at Murrayfield conscription was introduced and England would not play again for eight long years.

50 Greatest Players

BERNARD GADNEY Scrum-half

Clubs: Leicester, Headingley

Debut: v Ireland, 13 February 1932

No. of Caps: 14 **No. of Points:** 3

At a time when international rugby matches were low-scoring contests in which tight defences invariably stifled sides with attacking ambitions, Leicester's Gadney emerged as the outstanding scrum-half of the day, a player ideally suited to bear the pressures of the times and break the shackles of attentive flankers.

Tall for a scrum-half, he made his England debut in 1932 and quickly impressed the critics. 'He conforms to the modern conception of a workable scrum half, a man strong enough to get the ball away with a couple of opposing wing forwards on top of him,' remarked *The Times* after his first match.

Eighteen months later he was at the peak of his powers going into the England trials for 1933-34. He had a forceful break and his strength often carried him through defences for what became generally known as 'one of Gadney's characteristic tries'. Captaincy was also thrust upon him that season. He was to skipper Leicester later, but the novice proved a shrewd leader steering England to their first Triple Crown for six years.

Ankle injuries and the rival skills of Coventry's Jimmy Giles interrupted his run in the England side. Even so, he led them to a famous victory over the 1936 All Blacks (in Obolensky's match) and he returned to work the scrum when England regained the Triple Crown by winning for the first time at Murrayfield, in 1937. After taking up a headship in Yorkshire he joined Headingley the same year and played his last international against Wales at Cardiff in 1938.

Chapter Four: 1945-59
New Beginnings

For the best part of eight years the English public had been rationed not only of food and the bare essentials of life but also of outdoor spectator sport. In the post-war years there was a clamour to watch soccer and cricket and both sports had followings that far outstripped the crowds of the 1930s. International rugby union, however, took some time before it could return. The Second World War had taken a heavy toll on its playing strength and the sport's still-amateur players had to first resurrect their interrupted working lives.

During the war there had been service international matches and, in the immediate aftermath, a series of informal representative fixtures known as the 'Victory Internationals'. The Rugby Football Union picked an England XV for one such game against a Kiwi XV in November 1945 at Twickenham, a contest that ended in a heavy defeat for the home team by 18-3. Two months later the England team beat a Welsh XV in Cardiff 25-13. There were 14 of these fixtures with France and the other home unions also involved. England were to play two more of these games at Twickenham in the spring of 1946, beating Scotland and losing to Wales. There were no caps given for these matches, but the sport was in a revivalist mood, 40,000, including George VI and Princess Elizabeth, watching the University match and the Middlesex Sevens competition returned to Twickenham.

But for England the International Championship lay dormant until 18 January 1947 and a meeting with Wales at Cardiff Arms Park. It was a freezing winter, the country was in the grip of a fuel crisis with a ban on coal exports and a strike of transport workers had begun. The Churchill government was trying to appease a country that had grown tired of austerity and in Wales the anticipation of a game of rugby union against the English was at fever-pitch. There were only 44,000 tickets available as bomb damage had made the north stand unsafe, but there had been more than a quarter of a million applications for tickets.

Wales fancied their chances. They had a midfield trinity of Cardiff players in the brilliant fly-half Bleddyn Williams and the two centres Jack Matthews and Billy Cleaver. With their captain, the scrum-half Haydn Tanner, they were expected to profit from plenty of possession from a rugged pack. Matthews had just recovered from a bout of flu and amazingly, as the country was to be enveloped by fog the following day, the sun shone in an almost symbolic way on this fixture. The two countries had emerged from dark days to play rugby again but it was no classic. England won 9-6 in a match *The Times* called a 'crude and scrappy affair'.

Olympic Sprinter

Three players from before the war had survived to play in the fixture, Haydn Tanner and Howard Davies of Wales and the Waterloo wing Dickie Guest for England. Rees Stephens and Gwyn Evans, two back-row players, scored the tries for Wales who chose the Olympic sprinter Ken Jones on their right wing. The Welsh crowd were deflated after the game, a match which had no loudspeaker system so the team changes had to be given by a man carrying a board around the edge of the pitch.

England coped well with the much-vaunted Welsh eight despite, for most of the match, being reduced to seven forwards when Mickey Steele-Bodger, their Cambridge flanker, was shunted to the backs to fill in for the injured centre Keith Scott who damaged his knee after only 15 minutes. England's victory came via a try by the Northampton flanker Don White from a cross kick by the scrum-half Bill Moore. White, who that weekend was celebrating his 21st birthday, was later to play a major part in the revival of English rugby as a selector and coach.

Action from England's 'Victory International' against Wales at Twickenham in February 1946.

England knew they had been lucky but were just relieved to have finally played a match and begun the post-war era on a winning note. Their elation, though, lasted only three weeks by which time Ireland had trounced them 22-0 in Dublin, a record defeat in the fixture. Ireland were assembling their most successful side, built around a solid pack and an outstanding fly-half in the Queen's University player Jack Kyle. It was a raw day and the England players unusually left the field at the interval when they each had a glass of brandy to help revive their bodies for the second half. There was not much to raise English spirits, though. The Lansdowne Road pitch was half frozen and in a biting east wind Ireland scored five tries without a reply. The English pack were outplayed and the selectors made swingeing changes for the fixture with France, a game that was to be postponed until the end of the season because of the icy conditions that gripped the country. The student players were not thought up to it. Out went the Oxford three-quarters David Swarbrick and Martin Donnelly, the No. 8 Basil Travers and Cambridge lock Sam Perry. Donnelly never played for England again but the New Zealander became one of his country's leading cricketers.When England returned to play a full international at Twickenham on 15 March 1947, Scotland were beaten 24-5. The hard-tackling Waterloo centre Jack Heaton, much derided by critics for his performance against the Scots in that last match before the war, had a thick skin for he had returned to international action in Dublin and survived to captain the side here and convert one of England's four tries. In Nim Hall, the St Mary's fly-half, and Mickey Steele-Bodger, England looked to have found players of real quality.

The following month saw France, in that postponed fixture, beaten 6-3 when they eventually came to Twickenham. The hitherto disappointing Swarbrick showed some good touches at last and Dickie Guest and the Cornish forward Vic Roberts scored tries to end a more than satisfactory championship return for England. Roberts had replaced Don White in the back row, the selectors noting that White had played four games in five days on Northampton's trip to Wales that Easter and was looking stale.

The 'Third Wallabies'

England had a side that could match any of their European rivals but they invariably fell short when they played the southern hemisphere big three. There were isolated successes – Australia in 1928, New Zealand in 1936 – but when Australia called again at the beginning of 1948 England were once more found wanting. The 'Third Wallabies' won 11-0 at Twickenham and, as the old joke goes, England were lucky to get nil.

The Wallaby tour had begun badly when their captain, the Queensland forward Bill McLean, broke his leg in the sixth match against Combined Services but the trip became something of a triumph. They did not concede a try in their four internationals, although beaten 6-0 by Wales thanks to two Bill Tamplin penalties. On the day of the meeting with England, a damp mist covered the ground and 70,000 spectators saw the New South Wales Test debutant Alan Walker score a sensational try after receiving the ball from a scrum on the Australian 25. Two more tries spelt a demoralising defeat for England but there was to be a portent of better things to come. Making his debut in a less sensational way than Walker was a young Sale prop Eric Evans. In the next decade Evans was to lead one of the best sides in England's history and secure a place in the pantheon with a famous Grand Slam victory.

'Titanic Struggle'

In the meantime, it was a bleak period for England. They faced Wales at Twickenham a fortnight after the Wallaby defeat and only the Twickenham jinx that had haunted the Welsh again robbed them of victory. It was 3-3 but Wales should easily have won a game *The Times* called a 'Titanic struggle'. A quarter of an hour from time Newman broke his arm and Basil Travers had to drop back from the pack to cover. Travers had a bandage over his cut eye and England were given some scary moments. Amazingly they survived, but Newman, England's scorer, never played again. More controversially, neither did England's captain, the Richmond fly-half Tom Kemp, who refused to travel to Ireland for the next fixture. Although his England career ended abruptly Kemp was later to become the Rugby Football Union president in 1971.

At Twickenham, Karl Mullen's resurgent Irish team beat England 11-10 on their way to their one and only Grand Slam. This was despite a quite stunning try by Dickie Guest who ran in to score with a swerving run from inside England's 25. England's misery continued as they lost their following two games at Murrayfield and Stade Colombes.

Now in disarray, their 15-0 defeat by France was the worst in the history of the fixture. England finished the decade with another emphatic victory over the Scots, but the win only helped them avoid a wooden spoon. The season had opened with away defeats to Wales and Ireland when, once again, they resorted to an overseas student – this time the Oxford centre and South African Test cricketer Clive van Ryneveld – to bolster their back division. The team that entered the 1950s would have a makeshift look to it. In two seasons they had been led by five different captains – Keith Scott, Tom Kemp, Bob Weighill, Nim Hall and Ivor Preece.

For the first game of the new decade, against Wales at Twickenham, the crowd was a record 75,500 and the appetite for the game was never healthier. The gates were closed half an hour before kick-off and thousands were locked out. Eric Evans returned to the side as hooker, a position the Lancastrian was to make his own, but he made little immediate impact. Not only was Wales's 11-5 victory their first at Twickenham for 17 years, but it marked a high-water mark for Welsh rugby. Eighteen-year-old full-back Lewis Jones, the new star of Welsh rugby, constructed a brilliant try when he fielded a kick deep in his own half and began a swerving run to the English 25 beginning a move that ended with Cardiff's prop Cliff Davies crashing over.

One more crunching tackle in England's gruelling 3-8 defeat by South Africa in 1952.

Outmuscled

And again England were to be found wanting when southern hemisphere opposition came to call. The 1952 Springboks, led by Basil Kenyon, were one of the strongest sides to have left South Africa. Even with No. 8 Hennie Muller deputising for Kenyon, the tourists ran up an 8-3 win at Twickenham against an English side led by Nim Hall. The Springboks were not an attractive side but they had an outstanding stand-off in Hannes Brewis and outmuscled opponents up front while playing to strict tactics. Kenyon explained: 'Tight play was never neglected, but used to form the basis for second-phase attack which we knew we could win, possessing the speed to do so among the loose forwards. Once they mastered the ball they brought the tight forwards back into play, hence the many passing movements among the forwards. When the loose forwards were forced to form a loose scrum the ball went out to the backs who rounded off the movement. The tight play would soften up our opponents and the loose play would send backs away or bring the forwards back into play.'

The tactics were brutally effective and the Springboks had forwards like the Boland prop Chris Koch, the bald-headed flanker Basie van Wyk and the huge lock Salty du Rand who could carry them out. England were beaten but they fared a lot better than Scotland who were thrashed 44-0 at Murrayfield in a game of nine tries and no penalties. And if the England team of the early 1950s had a mix-and-match look it would soon regroup around Evans and evolve into the best English side since the heady days of Wavell Wakefield.

50 Greatest Players

NORMAN 'NIM' HALL Full-back/Fly-half

Clubs: St Mary's Hospital, Richmond

Debut: v Wales, 18 January 1947

No. of Caps: 17 **No. of Points:** 39

His father was Irish and his mother Scottish, but Norman 'Nim' Hall was the backbone of the England side for the best part of nine seasons when official internationals restarted after the Second World War.

He entered first-class rugby as a young 18-year-old medical student in 1943 and was a prominent member of the St Mary's Hospital back division that enjoyed a long period of success during the restricted programme of club matches staged in the war seasons. Later, though still in his playing prime, Hall was called 'Rugby's Methuselah' by critics who joked that he had been in the game for so long.

His exploits with the hospital side made him an automatic choice for England when organised Tests restarted in 1947. On his debut he helped sink Wales at Cardiff with one of his trademark dropped goals and he was the side's linchpin at fly-half in a season that brought a share of the International Championship. Only 23 when he was made captain in 1949, his appearances over the next three seasons were restricted through injury, but he returned as captain in 1952 when England were runners-up in the championship. As a converted full-back, he led an enterprising side to the title in 1953 when his style and certainty, as a then unprecedented round-the-corner place-kicker, yielded the two important penalties that earned England a lucky draw in Dublin. Still under 30, he last appeared in 1955 winding up a career in which he had led his country 13 times to match Wavell Wakefield's old record.

Enter Butterfield

England's zenith was the Grand Slam-winning team of 1957 but, in 1953, the year of the Matthews FA Cup final and England's victory in cricket's Ashes series, the national rugby team had something to celebrate. Still led by Nim Hall, who by now had moved to full-back, England won the International Championship, narrowly failing to win a Grand Slam with a 9-9 draw in Dublin where Jack Kyle was back to his mesmerising best. England found their own new star during the season in the Northampton centre Jeff Butterfield who crowned his debut against France at Twickenham with a late try. Butterfield, a sinewy runner, was to become a British Lion and one of the finest centres England had produced. By the end of the season he was to forge a partnership with the young hard-tackling Harlequins centre Phil 'WPC' Davies that would become a potent combination during the 1950s. Butterfield ran in one of six tries as England crushed Scotland 26-8 to win the championship outright for the first time since 1937.

Still, though, those hard-nosed visitors from the Land of the Long White Cloud were to puncture English optimism with a 5-0 victory at Twickenham the following year. Again England entertained New Zealand in a period of awful weather. Some 17 tons of straw just managed to preserve the Twickenham game on a day when there was a wholesale cancellation of club fixtures and

Action from England's match against New Zealand in January 1954 as Bob Scott (right) pounces on 'Tug' Wilson.

the postponement of the Wales-Scotland game at Swansea. The All Blacks had a genius at full-back in Bob Scott and a dominant pack. 'Heroic but hopeless' said *The Times* of England's failure to prevent the New Zealanders exacting revenge for that 1936 defeat. Oddly, a month earlier, Wales had beaten the All Blacks with a famous try by Ken Jones from a cross-kick by Clem Thomas but there was no such inspiration from England.

This was an historic season for France who for the first time in their history topped the championship, albeit with the same number of points as England and Wales. But it was England who grabbed the Triple Crown. Jeff Butterfield had been particularly brilliant at Twickenham when Jack Kyle had failed to make the team after pulling a thigh muscle in training in Belfast and the Lancashire half-back pair of Gordon Rimmer and Martin Regan were developing into a useful combination. England's only defeat of the 1954 season came in their final game in Paris when the English pack was made to look leaden-footed, and the boot of the legendary back-row forward Jean Prat and an opportunist try by his brother, the centre Maurice, condemned the visitors to an 11-3 defeat which deprived them of the Grand Slam.

Revamped Pack

England were led in their Triple Crown-winning year by Bob Stirling, the Wasps prop, who with Eric Evans and the Harlequin Donald 'Sandy' Sanders formed the cornerstone of an effective English pack. Stirling had been a heavyweight boxer in the RAF and England were punching their weight in the mid-1950s, but the French team's forwards handled like backs and the English looked stodgy in comparison. The selectors, for the next game in 1955 at Cardiff Arms Park, completely revamped the pack. Hooker Eric Evans was replaced by South African Nick Labuschagne, the last of a number of non-English students to be picked for the national team, and only Dublin Wanderers lock Peter Young survived the cull.

As a heavy Arthurian mist enveloped the stadium, 56,000 watched one of the most miserable internationals of all time. Wales won 3-0 with the only score coming from a penalty by the London Welsh full-back Arthur Edwards. There were mitigating circumstances for the awfulness of the occasion. The match had been postponed for a week because of heavy snow and the pitch was a morass of clinging mud. Even Bleddyn Williams, the legendary Welsh centre in his last season, played poorly. It was a miserable English squad that returned from Cardiff the following day.

From the wreckage of the 1955 season, when only Scotland were beaten in a dour final game at Twickenham, the English selectors looked to construct

50 Greatest Players

ERIC EVANS Prop/Hooker

Club: Sale

Debut: v Australia, 3 January 1948

No. of Caps: 30 **No. of Points:** 15

He won his first cap as a prop, but it was as an expert hooker and inspirational captain that Eric Evans is chiefly remembered. His England appearances were few and far between in the three years that followed his debut, but at length he resolved to improve his physical fitness and took himself off to train with the legendary Manchester United Busby Babes. He raised his stamina to levels that would not look out of place in today's demanding professional era, at the same time honing his skills to become one of the best technical exponents of the hooker's arts.

After featuring in the championship-winning side of 1953 and the Triple Crown success of 1954, he was recalled in 1956 as captain of an inexperienced team. Aged nearly 35, Evans relished the challenge of leading an England team that contained ten new caps and, although seeing the team narrowly beaten by Wales in the opening game, the selectors wisely resisted the temptation to make wholesale changes.

Evans' enthusiasm rubbed off on his side. He set them high standards with his own personal fitness and forged the entire team into such a formidable unit that over the three seasons he was in charge England lost only once more. They achieved the Grand Slam for the first time for 29 years in 1957 and won the championship title again in 1958 before Evans retired, safely among the top England captains of all-time.

a new side around the leadership of Eric Evans. Their search found Oxford's John Currie and Cambridge's David Marques, at 6ft 5in (1.85m) the tallest player of his era. They would become a permanent fixture in the second row until they went their separate ways in 1961. Also from Oxford came the open-side flanker Peter Robbins, a tough, uncompromising forward. However, Oxford University stand-off Mike Smith, was drafted in for the 1956 return against Wales and while he was to prove an able England cricket captain in the 1960s, he was out of his depth on the international rugby field. It was his only cap and Smith was to be a scapegoat for an 8-3 defeat.

The team quickly took shape. Dickie Jeeps, the British Lions scrum-half, found a perfect partner in the Harlequin stand-off Ricky Bartlett, while

England found themselves with a set of three-quarters as effective as any combination in world rugby. Jeff Butterfield found his perfect foil in Phil Davies and on the wings Coventry's Peter Jackson and Peter Thompson from Headingley were deadly finishers.

The Elusive Grand Slam

The 1957 England team was one of the strongest ever fielded and yet England might never have won that elusive Grand Slam if it were not for the Neath wing Keith Maddocks straying offside in the first half of the opening game at the Arms Park. Maddocks was slow to get back into position while a line-out was taking place at the other side of the field. His casual and quite unintentional error was spotted by the Scottish referee Mr Dickie and the Coventry full-back Fenwick Allison landed the penalty, the only score of the match. The contrast between England's mood after this 3-0 win and defeat by the same score in Cardiff two years earlier could not have been greater.

Lewis Cannell, who partnered Butterfield in the centre for the first two games of the Grand Slam year, had first appeared for England in 1948. The Northampton player was one of the most underrated players of the day but opportunities for three-quarters were rare in international rugby in the 1950s; Cannell scored only two tries in 19 games.

The 1957 Grand Slam-winning team only scored one try in their first two games, Peter Jackson's winning effort settling another close game in Dublin. Evans' team then opened up to beat France 9-5 at Twickenham with two tries by Jackson and one by Evans, before wrapping up their first Grand Slam since 1928 with a 16-3 victory over Scotland. Evans was carried off on the shoulders of his team. They used only 17 players all season with their muscular pack unchanged throughout the campaign. The phrase 'Grand Slam' was used for the first time in *The Times* and it has been the Holy Grail of sides in the championship ever since.

Evans, the sandy-haired bow-legged Lancastrian who could turn the air blue with his flow of colourful language, was the linchpin of the side. Although his opponents complained that he was over-physical, he had few rivals as hooker and was unlucky not to be picked by the British Lions. Through a mixture of shrewdness and toughness, he generated a drive and discipline that had not been seen in England sides of the past and this, combined with a set of outstanding backs who could capitalise on abundant possession, made England unstoppable. They were unbeaten for two seasons, although in 1958 Clem Thomas's Welsh team held England to a

50 Greatest Players

PETER JACKSON Wing

Club: Coventry

Debut: v Wales, 21 January 1956

No. of Caps: 20 **No. of Points:** 18

Peter Jackson was the most unorthodox wing to play for England since Alex Obolensky. Like the Russian prince, beating players came instinctively to him. He could tear defences apart with a lethal cut-in that wrong footed opponents, but the criticism levelled at him was that his unpredictability too often bamboozled his own colleagues.

He entered Eric Evans's England team alongside nine other new caps against Wales in 1956 and in the following match against Ireland scored the first of his six international tries.

Jackson was an inspiration to the 1957 Grand Slam side. His reputation as a tricky runner now well established, he had opponents jittery at the prospect of marking him. Against Wales his opposite number fell offside at a set-piece to present England with a penalty goal near the posts which proved to be the only score of the game. Jackson scored the only try of the match in Dublin and crossed for two beauties in the 9-5 defeat of France at Twickenham.

He thrilled Twickenham again in 1958, scoring the winning try against Australia with a mesmerising solo effort in the dying moments, and he was a success in New Zealand with the 1959 Lions before mysteriously losing form and favour. Jackson made only one more appearance in the next three seasons before returning, aged 32, to play in the side that won the championship title outright in 1963. His pace against Wales created the spectacular match-turning try by Malcolm Phillips in what was destined to be England's last Cardiff triumph for 28 years.

3-3 draw – there were hearts in English mouths near the end when Terry Davies's late long-range penalty struck a post – and Scotland earned an identical result. Evans summed up his winning philosophy: 'Ours was a disciplined approach and perhaps being mature in the game I was able to enforce that discipline. I received every encouragement from the chairman of selectors Carston Catcheside and I went to a lot of trouble to get and keep extremely fit.'

Evans' booming voice could be heard from the touchline berating his players. His hard-nosed approach did not go down well with everyone in the corridors of power at Twickenham, but in the late 1950s England had a team that could hold its own with the best in the world. When the Australians came to call in 1958, they knew they were in for a

Great Matches

FIVE NATIONS CHAMPIONSHIP — **Twickenham, 16 March 1957**
Attendance: 72,000

England 16 — **Scotland 3**

Forward dominance and a back division that snaffled up its chances helped England to their first Grand Slam for 29 years. They savoured the victory, and it was just as well – it would be their last for another 23 seasons.

In a tentative start, England reacted nervously to the few chances that came their way and an expectant crowd began to wonder if the enormity of the occasion would prove too burdensome for a young side. But doubts began to evaporate before half-time when Jeff Butterfield, at his creative best, carved out an opening for his co-centre Phil Davies to cross at the corner to give England a 6-3 lead.

It was a try that whetted appetites for the feast that was to follow late in the match, when the Scottish defence finally crumbled. Flanker Reg Higgins, who played a blinder, burst away to send Peter Thompson over and then scored the last try himself after unrelenting English pressure near the Scotland line.

Under Eric Evans' captaincy, England had enjoyed three successful seasons between 1956 and 1958, losing only two of their 13 internationals. Arguably their finest hour came in this three-try win set before the Queen, Prince Philip and Prince Charles and notably the term 'Grand Slam', referring to an invincible championship season, appeared for the first time in the press reviews of this match.

England: R. Challis; P.B. Jackson, J. Butterfield, W.P.C. Davies, P.H. Thompson; R.M. Bartlett, R.E.G. Jeeps; C.R. Jacobs, E. Evans (captain), G.W.D. Hastings, J.D. Currie, R.W.D. Marques, R. Higgins, A. Ashcroft, P.G.D. Robbins
Scorers: Tries Davies, Thompson, Higgins **Conversions** Challis 2 **Penalty Goal** Challis

Scotland: K.J.F. Scotland; A.R. Smith, T. McClung, K.R. Macdonald, J.L.F. Allan; G.H. Waddell, A.F. Dorward; H.F. McLeod, R.K.G. MacEwen, T. Elliot, E.J.S. Michie, J.W.Y. Kemp, A. Robson, J.T. Greenwood (captain), G.K. Smith
Scorer: Penalty Goal Scotland

Referee: R. Mitchell (Ireland)

Above: Peter Thompson touches down for England's second try. Opposite page: Bob Challis converts Thompson's try. Below: Eric Evans is chaired off by his Grand Slam winning team-mates.

tough game, but the match against the Wallabies proved to be a sensational one.

It was punctuated by stoppages for injuries and England played over half the match with 14 men when their stand-off Phil Horrocks-Taylor left the field, leaving Peter Robbins to fill a vacant berth in midfield. Then Jeff Butterfield, who had moved temporarily to fly-half to fill in for Horrocks-Taylor, was injured in a heavy tackle. A stretcher carried the centre off the field only for Butterfield to leap out of it and Lazarus-like resume his place at fly-half. The incident seemed to inspire England deep into injury-time when they launched one last desperate attack. The ball moved to the left wing where Peter Thompson was bundled into touch but managed to keep the ball alive. In the thick February mist Jeeps, Butterfield and Robbins kept the ball moving and transferred it to Jackson who was moving diagonally from the right wing. Without checking his speed he sped past three covering defenders before diving over in the corner for one of the greatest tries ever seen at Twickenham. England had their first win over one of the southern hemisphere big three since the war – the defining moment of English rugby in the 1950s and the highlight of the Coventry wing's career.

Lack of Decorum

The Wallabies argued that Jackson's try should not have stood as it occurred deep into injury-time, but the bruising game was already a controversial one. The tourists had picked the teenage centre Jim Lenehan whose crash-tackles had almost caused a riot when the tourists met Swansea. Early in the England match, Lenehan was in the thick of things again and his knees-first tackle on Peter Thompson caused the Twickenham crowd to boo him every time he touched the ball. In the 1950s this lack of decorum was unusual for a rugby crowd. The *Manchester Guardian* reported on this end to an age of innocence: 'The booing was of an ugliness even old campaigners could not recall at Twickenham.'

Evans' team could not survive more than two seasons, though, and the decade finished with new captain Jeff Butterfield's team being swamped in a Cardiff mudheap. A series of attritional matches between Wales and England continued with Clem Thomas leading his team to a 5-0 win at the Arms Park. It was a game remembered for one move when the Welsh wing Dewi Bebb somehow overcame the appalling conditions to mark his debut with a dazzling try. Jeff Butterfield's team ended the decade with more of a whimper than a bang, going five successive matches without scoring a try. With finishers of the likes of British Lions Butterfield and Peter Jackson at

Great Matches

TEST MATCH | **Twickenham, 1 February 1958**
Attendance: 60,000

England 9 | **Australia 6**

There have been more polished performances and more important victories. But for sheer guts or a more desperate grandstand finish there can be few among England's 500-plus Tests to match this winter win against Bob Davidson's Fourth Wallabies.

Several England players were concussed or injured during the course of a rough game and, 11 years before the use of substitutes was finally sanctioned at Test level, Eric Evans's team had to play for nearly an hour with only 14 men. Phil Horrocks-Taylor had been injured early on, necessitating a wholesale rearrangement of the back division.

In the dying minutes the scores were tied at 6-6 when, with Jeff Butterfield also lying injured, Eric Evans exhorted his men to raise one last effort to win the game. The player who turned the match with a sublime do-or-die run was right-wing, Peter Jackson. Receiving the ball on the Aussie 25, he deceived his opponent with a swerve and hand-off and ran clear to turn the full-back inside out with a wonderful feint and check. Then he raced on to the line, winning a race with Rod Phelps to lunge over at the corner flag for the score that gave the men in white their first success against a touring side for 22 years.

Match hero Peter Jackson kicks for touch.

England: J.G.G. Hetherington; P.B. Jackson, J. Butterfield, M.S. Phillips, P.H. Thompson; J.P. Horrocks-Taylor, R.E.G. Jeeps; C.R. Jacobs, E. Evans (captain), G.W.D. Hastings, J.D. Currie, R.W.D. Marques, R.E. Syrett, A. Ashcroft, P.G.D. Robbins
Scorers: Tries Jackson, Phillips **Penalty Goal** Hetherington

Australia: T.G.P. Curley; K.J. Donald, J.K. Lenehan, S.W. White, R. Phelps; A.J. Summons, D.M. Connor; G.N. Vaughan, J.V. Brown, R.A.L. Davidson (captain), A.R. Miller, D.M. Emanuel, N.M. Hughes, K.J. Ryan, P.T. Fenwicke
Scorers: Penalty Goal Lenehan **Drop Goal** Curley

Referee: R.C. Williams (Ireland)

their disposal, that was a serious indictment of their play. A crowd of 70,000 tramped out of Twickenham after the last match of the decade, yet another drab 3-3 draw with the Scots, in subdued mood given the pyrotechnics they had witnessed in that win over the Wallabies little more than 12 months earlier. But even if the 1950s had ended a bit of a damp squib, Eric Evans' Boys of 1957 had already written a size 13 footnote in English rugby history.

50 Greatest Players

JEFF BUTTERFIELD Centre

Club: Northampton

Debut: v France, 28 February 1953

No. of Caps: 28 **No. of Points:** 15

'At centre... England gained considerably in penetrative power through the introduction of Butterfield.' That was the considered opinion of *The Times*'s rugby correspondent, Owen Owen, after Jeff Butterfield's debut in 1953. Six years and 27 more successive matches which included four championship titles, two Triple Crowns and a Grand Slam would seem to support his judgement.

The hallmark of Butterfield's approach to Test rugby was personal fitness. He set high standards working to improve his strength and speed, but while the hours of training gave him the stamina to tackle opponents to a standstill, the striking feature of his play was his handling. A natural sportsman, he had the dexterity to take and give a pass in one smooth action and the vision to straighten a three-quarter attack. Often his carefully weighted transfers created tries for his wings, though he was a deadly finisher in his own right, well able to score tries from his searing breaks.

Butterfield's vision was a key element in England's successful years between 1953 and 1958. Just consider the statistics: during his career 26 of the 43 tries England scored were credited to three-quarters and England kept 15 clean try sheets. International rugby in the 1950s was not the fast-flowing spectacle that it is today, maybe. Yet Jeff Butterfield's skills would have shone like a beacon in any era.

Chapter Five: 1960-79
The Monochrome Years

The 1960s would be a decade that wasn't so much swinging for the national team as one that lurched from bad to not much better. But English rugby began the decade in search of a new hero and it found one, after just 16 days. In the 1959 season England had found a fly-half in the unlikely setting of the geography department of Manchester University.

Bev Risman was also an unlikely candidate to wear the white shirt of England. The son of Gus Risman, one of the all-time greats of rugby league, Risman junior was a great natural talent who had made such an impact in 1959 that he was selected for the Lions' tour of New Zealand and Australia. He played with easy-going precocity in winning Tests against the Wallabies in Brisbane and Sydney and in the first losing Test against the All Blacks, only to chip a bone in his ankle on the eve of the second Test. Returning for the final Test in Auckland, Risman won the match with a late try from a blindside run. He came home a hero and England expected to build their new-look championship around him in partnership with their new captain Dickie Jeeps. But fate had other plans.

As the 1960 season got underway, a tweaked hamstring caused Risman once again to cry off on the eve of a match. On the Friday afternoon, Twickenham cabled the Cornish home of Richard Sharp, a 21-year-old who had starred in the Varsity match for Oxford a month earlier. The following afternoon, Sharp's debut against Wales electrified Twickenham in much the same way Obolensky had a generation earlier. Despite the layers of straw on the pitch that had ensured the weather-ravaged fixture had gone ahead, Sharp ran rings around his marker, the flanker Haydn Morgan. His telling break from halfway gave another debutant, the Sale wing Jim Roberts, the second of his two tries to ensure a comfortable 14-6 win against a highly rated Welsh team. *The Times* was ecstatic: 'The signs are most encouraging to the hosts of lovers of the game who have hated the negative at-all-costs-don't-lose outlook which had been strangling an adventurous approach. Sharp came in at stand-off by a lucky fluke and few men have ever made a more telling first appearance. Tall and long-limbed, he moves fast with an elegant grace, can kick with either foot and can pick up a pass from anywhere.'

England's Bev Risman tries to jink his way down the near touchline in the championship match against Wales in 1961.

When Sharp played in England's next game against Ireland he landed a nonchalant drop goal to give them an 8-5 win and England's supporters knew they had the genuine article at fly-half, someone they could mention in the same breath as Ireland's Jack Kyle and Cliff Morgan of Wales. The England selectors, who had waited an eternity for a special fly-half to appear, were suddenly spoiled for choice. Risman played another two matches for England the following season but, edged out of the No. 10 spot by Sharp, soon left for a career in rugby league.

Cheekbone Smashed

Sharp, a modest, unassuming man who went on to become the *Sunday Telegraph*'s rugby correspondent, won 14 caps between 1960 and 1967 and captained England five times. He would have been a star too of the British Lions in South Africa in 1962 but Sharp had his cheekbone smashed as the result of a high tackle by the Northern Transvaal centre Mannetjies Roux in a warm-up match for the first Test in Pretoria.

He recovered, though, in time to lead England to their championship victory of 1963. Amazingly, it was their only championship victory of not only the 1960s but also the 1970s, a period of domination by Wales and France. The portents in 1963, though, looked good for English rugby. Sharp had taken over from Jeeps as captain and England had a new scrum-half in the Cambridge University No. 9, Simon Clarke. The only survivor from Evans' Grand Slam-winning side was Peter Jackson as Budge Rogers had seen off the challenge of Robbins for the open-side flanker's berth in a pack containing six new caps.

Again the Wales match in Cardiff was dogged by foul weather, England winning 13-6 on a pitch more suited to ice skating than rugby, but Sharp was

50 Greatest Players

PETER ROBBINS Flanker

Clubs: Oxford University, Coventry, Moseley

Debut: v Wales, 21 January 1956

No. of Caps: 19 **No. of Points:** 0

Peter Robbins was the out-and-out open-side flanker who tackled like a thunderbolt and covered the ground with lightning pace in the packs that dominated the Five Nations in 1957, 1958 and 1960.

An Oxford graduate, he lined up under Eric Evans among the ten new caps who faced Wales in 1956 and quickly gained a reputation as a canny flanker who used his sense of anticipation to nail opposing fly-halves. Robbins, like the Mounties, always got his man. Teams coming up against him in Five Nations matches between 1957 and 1960 – he was controversially dropped in 1959 because he didn't push in the scrums, the critics said – managed only three tries. That statistic underlines the effective defensive work of the team and of the flankers in particular.

Many critics lobbied for him as an England captain. Robbins had lifted an ordinary Oxford side into a fit and effective unit that outwitted Cambridge to win the 1957 Varsity match. But the call never came. He was succeeded on the open-side by Budge Rogers in 1961 and despite subsequently switching to the blind side for his club, his tally of appearances ended at 19 after a brief recall in 1962. He should, many felt, have won twice as a many caps.

more than a match for Wales's new fly-half prodigy David Watkins. Another of those points-free matches that continued to dog the championship gave England a slightly lucky share of the spoils in Dublin before France were beaten by a point 6-5 at Twickenham. England was in the grip of another freezing winter and for the first time hot-air blowers protected the pitch to ensure the French game went ahead. But England's victory was only ensured by two penalties from the British Lions full-back John Willcox. England were set for the championship, but they had saved the champagne rugby to last, and it was Richard Sharp who provided the sparkle.

Scotland, led by the fly-half Ken Scotland, came to Twickenham determined to end their bleak run in London and began the match with a swagger. They ran up an eight-point lead before Sharp took over. The prop Nick Drake-Lee had scored a try to give England an escape route and Sharp successfully hatched the escape plan. Early in the second half England won a scrum and Simon Clarke gave Sharp the opportunity for an open-side run.

Sharp worked a dummy scissors with his centres Mike Weston and Malcolm Phillips before straightening up and slicing between the Scottish centres. With only the Scottish full-back Blaikie between him and the line, Sharp threw an enormous dummy before gliding over the line without any change of pace. Twickenham erupted and Sharp was cheered back to the halfway line. John Willcox's conversion wrapped up the championship.

The game, remembered as 'Richard Sharp's March', was to herald a new golden era for English rugby but rather it was a peak in a flat period. Richard

Great Matches

FIVE NATIONS CHAMPIONSHIP — **Cardiff Arms Park, 19 January 1963**
Attendance: 51,500

Wales 6 — **England 13**

Two young and inexperienced sides faced each other in Arctic conditions yet presented the capacity crowd and a huge television audience (there being no other major outdoor sporting event to cover owing to the severe weather) with a wonderful exhibition of attacking rugby. The weather was so cold that the paint used to mark the pitch froze and the players were issued with thermal underwear.

England went on to take the championship title under new skipper, Richard Sharp. Forward dominance, a lively back row spearheaded by Budge Rogers, and of course Sharp to ignite a fast and talented back division were the notable ingredients in England's success.

Wales had several chances to open the scoring in the early stages but their failure to do so enabled the young visitors to grow in confidence. The first score came shortly before half time when Mike Weston took a long throw-in on his own 25 and sent Malcolm Phillips and Peter Jackson on a breathtaking length-of-the-pitch run for Phillips to score.

In a match destined to be England's last win in Cardiff for 28 years they never looked in danger of relinquishing their stranglehold on an unusually subdued Welsh pack in the second half.

Wales: G.T.R. Hodgson; D.R.R. Morgan, D.K. Jones, D.B. Davies, D.I.E. Bebb; D. Watkins, D.C.T. Rowlands (captain); K.D. Jones, N.R. Gale, D. Williams, B. Thomas, B. Price, A.E.I. Pask, R.C.B. Michaelson, D.J. Hayward
Scorers: Try Hayward **Penalty Goal** Hodgson

England: J.G. Willcox; P.B. Jackson, M.S. Phillips, M.P. Weston, J. Roberts; R.A.W. Sharp (captain), S.J.S. Clarke; N.J. Drake-Lee, J.D. Thorne, B.A. Dovey, A.M. Davis, J.E. Owen, D.C. Manley, B.J. Wightman, D.P. Rogers
Scorers: Tries Owen, Phillips **Conversions** Sharp 2 **Drop Goal** Sharp

Referee: K.D. Kelleher (Ireland)

Sharp was to play only one more game for England when Australia hammered them at Twickenham four years later. He retired prematurely to concentrate on his day job as a master at Sherborne School in Dorset. He was a classic running fly-half and he did not enjoy his bruising encounter with the All Blacks when he played for the Barbarians 10 months after guiding England to the championship and, at 25, his international career was effectively over.

Sharp was gone and England were caught at the sharp end. Without their fly-half genius, England's championship side made history when they became the first of the home nations to tour New Zealand in the spring of 1963. Made history off the pitch, that is. On it, Wilson Whineray's All Blacks were absolutely in control, winning 21-11 in Auckland and 9-6 in Christchurch. England, led by Mike Weston, were without several leading players and the pack, shored up by the return of the veteran prop Ron Jacobs, were

50 Greatest Players

BEV RISMAN Fly-half/Centre

Clubs: Manchester University, Loughborough Colleges

Debut: v Wales, 17 January 1959

No. of Caps: 8 **No. of Points:** 8

Few English fly-halves cultivated more finesse than Bev Risman. His flawless basic skills, ability to create openings for his three-quarters and his knack of hypnotising opponents with his clean outside breaks made him stand out in the England trials at the start of the 1958-59 season.

He was subsequently capped against Wales in 1959 in the Cardiff mud while playing for the Manchester University club and kept his place throughout a lacklustre season. These were lean times for England: between 1958 and 1960 the national side failed to score a try in five internationals. Still, with Risman in the ranks, at least selectors and supporters felt they had the talent available to bring out the best in the back division.

He was the automatic choice for the opening match of the 1960 season, but at the eleventh hour he had to withdraw from the side to face Wales. He was unlucky. Richard Sharp stepped in, played a blinder to launch a Triple Crown year and Risman had to wait another season before taking his next chance for England.

When it came, he found himself on the losing side against both South Africa and Wales. Anxious to restore Sharp as fly-half, the selectors could not bear to omit Risman and unwisely chose to experiment with him at centre. The switch failed and by the start of the next season he had followed his famous father, Gus, to rugby league.

steamrollered by the All Blacks. With Colin Meads, Waka Nathan and Kel Tremain in their pomp, the Kiwis were utterly ruthless, their trademark rucking game enabling them to recover from a six-point deficit at the interval of the first Test.

England were defiant, though, in the second Test when they were unlucky not to draw the series. Defiant and heroic. Mike Davis, their young lock from Devon, dislocated his shoulder early in the match and, these being the days before replacements, returned to give the greatest display of one-handed catching ever from the line-outs. Malcolm Phillips looked to have given England victory with a breakaway try from a kick ahead by Budge Rogers, but late in the game when New Zealand's full-back Don Clarke called for a mark inside his own half, England were penalised for rushing at his kick and

50 Greatest Players

MALCOLM PHILLIPS Centre/Wing

Clubs: Oxford University, Fylde

Debut: v Australia, 1 February 1958

No. of Caps: 25 **No. of Points:** 15

The player wings wanted inside them in England's honours-laden seasons of 1958, 1960 and 1963 was Malcolm Phillips. He was the unsung hero whose direct running, determined bursts and carefully flighted passes created the opportunities for Peter Jackson, Jim Roberts, John Young and Peter Thompson to score vital tries.

Phillips broke into the England side against Australia early in 1958 on the strength of an outstanding display in the University match and became a fixture in the side. In 1960, playing beside his old Oxford colleague Richard Sharp, he took a lead role in the Triple Crown campaign. Phillips's brilliance lit up the three-quarter line that sparkled against Wales, his lighning dart set up the winning score against Ireland and he had a loud say in John Young's try when the Triple Crown was claimed at Murrayfield.

Then he was unkindly made the scapegoat of a defeat in Cardiff the year later and two seasons passed before his guile and speed were again seen in England colours. In the never-to-be-forgotten match at Cardiff in 1963 his 70-yard attack with Peter Jackson culminated in his scoring the match breaking try as England launched a memorable championship winning season.

He toured Australia and New Zealand in 1963 as England's most experienced back, scoring tries in the Tests at Christchurch and Sydney. Since hanging up his international boots the season later Phillips has concentrated on putting something back into the game as an astute administrator at club, national and international level.

Clarke landed the winning goal. By the time they reached Sydney for a Test against the Wallabies only three days later, England were spent. In the wet conditions, they went down 18-9 to John Thornett's side.

England, though, continued to be misguidedly optimistic. The tour had been gruelling but they had almost won in Christchurch and they felt they could gain revenge over Whineray's touring All Blacks the following year. But the match at Twickenham on 4 January 1964 was a massive setback for England. The 14-0 defeat was the biggest winning margin at the ground since internationals began there 54 years earlier. The All Blacks' flat defence formed an impenetrable wall and 65,000 spectators on a foggy day saw little in the gloom to lighten their spirits. The England team, in the middle of a run of six games without a win, had lost their way.

There were shafts of light in the gloom, though, and English teams continued to illuminate games with moments of individual brilliance. Andy Hancock, the 25-year-old Northampton wing, had only made his debut against France in February 1965, but he kept his place for the next game against Scotland, a match where a wooden spoon was at stake. Heavy rain in the morning had left

England against Scotland in 1963 and Malcolm Phillips (centre) makes a storming run for the corner.

50 Greatest Players

DICKIE JEEPS Scrum-half

Club: Northampton

Debut: v Wales, 21 January 1956

No. of Caps: 24 **No. of Points:** 0

Competitive, courageous, stroppy even. Dickie Jeeps was the scrum-half England's forwards loved to have aboard. He never hesitated to stick his oar into the tide of players bearing down on him and made life hell for his opponents.

One of the rare band of international players to play in a Test for the Lions (1955) before winning his cap for his country (1956), he came to the fore in the 1957 Grand Slam season. His immaculate service from the scrum was the stuff of dreams for an attacking fly-half like his partner that year, Ricky Bartlett. Jeeps was a fast and accurate passer during a period when tight marking was the norm in international matches. Jeeps's short passes just in front of his partner tempted the fly-half to take the ball on the run. That way Bartlett was able to engage his talented three-quarter line to unlock defences.

Jeeps's finest hour came in the match against Scotland when England wrapped up all the silverware the championship had to offer. He bobbed about the field like a cork floating in choppy waters, at first bearing the brunt of Scottish back-row attacks before settling to take a hand in all three of England's tries.

In 1960 he was England's new captain for a season which brought another Triple Crown and a share with France of the Five Nations title. Jeeps was an inspiring captain who tackled resolutely and shrugged off the constant batterings he received, particularly from a rampaging French pack in Paris. He retired in 1962 after leading the side in 13 successive Tests. At the time he was England's most-capped scrum-half.

the pitch soggy and the match was equally heavy going for England's supporters until the final minute when Hancock unexpectedly joined Adrian Stoop, Prince Obolensky and Richard Sharp as a Twickenham legend.

England were three points adrift and the newspaper reporters in the press box had already filed their stories, recording yet another soggy English defeat, their first to the Scots at Twickenham in the post-war era. That was until, with ten seconds of the game left, Mike Weston gathered a loose ball in his 25 and delivered a pass to Andy Hancock standing on the left wing. Hancock was expected to hoof the ball into touch and perhaps set up a line-out for one last desperate attack. Instead he set off on a run, at first appearing only to be trotting while sizing up the Scottish defensive pattern. He increased his pace, swerving past one defender until he reached the halfway line. Passing the Royal Box, he swerved infield, hoping to take the English back row with him. Probably to his horror, nobody was there but it was then that the Scottish captain, full-back Stuart Wilson, made a terrible error, diving at Hancock who swerved outside, recovered his balance and ran the remaining 35 yards to the corner.

Unlikely Hero

Hancock had run 90 yards, the longest run for a try in international history. Don Rutherford failed to convert but England had avoided defeat. The unlikely hero said afterwards: 'I knew there was no point in kicking as the match was almost over. So I tried to find an opening. Eventually there were no more blue shirts but the line was still a long way ahead and my lungs and head were bursting but I dared not slow down because I knew someone was just behind me.'

Hancock, though, played only one more game for England and it was less than glorious. He tore a hamstring just before the break the following season at Stade Colombes and hobbled on in agony as England limped to a 13-0 defeat by the French. Budge Rogers's team were hopelessly outclassed by France for whom the Boniface brothers in the centre were superb and England won the wooden spoon in 1966.

In a year that England's soccer players proved themselves to be the best in the world, the national rugby side's measly one point from their four games was the worst return in the International Championship since 1948. The French and Welsh teams were taking the game to new levels; England were hopelessly lagging behind. And hopelessly outmoded in their thinking. When the Australians toured the following winter another Twickenham record fell. The 23 points the Wallabies scored at Twickenham were a record score by any opposition there since the stadium was opened. This was another watershed match for England, as significant as that defeat by the All Blacks had been 62 years earlier. England had brought back Richard Sharp for his valedictory game but he looked like a player from another era. The Wallabies had peerless half-backs in their captain Ken Catchpole at scrum-half and Phil Hawthorne at fly-half. Catchpole had a superb accurate pass but in this game he rarely used the traditional dive pass and the half-backs hardly used long passes to move the ball to their wings. Instead Catchpole and Hawthorne used shorter more accurate passes to probe away at the opposition defence. It was revolutionary thinking at the time but it was devastatingly effective.

England's Phil Judd (left) chases the loose ball in the 1967 Five Nations match against France.

Hawthorne dropped three goals, becoming only the second player after France's Pierre Albaladejo to do so in an international.

Lagging Behind

Meanwhile, across Offa's Dyke, Wales were assembling one of the greatest of modern international sides. When England went to Cardiff on a sunny spring day in April 1967 in search of a victory that would have brought them a Triple Crown, an 18-year-old full-back called Keith Jarrett buried their hopes of a revival with a virtuoso display of 19 points that included an individual try that shook the Arms Park to its foundations. Jarrett even converted his try from the touchline. The winning score of 34-21 was Wales's highest since a 49-14 thrashing of France 57 years earlier.

In 1967, the year of flower power, the red rose looked well and truly wilted. Brian Lochore's All Blacks arrived in the autumn for a 15-match tour of Britain and France and, like Wilson Whineray's all-conquering team of four years earlier, laid all opposition to waste. There was not a lot for English rugby to be cheery about. There was even less when the talented Bedford centre Danny Hearn, who had made his England debut against France 18 months earlier and was playing for his Test place in a Midland Counties game against the tourists at Leicester, broke his neck in a tackle on his opposite number Ian McRae. The tragedy confined Hearn to a wheelchair and provoked a fresh debate about the dangers of this contact sport. It also cast a pall over the English squad as they prepared to face the All Blacks at Twickenham. Not surprisingly England were well beaten by 23-11.

It was not that England lacked good players; France, Wales and Scotland were also beaten by Lochore's All Blacks. What England lacked was coaching and organisation, a system more sophisticated than picking the cream of players from a select number of clubs, throwing them together for infrequent training sessions and hoping that the right blend would emerge.

After the 1967 defeat by the All Blacks, England's doleful record against the southern hemisphere big three was a single win against the Wallabies since the far-off days of Prince Obolensky. The 1967 All Blacks had shown the virtues of good coaching. Fred Allen managed to combine a team ethic with finely honed individual skills to create a template for the 15-man game. The All Blacks under Allen and Lochore were one of the most attractive, as well as one of the most successful, sides to leave New Zealand and England

50 Greatest Players

RICHARD SHARP Fly-half

Clubs: Oxford University, Wasps, Bristol

Debut: v Wales, 16 January 1960

No. of Caps: 14 **No. of Points:** 26

Wales journeyed to Twickenham in 1960 with seven players whose reputations were enhanced by their displays for the 1959 Lions in New Zealand. Yet they returned home with their pride destroyed, cut to ribbons by a young blond Cornishman who had only entered the England side as an eleventh-hour replacement for the injured Risman.

Richard Sharp was the destroyer. His name hadn't even featured in the match programme, yet 48 hours after the game every rugby column carried his name in banner headlines. He had the Welsh at sixes and sevens and his adventurous running and bold breaks brought a breath of fresh air to a side that hadn't managed to score a try for nearly two seasons. England kept the same side for the entire championship season and with Sharp in the lead role behind the scrum, the Triple Crown and a share of the championship came their way.

He always wanted to play with panache – born into a later generation playing under the dispensation laws he would have been a brilliant attacking full-back. But at a time when international rugby was shackled by touch kicking and tight marking, his methods did not always pay off. Still, his Five Nations record made impressive reading: only two defeats in 13 matches before retiring, aged only 27, after scoring an exquisite match-winning try as captain against Scotland in 1963. He was tempted back to lead the side against Australia four years later by which time he was past his best.

50 Greatest Players

BUDGE ROGERS Flanker

Club: Bedford

Debut: v Ireland, 11 February 1961

No. of Caps: 34 **No. of Points:** 9

England's most dynamic open side flanker during the 1960s was Budge Rogers. Early on he made his name as a destructive loose forward whose fitness and stamina carried him to parts of the field which lesser flankers could not reach. In his first three seasons in the England set-up the side conceded only one try to backs, a fitting tribute to Rogers's exceptional talent as a snuffer-out of attacks. That span included 1963, the best season of the Rogers years, England picking up their only championship title of the decade.

In the mid-1960s significant changes were made to the game's laws affecting the activities of flankers. Rogers had to reassess his approach and temporarily lost his edge. Typically, though, he remained dedicated in his preparations and for fitness and stamina had no equal on the club scene.

At length he developed subtle changes in his lines of defence. He was among the pioneers at perfecting a drift approach which forced opponents sideways, so stifling attacks. In addition, he still used his fitness to ensure that he was the first forward to arrive at breakdowns, but now worked on building a reputation as a constructive agent who was an invaluable asset in setting up second phase possession.

He later captained his country and ended a distinguished international career in 1969 by breaking Wavell Wakefield's long-standing cap record. Later, he was awarded the OBE for services to rugby.

knew that as an unsuccessful decade headed to its conclusion they would have to adopt some of the All Blacks' methods.

The 1960s had seen a decline in back play in the northern hemisphere but some brilliant players were beginning to emerge in Britain who would form the core of the Lions side that won in New Zealand in 1971. The Welsh half-backs Barry John and Gareth Edwards, the full-back J.P.R. Williams and the Ireland centre Mike Gibson emerged at the same time as David Duckham, the Coventry three-quarter whose unfettered style would define the time. Duckham, who made his England debut alongside another debutant, John Spencer, in Dublin in 1969, had the long blond hair that was so fashionable in the 1960s but not yet de rigueur among rugby players. He had electrifying speed and a sidestep that shredded club defences. This singled him out as a rugby star whose charisma rivalled Edwards and Gibson.

Fielding's Debut

Also making his debut against Ireland that February was the 19-year-old Loughborough Colleges wing Keith Fielding, a real sprinter with a tremendous swerving running style. England had a back division of real artistry but the Ireland game summed up the time. They lost 17-15, despite a breathtaking try by Duckham. But when the Bedford flanker Budge Rogers took over as captain against the French, England ran up a 22-8 victory and then beat Scotland with two Duckham tries. Wales, though, soon to set out on a decade of ravishing success, were a different quality. The white jerseys were overwhelmed in Cardiff as their hosts secured the Triple Crown.

A quiet revolution was needed to harness England's talent and Don White, the former Northampton captain and flanker who had scored England's first post-war try, was called from the shires to lead it. White was an uncompromising player with a vision to take the game forward. His playing days had ended in 1961, but as chairman of the East Midlands coaching committee, with the help of Ron Jacobs, Jeff Butterfield and Frank Sykes, he had organised fitness programmes for the junior clubs of that area. White also helped compile a manual of rugby skills which in 1969 impressed Twickenham enough for it to offer him the post of England's first coach. The Rugby Football Union did not go as far as calling him coach. White was called England's team manager. He agreed to do the job for two seasons, unpaid, as he continued to be managing director of a shoe company.

Squash Accident

In August, 1969, on a blazing hot afternoon at Twickenham, 30 players prepared to meet the Springboks at the same venue four months later. The emphasis was on fitness training and Don White had enlisted the help of his old club-mate Jeff Butterfield to put the first England squad through their paces. An unfortunate consequence of his strict new regime was the dislocation of David Duckham's jaw by the elbow of England's former captain Dick Greenwood. Greenwood's own playing career had ended on the eve of the game against France the February before. The Waterloo flanker had been playing squash when a racquet caught him in the face and shattered his glasses, causing splinters of glass to enter his eye. His retirement after winning only five caps was a huge blow, but he would later coach his country and his son Will would star in the centre for England and the Lions.

Duckham only just recovered in time to play for England against the South Africans that December, but the match was to end the 1960s in thrilling style and herald the coaching career of Don White in electrifying style. White picked a new captain for Twickenham in the Harlequins full-back Bob Hiller. Hiller was making a name for himself with his deliberate, but highly successful, style of kicking which would rescue all manner of lost causes for England. The two new half-backs were Nigel Starmer-Smith, later to become the distinctive voice of English rugby, and the Cambridge stand-off Roger Shackleton. White also picked, among five new caps, the Cornish prop Claude Brian, better known as 'Stack' Stevens.

The 1969 Springbok tour was an unhappy one, marred by anti-apartheid demonstrations. The South Africans were becoming more and more entrenched and detached from the rest of the rugby world, but Dawie de Villiers' side was still a force. The Springboks had destroyed the Lions a year earlier and Don White knew his side was in for a physical confrontation. Starmer-Smith and another new cap, the Richmond flanker Tony Bucknall, who had both played at Oxford University alongside the Springbok No. 8 Tommy Bedford, warned his young colleagues what to expect. But England gained an 11-8 victory and it was Bucknall who gave the scrum-half de

England's David Duckham dives to touch the ball down in defence as England defeat the touring Springboks in December 1969.

Villiers a thoroughly unproductive afternoon with tries from Peter Larter and John Pullin and a conversion and penalty from Bob Hiller ensuring a well-earned victory.

The Springboks failed to win a Test. Their rugby was going rapidly backwards and at the end of the tour their coach Avril Malan admitted it would get worse. Malan's pessimism was justified five years later when Willie-John McBride's Lions thumped the Springboks in their own backyard. But when England began the 1970s it appeared they had a team that could match the brilliant new Welsh side. It was not to be. The selectors insisted that England should hold a final trial and told Don White that he could not hold any more squad sessions during the 1970 championship. This was to prove a retrograde step. White saw this as an affront to his new authority. His England players had just beaten the Springboks and seemed destined for great things, but had once more been left anxious and insecure.

By the time the championship season had ended, Bob Hiller had been dropped and replaced by Don White's Northampton flanker Bob Taylor as captain and England had lost three of their four games, ending with a 35-13 capitulation in Paris to a brilliant French side. It was the most points any team had scored against England in 100 years. England's selection policy was once more in disarray and sharing the wooden spoon with Scotland was not exactly what Don White had in mind when his players were put through their paces in those hot August days eight months earlier.

Centenary Celebrations

Twickenham badly needed 1971 to be a bigger success. It was the centenary of the Rugby Football Union and a host of events in 1970-1 gave the season a party feel. The Fijians visited with their unique brand of running rugby. They slaughtered a strong Barbarians side and almost beat an England Under-25 team at Twickenham. In the spring an RFU President's XV, essentially a world team led by Brian Lochore, beat England 28-11. England finished third in the championship, their only win coming off the back of three Bob Hiller penalties in a drab win in Dublin. They even played Scotland twice, but lost in the championship at Twickenham and again, a week later, at Murrayfield in a game to mark the centenary of the first international fixture. In the second match John Spencer dropped the ball after 13 seconds to hand the Scots a try and they ran out eventual 26-6 winners. The centenary party fell a little flat.

It would be followed by the biggest hangover ever. In 1972 England suffered the first whitewash in their history. A knockout cup was introduced in England to improve competitive standards in the clubs, but it had the

Captain Bob Hiller leads the team out at Twickenham for the match against Ireland in 1972.

opposite effect on the national side who were now being coached by the schoolmaster John Elders. Bob Hiller began the season as captain but was ditched after a home defeat by Ireland and replaced as skipper by the flanker Peter Dixon. England had a good pack with the likes of Stevens, Pullin, Dixon and the emerging high-stepping No. 8 Andy Ripley but they could not score tries. Duckham, by now shunted to the wing, had been a star for the Lions in New Zealand the summer before but he hardly received a pass, let alone crossed the line. Yet again England were thumped in Paris, Walter Spanghero's side winning 37-12 with some brilliant rugby to bid Stade Colombes adieu. It was France's biggest ever win over England, the lowest point English rugby reached in an inglorious decade.

John Elders had taken over the reins in preference to another highly respected coach John Burgess. The Lancastrian Burgess had taken charge of an England tour to the Far East at the beginning of the 1971-2 season. It did not include the English Lions who had won in New Zealand that summer, but Budge Rogers's team included new faces who were to play an important role for England during the next decade; the Leicester hooker Peter Wheeler was a reserve along with Roger Uttley, Fran Cotton and Tony Neary. Cotton and Neary had already played for England the previous season and Uttley and Wheeler would soon break through. England won all their games on tour in Japan, Hong Kong and Sri Lanka but ten days after their return, Elders was given the coaching role ahead of Burgess who would bide his time and eventually succeed Elders two years later.

Having had their worst ever season in the championship, England looked in no fit state to tour South Africa in the summer of 1972. But three months after that depressing defeat at Murrayfield, the rugby world turned upside down.

John Pullin's side became the first tourists since 1891 to leave South Africa unbeaten. The Test in Johannesburg was a triumph, England winning 18-9 with a try by the Bristol wing Alan Morley from a high kick by Jan Webster. Webster, the tiny Moseley scrum-half, created all sorts of problems for the ponderous Springboks with his darting runs. Morley was one of four new caps at Ellis Park along with flanker John Watkins, centre Peter Preece and full-back Sam Doble. Doble was a reliable kicker in the mould of Bob Hiller and his four penalties and conversion kept England's noses in front.

England's tour, in which they won six and drew one game, looked to be a turning point. The squad was buoyant and, following the success of the Lions in New Zealand a year earlier, it appeared that northern hemisphere rugby was on the up. Even at 6,000ft altitude, England seemed fitter than the opposition and the tour showed how South African provincial rugby during political isolation was gasping for air. England's win gave fresh hope to non-white rugby players in the blighted land. England's two matches against 'coloured' and African teams were the first played in South Africa by touring white sides. The president of the South African Rugby Board, Grant Khomo, was delighted: 'We are proud to be associated with this historic match. It heralds the beginning of bigger things to come for all in this country.'

Optimism Evaporates

The optimism generated from that unexpected win in South Africa evaporated by the new year. The Barbarians were to beat the touring All Blacks in perhaps the most famous game of the televised age in Cardiff, but Ian Kirkpatrick's men were too strong for England who went down to a 9-0 defeat at Twickenham on 6 January 1973. England could ill afford to lose Fran Cotton whose last-minute injury allowed Frank Anderson to become the first player from Orrell to win a cap and the All Black forwards gained a stranglehold on the match. Peter Preece thought he had scored a try but the move was pulled back for a forward pass. Kirkpatrick did score a try, Joe Karam landed a penalty and Bryan Williams a drop goal.

England's bleak run in the championship continued with defeats in Cardiff and then Dublin. Against Wales, England were overwhelmed 25-9 for Wales's fifth successive win in the fixture. Against Ireland they were beaten 18-9 but the game provided one of the more heartwarming sporting stories of the year.

The Troubles were at their height and in the previous season both Wales and Scotland had refused to travel to Dublin. This robbed Ireland, who at the time had a very strong side with the likes of Willie-John McBride, Mike

50 Greatest Players

JOHN PULLIN Hooker

Club: Bristol

Debut: v Wales, 15 January 1966

No. of Caps: 42 **No. of Points:** 3

The outstanding far-foot striker of the ball in English front-rows of the late 1960s and early 1970s was the Bristol hooker, John Pullin. A tough customer who farmed in the shadow of the Severn Bridge, Pullin's simple but effective technique allied to his remarkable positional sense made him an automatic choice during an admittedly lean period for English rugby. That the selectors kept faith with him, at a time when countless England players were capped only a handful or so times before being discarded, spoke volumes for Pullin's tenacity and skills.

The selectors even turned to him in an hour of need to lead the side in 1972, and what a miraculous job he performed. England had been whitewashed in that season's International Championship before Pullin was entrusted with the captaincy for the difficult tour to South Africa. Yet the Bristol man inspired his side to a stunning 18-9 victory in the only Test of the visit and proceeded to lead England to further famous wins against New Zealand (in Auckland in 1973) and Australia (at Twickenham later the same year). Only Will Carling and Martin Johnson, with sides that sustained their excellence over longer periods, have managed England wins over the big three southern hemisphere forces. Pullin played his 42nd and last match for England in 1976 before standing down as his country's then most-capped player.

Gibson and Ray McLoughlin in their pomp, of a possible Grand Slam as they had already won in Paris and London. England, though, did travel in February 1973 and their fixture has entered rugby folklore. The players were told that the decision to travel was theirs and Nigel Horton, a policeman, and Peter Larter, who was in the RAF, feared they might be IRA targets and opted to stay at home. Their absence gave Roger Uttley, the tough Gosforth forward, his debut. He remembers the day: 'We stayed at the Shelbourne in the centre of Dublin and as a young bloke I was just pleased to be playing for my country. The reception we got proved it was the right decision.' Indeed, when John Pullin led his team out on to the pitch the ovation lasted for around five minutes. Edmund van Esbeck, the veteran chronicler of the

Irish Times, said: 'I have been going to Lansdowne Road for 50 years and I have never seen emotion as when England ran out. There was a huge warmth for the English. It was a very moving experience.'

At Least We Turn Up

McBride was playing his 50th match for Ireland who eventually ran out winners with tries from Tom Grace and Dick Milliken, with the boot of Barry McGann doing the rest. It was England's seventh defeat in a row in the championship but, at the post-match dinner, Pullin captured the mood perfectly. In his speech the England captain modestly remarked: 'We may not be much good, but at least we turn up.' For the second time that day the skipper bought the house down. Years later Pullin remembered the day vividly: 'Normally on a Friday night we would go out to the nearest pub. But we all stayed around the hotel. Some of the players definitely didn't play as well as they could because of the trepidation they felt. Being on the wing you felt pretty isolated. In the forwards you were OK.' Uttley also remembers the day well. 'I said to Chris Ralston, my second-row partner, that I felt a bit sick about losing in my first game. He told me not to worry as it was his 10th game and he still hadn't been on a winning side.'

These, then, were times that England's players had to laugh or they would have cried. They had some of the world's top forwards in John Pullin, Fran Cotton, Tony Neary and Roger Uttley, some terrific backs like David Duckham and Peter Preece, but they continually fell short. Ralston did, though, finally taste the fruits of victory. Walter Spanghero's French team came to Twickenham and were fancied to give the English pack an uncomfortable time. But the English forwards prevailed and at last Duckham received some ball. He took a pass from Stack Stevens to score a try after earlier combining with Preece to zip over in the corner. Tony Jorden's penalties nudged England ahead and with the miserable run over, England deprived Scotland of a Triple Crown with a 20-13 win at Twickenham three weeks later. By now Preece, Duckham and the other Coventry three-quarter Geoff Evans were proving an irresistible combination behind a powerful scrum and the young Sale scrum-half Steve Smith. Moseley's stand-off Martin Cooper played an essentially conservative game that day but he provided a good try for Peter Squires. Evans pounced on a diagonal kick by Preece for another and Peter Dixon powered over for two more.

The year had begun with three defeats but it soon proved England's best of the decade. During the summer they were supposed to travel to Argentina but the tour fell through and instead arranged a short tour to Fiji and New

Great Matches

TOUR MATCH **Eden Park, Auckland, 15 September 1973**
Attendance: 56,000

New Zealand 10 **England 16**

England had surprised the rugby world in the summer of 1972 when they walloped South Africa in Johannesburg. A year later John Pullin again led England to a famous overseas victory, this time in the land of the All Black.

England's tour had been hastily arranged after the cancellation of a proposed visit to Argentina. Pullin's side lost its first three provincial matches before pulling out all the stops to overwhelm New Zealand in the Test. 'England played with admirable efficiency,' wrote John Brooks of the *Christchurch Press*. 'New Zealand showed a great lack of tactical appreciation and serious flaws in technique,' he added.

Kent Lambert tries in vain to stop Stack Stevens.

England wisely played to their strengths. Controlled ten-man rugby was the order of the day from John Pullin and it paid handsome dividends in the form of three tries in the second half, after New Zealand had held a 10-6 lead at the break.

Scrum-half Jan Webster was the mainspring of the English attack, posing his famous opponent, Sid Going, countless problems with darting runs that twice led to tries. Webster was the essential link with the forwards for the round of passing that led to England's first try and he created the move that led to Tony Neary's winning try five minutes from time.

New Zealand: R.N. Lendrum; G.B. Batty, I.A. Hurst, B.G. Williams; R.M. Parkinson, J.P. Dougan, S.M. Going; K.K. Lambert, R.W. Norton, M.G. Jones, H.H. Macdonald, S.C. Strahan, K.W. Stewart, A.J. Wyllie, I.A. Kirkpatrick (captain) Replacement: T.G. Morrison for Parkinson
Scorers: Tries Batty, Hurst **Conversion** Lendrum

England: P.A. Rossborough; P.J. Squires, P.S. Preece, G.W. Evans, D. J Duckham; A.G.B. Old, J.G. Webster; C.B. Stevens, J.V. Pullin (captain), F.E. Cotton, R.M. Uttley, C.W. Ralston, J.A. Watkins, A.G. Ripley, A. Neary; Replacement: M.J. Cooper for Evans
Scorers: Tries Squires, Stevens, Neary **Conversions** Rossborough 2

Referee: R.F. McMullen (New Zealand)

Zealand. At the time, meeting Ian Kirkpatrick's team, who were finely tuned at the end of their winter, seemed foolhardy but nobody told John Pullin. Jan Webster was recalled at scrum-half behind a formidable pack and England won 16-10 in Auckland, one of the more staggering results of the era. Playing controlled ten-man rugby with Alan Old now at fly-half, they scored tries through Tony Neary, Peter Squires and the redoubtable Stack Stevens. 'This was better than beating the Springboks last year because the All Blacks are a stronger team,' said Pullin. As at Ellis Park, the most eye-catching display came from Jan Webster whose little twisting runs were too much for his opposite-number Sid Going and the concentrated onslaught of the English forwards destroyed the All Black pack.

Heady days continued as the less-fancied Australians, captained by John Hipwell, visited England and Wales in the autumn and were well beaten at Twickenham with Neary, Old and Andy Ripley scoring tries. In 18 months

John Pullin breaks through for England against France in the Paris air disaster non-cap match in April 1974.

John Pullin had led England, who so often failed to get their act together against the home nations, to victories against the southern hemisphere's big three. Pullin was arguably the best hooker who ever played for England, forever immortalised for his part in Gareth Edwards's famous try for the 1973 Barbarians against the All Blacks. He led England into the 1974 championship, by the end of which England were laying claims to be the strongest pack in the competition. But by the end of the championship they had still only won one game, albeit a highly credible 16-12 win over Wales at Twickenham when the Nottinghamshire farmer William 'Dusty' Hare made his debut at full-back. Hare was a no-frills player who, like Bob Hiller, was to save England's bacon on countless occasions with his accurate place-kicking.

John Burgess eventually received the call to rescue England's lost cause. The Lancastrian had masterminded a memorable win by the North-West

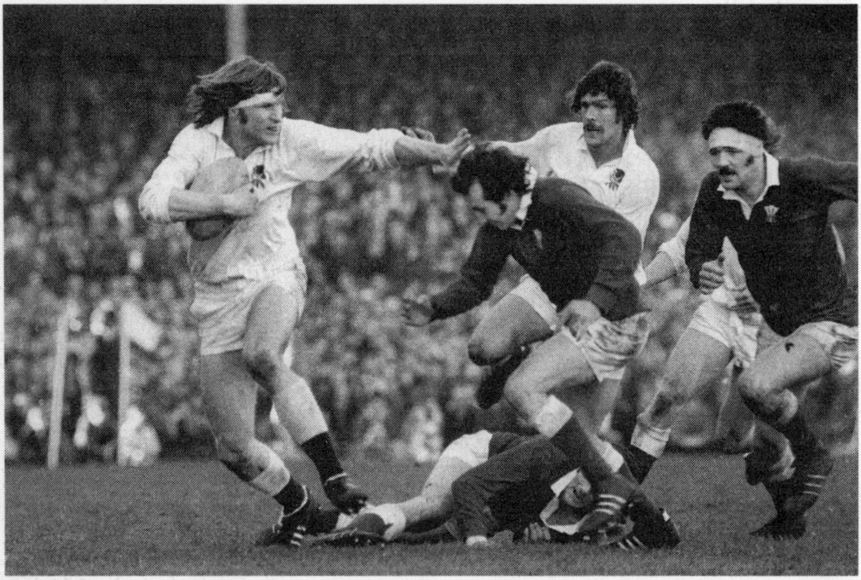

Andy Ripley fends off Gareth Edwards as England take on Wales at Twickenham in 1974.

Counties over Ian Kirkpatrick's All Blacks at Workington in November 1972, New Zealand's first defeat in England outside the Test arena. Burgess had watched the 1967 All Blacks and decided he wanted England to emulate their style with Lancashire, a 15-man game with a fiercely competitive pack blending with hard-running backs. Lancashire, a poor county in the 1960s, became, under Burgess, the powerhouse of English rugby in the 1970s.

Burgess turned to another Lancastrian, Fran Cotton, already established as England's tight-head prop, to captain his first side against Ireland in Dublin. He also awarded a first cap to a player who began life as sixth-team full-back at the Fylde club near Blackpool. Bill Beaumont packed down in the scrum alongside Chris Ralston to begin an England career that within seven years would make him one of the most recognisable sporting figures in the country. Beaumont's rise had been fast. The summer before his first cap he had toured South Africa with Lancashire and had played against the touring Tongans for the North of England. At the turn of the year Roger Uttley was favourite to retain his place in the second row, but when he ricked his back bending over to pick up a piece of apple pie, Beaumont took his chance.

Like Uttley, though, England did not receive their just deserts in Dublin. On Beaumont's debut England lost 12-9, leading until late in the game when they got into a muddle at a scrum close to their own posts. England heeled the ball but Peter Preece slipped as Jan Webster passed back and the Irish fly-half Billy McCombe gathered the ball to score the winning try. Though Beaumont had played well against Willie-John McBride he could not prevent Uttley's return when France visited Twickenham. There was one new face in Peter Wheeler who replaced the old warrior John Pullin to begin an England

50 Greatest Players

DAVID DUCKHAM Centre/Wing

Club: Coventry

Debut: v Ireland, 8 February 1969

No. of Caps: 36 **No. of Points:** 36

Strongly built, fast and a graceful runner who could leave defenders standing with his electric sidestep, David Duckham was the most powerful and exciting runner in the British game in the early 1970s. He had no equal for sheer zest and it was his misfortune that he appeared at a time when English rugby was in the doldrums.

Even so, his incisive running was an integral part of several famous England wins. True, sometimes his play lacked vision, but the element of surprise in his attacks often embarrassed opponents. The French, in particular, were left to rue their failure to deal with him in the 1973 match at Twickenham. That day Duckham thrilled the home crowd with his tricky running and collected two tries to sink French championship hopes. At length, England went on to claim their share in a unique quintuple tie in the championship, each of the Five Nations winning their two home matches but failing away. Later the same year he was a part of England's famous defeat of the All Blacks in Auckland.

He retired as England's most-capped three-quarter in 1976. If his achievements for his country look modest in retrospect, he seemed to epitomise the spirit of running rugby which uplifted British credentials in his time.

career in which he would challenge the Bristol man for the title of England's greatest hooker. But Claude Dourthe's team outplayed the English, their total of 27 points a new record haul at Twickenham, their artistry behind the scrum mocking Burgess's pretensions to play 15-man rugby. After a heavy defeat in Cardiff only a 7-6 defeat of Scotland in a dreary finale to the season prevented another whitewash. It did not prevent England from a wooden spoon. Burgess's revolution had been thwarted.

Things would go from bad to worse that summer. England sent a raw squad to travel Australia, leaving out experienced forwards like Nigel Horton and Chris Ralston and seasoned half-backs Steve Smith and Alan Old. The tour was an unmitigated disaster. Tony Neary's side were beaten 16-9 in the first Test in Sydney and 30-21 in the second Test in Brisbane. One

50 Greatest Players

ANDY RIPLEY No. 8

Club: Rosslyn Park

Debut: v Wales, 15 January 1972

No. of Caps: 24 **No. of Points:** 8

'I have little natural ball-playing ability,' Andy Ripley once divulged. True, he enjoyed sending himself up, but the modesty only told part of the story: on the hoof he was a player who put the fear of God into would-be tacklers during his 24-cap career with England between 1972 and 1976.

He played football until he was 18, but realising that he was 'too lanky and clumsy' converted to basketball before finding his physical competitive edge better rewarded on the rugby field. He took up the game at East Anglia University, joined Rosslyn Park in 1970 and a season later lined up at No. 8 for his first cap in a 12-3 defeat by Wales.

Instantly recognisable with his hippy-style shoulder-length hair, he quickly became one of the hottest properties in the side. The storming runs and searing pace of England's beanpole cut swathes through opposition defences and he was a star in the teams that carried off unlikely yet deserved victories overseas against South Africa and New Zealand in 1972 and 1973 respectively. Although smother tackling was the weakness in his armour, he was an England regular until 1976 when he played his last international against Scotland, bowing out of the national squad as his country's then most-capped No. 8.

of the few experienced forwards, Neary was injured by the time the Brisbane game came round and Pullin was brought back to replace him as skipper. The tour was scarred by ill discipline. In an early game against Sydney, Beaumont was almost knocked cold by a punch from the Sydney prop Steve Finnane who had already laid out Mike Burton. In the second half of that defeat Fran Cotton trapped a nerve in his back and played no further part in the tour. Finnane was picked for the first Test which again was marred by violence and Beaumont replaced Neary who injured his ribs.

England were flattered by the score but in Brisbane they were well-beaten in a game that will only be remembered for its naked aggression. Finnane had been dropped, but early in the match the England prop Barry Nelmes fell on the ball and was trampled on. From the ensuing line-out England's other prop Mike Burton and his opposite number Stuart MacDougall had a verbal spat before the line-out broke into a flurry of punches. Burton was reprimanded by the referee Bob Burnett but while Beaumont was off the field having a cut stitched up, Burton was sent off for a late tackle. He became the first England player to be sent off in an international in 104 years. The game then descended into one of the most brutal internationals in modern times.

The violence in Brisbane did untold harm to the relations between the two countries, but moreover it damaged the reputation of John Burgess as a coach. After only six games and five defeats he was replaced by Peter Colston of Bristol, who had been in charge of England's Under-23 side.

David Duckham played a big part in England's record defeat of Australia in 1976.

His parting-shot was 'Oh ye of little faith'. A charitable view of Burgess was that he had been given too inexperienced a squad to tour and not enough time to develop his vision. Burgess later became the president of the Rugby Football Union and one of the game's great thinkers, but his year as England coach had been chastening. He also had his detractors in Twickenham who didn't take kindly to his passionate style of motivational coaching. He would even march around the pitch before England matches, roaring at the crowd to give the team support, and sweat would pour from his brow in his highly charged team talks. In a conservative sport, Burgess was a radical and ahead of his time but the English game was not ready for his methods. Twickenham's own thinking seemed to be muddle-headed. The squad system

50 Greatest Players

TONY NEARY Flanker

Club: Broughton Park

Debut: v Wales, 16 January 1971

No. of Caps: 43 **No. of Points:** 19

Only the fourth player to win England honours at Under-15, Under-19 and senior level, Tony Neary was an automatic choice for his country in 27 successive Tests before injury removed him from the side he captained in Australia in 1975.

From an early age he shone as a flanker of speed and agility and his basketball-playing enhanced his handling skills in the loose. What set Neary apart from the run-of-the-mill flankers was his willingness to become involved at the breakdown and use his upper-body strength to recycle ball at the mauls.

By 1976 he had appeared in Test victories against the big three from the southern hemisphere, but his career reached a watershed after he lost the England captaincy in 1977. He was virtually rejected for the next two seasons before bouncing back to replace Peter Dixon for the 1979 Five Nations Championship.

Interviewed early in his career 'Nero' had said that his ambition was to take part in an England rugby revival. That wish came true in 1980 when he played a prominent part in the pack that laid the foundations for a Grand Slam, but later the same year he sprang a rib cartilage in a national squad training session and never again played international rugby.

Then England's most-capped player, he built a successful career as a solicitor and co-founder of Cotton Traders, the leisurewear group, but the man who seemed to have it all had a spectacular fall from grace in 1998 when he was jailed for stealing nearly £300,000.

developed by Don White had long been ditched. Instead there were trials which only served to muddy the waters. When England prepared for the Wallabies' visit three days into 1976, Peter Wheeler's North and Midlands side beat England, forcing the selectors to make desperate changes to the eventual England line-up. It hardly mattered. Australia had already lost to Wales and Scotland when they came to Twickenham to play a side with most of their pack, Cotton, Wheeler and Neary included, fit again and hungry for retribution. Mike Burton was forgiven and played at tight-head prop, packing down against Steve Finnane. England, with a new scrum-half in the physical Headingley No. 9 Mike Lampkowski, recorded a 23-6 win, their biggest ever margin of victory over the Wallabies. David Duckham was back, running in one of three tries. It was to be Duckham's last season, a collision with the Scottish wing David Shedden putting both players out of the Calcutta Cup match at Twickenham and ending Duckham's career.

Strange Selections

Tony Neary's side suffered another whitewash season, scoring only two tries and Wales winning at Twickenham by a record margin. England were rudderless. They had a strong pack but had no idea of how to play. Instead of opting to play ten-man rugby they tried to emulate Wales and France with nothing like the effectiveness and instead of picking the two best half-backs in Smith and Old, they refused to match the pair all season. More strange selections followed. For the final match in Paris England called up Chris Williams of Gloucester for his one and only cap and continued with the smaller No. 8 Gary Adey, who replaced Andy Ripley. The result was a humiliating 30-9 defeat, an inauspicious end to the career of John Pullin.

The 1976 whitewash laid bare a few facts about England. The country had the biggest playing-base but it was not selecting the right players and the competitive rugby England's players were playing each week was not preparing them for the rigours of international rugby. England again revamped their selection process with the former international prop Sandy Sanders stepping up as chairman of selectors, helped by a new panel of experts in former internationals Mike Weston, Derek Morgan and Budge Rogers. The new panel combined wisdom with a more sympathetic approach, and England's fortunes improved, not by leaps and bounds but gradually. The approach was more pragmatic. They knew that the strapping Oxford University centre Charles Kent was no Duckham but that he could punch holes in the middle of the Scottish defence. Kent's crash-ball tactics duly led to two tries in a crushing 26-6 Calcutta Cup win

Fran Cotton (centre) in the thick of things for England against Wales in 1977.

in 1977. England, captained by Roger Uttley, were still beaten by the French and Welsh in 1977 but narrowly, their powerful pack by now the best in the championship.

Kent only lasted one season, and was replaced by the equally physical young Leicester centre Paul Dodge. After the Lions defeat in New Zealand in 1977, England turned to one of the Lions' forwards to lead them into the next campaign. Bill Beaumont had already captained an England XV in a charity match against the United States to celebrate the Queen's Jubilee when he was given the call to captain England in 1978. Beaumont's start was inauspicious. Though difficult to beat in the last two years of another frustrating decade, they continued to fall short against Wales and France. And they were beaten twice in 12 months by Graham Mourie's All Blacks, each time failing to score a try. The 1979 defeat was especially frustrating, losing by a point to a team that the North side had beaten in a stirring game. Fred Allen, the former All Black coach whose vision had led England to appoint their first coach 10 years earlier, said the North's display was the greatest he had ever seen against the All Blacks. Though England ended the decade with the narrowest of defeats, 10-9 by the All Blacks, the red rose was about to blossom.

Chapter Six: 1980-87
From Bill to Old Bill

The sight England fans had waited 23 years to see, a Grand Slam victory.

For the English sports fan, 1980 was a heady year. In the space of a few weeks Sebastian Coe and Steve Ovett both took memorable middle-distance gold medals at the Moscow Olympics; Brian Clough's unfashionable Nottingham Forest won the European Cup on a balmy night in Madrid and England's rugby players ended a barren run in the Five Nations Championship that had stretched back an entire generation.

For the first time in 23 years England had won the northern hemisphere's holy grail, the Grand Slam. England rugby supporters of a certain age can still reel off the names of the 1980 team like a litany: Hare; Carleton, Woodward, Dodge, Slemen; Horton, Smith; Cotton, Wheeler, Blakeway, Beaumont, Colclough, Uttley, Neary, Scott. There were walk-on parts, too, for the centres Nick Preston of Richmond and Sale's Tony Bond and the Moseley lock Nigel Horton. It was a solid, experienced side with a powerful set of forwards and backs of real flair. Eight of this squad had helped the North beat the All Blacks the previous year.

For once, England, coached by Mike Davis, had a settled look that had been absent through the 1970s when no one seemed sure of retaining their place. Under Bill Beaumont's captaincy England had their best side for years. The great Welsh team of the 1970s had broken up, France were inconsistent, Scotland ordinary and only the Irish pack, with its aged warriors Duggan, Keane and Orr, looked a match for the English eight.

Mike Davis was a schoolteacher and a former lock with Harlequins who had won 16 caps in the 1960s. His book *Science of Rugby Football* had established his credentials as a coach and he took the England job in 1979 when he led an experimental squad in Japan in May of that year. The memory of taking a raw squad to Australia four years earlier still haunted England and the Japanese trip hardly hinted at great things. In the first Test in Osaka, it

50 Greatest Players

FRAN COTTON Prop

Clubs: Loughborough Colleges, Coventry, Sale

Debut: v Scotland, 20 March 1971

No. of Caps: 31 **No. of Points:** 4

English rugby was passing through its dark ages when Fran Cotton entered the side in 1971. He was on the losing side in each of his first five internationals, but his down-to-earth attitude, sense of self-belief and uncompromising rugby values enabled him to ride out the early setbacks.

Outside the England camp he captained the North-West to a victory over the sixth All Blacks in 1972 and was the Lions' tight-head for the famous series win in South Africa in 1974. By 1977, he was one of the most respected players among a squad that began to pull English rugby out of international obscurity.

Equally at home on either side of the front-row, it was at loose-head that he brought remorseless pressure to bear on opponents in 1980. He had the ideal temperament for scrum operations and played an important part in the subdue-and-exploit approach so effectively used by Bill Beaumont's boys during the Grand Slam season.

A serious injury put an end to his career a year later, when he retired as his country's then most-capped prop. Fortunately he has stuck around the national set-up as a valued member of the RFU Council, where his dogged determination has proved every ounce as effective as in a playing career that spanned the heights and depths of England's rugby fortunes.

needed a late try from Peter Squires to beat Japan 21-19 and although the second Test was won more comfortably 38-18, the ingenuity of the Japanese forwards unsettled Beaumont's team. Usefully, Davis was able to use the tour to sift out players who he knew would not reach international standard while others, such as the strapping Orrell wing John Carleton, the lock Maurice Colclough and the skilful Wasps stand-off Huw Davies clearly measured up.

Later in the summer another tour helped lay the foundations for the all-conquering England team. The North-West Counties team toured South Africa under their coach Des Seabrook. Their back division would contain the core of the England line-up, John Carleton, Mike Slemen, Steve Smith and Tony Bond. Fran Cotton, the cornerstone of the pack, used the tour to test the Achilles injury that had caused him to be sidelined for months. In the high altitude of South Africa many of the England team were able to reach new fitness levels which enabled them to help the North team beat the All Blacks that autumn and England to banish their ghosts the following year.

Quixotic Skills

The 1980 England side had only two new caps, Clive Woodward and Phil Blakeway, the Gloucester fruit and vegetable trader who was hardly as green as his cabbages. He was 29, tough as teak and had broken his neck a few years earlier. Davis switched Fran Cotton to loose-head prop and played Blakeway at tight-head. The front row, with Peter Wheeler established as hooker, was as solid as England have ever had. England's one contentious position was fly-half where Bath's John Horton was given the nod over Leicester's Les Cusworth who had made his debut against the All Blacks two months earlier. Cusworth had quixotic skills but was never given a run in the England team. Davis favoured the more pragmatic Horton.

Nigel Horton partnered Bill Beaumont in the second row for the opening game against Ireland, a match that looked difficult on paper but turned into the first stage of a triumphant two months. England won 24-9 with Horton and Steve Smith composed behind a dominant pack in which Blakeway was outstanding against the dangerous Phil Orr. John Scott, Mike Slemen and Steve Smith ran in tries but there was a downside. Tony Bond broke his leg in the 20th minute to give the 24-year-old Leicester centre Clive Woodward his first full international. Though an elusive runner, Woodward was to make an error that blighted his international career. He would make his name in another context, as the England head coach that masterminded a Grand Slam and saw a few others slip through his fingers.

France's Grand Slam pack was breaking up and their fears of the English forwards looked justified when an efficient display by the pack, in which Nigel Horton had been displaced by Maurice Colclough, helped England win 17-13 in Paris. Nick Preston and John Carleton scored tries in England's first victory in the French capital for 16 years, but the French began and finished the game strongly. John Horton kicked two priceless drop goals while Roger Uttley was off the field having treatment to a head injury. It was a remorseless match but nothing like as brutal as the game that followed.

Highly Charged

To say the meeting with Wales at Twickenham was highly charged would be something of an understatement. When they came to London on 16 February, Wales had already beaten France but that had been a spiteful match in which the Wales and Lions prop Graham Price had been accused of collapsing scrums, a charge he bitterly rejected and which led to a siege mentality in the Welsh squad. In the build-up to the match the newspapers picked up on this mood of recrimination and what followed, once the match began, was a pressure-cooker atmosphere that boiled over into violence. After a quarter of an hour Paul Ringer, the Llanelli flanker, was sent off by David Burnett for a high tackle on John Horton for which Dusty Hare exacted retribution with a successful penalty. Hare kicked his third penalty in injury-time to cancel out two tries by Jeff Squire and Elgan Rees. Though down to 14 men Wales had raised their game but the mystery was why England, with their pack so dominant, had made such hard work of their 9-8 victory.

The match set up a famous victory at Murrayfield when England won a Grand Slam in the style that had been missing in the attritional warfare of their game against Wales. England won 30-18 with a hat-trick from John Carleton and tries by Mike Slemen and Steve Smith. It was emphatic and the Scots were overwhelmed by scrummaging power. Peter Wheeler remembered: 'There was one scrum which I regard as the best I have ever been part of. It took place near Scotland's line and Billy called for a double shove. I can still recall the feeling as we surged forward, like a supercharged car in overdrive. The sensation from that scrum was an uncommon experience. Occasionally it happens at the end of a club game but you do not expect that sort of surge in the early stages of an international game.'

From that surge John Carleton scored a blind-side try and although the Scots rallied England were never going to be denied. Bill Beaumont was chaired from the field, England had assured themselves of a place in the record books, and Beaumont was given the captaincy of the 1980 Lions in

Highly charged? Bill Beaumont leads the attack on the Scottish lines in 1980.

South Africa. Beaumont later remembered 1980: 'When you look back, those lads didn't need much captaincy. They were the most experienced bunch I've ever played with. But what many people do not know was that for most of the game Roger Uttley and Phil Blakeway were suffering from serious rib injuries and Fran Cotton had concussion. We got away with it for most of the game but towards the end the injuries started to show.'

Farewell to Neary

At the end of the match Beaumont presented Tony Neary with a tankard to mark his record-breaking 43rd cap. It was to be the former captain's last international, a sweet end for the flanker who only four years earlier had been tarnished as the first man to lead England to a whitewash. Neary was perhaps the greatest of England flankers. Ireland's outstanding No. 7 Fergus Slattery said: 'During my playing days he was easily England's finest flanker, far better than Jean-Pierre Rives. A complete footballer.'

But by the next season Neary was gone and so had Roger Uttley. Fran Cotton lasted only the first match against Wales in Cardiff. The Grand Slam pack was breaking up but England had gone to Cardiff still confident they could repeat their triumph of 12 months earlier. Bill Beaumont was captaining

50 Greatest Players

ROGER UTTLEY Lock/No. 8/Flanker

Clubs: Gosforth, Wasps

Debut: v Ireland, 10 February 1973

No. of Caps: 23 **No. of Points:** 8

Primarily a big tight forward of strength, determination and vigour, Roger Uttley forced his way into the England set-up in 1973 with a series of high octane performances for the Newcastle club, Gosforth. His high work-rate, tremendous scrummaging power and ball-winning capacity mainly at the tail of the line-out made him an automatic choice as either lock or No. 8 for his country.

Injuries, however, dogged his career and it was not until 1977 that he enjoyed a sustained run of appearances in the national side. He was such an inspiration to the forwards around him that the selectors appointed him captain for a campaign that opened with morale raising wins over Scotland and Ireland. Though defeats followed against France and Wales, Uttley had sown the seeds of self-belief in a side whose resurgence continued in 1978, when he was absent with back problems.

He returned for one last season in 1980 to see England reap the benefit of his earlier work. Uttley played on the blind-side flank, the position he had so successfully filled for the 1974 Lions in a pack whose urgency and power overwhelmed opponents.

Later, in a coaching capacity, his expertise as a motivator benefited the 1989 Lions and he helped Geoff Cooke to fuse the England sides of the early 1990s into the confident and purposeful outfit that went on to dominate the Five Nations.

the side for the 14th time, passing the record held by Wakefield, Hall, Evans, Jeeps and Pullin. Mike Rafter returned to the back row and the Harlequins flanker David Cooke made his debut as an open-side flanker.

It was a game that Wales, in their centenary season, desperately wanted to win. An early injury to Cotton in his final match disrupted the English scrum but England held on to a 19-18 lead until the final minute when Clive Woodward was ruled offside by the margin of a boot-cap at a scrum. Steve Fenwick kicked the winning penalty. For England the incident had echoes of 1957 when a Grand Slam had been won thanks to victory at Cardiff when Keith Maddocks was harshly judged offside. Woodward felt as wretched this day as Maddocks and a Grand Slam opportunity had disappeared.

Victories over Scotland and Ireland, though, restored England's equilibrium with Woodward bagging the winning try against the Scots to atone for his error. Huw Davies had by now replaced John Horton at stand-off and the powerful Newport prop Colin Smart had filled the huge hole left by Fran Cotton and England still had the chance of a share of the championship when they met France at Twickenham.

Clive Woodward, whose England season got off to a terrible start against Wales in 1981.

Refereeing Error

France won the Grand Slam thanks to a refereeing error by the Scot Allan Hosie. England lost 16-12 with France scoring an illegal try. A quick throw-in on the English 22 saw the French flanker Jean-Pierre Rives create space for Pierre Lacans to score near the posts. But the try should not have been allowed. Pierre Berbizier had thrown into the line-out a ball that he had received from a bystander rather than the match ball. For a quick throw-in only a ball that has not been touched by a spectator must be used. England, whose points were scored by new full-back Marcus Rose, were furious.

England went to Argentina that spring, just a few months before war broke out between the countries, and drew the first Test 19-19 against the Pumas in Buenos Aires, but with only two of the Grand Slam pack that triumphed at Murrayfield 14 months earlier. It needed a late try by Clive Woodward to secure the draw. A week later a physical, often brutal, second Test saw England win 12-6, Mike Rafter subduing the threat of the world's leading fly-half Hugo Porta and Huw Davies scoring the try.

Beaumont's England looked a match for any side in the world and the visit of Mark Loane's Australians that autumn would measure how far they had come. The 1981-82 Wallabies, with the brilliant Mark Ella at fly-half, were hailed by the southern hemisphere press as world champions at the time on account of beating the All Blacks, who had beaten the South Africans who had beaten Beaumont's 1980 Lions. It was a billing the Wallabies could not live up to in January 1982 when England beat them 15-11 at Twickenham – thanks to a try by Nick Jeavons who rolled off a maul to crash over in the corner. It was a match that will be remembered for a half-time pitch invasion by 24-year-old Erika Roe. Beaumont found the minds of his players wandering during his on-field pep talk. Erika Roe had decided to take up the peculiar but strangely popular trend of streaking. Perhaps the most tasteful description came in *Rothmans Rugby Union Yearbook* whose editor, Viv Jenkins, described this highlight of the season as being: 'when a lady named Erika erupted on to the field like a galleon in full sail but minus her spinnakers.'

England had beaten the much-fancied Australians but they, too, were exposed in the New Year, drawing at Murrayfield before losing at home to

50 Greatest Players

BILL BEAUMONT Lock

Club: Fylde

Debut: v Ireland, 18 January 1975

No. of Caps: 34 **No. of Points:** 0

The player who more than any other was responsible for England's rugby revival in 1980 was the British Bulldog from Fylde and Lancashire, Bill Beaumont. He came into the side in the mid-1970s and soon commanded a regular place through his technical expertise and special skills as a front-of-the-line jumper.

It was the quality of his captaincy, however, that was to drive up England's rugby stock. He stepped in as leader in 1978 and quickly showed his knack for player management. Never one to bawl out his players, Beaumont implemented his belief that mutual respect on the field grew from trust and good relations formed off it.

Players warmed to his example and results steadily improved. With the nucleus of his successful Lancashire county side he led the Northern Division to a famous victory over the 1979 All Blacks before his rebuilding work with England reached its peak in 1980. A national side bursting with the confidence instilled by Beaumont carried off its first Grand Slam for 23 years.

He remained as captain for another two years until advised on medical grounds to take early retirement. After leading his nation on a then record 21 occasions, it was a sad way for one of England's finest servants to leave the game he deeply loved.

Ireland when the Munster prop Ginger McLoughlin crashed over for a try that has been shown endlessly in television replays ever since. They were two sobering results but, for England, the real loss was that of the captain who had led them to their Grand Slam triumph. Bill Beaumont received a knock on the head leading Lancashire in the County Championship a week before the Ireland game. It was the third similar injury he had received in 12 months and his sight became impaired. After neurological tests he was advised to give up the game. Beaumont's run of 33 successive England games came to a shuddering halt and with it England's run of successes.

Steve Smith took over the captaincy and England without their popular leader managed to rouse themselves from the trough of despair that followed Beaumont's departure and the Irish defeat. Dusty Hare was recalled at full-back and England repeated their win in Paris of two years earlier with a 27-15 victory thanks to 19 points from the Leicester man and two tries by Clive Woodward and John Carleton. A fortnight later England played with similar enterprise to dispatch Wales 17-7. And despite their captain's departure the England team still found ways to enjoy themselves. After the Paris win, Colin Smart had his 15 minutes of fame when, at the after-match dinner, he drank his gift bottle of after-shave and passed out. His team-mates had tricked the prop into thinking they were drinking the same cologne but had emptied the contents and replaced it with wine. Smart recovered, though, and as his captain Steve Smith remarked at the time: 'He was in a bad way but his breath smelt lovely.'

Turning Wine into Water

England themselves would complete the year smelling of roses. They were unearthing some outstanding players, too. Peter Winterbottom, the Yorkshire farmer with the hayrick hair, had filled the huge gap left by Tony Neary on the open-side flank. Winterbottom's athleticism had already made him one of the world's leading No. 7s. The scrum-half Nigel Melville, another Yorkshireman, was attracting the attention of the selectors with a lightning quick pass that was already helping draw comparisons with the All Black Dave Loveridge. And Tony Bond was restored to full fitness to become another bludgeon to link with the rapier skills of Clive Woodward in the centre. All three took part in an end-of-season tour to North America when England beat Canada, an emerging force in the game, 43-6 in Vancouver before thrashing the college boys of the United States 59-0 in Hartford, Connecticut. England were breaking records in 1982 with the size of their victories over lesser nations. Fiji, who still clung to the memories of their triumphant 1970 tour, came to Scotland and England in the dank autumn and were blown away on a

50 Greatest Players

PETER WHEELER Hooker

Club: Leicester

Debut: v France, 1 February 1975

No. of Caps: 41 **No. of Points:** 0

Looking back, it seems astonishing that Peter Wheeler first caught the selectors' attention with his place-kicking. It was a duty he performed for Leicester in the early 1970s, yet in a distinguished career of 41 England caps he never scored a point in an international match.

He had to live in the shadow of John Pullin for a number of seasons before his livewire performances in the loose and his technical expertise in the front-row finally made the selectors realise that they could not overlook him any longer. He forced his way ahead of Pullin for a couple of matches in 1975 until injury sidelined him.

By 1977 he was first-choice hooker in an England side that steeled itself to erase memories of the indifferent form of the 1970s. Wheeler's polished contributions as a fast-striking right-footed hooker in the tight and as an indefatigable all-rounder in the loose were invaluable to the side's rehabilitation. Needless to say he was one of the elder statesmen of the pack that three years later collected all the Five Nations' silverware and he remained an important part of the national set-up until 1983-84.

He was captain in his last season, beginning with a spirited 15-9 win against the All Blacks in an autumn Test. His side, however, never quite realised its potential thereafter and a season that had started with such promise petered out with the loss of three of the four matches in the Five Nations. Somehow, even neutral observers felt that Wheeler deserved a more fitting Test farewell.

disastrous tour that ended with a 60-19 beating by an England XV at Twickenham. The Bath flier David Trick ran in a hat-trick of tries. It was their tenth successive defeat on the trip.

Steve Bainbridge, a 6ft 7in (1.9m) athletic lock from Gosforth, had now taken over Bill Beaumont's role as the foil for the hugely effective Maurice Colclough in the second row and Steve Smith, a bundle of energy at scrum-half, was proving a noisy, restless but effective captain with a style that couldn't be more different to the calm, matey Beaumont.

Smith's England were expected to prosper after a golden autumn in which a young fly-half, Rob Andrew, was making a name for himself at Cambridge.

But the 1983 championship was an anticlimax, not helped by an injury in the first game against France to Maurice Colclough and the retirement of Phil Blakeway. The 1980 Grand Slam pack was breaking up rather too quickly for the liking of Mike Davis and in the 1983 season England managed only one try. Smith made public criticisms of the selectors. In particular the omission of Mike Slemen from the trial was particularly crass. The Swansea right-wing Tony Swift lived up to his name but he played on the left-wing for England's first three matches and was immediately exposed against France when Philippe Sella zigzagged inside and outside him for the first try in a 19-15 win. France eventually took the championship and England finished bottom with just one point from a 13-13 draw in Cardiff against Wales, a game they should have won with a cracking try from John Carleton that was to be a shaft a of light in a gloomy three months. England finished the tournament with a 22-12 defeat at home to Scotland who had not won at Twickenham for a dozen years and a 15-25 reverse in Dublin. By the end of the season John Scott had taken over the captaincy from Smith. Mike Davis resigned, though he was being a little harsh on himself with his parting shot: 'I'm the first man to turn wine into water.'

Rugby Circus

It was an unhappy time for English rugby and northern hemisphere rugby in general. During the year an Australian businessman, David Lord, approached many of the England team with offers to join a professional rugby circus. Cracks were appearing in the amateur facade of the international game. Two England captains, Peter Wheeler and Steve Smith, met Lord in Manchester. His grandiose plan was to recruit over 200 of the world's top players and bring them together to play exhibitions around the world's top venues.

The scheme never materialised but the fact that it was being touted revealed that amateur rugby union at international level was at a crossroads. Its leading players were finding it difficult to hold down jobs while at the same time devoting hours to the sport without financial reward. There was growing resentment among the England players that in a country like New Zealand players were openly earning money for rugby-related activities. In England a player could not even profit from writing a book. If like David Duckham he did, he was not allowed to contribute to the game, as a coach for instance, and valuable expertise was lost. It was clearly a contradictory and grossly unfair arrangement.

The consequences of the moribund season for England had an impact on the selection of the Lions squad for the tour of New Zealand that summer.

The Lions suffered a 4-0 whitewash and the low standards of British rugby, particularly back play at the time, were exposed. Peter Wheeler, regarded by most as the leading hooker in the world, was left at home as the horse-trading of the selectors had resulted in Ciaran Fitzgerald being picked as tour captain and Scotland's in-form Colin Deans being chosen as the Irishman's number two. Andy Dalton's All Blacks were completely dominant.

Changes had been rung by the time the New Zealanders visited in the winter. England had a new chairman of selectors in Derek Morgan, a new coach in Dick Greenwood, and yet another new captain in Peter Wheeler, the man discarded by the Lions. Wheeler had a point to prove and he did it emphatically on 19 November when the All Blacks were defeated 15-9. Maurice Colclough, who had played most of his rugby in France but had now returned to play for Wasps, achieved immortality with the England try and his victorious skipper tagging him 'The Marquis de Colclough'. England did not win with quite the panache of 1936. It was an attritional victory built on a solid forward platform in which the new No. 8 Paul Simpson was outstanding. It was the All Blacks' first defeat in a Test in Britain for 30 years and it was not a proud day for their rugby. Three players, including Simpson, needed stitches and Mike Slemen was badly raked, but England had lurched from the ridiculous to the sublime in the space of six months.

Underwood Underused

And back to the ridiculous. For England's plan to take the crushing forward-orientated style of rugby into the International Championship backfired. Behind their pack they played the Leicester scrum-half Nick Youngs, a farmer who was very much in the mould of Wales's ninth forward Terry Holmes. But England were swept off their feet by Scotland at Murrayfield and never recovered, while the Scots went on to take a rare Grand Slam. All England had to show against Scotland and Ireland were penalties by Dusty Hare and a Les Cusworth drop goal, and although the Irish were beaten at Twickenham, the sterile style of rugby made England few friends. France duly walloped them 32-18 in Paris with a breathtaking display of attacking rugby but there was at least a try from their new wing Rory Underwood, a trainee pilot whose vapour trails were soon to be seen across the rugby stadiums of the world. Underwood would become England's most-capped and most prolific wing, but in the mid-1980s he could have played games in a sheepskin coat with his hands thrust into its pockets, so little of the ball did he see.

England's supporters had little to refresh them in this arid era. There was discord in the England camp at the time. The forwards wanted a tight simple

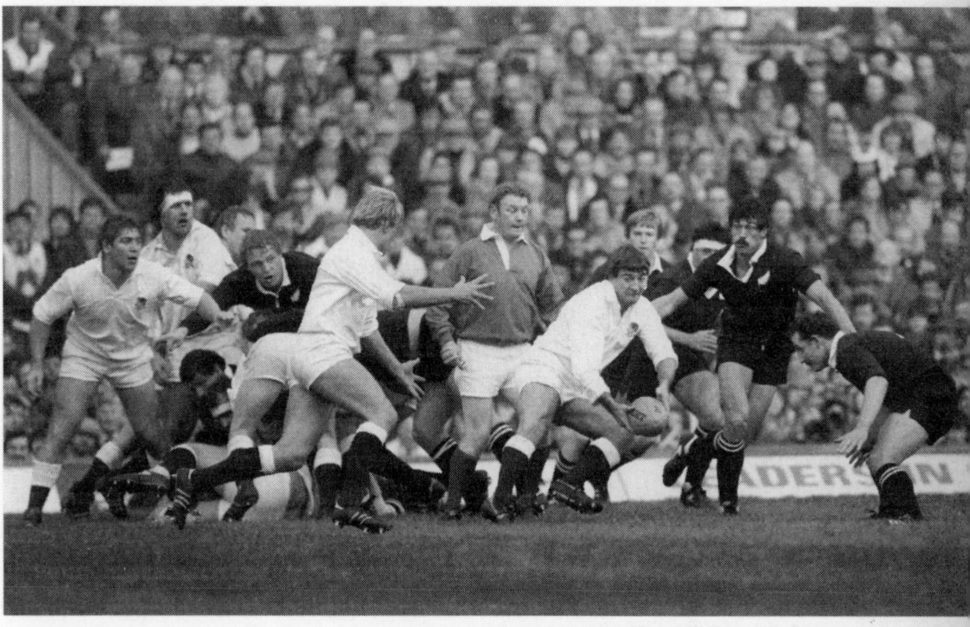

England's Nick Youngs (centre) lays the ball off to the charging Peter Winterbottom (left) in the amazing 15-9 defeat of New Zealand in November 1983.

game, others such as the Leicester stand-off Les Cusworth wanted to run the ball and, with backs of the calibre of Underwood, Mark Bailey, Bryan Barley and Swift, many felt that England were too constricted. Meanwhile, they faced greater challenges with a tour to South Africa and a visit from the Australians, now playing a 15-man game that made England's style of rugby look prehistoric.

The South African trip was fraught with problems and not only on the playing field. Nelson Mandela was still a political prisoner and South Africa still off-limits for most of the world's sportsmen and women. England toured the Republic in the summer of 1984 in spite of pressure from the Labour party at home, churches and the anti-apartheid movement. And as well as the hue-and-cry at home, many of the players were reluctant to make the trip.

England left under their restored captain John Scott without 18 regulars and were as exposed as the Lions had been in New Zealand 12 months earlier. They lost the first Test in Port Elizabeth 33-15 and in Johannesburg were beaten 35-9, their heaviest-ever defeat. Danie Gerber, the world's leading centre, who the world knew little about, made up for lost time with four tries in the two Tests, precisely four more than England were to manage themselves. The trip was a test of fire for an inexperienced squad and it ended careers before they had begun. When the next International Championship came round, only five of the tourists were selected for the first game against France.

It was, then, no real surprise or disgrace when England, who featured a new fly-half in Bristol's Stuart Barnes, lost to the Wallabies that autumn. Australia ran roughshod over all the home nations on their tour and were widely considered to be, under their innovative coach Alan Jones, one of the finest and most attractive of international sides.

England, with a set of backs – Rob Andrew, Kevin Simms and Simon Smith – lifted from the brilliant Cambridge side alongside Rory Underwood, looked to be brimming with pace for the next match, against Romania. Nigel Melville had been succeeded by Paul Dodge as captain, a job that was becoming something of a hot potato, and Dick Greenwood had found a lock forward in the unlikely setting of his club Preston Grasshoppers. The coach later recalled: 'I was at the club having a pee, when it suddenly became dark and this enormous lad came in.' The 6ft 8in (1.92m) community policeman Wade Dooley was to become one of the most imposing figures in rugby. In his championship debut against the much-vaunted French team of 1985 he took few prisoners. England drew 9-9 thanks to a famous tackle by their scrum-half Richard Harding who nailed the French wing Patrick Esteve after he had crossed the line.

England regained the Calcutta Cup with a 10-7 victory over the Scots but Ireland, who won the championship, and Wales beat them to leave England mired in mid-table mediocrity. It was progress of sorts but England had a scapegoat to rival the wretched Esteve in Chris Martin, Bath's Cornish full-back, who dropped a high kick from Jonathan Davies and conceded a try in Cardiff that ensured England's melancholy run there continued.

England Under-23 coach, Martin Green, had replaced Dick Greenwood by the time England travelled to New Zealand that summer. Greenwood left the post for business reasons, but he probably would not have survived long. In a nightmarish 12 months England had used 51 players in eight internationals and had been put in their place by two of the best sides in the world.

Mastermind

Martin Green had credentials. He had masterminded the Midlands defeat of the All Blacks in 1983, a result that England used as a blueprint for their own win, but any trip to meet the All Blacks in their own backyard is ferociously difficult. The tour began with a bomb scare at Auckland airport and ended with England imploding in the second Test at Wellington when they went down to a 42-15 defeat, their worst in history.

Paul Dodge's team had performed with great credit in the first Test, going down 18-13 in Christchurch. England were also beaten by Auckland and

50 Greatest Players

PETER WINTERBOTTOM Flanker

Clubs: Headingley, Harlequins

Debut: v Australia, 2 January 1982

No. of Caps: 58 **No. of Points:** 13

In his first season as an international player Peter Winterbottom earned a reputation as an out and out open side flanker who made an art of flattening opponents with vigorous tackles. Even as a young player he possessed immense upper body strength – the legacy of a vigorous spare time job as an agricultural labourer on his uncle's farm.

He was hell bent on winning possession in the loose and was never more than three or four metres from the ball. He had sharpened his aggressive defence by spending a summer abroad in New Zealand playing for Hawke's Bay and on his return was the strong man among the national packs of the 1980s.

After comfortably making the transition from the cosy club atmosphere at Headingley to the slick city outfit at Harlequins he became an integral part of Geoff Cooke's plans to transform the fortunes of the England side in 1990. Winterbottom retained the hardness of his youth, but it was his contribution as a constructive forward that made him the key man. He invariably set up the rucks and mauls that provided the platform for the backs to use second-phase possession to dictate the tactical pattern of matches.

An ever present in the back to back Grand Slams of 1991 and 1992 and a member of the World Cup runners-up team in 1991, he retired as England's most-capped forward in 1993.

although they won their other four games, the gap between northern and southern hemisphere rugby was widening to a chasm. The just-retired Maurice Colclough, who announced he would like to make the trip, was disappointingly turned down as England forwards were no match for Andy Dalton's pack. The first Test showed what might have been, had they taken on the All Blacks up front. England scored the only tries of the match, the first by the Yorkshire wing Mike Harrison who intercepted Steve Pokere's pass to run half the length of the field to score memorably on his debut.

The second Test was a malevolent affair. Kicking and stamping by the All Blacks went unpunished and, in the words of one report, the England dressing-room later saw 'more stitches than the Bayeux Tapestry'. Wade

Dooley later recalled: 'The All Blacks got slaughtered by the press and public for only beating us 18-13. They reacted accordingly because the press and the public had them so wound up. That was the most violent match I have ever played in and I didn't come on until the last 20 minutes. They were determined to give our boys a seeing to... The ironic thing is that they would probably have won just as convincingly if they had concentrated on the rugby rather than the intimidation.'

Colclough did return to partner Wade Dooley the following year and there were green shoots of some kind of recovery. Rob Andrew gave a virtuoso performance in kicking all 21 points in a three-point victory over Wales and the Leicester policeman Dean Richards marked a memorable debut with two tries in a 25-20 win over the Irish. But England were thumped in Edinburgh and Paris and there was still an absence of flair in the English game.

Martin Green knew that in the first World Cup, taking place the following spring, England would have to inject more pace into their game to have any chance of competing with the host Australians and New Zealanders, let alone France, whose brilliant full-back Serge Blanco helped them become top dogs in Europe in 1986. Green, though, remained optimistic, responding to accusations that England's players lacked the necessary athleticism by hiring athletics coach Tom McNab to inject a more explosive running style among the players. Green, a lugubrious man not comfortable with the media demands of his new job, recognised that England's continued failings lay with the poor quality club rugby its internationals were playing week in week out and that the system was not sifting out talent.

Notorious International

Martin Green's ambitions for England in the first World Cup of 1987 were undermined, though, in one game in the championship of that year. England had already lost badly in Dublin, by 17-0 in wretched conditions, and at home to France, when they travelled to Cardiff under the leadership of the Bath scrum-half Richard Hill for what became a notorious international. Wales inflicted a third defeat on Green's team but it was a bitter affair to rank with that at Twickenham seven years earlier. Wade Dooley floored the Welsh No. 8 Phil Davies and the referee Ray Megson gave warnings to the lock, the hooker Graham Dawe and his Bath team-mate Gareth Chilcott.

All three, along with captain Richard Hill, were banned for the final game of the season against Scotland which England won under their new captain Mike Harrison. England won 21-12, playing some of their best rugby for years, with Brian Moore replacing Dawe as hooker and Paul Rendall taking Chilcott's place alongside him. Green's plans for the World Cup had become confused but the one good match of the championship left him in no doubt that Mike Harrison should lead England in the World Cup.

Martin Green's right-hand man in Australia was Mike Weston, the genial chairman of selectors who had won 29 caps as a centre and fly-half. The estate agent had also led England in 1968 and had been a selector in the Grand Slam year. Harrison retained the captaincy. Wade Dooley, Richard Hill, Graham Dawe and Gareth Chilcott were also forgiven and rejoined the squad. But although Dooley was to become a key player, the Bath trio were now supplanted in the England first team. Brian Moore was now the first-choice hooker and would be for years to come and his rivalry with the Cornish farmer Dawe was always intense.

With a wing as captain, it was clear England were going to put some emphasis on the ball reaching him and Rory Underwood. But it was a wing who England left behind that may have made the difference between winning and losing in Australia. Martin Offiah had suddenly become hot property at Rosslyn Park and had electrified matches in Wales where he turned out in the colours of the Barbarians that Easter. Offiah's unorthodox play, particularly

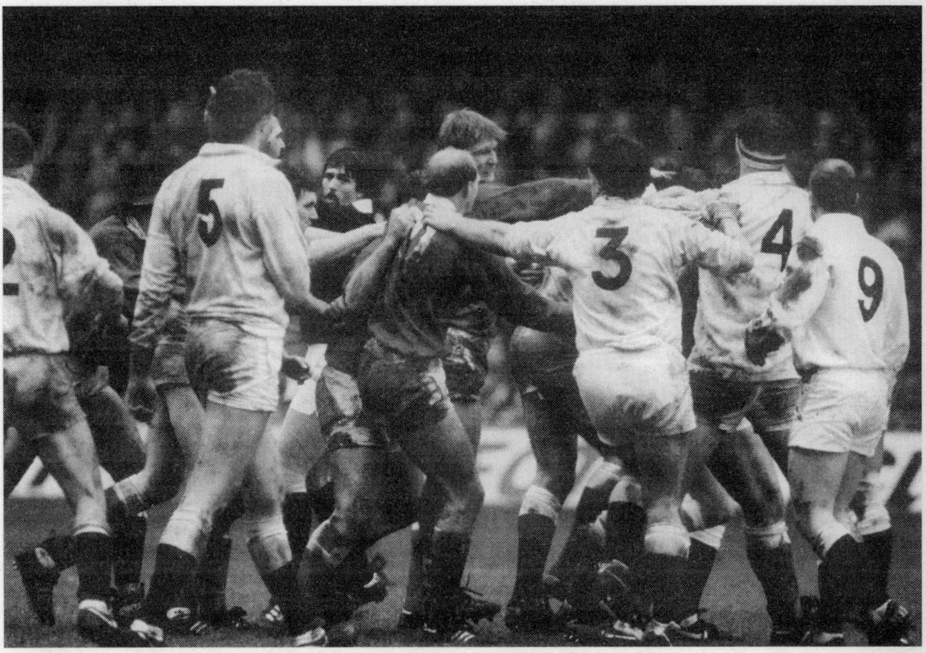

Paul Moriarty (blond hair) launches at Wade Dooley (No. 4) as Richie Collins and Gary Pearce (No. 3) grapple. Wales v England, Five Nations Championship, Cardiff, 1987.

when he scored a hat-trick of tries against Swansea, brought him to the attention of the England selectors but too late for inclusion in the World Cup party. Another few months and he would have walked into the England team. Instead that summer Widnes came up with an offer the 21-year-old could not refuse and Offiah went on to smash records in rugby league.

England were taking a no-risks policy at this time as they stepped into unknown territory and the game took a seismic shift forwards with the first World Cup. A handsome gold trophy called the William Webb Ellis Cup awaited the winners. Australia, co-hosts with New Zealand, would soon refer to it as 'Old Bill'.

It was Australia who England met in a fiendishly difficult first game at the Concord Oval in Sydney. Australia included 18 of the players in their squad who had taken part in the all-conquering 1984 tour of Britain and Ireland and they had the biggest pack in world rugby, personified by the 17st hooker Tommy Lawton, a Great Dane to England's so-called 'Pit Bull' Brian Moore. Although injury robbed England of the services of two key forwards Steve Bainbridge and Jon Hall, England gave a good account of themselves in Sydney before going down 19-6. The defeat was hardly a disaster. England had the United States and Japan in their pool and wins over both would ensure a safe passage to the quarter-finals.

England set a new record in beating Japan 60-7 with Mike Harrison bagging a hat-trick of tries. Then the Americans were seen off 34-6 with Peter Winterbottom scoring his first international tries. Jonathan Webb, who took over at full-back in place of Marcus Rose, was one of a number of players drafted in to allow Green's first choices to rest before flying to Brisbane for a quarter-final with Wales. The plan to rest players had worked handsomely and England, with 110 points from their three games, had plenty of reasons to be cheerful as they flew north to Queensland.

Breakfast Blues

Wales were struggling to hit any real form. Their captain Richard Moriarty had even been dropped for the game against Canada with Jonathan Davies taking over as skipper. England had injuries, notably to their fly-half Peter Williams who had turned his ankle, but they insisted the game at Ballymore would not be a grudge match and were convinced that they could reach the last four. England's supporters watching at home on television, though, were given a severe dose of Monday morning blues as England limply lost 16-3. Moriarty returned to form in conditions that were not so much sub-tropical as like a murky, muddy November day in Swansea. While Paul Rendall was being replaced at prop by Gareth Chilcott and Nigel Redman was playing as a stop-gap loose-head, the ball squirted out of a scrum for the Cardiff flanker Gareth Roberts to score a try. In the final minute John Devereux intercepted a pass to score a second try and England were on their way home.

The red rose of England had simply wilted. Even the English scrum had come off second-best against the Welsh pack whose experiment of playing with a 19-year-old prop David Young had paid off. It was a measure of how ordinary England were that the All Blacks crushed Wales 49-6 a week later, although the Welsh were able to claim third place in the tournament by beating Australia. New Zealand won the first World Cup with a 29-9 victory over the French in Auckland.

After their heavy defeat by the All Blacks, the Wales manager Clive Rowlands was asked where his side would go from there. 'Back to beating England every year,' was his reply. Nobody was going to spare England's blushes. The Brisbane defeat revealed serious cracks in the England game. It was not so much the result as the way they lost that was so depressing. Tom McNab had spent a year helping raise the fitness levels of the players but in the pressure of big matches England seemed to freeze. Mike Weston was realistic: 'We realised our shortcomings a year ago and we tried to do something about it. We thought we were on course and we're hoping to get the structure

Jamie Salmon takes up the running in the 34-6 win over USA in the 1987 World Cup.

changed and maybe we have set the ball rolling for English rugby.'

The coaches were not around for long. The debacle over, Mike Weston resigned and Martin Green was sacked. It had been a depressing few months for England, from the capitulation at Lansdowne Road, to the violence at Cardiff, to the tepid early exit from the World Cup party. Peter Williams and Jamie Salmon never played for England again and Williams would soon defect to rugby league. The super-fit, highly motivated, well-drilled players of New Zealand had shown they were way ahead of England on the road to professionalism.

50 Greatest Players

WADE DOOLEY Lock

Clubs: Preston Grasshoppers, Fylde

Debut: v Romania, 5 January 1985

No. of Caps: 55 **No. of Points:** 12

They called him the throwback. At a time when domestic rugby in England was organising itself into leagues, Wade Dooley was the player who plied his trade playing with an unfashionable fourth division club (Preston Grasshoppers), yet pushed hard for England honours and went on to win 55 caps before retiring in 1993 as his country's most-capped lock.

Sheer willpower and a healthy competitive edge carried him to national honours in 1985 and he quickly cornered the middle-of-the-line-out position in the England set-up. It's true that his edge landed him in trouble in a brutal match at Cardiff in 1987, but after serving a brief suspension he retained his place when Geoff Cooke began assembling his team of all the talents in 1988. Dooley was to play his part among the nucleus of hard-core forwards who generated quiet confidence in that squad.

His line-out work partnering first Paul Ackford and then Martin Bayfield was an important factor in the back-to-back Grand Slam seasons of 1991 and 1992. After a measured first 40 minutes he invariably cleaned out his opponents with his second-half performances to provide England with the platform for victory. Indeed, when he retired in 1993, the statistic that arguably summed up most effectively his contribution was that England won the battle for line-out possession in 85 per cent of the Five Nations matches in which Big Wade featured.

Chapter Seven: 1987-94
Wind of Change

On 15 October 1987 gale-force winds swept across Britain, uprooting trees and changing the landscape of the south of England for ever. On the same day Geoff Cooke became the new manager of England's rugby team and a wind of change was to transform the fortunes of a national side deep in the doldrums after their abject failure in the World Cup that spring.

Outside Yorkshire, Cooke was hardly a high-profile figure. He was the principal sports development officer with Leeds City Council and had been Yorkshire's coach and later chairman of selectors. He had helped select the North side that memorably beat the All Blacks at Otley eight years earlier and his most recent triumph had been as a coach and selector of the North side that had won the Divisional Championship.

Unwieldy committees would no longer take decisions about the preparation and selection of the England team. They were to be taken by Geoff Cooke, England's first manager. He quickly appointed fitness and medical officers, John Elliott was nominated as a selector, the doughty former England captain and warrior forward Roger Uttley became coach and the Nottingham coach Alan Davies was put in charge of the England B team. The pragmatic Cooke had watched the World Cup unfold with a mixture of horror and frustration. 'We have to be honest enough to face up to the fact that we're in the second division,' he said. 'We've had a poor time since 1980, nine wins out of the last 20 in the Five Nations endorses that view. We need to arrive quickly at our best side and look to improved performance by the players once they reach international level.'

Cooke wanted to expand England's horizons and it was his great fortune that a revolution in the England club game at this time gave him the ingredients for his ambitious recipe. A month before he began his job the club game in England underwent a massive change with the introduction of the Courage Club Championship. Every club in the land was ranked and joined a league, a towering pyramid of 1,128 clubs in which the leading first-class clubs, those that charged money at the gate, were at the apex. For tiny junior clubs there was the incentive of promotion through the pyramid and throughout the shires fixtures became more meaningful, more competitive.

For Geoff Cooke's new England, talent would be quickly filtered through to the top clubs and he would be able to concentrate on watching fixtures in National Leagues One and Two. The first winners of the Courage Championship were Leicester, followed by Wasps, Harlequins, Bath and Gloucester. These were the kinds of clubs who would prosper and who would provide Cooke with the majority of his England players. There were exceptions, Wade Dooley was selected from Preston Grasshoppers for instance, but the cream in the English club game would soon rise to the top.

Rugby World magazine questioned some major figures in the game during the first league season and most were enthusiastic. John Carleton, still plying his trade on the wing at Orrell, was in no doubt: 'They are five to ten years overdue and it will take two or three years to produce what we are looking for – a migration of the best players to better clubs. The England team will benefit accordingly,' he said. Interestingly, the Harlequins flanker Micky Skinner, who was just establishing himself in the England side, was less sure: 'The pressures on players were big enough last year. The arrival of the leagues has only served to increase those pressures on the players, coaches and administrators. The training is more severe and the game on a Saturday afternoon more intense. The game is in danger of not being fun any more.'

As usual, there was also the alternative view from Andy Ripley, the great Corinthian England player of the early 1970s. Ripley was a one-off in rugby. There weren't too many rugby players who had appeared on the *Wogan* TV

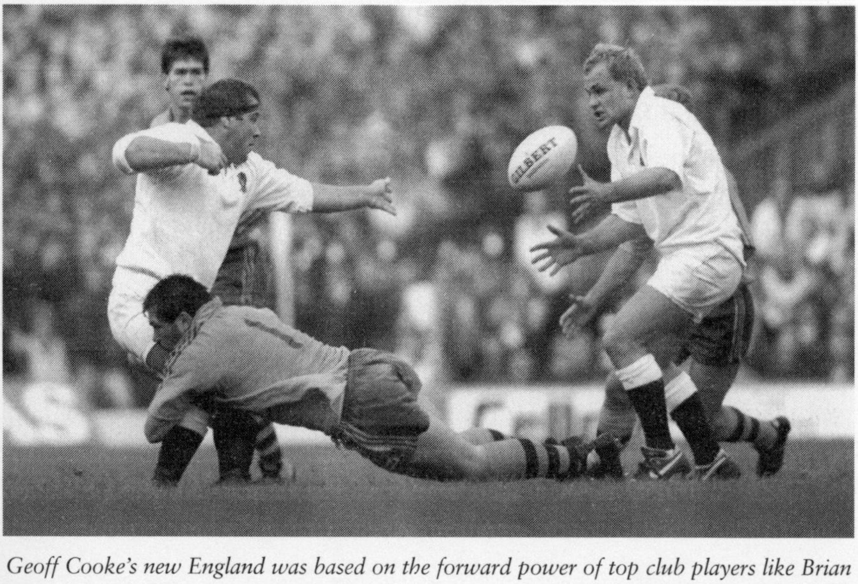

Geoff Cooke's new England was based on the forward power of top club players like Brian Moore (left) and Andy Robinson (right).

programme to plug a book or on BBC's *Superstars*. His Rosslyn Park club in south-west London were to slip from grace with the advent of league rugby. Though their rugby was serious, it was not serious enough to get in the way of a good time. Ripley said: 'League rugby is a curate's egg – the players basically like it, especially the team that is doing well. However, it is going to generate a down-side and one should appreciate that although it brings benefits, notably a degree of professionalism which will develop, I am not too sure the RFU in its current structure is either aware of or can actually handle them.'

All three men were essentially spot on. It did take two or three years before the benefits of the leagues were felt by the national side, rugby did cease to be fun for players at the apex of the pyramid and the professionalism that came with the restructuring of rugby at top club and country level did eventually lead to the end of amateur rugby. Cooke, though, could afford not to listen to siren voices. He knew he had the tools to change the underachieving England team and a pool of special experts in fitness and preparation that would utilise the biggest player-base in the world. No longer would it be possible to play well in the Varsity match and be thrust into the England set-up a month later. Cooke would build his team around a group of talented players emerging from the north and from the clubs making the biggest impact in the Courage League. And it was one of these little-known players from the north of England who was to become Cooke's key brick in the foundations of one of the greatest England teams.

Carling – A Special Brew

Will Carling was the son of army brigadier, Bill Carling, who had played prop for Cardiff. Carling was a hard-running centre at Sedbergh School in Cumbria, a notable rugby academy whose old boys also included another great England centre in John Spencer. Carling had captained England Schools in 1984 and had played for the Army side while on a scholarship at Sandhurst. He would soon resign his commission, however, after Geoff Cooke, whose first choices Simon Halliday and John Buckton were injured, named the Durham University student in his first England side to face France in Paris in January 1988. Mike Harrison was retained as captain but his days were numbered.

World Cup failures England were expected to be well beaten, after all France were still buzzing from an epic winning World Cup semi-final against Australia – one of the greatest games of all-time – but they turned out one of their best displays for a long time in losing 10-9. If Carling's centre partner Kevin Simms had not looked to pass rather than let his momentum carry him over the line, England could have won the match. The England forwards

50 Greatest Players

BRIAN MOORE Hooker

Clubs: Nottingham, Harlequins

Debut: v Scotland, 4 April 1987

No. of Caps: 64 **No. of Points:** 4

The hooker whose mental steel and all-round skills epitomised the new breed of England forward in the late 1980s was Brian Moore. For years English forwards had been viewed as gentle giants by their opponents. Moore and the packs he fronted in the Carling era were tough-minded with a hatred of losing.

From an early stage in his career a strike against his head or a take against his line-out throw, one sensed, were painful losses for Moore. Once he became a fixture in the Test side, he went on to play a significant role in England's resurgence.

Underwood, Carling and Andrew were the public figureheads of the Grand Slam years. But the key to England's successes was forward dominance, and that's where Moore figured prominently. He was the catalyst who urged the pack into a unit capable of subduing any opposition scrum. For sheer energy and determination he had no peer, whether leading by example or exhorting his colleagues to raise their game. He managed to hold his eight together at critical moments invariably snapping their efforts into championship-winning performances.

His other great assets were courage and stamina. As England's first-choice hooker for eight years he was never dropped and never once required replacement in a Test match.

Wade Dooley, Peter Winterbottom and Micky Skinner were outstanding. Cooke's first game showed glimpses of what the new regime could achieve.

There were high expectations when Wales rolled into Twickenham a fortnight later but again England's bubble was pricked. An 11-3 defeat thanks to two tries by Adrian Hadley was a depressing comedown after the promise of Paris. If he didn't know already, here was proof that Cooke's job would not be easy. There was little of the adventure of Paris with Wales, who had boldly chosen four fly-halves, including the 20-year-old Tony Clement, displaying all the attacking nous. Carling barely had a run and Twickenham's first glimpse of this new prodigy did not reveal much of what lay ahead.

Cooke cleared out the old guard for Murrayfield. Out went Mike Harrison, Kevin Simms and Les Cusworth. In came Chris Oti, a black wing who had scored two tries in the 1987 Varsity match and as a 17-year-old at Millfield School had set a sprint record of 10.8 seconds. Rory Underwood moved to the right wing to accommodate Oti and, if nothing else, this new-look English back division, which now had Simon Halliday to partner the young Carling in the centre, had plenty of gas. Lots of gas but the engine was still spluttering in the cold of the 1988 winter. England, under their new captain Nigel Melville, won at Murrayfield but only thanks to two Jon Webb penalties and a drop goal from Rob Andrew.

The 9-6 win was enough to give England the Calcutta Cup but the game, and the old trophy, suffered. Scotland's coach Derrick Grant, in his last game in charge, accused England of negative tactics. Geoff Cooke claimed England had been prevented from playing much rugby because of the negative tactics of the Scots. After the match the Calcutta Cup itself featured in an impromptu game of football in the streets of Edinburgh and Scotland's John Jeffrey and England's Dean Richards were singled out for disciplinary action.

Swing Low Sweet Chariot

The patience of England's supporters was being tested. This supposed new dawn was proving less than sunny. England had gone three games in the championship without a try and at half-time in their final game, the meeting with Ireland at Twickenham, matters had not improved. No tries, a Michael Kiernan drop goal separating the sides and their captain Melville taken off on a stretcher. What Geoff Cooke said to his side at the interval was anybody's guess but the transformation was startling. In the second half England scored six tries, including a hat-trick from Chris Oti who bamboozled the Irish with his ability to change direction in a space little bigger than a telephone box. The sounds of 'Swing Low Sweet Chariot' echoed from Twickenham's stands for the first time and suddenly, in the space of 40 minutes, England's supporters had found their voice and England had found a team.

Geoff Cooke had said that he aimed to make England a leading force in the world, but there were only weeks to prepare for a tour to Australia that would pitch his team against one of the best. The Bedford lock John Orwin was handed the captaincy in place of Melville whose international career was over after breaking his leg against Ireland. Melville could have been the greatest scrum-half England ever had – he had the quickest, most fluent, pass around – but injuries plagued him. On the 1983 Lions tour he returned home with a neck injury after one match and Cooke turned back to the tried and tested Richard Harding for the Australian trip and Melville became one of the great unfulfilled talents.

Chris Oti takes the plaudits after scoring a hat-trick of tries against Ireland at Twickenham in 1988.

It was a demoralising tour. England lost the first Test 22-16 in Brisbane but outscored the Wallabies by two tries to one, Rory Underwood and John Bentley crossing the line. But Nick Farr-Jones and Michael Lynagh, the Australian half-backs, gave the Wallabies a control that Richard Harding and Rob Andrew could not match. In the second Test in Sydney England were thumped 28-8, a hugely disappointing display in which David Campese, the wing who was so often to prove England's crowing nemesis, made them look leaden-footed. England were even beaten by New South Wales and their back play on the tour was, at best, ordinary while the forwards were in decline, Orwin lucky to keep his Test place ahead of the promising Nigel Redman. A win in Suva over Fiji could hardly be described as a consolation. England needed to regroup quickly, especially as Australia were their next opponents that autumn at Twickenham.

Everything on the tour was wrong. And the trip set the blunt-speaking Cooke at odds with Twickenham for the first, but not the last, time. The players had trouble on the hard grounds with their boots. Cooke cabled home, claiming the players' boots were unsuitable. Dudley Wood, the Rugby Football Union secretary, replied from the other side of the globe: 'The suitability of the boots, which have been used for two seasons, is not in question.' The point Cooke was making may have seemed trivial to Twickenham but it was a valid one. How could rugby players play in boots that hurt their feet. Twickenham's attitude was that rugby boots were rugby boots. It was a classic case of the old world meeting the new head on.

But Geoff Cooke and John Elliott had seen something earlier that spring in Will Carling that made them sit up. In the greatest final of its 17-year history, Carling had helped his new club Harlequins become the first London side to win the English cup in a match against Bristol played at the kind of blistering pace rarely seen in an English club game. Carling, who scored two tries, was in barnstorming form. His second try was from an 80-metre run. Cooke was convinced that in this diffident 22-year-old he had a captain who could inspire through his own deeds on the field. Rob Andrew would have been Cooke's first choice but in 1988 the fly-half who would become England's greatest pivot was not sure of his place in the team. Carling was.

Landmark Game

Carling had had to join the Australian tour late because he stayed at home to finish university psychology exams. Now for his greatest test. On 5 November 1988 he was chosen to lead England for the first time. Carling was the youngest captain of England for 57 years. It was a landmark game with fireworks all over the pitch and one that erased the memories of the Australian tour that spring for which John Orwin became a scapegoat. England beat the Wallabies 28-19 with a display of refreshing attacking rugby that had not been seen at Twickenham since the days of Bill Beaumont's Grand Slam side. Rory Underwood scored two of four tries, and Carling made another for Simon Halliday, only to be knocked cold in the process. The new captain was concussed and did not finish the match. He was not the only one dazed – England's careworn supporters had seen ten tries in two successive matches at Twickenham.

Cooke built his team around Carling but it was a team that relied heavily on forward power. For the Australian win, England had introduced the Harlequins lock Paul Ackford who would provide a formidable second-row foil to the enormous, intimidating Wade Dooley. The front row of Wasps props Paul Rendall and Jeff Probyn, with the aggressive Nottingham hooker Brian Moore in between, would complete a ferocious front five. Behind them the likes of Dean Richards, Mike Teague, Peter Winterbottom, Micky Skinner and the emerging grafting flanker Andy Robinson would ensure that England packs in the 1990s would not take too many backward steps. Dewi Morris was another debutant in the win over

Will Carling led England for the first time in the Test against Australia in November 1988.

Australia. Born in Crickhowell, Wales were to rue the day they let this ultra-physical scrum-half slip through their fingers. Morris was the antithesis of the slim Nigel Melville with his super-charged pass. He was more akin to a ninth member of the pack and would suit Cooke's forward-orientated side to a T.

The last year of the decade that had started with the Grand Slam was to provide a hint that England could achieve a similar feat under Cooke and Carling. The Lions toured Australia in 1989 and England forwards Dean Richards, Wade Dooley, Andy Robinson, Brian Moore and Mike Teague featured notably in Finlay Calder's team that beat the Wallabies 2-1. The Lions used a battering-ram style, forward-dominated approach to win in Australia. It was not popular with the Wallaby supporters who claimed the Lions were over-physical but it was a winning method and it was one adopted by Geoff Cooke.

At Bath, the coach Jack Rowell was developing a style of play that was to be easy-on-the-eye as well as successful. The Bath club side concentrated on backs and forwards crossing the gainline and on constant quick recycling of the ball; England began to win matches through winning set-piece possession, in grinding down opponents before unleashing their backs in the second half. It was not so pretty but it was effective. Cooke had the forwards and, in Dewi Morris and the steady, hard-tackling stand-off Rob Andrew, he had two half-backs who could play to a strict pattern. Andrew was preferred to Bath's more adventurous Stuart Barnes and the rivalry between this pair was to provide an interesting sub-plot to the England drama.

But if England began 1989 buoyed with optimism after the win over the Wallabies, the championship began with them displaying all their old failings. Finlay Calder's rapidly improving Scottish team came to Twickenham and held England to a 12-12 draw with Rob Andrew and Jon Webb contriving to miss seven kicks between them. There was more to cheer in the visit to Dublin when England ground out a 16-3 win with Brian Moore and Dean Richards' tries separating the sides in a bitter, bruising encounter. And, in the 11-0 win over Pierre Berbizier's French team at Twickenham, England really looked the part only to squander their chance of the championship with another defeat in Cardiff when they lost Mike Teague to an injury early in the game.

'New' England

The game against France was typical of the new style of England. It was a highly charged affair, a thumping clash of two muscular packs with the 18 stone French prop Claude Portolan leaving the field with broken ribs.

Carling sliced through the French defence to score his first try for England. Pierre Villepreux, the former coach of Toulouse and France full-back, who crossed the Channel to help coach England, said, only half in jest: 'Maybe now England will do even better if I teach them to link the forwards with the backs.' Villepreux may have had a good point about England's limited approach, but the fact that Geoff Cooke and Roger Uttley hired his services was quite a revolutionary move at the time. Villepreux was always something of a prophet without honour in his own country but the England management knew his knowledge about the game would be priceless.

France had, like England, developed a team that, under its former scrum-half Jacques Fouroux, developed an obsession with forward power and Villepreux became the cavalier to Fouroux's roundhead. Villepreux espoused a more romantic idea of total rugby and made several visits to England, including an instructive trip to Bath, to swap ideas. His philosophy had long been admired by Twickenham's coaching organiser Don Rutherford and Villepreux was invited to England's training camp before the 1989 Five Nations. Villepreux's basic philosophy was: do not kick if you can run. Cooke's players absorbed that message, beginning the new decade with a brand of rugby that would make the world sit up and give them a chance of winning the World Cup when it came to Britain, Ireland and France in 1991.

Guscott Gets the Call

England, meanwhile, lost their captain for an international in Bucharest against Romania because of a shin injury. The injury also prevented him from touring with the Lions in Australia, but during the Bucharest trip England unearthed a new centre who perfectly complemented the new captain. Jeremy Guscott had just helped Bath land a league and cup double when he received the call from Twickenham. They were pre-revolutionary days in Romania and the national side were in decline. At the 23 August Stadium, England won 58-3 and Guscott scored three tries with Oti going one better with four. Simon Hodgkinson landed 19 points, converting eight of England's nine tries.

In 80 minutes of glorious spring sunshine Guscott was propelled into the Lions team, where he helped turn the series with a piece of individual brilliance in the second Test in Brisbane. England had found a new star centre who was to become a permanent fixture alongside Will Carling. No English three-quarter since the days of David Duckham had made such an immediate impact. Guscott's luck was that he learned his rugby at Bath, where he formed a formidable midfield trinity with Stuart Barnes and Simon Halliday. One of their trademark moves was running close to the ball-carrier and taking a short pass just as he was tackled. This proved effective against tight defences as an altered angle of the run would frequently open a gap which Guscott's pace could exploit. Guscott had played in Bath's first team since the age of 19 and at 23 he bridged the gulf between club and country with ease.

Dudley Wood, the Rugby Football Union secretary, described the 1988-89 season as a 'momentous season for English rugby' and Don Rutherford described the May day in Bucharest as 'breathtaking'. Rutherford highlighted how the fitness levels of the forwards had improved beyond measure, enabling them to run for 80 minutes in the energy-sapping heat. There was praise too for the B team and, in particular, their young flanker Neil Back. And, for the first time in history, an England manager compiled a report that was made public. Cooke highlighted problems such as indifferent decision-making and inconsistent goalkicking and he added: 'The most disappointing feature has been the reluctance or inability of the players to fully embrace a concept of total rugby which is, I believe, largely a reflection of what is happening in our clubs every Saturday.'

Soon England would embrace Cooke and Pierre Villepreux's idea of total rugby. The 1990 season was perhaps the most memorable in the history of the Five Nations Championship and it contained a finale that has never been matched for drama. England cast off their shackles, beating Ireland 23-0 at Twickenham in some style, although it was not until the last quarter that they really sprang into life, running in three tries in the final eight minutes. Richard Hill had replaced Dewi Morris at scrum-half and Hill's Bath club-mate Dave Egerton was in for the injured Dean Richards at No. 8. When Rory Underwood scored a typical try in the corner, he beat Cyril Lowe's record of 18 tries that had been set in the early 1920s.

Running Rugby

It had taken some time for the England juggernaut to get into gear but it now looked unstoppable. In Paris a fortnight later Carling's team produced one of the great England performances. A mediocre French team were ripped apart 26-7 with Underwood, Carling and Guscott scoring tries. Out came all those 'England's Stroll in the Parc' headlines and for once they were justified. It was the complete display, forward power linked with real flair behind the scrum. Mike Teague returned after a shoulder injury, and was outstanding in the back row. With Simon Hodgkinson kicking superbly in the strong wind, France were blown away. England just kept getting better and Wales were hammered 34-6 at Twickenham. Geoff Cooke brought the burlier Simon Halliday in to replace Mark Bailey on the wing in an effort to neutralise the

50 Greatest Players

PAUL ACKFORD Lock

Club: Harlequins

Debut: v Australia, 5 November 1988

No. of Caps: 22 **No. of Points:** 4

There were three policemen in the England pack when Will Carling became captain against Australia in 1988. Dean Richards and Wade Dooley were already seasoned campaigners. The third was a new cap, Paul Ackford.

The rookie was a late developer as a Test player. He had won England B honours as early as 1979, but he was north of 30 when a strong all-round performance for the London Division against the 1988 Wallabies earned him promotion to the full England side.

His athleticism and front-of-the-line-out skills made critics sit up and wonder why he had been left on the shelf for so long. Manager Geoff Cooke recognised Ackford's potential and the 6 foot 7 inch lock became a fixture in the side. He was a prominent winner of line-out possession in both the 1989 and 1990 Five Nations campaigns, when England challenged strongly but narrowly failed in their quest for honours, and the impressive run of consistent personal displays strengthened his reputation.

Ackford's untiring energy helped England lay the foundations for the Grand Slam victories of 1991. Confident and always one to rise to the big occasion, he denied opponents line-out ball, proved an imposing presence in the loose and was the perfect exponent of the driving forward game Geoff Cooke favoured. He remained an integral part of the squad for the Rugby World Cup in 1991 before announcing his retirement at the top of his trade immediately after the World Cup final.

threat of Wales's dangerous Arthur Emyr. But all the running rugby was done by England. Underwood scored two more tries; Carling and Richard Hill also scored. After the rout the Wales coach John Ryan resigned.

This was real total rugby and England looked to have the momentum that would carry them to a Grand Slam. They had scored 83 points and illuminated the championship. When they travelled to Murrayfield in March to inflict another emphatic defeat on the Scots it would be ten years, almost to the day, since Bill Beaumont's team had made the same journey to wrap up their Grand Slam. The omens were everywhere.

David Sole's Scottish team, though, were having a just as successful, if less spectacular time in the competition. They too had won all three of their games, but not in such style. Their win in Cardiff had come via the boot of Craig Chalmers and they had just squeezed past the Irish in Dublin. There were signs that this was one of the greatest Scottish sides in a 21-0 demolition of France. But England looked destined to make their mark in history. Will Carling had become the darling of the English tabloid press. He spoke in the build-up to the match of 'Going in like the SAS'. For Scotland's supporters the clipped-tones of this public schoolboy and army officer's son were too much and it added spice to what promised to be a molten occasion at Murrayfield when the Grand Slam, the championship, the Triple Crown and the Calcutta Cup would all be up for grabs. Bill McLaren reported on seeing England go through their paces on the eve of the match and looking frighteningly good. Even in their practice drills England never dropped a ball.

And so England ran out on the afternoon of 17 March in an atmosphere that would make a cauldron seem like a lukewarm bath. David Sole led his team out in a dramatic slow march. England had retained Halliday on the wing to counter the threat of Iwan Tukalo. They also kept Mike Teague at No. 8 in place of the slower Dean Richards. That was one selectorial decision that, in hindsight, would be England's undoing. The Scottish back row tackled until they dropped, cutting off England's expected midfield possession at source. The England pack were never allowed any momentum and although a splendid move gave Guscott the chance to arrow through for a try, Chalmers's penalties kept the Scots ahead.

Peter Winterbottom dodges Scotland's Sean Lineen in the tense Grand Slam decider at Murrayfield in March 1990.

In the second half Gavin Hastings hoisted a ball to the corner and the right wing Tony Stanger followed up to plunge over for a try. Bill McLaren, who had taught Stanger at primary school in Hawick, needed all his fabled cool professionalism in the commentary box to keep calm. England chased the game but they were cut down by ferocious tackles, most notably Scott Hastings thumping into Rory Underwood to prevent a certain try. Scotland won 13-7 for only the third Grand Slam in their history. England's dream Five Nations season had ended in a nightmare.

Scotland had been well-prepared by their coaches Ian McGeechan and Jim Telfer and the team, with players like John Jeffrey, David Sole and Finlay Calder, were at the height of their powers, but England knew they had let themselves down and underestimated the passionate intensity of the Scottish game. The underdogs yapped at England's heels for 80 minutes. Scotland played with a flat-out intensity that some of the older English forwards could not match. As well as the increased tempo, the Scottish scrum held up better than expected and the players varied their line-out ploys masterfully. When England did win ball from set-pieces it was usually pretty scrappy.

Shared Responsibility

England's Grand Slam 1990 sweat shirts that had been printed soon after the Wales game never did find a market on a day the streets of Edinburgh resembled something from VE Day. For the first time Carling's role as captain was questioned and the scrutiny angered Geoff Cooke. There was some resentment that Carling had been appointed captain until 'at least the 1991 World Cup'. Cooke's critics thought this an unfair privilege for an England skipper. Cooke's view was that the defeat at Murrayfield was a shared responsibility. A few days before the match the unheralded Buster Douglas had flattened the supposedly invincible Mike Tyson. England, too, had been hit by a sucker punch. The following season they would keep their guard up in pursuit of the Grand Slam that had been lost in Edinburgh.

Carling himself began to question his role as captain and a resentment built up in the squad when England were whisked away for a weekend in May to play a non-cap international in Italy. Wives and girlfriends had originally been invited on the trip which was to have celebrated the Grand Slam. But as they had not won it, the players had to go on their own. Many felt that this was an unfair punishment for letting the Murrayfield match slip. Carling captained an England XV to a 33-15 win over the Italians in Rovigo. Asti Spumante had replaced the champagne rugby of the season. It was a flat affair, even more so when England's players, worn by their efforts during a long season, were

50 Greatest Players

DEAN RICHARDS No. 8

Club: Leicester

Debut: v Ireland, 1 March 1986

No. of Caps: 48 **No. of Points:** 24

Dean Richards forced his way into the England back row with a series of strong, bustling performances for Leicester and signalled his Test arrival with two tries on his debut against Ireland in 1986.

By the 1987 World Cup he had made the England No. 8 position his own with a series of dominant performances against the best players in the world. The broad shouldered bobby developed into a constructive agent in the loose capable of phenomenal clearing operations in defence.

He was the integral forward element in the 1991 Grand Slam. A tower of strength at the back of the pack, the hallmark of the player was his stamina and undying support for his colleagues. When the side was going forward, he was the player most likely to arrive at the breakdown and recycle possession. In defence, Richards was the guy with the rolled-down socks whose free-ranging covering and tackling snuffed out danger.

During the World Cup in 1991 he took the disappointment of being left out for the knockout stages and final in his typically phlegmatic way, supporting his successor Mike Teague without the slightest rancour. Then, halfway through the 1992 season, Geoff Cooke recalled 'Deano' to play with his usual drive in the demolitions of France and Wales on the way to the back-to-back Grand Slam.

In 1995, though slightly slower than in his youth, he nevertheless remained an ominous sight in arguably England's best Grand Slam pack of the decade. A year later, as his country's most-capped No. 8, he brought the curtain down on a distinguished career in a win against Ireland that sealed the Triple Crown.

forced to contemplate a summer tour of Argentina, never the place to go when a soothing balm rather than another bruising match is needed.

Several players decided enough was enough. There was no Richards, Teague, Ackford, Rory Underwood, Guscott or Andrew in Argentina. It was eight years after the Falklands War but the atmosphere in the Tests was intimidating, Union Jack flags being burned on the terraces. But England did discover a new prop: Jason Leonard of Saracens made his name against the hard scrummaging Pumas and never looked back.

The tour began dreadfully, England losing the first two Saturday matches before they responded with an excellent display in the first Test which they won 25-12. The tour had several flashpoints with the midweek captain Jon Olver, the Harlequins hooker, nearly taking the team off the field in the win over Cordoba in a protest at incompetent refereeing. England were looking to become the first tourists to win a series in Argentina since France in 1974. This makeshift team came within a penalty kick of doing just that but Hernan Vidou's accuracy won the second Test 15-13 for the Pumas.

Cooke Criticises Club Coaches

Cooke's frustration boiled over into criticisms of how clubs were treating the England players. He was especially critical of coaches who he said did not attend meetings on how to bridge the gap between the clubs and the national team and how to condition the players. Once again, his comments were unlikely to win him friends at home. Will Carling also fell out with Roger Uttley on the tour and the coach was angry when his captain asked Dick Best, Carling's coach at Harlequins, to coach some sessions in Argentina. Best was working as a travel agent at the time and Uttley saw his authority being undermined. Carling's first tour as captain had not been a success.

The amateur game was in a state of flux. Almost by the week huge changes were taking place. Even in 1990 most players stayed loyal to one club but this was about to change. Jason Leonard moved across London from Saracens to Harlequins after the Argentinian tour. There was a furious reaction from Saracens who claimed Will Carling had tapped up their young prop on tour. France already had a rule that prevented players appearing for their new clubs for 12 months after a switch and there were calls for Twickenham to prevent a transfer system that favoured the wealthy clubs.

Off the pitch the leading players were attempting to change the rules that prevented them from earning money from 'non-rugby related activities'. Twickenham, now making vast amounts of money that was enabling it to transform the stadium, was well aware that its England players could no longer afford to devote as much time and energy as full-time professional sportsmen and hold down jobs at the same time. Jon Webb, the Bath and England full-back, was training to become a surgeon at the same time as playing for England. Webb never had a free evening. Mike Teague, a self-employed builder, later estimated that playing in the 1991 World Cup cost him around £15,000. Players like Will Carling and Jeremy Guscott were now extremely high-profile figures in a way unimaginable even a decade earlier in the playing days of Bill Beaumont.

There was a hint of revolution in the air but on the pitch England continued to prosper. In the autumn they faced a star-studded Barbarians team that included Campese, Lynagh and Ian Jones and beat them 18-16. Then Argentina arrived in England to try and carry on where they left off in the summer, but England's leading men were back and they demolished the Pumas 51-0, a message of intent to their Five Nations opponents.

There was a debate before the match about whether Argentina's 18-year-old schoolboy Federico Mendez was the youngest prop ever to appear in an international. He certainly became the youngest to be sent off at Twickenham when he floored Paul Ackford with a punch from behind. Mendez later played successfully for Bath and Northampton but his infamous right hook blotted out the memory of a record haul of 23 points by Simon Hodgkinson and blotted out the entire afternoon for Ackford.

England Save the Best Till Last

Clear heads were needed as England embarked on the 1991 Five Nations campaign, still haunted by the one that got away. Carling's team knew that they had to nail down the Grand Slam in 1991 even if it meant abandoning the refreshing style of the previous year. Their dilemma was that they knew a 10-man game would not be enough to match the All Blacks, Australia and France a few months later when the World Cup came to Europe.

In the event, a no-risk policy was adopted to win all four Five Nations games. In Cardiff, where, as England were ceaselessly reminded, they had not won since 1963, Carling's team won 25-6 with a Teague try and seven Hodgkinson penalties. England then exacted revenge for the Murrayfield debacle with a solid 21-12 defeat of the Scots, Nigel Heslop's try and the boot of Hodgkinson accounting for their points, before the Triple Crown was completed with a 16-7 win in Dublin, Rory Underwood and Teague tries breaking stubborn Irish resistance. The best was saved until last when France were beaten 21-19 in an epic contest at Twickenham. For the second successive year the last day of the tournament saw two teams playing each other, each with the Grand Slam at stake.

Behind England's 1991 Grand Slam victory were two stories – one off the field, one on the field. After the win in Cardiff, England refused to discuss the match with the media and the whole game had a surreal feel. Towards the end of the match the Arms Park, normally a cacophony of noise on international days, had fallen so silent that you could practically hear the players on the pitch. But it was the self-imposed silence of the England players and management afterwards that spoke loudest.

The England team had become angry at the intransigence of Twickenham over the issue of players earning money from off-the-field activities. In 1990 the sport's governing body, the International Board, had lifted the ban on certain sorts of commercial activity, but the England players claimed that the Rugby Football Union was obstructing these moves.

Money Talks

Before the 1991 Five Nations the England team had hired a company run by the former England fast bowler Bob Willis to market the team. The players had also set up their own company, spearheaded by Will Carling, to examine ways that money could be earned from ancillary activities. Bob Willis asked the BBC for a sum of money to be given to the players' company, Playervision, in exchange for co-operation during the season. The RFU told the BBC not to pay the money and the corporation followed the Twickenham line. The players, livid at what they saw as obstruction to their commercial plans, then agreed not to talk to the BBC before some, including Geoff Cooke, widened their ban on the entire broadcast and print media. The furore created by a scorned press backfired on Carling's team. Within 24 hours the exorcising of the Cardiff ghost was forgotten and the players were being presented as grasping mercenaries.

There was even talk in the days after Cardiff that Geoff Cooke would be sacked. But for all the antagonism, by the end of the season, the RFU agreed that players could be paid for non-rugby related work. It was clear that Twickenham could no longer let international rugby union ride roughshod on the broken backs of its amateur players. The 1990s were drawing to a close with a situation that mirrored the row over broken-time payments at the end of the previous century. Dudley Wood, the Rugby Football Union's secretary, was adamant that amateurism was not about to crumble.

On the field the story of England's Grand Slam was how Will Carling's team, unchanged during the tournament, came close to seeing it prised from their grasp in that electrifying win over France. England's win on the day was thoroughly deserved, their pack dominating the French forwards but they were outscored on tries by three to one and one of those French tries ranks with the greatest ever seen in a major match at Twickenham.

It was great because of the context of the match. Serge Blanco was playing his 85th match and his last in the Championship. The peerless full-back naturally went out in style, initiating a move from behind his own line that ended under the English posts. The style of the try was something that Geoff Cooke could only dream about and one that, for all England's successful

Great Matches

FIVE NATIONS CHAMPIONSHIP **Twickenham, 16 March 1991**
Attendance: 58,950

England 21 **France 19**

This was only the fourth Grand Slam showdown in championship history. And in a marvellous spectacle, an epic battle was fought in a match of continuous excitement.

England had been denied the Grand Slam by Scotland the previous season. But on this occasion, the side showed its depth of character by responding positively to an early blow. Simon Hodgkinson, who had nudged England ahead with an early penalty, missed with another attempt ten minutes later. As the English prepared for the customary drop-out to restart the game, they were caught napping by an extraordinary counter-attack launched by Serge Blanco from his own dead-ball-line. It was a sublime move that culminated in a try for Saint-André.

Slowly but surely, the hosts responded. The forwards were immense in the scrums, line-outs and loose, and the composure of the entire team in the face of breathtaking French attacks underpinned England's confidence.

Rory Underwood is cheered on as he goes over for England's try.

England led 18-9 by the interval, a score that included a Rory Underwood special when he raced past Lafond to finish a slick move from possession set up by the tireless Mike Teague.

In the second half, France launched a succession of frantic attacks in a bid to steal victory. Through sheer guts and a little luck, England hung on to achieve the first title of the Carling era.

England: S.D. Hodgkinson; N.J. Heslop, W.D.C. Carling (captain), J.C. Guscott, R. Underwood; C.R. Andrew, R.J. Hill; J. Leonard, B.C. Moore, J.A. Probyn, P.J. Ackford, W.A. Dooley, M.C. Teague, D. Richards, P.J. Winterbottom
Scorers: Try Underwood **Conversion** Hodgkinson **Penalty Goals** Hodgkinson 4 **Drop Goal** Andrew

France: S. Blanco (captain); J-B Lafond, P. Sella, F. Mesnel, P. Saint-André; D. Camberabero, P. Berbizier; G. Lascubé, P. Marocco, P. Ondarts, M. Tachdjian, O. Roumat, X. Blond, A. Benazzi, L. Cabannes Replacement: M. Cecillon for Tachdjian
Scorers: Tries Saint-André, Camberabero, Mesnel **Conversions** Camberabero 2 **Penalty Goal** Camberabero

Referee: L.J. Peard (Wales)

grinding forward power, emphasised how far they had to go before they could become world champions. In 1991 England had, perhaps, the most powerful team the country had possessed in 120 years but, as if to emphasise the gulf between northern and southern hemisphere rugby, England travelled to Australia in the summer and were thumped 40-15 by the Wallabies.

Geoff Cooke had said that he did not want his team to stay at home and live in a fool's paradise, but taking a team at the end of a long season to face the best side in the world in the middle of theirs was dumping them in the devil's playground. England lost four of their seven matches and, rather than looking world beaters, the tour revealed cracks in the England façade that were to be opened up again when the Wallabies played England in the World Cup final four months later. Australian rugby had improved in leaps and bounds in the two years since their defeat by the Lions. Half-backs Nick Farr-Jones and Mike Lynagh were just about the best in the world, David Campese gave them a cutting-edge behind a powerful scrum and, in John Eales, Australia had discovered a lock who was every bit as good as Ackford and Dooley but more athletic to boot.

The tour shattered any illusions that England could conquer the world with their limited ten-man game. And if the 1991 World Cup did anything it was to expose the hollowness of Five Nations rugby. Wales were beaten by Western Samoa and England opened and finished with defeats by New Zealand and the Wallabies at Twickenham. In the opening game England were racked with tension in losing 18-12 to the All Blacks whose try by the brilliant flanker Michael Jones was the difference between the sides. There were routine wins, by 36-6 and 37-9, over Italy and the United States to ensure a quarter-final trip to Paris and a meeting with a French side convinced they could succeed where they had failed seven months earlier at Twickenham.

Biggest Day

England's 19-10 win was one of the greatest games in World Cup history. It was also a game when rugby union lost its innocence. In the tunnel afterwards the French coach Daniel Dubroca manhandled the referee, the New Zealander David Bishop, and was later forced into resignation for breaking the sport's most sacred code. On the field the game was brutal, Carling later describing it as the hardest game he had ever played. Serge Blanco, for whom this was to be his final and less than glorious match, floored Nigel Heslop with a flurry of punches and should have been dismissed. England then made their own legitimate statement of intent when Micky Skinner made a monumental tackle on the French flanker Marc Cecillon.

The England forwards gradually got on top and Underwood and Carling scored the tries that sent England into the last four. It was a performance of great resolution and courage under enormous pressure and for the first time in months they began to be spoken about as potential world champions. The Australians had some difficulty in beating Ireland in their quarter-final and Canada's pack impressively fronted up to the All Blacks in Lille before losing.

England, though, had a fight on their hands against Scotland, for whom John Jeffrey was playing his last game, at Murrayfield in the semi-final. In the event England went through with a 9-6 victory through a late drop goal by Rob Andrew and two penalties by Jonathan Webb. Ian McGeechan, the Scottish coach, claimed that England had strangled the life out of the semi-final while John Hart, the assistant manager of the All Blacks, was even more blunt: 'If England win the World Cup, God help rugby.'

Thanks to David Campese's brilliance in their semi-final against New Zealand, Australia met England in the final on 2 November 1991, the biggest day in the history of the England rugby team. England faced up to their critics and tried to play champagne rugby but still lost 12-6. Each attempt to spin the ball across the field being met with brickwall resistance by the Australian defence in which their centres Tim Horan and Jason Little were outstanding. Ironically the game's only try came not from a scintillating back move, but from short range when the podgy prop Tony Daly was driven over the line from a line-out. And another irony saw Campese, a leading critic of England during that autumn, commit rugby union's version of a professional foul as he deliberately knocked on a pass from Peter Winterbottom that was bound for Rory Underwood in a scoring position.

It was the end of Roger Uttley's time as coach and he left with regret. Uttley and the England pack believed they should have persevered with the style of play that had served them so well against France and Scotland. The one consolation for Will Carling's men in the World Cup of 1991 was that, just as it was for Bogart and Bergman, there would always be Paris.

Next, Best

England turned to Dick Best, the spiky, articulate coach of the London Division team that had thumped the touring Wallabies in 1988, to help erase the bittersweet memories of 1991. Best had a close working relationship with Will Carling and London had dominated the Divisional Championship but Best's detractors pointed out that as a coach at Harlequins, his record was less than glorious. Coaches like Alan Davies at Nottingham and Jack Rowell at Bath may have had better club records but Best, nicknamed 'Sulphuric' for his often explosive personality on the training pitch, had a simple formula: attack is the best form of defence.

England had to raise the tempo to compete with the likes of Australia and in 1992 they did just that with a second successive Grand Slam for the first time since the days of Wavell Wakefield. And they won it in style, 118 points for and 29 against was about as emphatic as it gets. Scotland were beaten 25-7, Ireland thumped 38-9, France 31-13 and Wales 24-0. England's points tally was a championship record as was Jonathan Webb's personal haul of 67, his points taking him past Dusty Hare's England record of 240 points. Everywhere

Wade Dooley crashes over for a try against Wales in the 1992 Five Nations match.

records were disappearing and Will Carling could claim to be the most successful captain in English history. Their detractors claimed that the opposition was token and there is some merit in this argument. Scotland had peaked two years earlier but were never able to build on their 1990 success and France, who could have rivalled England, were hamstrung by ill-discipline.

Sang-froid in Paris

The key game of the 1992 championship was in Paris where England's pack gave a brilliant display of controlled rugby and the French pack completely lost their heads. Two front-rowers were sent off: part-time boxer Vincent Moscato for punching and Gregoire Lascube for stamping on Martin Bayfield's head. England kept theirs. For the second time in four months a too pumped-up French side had been undermined by English sang-froid in Paris.

England were pushing at doors and they were opening. South Africa came to Twickenham in the autumn of 1992 for their first visit to the ground since 1969 when Don White's coaching revolution had inspired England's historic first win against the Springboks. After years of isolation South Africa had missed two World Cups but, arrogantly and misguidedly, still regarded themselves as the top side in the world. Will Carling's team swiftly disabused them of notions of superiority with a 33-16 win on a dank November afternoon with tries coming from Tony Underwood, now occupying the right wing with brother Rory on the left, Carling, Jeremy Guscott and Dewi Morris.

England looked in good heart to become the first team to win three Grand Slams in a row. But it was not to be. Geoff Cooke had said that his side had to shoot themselves in the foot not to win three on the trot. But they should have been looking over their shoulders. Or rather Rory Underwood should have been looking over his in Cardiff when he sauntered back after Emyr Lewis had kicked ahead and failed to notice that Ieuan Evans was haring up behind him. Evans kicked the ball ahead to score the only try in Wales's 10-9 win, though Dewi Morris appeared to have scored a try which was ruled out because of a double movement. On such marginal decisions games are won and lost. But there was nothing marginal in England's 17-3 defeat in Dublin. A frenzied Irish display caught England on the back foot and France took the championship despite a narrow defeat at Twickenham.

England's two victories in the 1993 championship provided a couple of sub-plots to the main drama. Stuart Barnes had made his England debut back in 1984 against the touring Wallabies. England had fielded a raw team and were soundly beaten. Two months later Rob Andrew transfixed Twickenham when the Cambridge University student ran the game from the opening minute on a freezing day and orchestrated a narrow win over the touring Romanians. From then on Andrew was always to get the selectors' nod over Barnes and Andrew became an important pivot in Geoff Cooke's teams.

The rivalry between the two fly-halves divided England's rugby followers. Rob Andrew had a tough time in an England shirt at first but after a spell in France his confidence improved and he became the reliable fulcrum of the national team, a thumping tackler and top-quality kicker. Stuart Barnes, though, soon became an influential figure in the dominant Bath side. He was the more daring, instinctive player, more like a Welsh fly-half. The two were like chalk and cheese. Rob Andrew from the north, public school and

Cambridge University, conservative, polite, fresh-faced; Stuart Barnes, from the south and educated in a state school in Wales and Oxford University, a Labour man, opinionated and unpredictable. Barnes was a non-conformist in a conformist sport.

Andrew had not been picked for the Lions tour in 1989 and got his chance when the Ireland No. 10 Paul Dean broke his leg in the first match and the Englishman was sent for as a replacement. He never looked back and for almost a decade after winning his first cap, Barnes was restricted to walk-on roles for England. Twice this restless man asked not to be considered, having become brassed off with sitting on the replacements bench. Barnes joked that his hair had gone grey while waiting in the wings for Andrew to make a slip. But after the defeat in Cardiff, Andrew was jettisoned and Barnes was called up for the Calcutta Cup match at Twickenham.

50 Greatest Players

ROB ANDREW Fly-half/Full-back

Clubs: Cambridge University, Nottingham, Wasps, Toulouse, Newcastle

Debut: v Romania, 5 January 1985

No. of Caps: 71 **No. of Points:** 396

Every successful side needs a reliable performer. That was the role Rob Andrew filled in England's honour-laden seasons of the early 1990s when they won three Grand Slams and reached the World Cup final in 1991.

He stamped his influence on the England team early in his career, dropping a goal in the first minutes of his debut international in 1985 and finishing that match with 18 points. By 1990 he had evolved into a tactical controller who, behind a winning pack, showed vision and sound judgement. There were critics of his style. Many felt he was too defensive and that his great rival, Stuart Barnes, could better kick-start the three-quarter line. Occasionally Barnes shone in the white shirt, but it was always to Andrew that the selectors turned when difficult decisions had to be made.

Towards the end of his Test days Andrew became the first in a line of deadly accurate England place kickers. His 396 points stood as the England Test record until surpassed by Jonny Wilkinson, the man Andrew groomed for stardom in his professional role as Director of Rugby at Newcastle Falcons.

Barnes' Storming Performance

All week Stuart Barnes told everybody who cared to listen that he was going to make an impact at Twickenham and the three-quarters would be getting a run. 'Everybody knows that I'm a gambler, gambling's in my blood. Of course I'll give it a go. There's no way you will find me walking off at the final whistle today, like some fly-halves have done, and saying that went well, I didn't do anything wrong.' The three-quarters did get a run and it was Barnes's characteristic scuttling run from just outside the English 22 that sent Jeremy Guscott away and Rory Underwood was given a clear run to the line. It was one of three tries by three-quarters with Guscott and Tony Underwood also scoring. Barnes had been true to his word and for once Rob Andrew had the bittersweet experience of watching it all from the bench.

After their playing days, both prospered in the fast-changing world of English rugby. Barnes continued talking, and got paid large amounts of money for his opinions as the voice of rugby on Sky TV and as a trenchant newspaper columnist. Rob Andrew left Wasps when rugby became a professional sport in 1995 to become first the key player and then director of rugby at Sir John Hall's Newcastle club.

The debate over the merits of Stuart Barnes did not end there, but England answered another question during the 1993 campaign. When Wade Dooley was injured on the eve of the opening game against France, England found a ready-made replacement for the great lock. Martin Johnson was given a call at his Leicestershire building society the day before and drove down the M1 just in time for the England team meeting. The next day he packed down alongside Martin Bayfield and gave the sort of wholehearted no-frills contribution to England's steaming forward effort that was to characterise the play of the man who would not only lead England but become the first man to lead successive Lions tours.

Hard School

Johnson had been partly schooled in his rugby in New Zealand where he played for New Zealand Colts. It was a hard school and England have had no harder lock forward. He would soon become Dooley's permanent replacement. England won the game against the French 16-15 when a penalty from Jon Webb struck the crossbar and fell into the hands of the right-wing Ian Hunter who plundered their only try.

The two championship defeats had serious implications for the selection of the Lions squad to New Zealand that summer. Will Carling was overlooked as captain in favour of the Scotland full-back Gavin Hastings. Andrew and Barnes were both picked, but it was Andrew who was to reassert himself and win his place in the Test team. It was the end for two key England forwards Dooley and Winterbottom and the end of England's dominance of Europe. England were suffering under the new laws about ruck and maul which helped prevent teams with dominant packs dictate the pattern of matches.

The Geoff Cooke era was drawing to a close but not before the meeting with the All Blacks in November 1993 that would define England under their revolutionary manager. Brian Moore remembered it as 'one of the great one-off performances of the era'. Nigel Redman remembered the night before when the lock was wide-awake with food poisoning. Jon Callard remembered it as the day he stepped from beneath the shadow of Jon Webb to create a little bit of personal history. England supporters remember it as the day the All Blacks were brought to earth. That day was 27 November 1993. That year the All Blacks had won every other game on their 13-match tour of England and Scotland but, as their captain Sean Fitzpatrick remarked on the eve of this meeting on a grey autumnal afternoon at Twickenham, those dozen wins would be forgotten if the All Blacks lost to England. And he was right.

An Era Draws to a Close

And yet England were hardly given a prayer by the bookmakers who had rated this outstanding All Blacks side 7-1 favourites to win. At the time those odds were not as generous as they seem in hindsight. The summer before the All Blacks had once more beaten Gavin Hastings's Lions side that contained a large smattering of Englishmen, while England's Five Nations season eight months earlier had once more ended in disappointing defeat in Cardiff. An era was drawing to a close. Paul Ackford, Wade Dooley, Peter Winterbottom, Mike Teague and Jeff Probyn had gone from the pack that ruled the northern hemisphere roost. Not only were England rebuilding, they had injuries to key players – the scrum-half Dewi Morris, the centre Jeremy Guscott and, perhaps, most worryingly, the giant lock Martin Bayfield who was needed to counter the threat of the imperious Ian Jones. The All Blacks were on a roll. They were a mixture of old warriors and emerging new talent who a week earlier had seen off Scotland 51-15, the highest score the All Blacks had ever posted in a Test in Europe.

England were forced to select a fledgling scrum-half in Bristol's Kyran Bracken and Jon Callard, the Bath full-back, for first caps. They also replaced Bayfield with Callard's club-mate Nigel Redman who had won his first cap against Australia as a 20-year-old nine years earlier and who simply refused to go away despite being constantly dropped and recalled.

During the week of the international, the All Blacks seemed to have the psychological edge on their opponents. Geoff Cooke and his coach Dick Best bemoaned their side's lack of match practice and stressed the strength of the All Blacks. But in private their thoughts were different. They believed they had the better of things. 'The things we were saying in public weren't the same as those we were saying in private,' admitted Cooke later. England still included seven of the Lions side that had beaten New Zealand in Wellington five months earlier and with discipline, control and an iron will they knew they could beat them again.

Best's dictum was 'tackle, tackle, tackle' and on the day they did just that. They picked a huge back row of Dean Richards, Tim Rodber and Ben Clarke, who were fast in the loose, and the bald-headed Redman skinned the New Zealand forwards at the line-outs. Callard kicked four penalties – to break Dusty Hare's individual scoring record of 11 against the All Blacks in the 1983 win – Rob Andrew landed a drop goal and the All Blacks could only muster three penalties from Jeff Wilson – who also missed five kickable attempts at goal – in a 15-9 victory for England. Nobody breached the tryline but the England wing Tony Underwood came close while his opposite number John Timu actually crossed the line but was judged by the Irish

'Tackle, tackle, tackle'. Tim Rodber takes his coach's words to heart as he grips the All Blacks' Jeff Wilson in the thrilling Twickenham clash in 1993.

touch-judge Stephen Hilditch to have put a foot into touch. The game was also remembered for a cynical stamp by the New Zealand flanker Jamie Joseph on Bracken.

Muscular Chess

Redman remembered: 'I had food poisoning the night before, either that or I was savaged by an attack of nerves. Anyway, by the morning of the match I was fully pumped up with adrenalin. A lot of the England players had already played for the A-team or for the South-West against the All Blacks. We felt we had a feel for how they would play. The actual match was like a muscular version of chess. We knew we had to be patient as the All Blacks game was built on pressure and wearing down defences. So there were lots of long drop-outs and the ball was constantly pinging to and fro. At one stage there were 28 players pinned in between the 10-metre lines. I remember Dean Richards finally losing patience and hoofing the ball into the third tier of the stand. It was a relentless game and must have been boring for any neutral to watch but I don't think there were too many of those in the crowd.'

Jon Callard became the day's human-interest story. Three weeks earlier, at Gateshead, the schoolmaster had seen his pass intercepted near the halfway line and watched Jeff Wilson storm away for a try. That mistake was followed by a nervy display for the South-West in which the division had been pipped 19-15, a game they should have won. Callard was by no means a certainty for a first cap, but his nerve held out while Wilson's was shot to pieces at Twickenham. Callard said: 'It was an atrocious time for me. Everything that could have gone wrong in the build-up did. I had missed four out of eight kicks for the South-West and we would have won that game if it hadn't been for a missed tackle but there was a feeling that things could only get better. I'd convince myself that the posts at Twickenham were no different from those at the Rec or at Downside School where I taught. But I was still working on my kicking technique. It was bizarre really.'

The win over the All Blacks was a time for celebration but it was also a time for some serious analysis of where the game was heading. A high-profile injury or a bout of violence on the pitch will always provoke a national debate on the seemier side of the sport. Phil de Glanville would go on to lead England, but when the All Blacks beat the South-West his face was to appear in the newpapers accompanied by some lurid headlines. The Bath centre needed 15 stitches to a wound over his left eye after being stamped at Redruth. The injury was bad enough but the reaction of the All Blacks management was just as depressing. Neil Gray, the tour manager, said: 'After viewing the passage of play several times on video it is clear to us that the injury was an unfortunate accident.' Sean Fitzpatrick, his alleged assailant, kept quiet. Gray was sacked on his return to New Zealand, but more it would seem as a consequence of losing one match in 13 than as a result of an act of violence that scarred the game.

Callard Continues

Geoff Cooke, Dick Best and Will Carling could all enjoy Christmas in 1993 with a memorable win over the All Blacks under their belts. And Callard's deeds were not over. In England's next game at Murrayfield the new full-back reduced Gavin Hastings to tears and a whole nation to indignation when his last-second penalty from 40 yards sailed between the posts to hand England a fortuitous 15-14 win. Scotland had been penalised for offside but Rob Andrew appeared to be the transgressor with a hand in a ruck. No matter, England were off and running in the 1994 Five Nations even if it was thanks only to five penalties.

At Twickenham a fortnight later, though, the wheels came off the chariot. Callard was England's only scorer again with four penalties against Ireland but Simon Geoghegan's brilliant try gave the Irish a quite unexpected one-point victory. Something more unexpected followed the next month, however. In the week of the match against the French in Paris, Geoff Cooke resigned. The manager who had masterminded two Grand Slams and a World Cup final appearance in more than six years claimed he was 'tired of living inside a goldfish bowl'.

The rumours circulated that he had jumped before he was pushed. Not everybody liked his blunt-speaking style. There were those in the media who never forgave him for the England team's silence after the 1991 win in Wales but Cooke's great legacy was that he transformed what he rightly saw as a second-division rugby nation that had dragged its feet for years into a major force in the world game. That legacy was establishing a framework for proper professional England sides, one that recognises talent from an early age and nurtures it. With the bluntness also came a refreshing honesty.

For a few days after Geoff Cooke left the goldfish bowl nothing much on the surface changed. England won in Paris thanks to the kicks of one of his key lieutenants, Rob Andrew. Indeed England went on to share the 1994 championship after beating Wales but the players were looking weary and a sea change in the game was needed if the national team was to prosper in the 1995 World Cup in South Africa. The English game came under intense

50 Greatest Players

RORY UNDERWOOD Wing

Clubs: Leicester, RAF

Debut: v Ireland, 18 February 1984

No. of Caps: 85 **No. of Points:** 210

Time and again the player who turned matches in England's favour during the successful early 1990s was the Leicester flyer, Rory Underwood. A surge of pace and the instinctive genius for popping up in the right place at the right time would enable him to take a vital pass and dash over in the corner for a match-winning try.

Arguably the most important try he scored was the one against France that clinched the 1991 Grand Slam. The forwards had made inroads into French territory before Simon Hodgkinson shipped a pass to Underwood wide out on the left. With plenty still to do, the wing accelerated effortlessly on a wide arc around his opponent to score in the corner.

Underwood announced his retirement in 1992, a decision he revoked a couple of months later in order to return to England colours to line up with his brother Tony on England's other wing. It was a happy partnership that lasted three years through to the 1995 Grand Slam, when England played their best rugby of the decade.

When he finally retired in 1996, Rory Underwood had collected numerous England Test records with the unassuming modesty that rugby followers expect of their heroes. Even so, his 49 tries and 85 caps in a period that included three Grand Slams were overall England career records that were richly deserved.

scrutiny. The Rugby Football Union president Ian Beer instigated a commission that looked into the playing structure. England players were playing too many games and the amateur walls were beginning to crack.

While Will Carling had become perhaps the most famous face in world rugby in the first half of the decade, these were the Geoff Cooke years. Without his vision Carling would not have been made England captain. Carling recognised that. He tells the story of when he was giving a stirring speech in the dressing-room before a match as the grizzled England forwards, Dooley, Moore, Winterbottom stared not at him but at their feet. 'I want this, I want that,' stormed the young captain. Cooke took him to one side and quietly suggested: 'You've got to say "we"; maybe "we" could do this, perhaps "we" could change that, but don't just stand there and say "I".' Under Cooke, England became a team rather than a selection of talented individuals. Carling was its dimple-chinned public face but Cooke was the real power behind the throne.

50 Greatest Players

WILL CARLING Centre

Clubs: Durham University, Harlequins

Debut: v France, 16 January 1988

No. of Caps: 72 **No. of Points:** 54

The public face of the English rugby successes between 1988 and 1996 undoubtedly belonged to its long-serving captain, Will Carling.

It was his polished three-quarter play that propelled him into an England side that was given little chance of beating France in Paris in 1988. Yet new manager Geoff Cooke's young bloods went down by only a point and Carling held his place in a Five Nations season of mixed fortunes, sharpening his defensive qualities and acclimatising to the extra pace of Test rugby.

By the end of the year, having established himself as a world-class player with a flair for the outside break, he was installed as captain, at 22 years and 329 days becoming the youngest man for 57 years to hold the honour for England. He led the side to a 28-19 victory against Australia and never looked back after that.

A psychology student, Carling did not follow the tub-thumping school of leadership. Instead he worked closely with first Geoff Cooke and later Jack Rowell to engender in his sides a collective responsibility to adhere to game plans worked out at squad training. A purposeful, friendly atmosphere developed around a side that went on to claim four Triple Crowns, three Grand Slams and reached the World Cup final in 1991 and the semi-final four years later. Carling's final record read 44 wins from 59 matches as captain. There can be no better testimony to the effectiveness of his approach.

A great captain. Will Carling in inspirational mood against Natal in Durban in May 1994.

Chapter Eight: 1994-97
Trampled Underfoot

Jack Rowell was an obvious choice to take over as manager of England after the departure of Geoff Cooke. Rowell had helped make the unfashionable Gosforth club one of the strongest clubs in England in the 1970s, before moving to Bath where, alongside the coach Brian Ashton, he had created the most successful side in the land. When Cooke departed the England job during the 1994 championship, Bath were about to wrap up their fourth successive league victory. Bath were not just about winning. They won in style, playing often breathtaking 15-man rugby. Bath were also innovative, hiring people like the fitness coach Tom Hudson, a former British pentathlon champion who had worked with the legendary Lions coach Carwyn James at Llanelli. And in the pre-professional era Bath played fixtures against some top European club sides such as Toulon and Toulouse. Bath had stayed in the forefront of English club rugby because they were professional in their outlook when the sport was still rooted in amateurism. Rowell would slyly say that a player was 'good enough for England but not good enough for Bath'. Now it was time for Rowell to test himself on the national stage.

Rowell's three years as manager, and then coach, were not easy. But they were three years in which the sport of rugby union changed forever. Rowell's tenure would be overshadowed by two momentous events in the summer of 1995, the unforgettable World Cup in South Africa and the announcement by the game's ruling body the International Board in Paris shortly afterwards that rugby union was no longer an amateur sport.

Rowell's reign began with a dramatic, and often disturbing, tour to South Africa. That country was emerging from the dark days of apartheid and in 1994 had made up for the famine of rugby with a feast of fixtures. The Springboks were to play nine Tests during the year, including two against England. The Springboks were led by Francois Pienaar, the new enlightened acceptable face of South African rugby. Pienaar drove a sleek white sports car. He was open and intelligent. He was from Transvaal, South Africa's rugby heartlands, and he was the polar opposite of the surly Boer. England's tour in May 1994 was supposed to bridge a gap in understanding between the nations but it was far from being just about rugby fellowship. It was often seamy and violent and some of the scenes brought the game into disrepute.

England, led by Will Carling and still with Dick Best as coach, won the first Test 32-15 in memorable style. Tim Rodber in the back row, who had been so important in the win over the All Blacks six months earlier, played the game of his life and Rob Andrew kicked 27 points, including a record 17th drop goal for England.

Brutal Game

In the second Test an injury-ravaged side went down to their heaviest defeat in three years. Overwhelmed by Pienaar's pack, they lost 27-9, but what happened in the week between the Tests partly explains the reversal in fortunes. That week saw a brutal game in Port Elizabeth against Eastern Province in which Tim Rodber became only the second player in England's history to be sent off and in which England's full-back Jon Callard finished the match with 25 stitches in two head wounds. The photographs of Callard's ugly scars went around the world, sullying the reputation of the sport. Callard was quoted as saying he was concerned for the game's image. 'Is it a game for thugs, or is it still a game for all the qualities which has made it great?' After the match the England management invited cameras into a dressing-room that resembled a MASH unit. The scars on the backs of their forwards Lawrence Dallaglio and John Mallett were wide and deep.

Players squared up to each other during England's brutal match against Eastern Province on the 1994 tour of South Africa.

Sent off for a flurry of punches into the body of the flanker Simon Tremain, Rodber was hardly an innocent in the Port Elizabeth brawl, but the Eastern Province forward Elandre van den Bergh, whose stamping could have cost Callard an eye, was far more guilty. After the violence of the tour, and a lot more incidents at international level, the International Board agreed to initiate a drive to end brutal play. At the top level it was threatening not only the bodies of the young men on the field, but the crowds, television and sponsors' revenue – and turning children away from wanting to take up the game.

The tour was also blighted by weak refereeing. Vernon Pugh, the IB chairman, was adamant: 'More instantaneous and effective punishment is essential for players who indulge in deliberate acts of violence. Rugby league teaches us a very good lesson because, despite the aggression in the sport, referees are exceptionally strict on any deliberate violence. With the current law commission paper looking into violence in sport, there is a possibility that their initial recommendations are adopted by the government and we could end up having the police running on the pitch every ten minutes. We're going to have to clean up the game pretty quickly.'

Under the Carpet

The Port Elizabeth affair won England few friends. Tim Rodber was allowed to escape suspension and play in the second Test, while Simon Tremain was suspended for a fortnight by Eastern Province. The whole incident reeked of England sweeping a problem under a very big carpet. The omens weren't great for the tourists. They were supposed to return to South Africa the following year to make a fist of winning the World Cup, but in the space of a week the team had imploded. Rob Andrew had been peerless in Pretoria but could do nothing right in Cape Town. His simple pass from the base of a scrum had gifted Hennie le Roux a decisive try. Jack Rowell had urged his team to go up a gear for the second Test but they had been stuck in neutral. The psychological scars might take longer to heal than the real ones.

South Africa in the summer of 1994 was a baptism of fire for Jack Rowell as the game at international level prepared to take a seismic shift. England had toured South Africa and had been shocked by the unashamed professionalism that was taking root in the game in the southern hemisphere. England soon began to debate the option of not taking part in future World Cups if amateurism was ignored in South Africa the following summer. The isolation of South Africa had allowed the rapid spread of professionalism to the upper reaches of the sport in the country. By the time England toured there, players in provincial competitions were being paid up to 1,000 rand a game. Carling and his team were not blind to this as they took time off, mostly unpaid, to be raked and kicked on the hard grounds of South Africa.

Will Carling had grown rich, as well as famous, as England captain. He had set up his own company in 1990, giving short motivational speeches to businessmen and running training seminars with other sporting personalities of the time such as the swimmer Adrian Moorhouse and the England striker Gary Lineker. To the blazered King Canutes at Twickenham, still grimly clinging on to the tenets of amateurism as if they were holy scripts, the thought of Will Carling PLC raking in large dollops of lucre was too much to take. In May 1995 the new and old worlds of international rugby, represented by Will Carling and RFU president Dennis Easby respectively, collided head-on with painful, if comic, consequences.

Gotcha!

Carling had just led England to their third Grand Slam in five years but that was quickly forgotten when he appeared on a Channel 4 programme about the modern game of rugby union which examined the changing face of the sport. Carling had not always been comfortable with the celebrity side of his job, despite being married to public relations executive Julia Smith. The England captain was particularly uncomfortable on television. His England team-mates had set him up to be humiliated by the grotesque pink monster Mr Blobby on the TV show *Noel's House Party*, but Carling did an even better job for himself at the end of the Channel 4 exposé, making what he thought were some off-microphone remarks about Twickenham's '57 old farts'. The comments were broadcast as the credits rolled and a few days of farce followed.

On 6 May 1995 and with crass timing, the Pilkington Cup final between Bath and Wasps was removed from the sports page headlines by the news that the most successful rugby captain in England's history had been sacked for bringing the game into disrepute. Will Carling had not punched anyone senseless or inflicted scars on the rugby field. He had made a mild off-hand joke, a remark that had already passed into the rugby lexicon. And he had been made an example of, like a naughty schoolboy, with the biggest tournament in the sport's history all of three weeks away. The decision had been reached in London's East India Club, with all its trappings of Empire and Old Fartdom, by Dennis Easby, past president Ian Beer and president-elect Bill Bishop, all mature men for whom Carling's little jibe should have been water off a duck's back. At a time when Jack Rowell's men should have been preparing for the World Cup it was a preposterous distraction.

50 Greatest Players

JEREMY GUSCOTT Centre

Club: Bath

Debut: v Romania, 13 May 1989

No. of Caps: 65 **No. of Points:** 143

The player whose inventiveness and silky skills placed him planes above his worldwide rivals in the outside centre position for the decade from 1989 was Jeremy Guscott. He hit the England side running with four tries on his debut as a stand-in for the injured Will Carling against Romania in Bucharest in 1989 and went on to form with Carling an outstandingly successful midfield partnership in three Grand Slam wins.

Although his defensive qualities were sometimes questioned early in his career, Guscott had no superior as an attacker. He could run and kick exquisitely, but it was for his creation of openings for others, most notably Rory Underwood, that he won the hearts of Twickenham crowds. He could rip through packed defences before invariably completing a move by giving a perfectly timed scoring pass. Some tend to forget, too, that his clear-cut breaks brought him a staggering 30 tries in an England shirt, a figure exceeded only by Underwood.

A self-confessed rebel as a teenager, Guscott grew into an assured and easy-going character outside rugby. He said he owed much to Bath, his only club during a career that often saw him targeted by rugby league scouts. Certainly the role models at the club helped mould a personality that had an iron will to succeed both on and off the pitch.

The England players, not all of them great friends of Carling, sprang instantly to the defence of their captain. Among them Dean Richards and Rob Andrew said that if Carling was not going to lead the team into the next World Cup, they weren't going to either. A couple of days later Will Carling and Dennis Easby appeared at an uneasy press conference. The captain apologised and was forgiven and all over the southern hemisphere England's opponents laughed like drains. This storm in a gin-and-tonic glass was hilarious in some ways but it also highlighted the appalling public relations of the Rugby Football Union. Dudley Wood, the RFU secretary, was proving a very capable administrator without a trace of pomposity, but the season had gone from the controversial sacking of the England coach Dick Best to this ridiculous and embarrassing incident.

Jack Rowell had taken over as coach by the time the 1995 Grand Slam year began. Two crushing autumn victories over Romania and Canada were followed by a championship in which England played with power and purpose. England and their captain Will Carling made history in a championship that, as a loosener for the World Cup, was perfect. England became the sixth side to go through the tournament unchanged and Carling the first captain in history to lead a team to a trio of Grand Slams. The South African-born Mike Catt had taken over from the injured Paul Hull at full-back and Martin Johnson and Martin Bayfield had formed a second-row to rival the Dooley-Ackford pairing of the first Grand Slam years.

Hard as Nails

Leicester's Johnson, a man once described memorably as '6 foot 6 of rolled-up barbed wire', was making his mark in world rugby. Johnson was a real athlete – his mother was an ultra-marathon runner – and he was as hard as nails. He never used ten words where one would do, but on the pitch he was eloquence itself. In Dublin Ireland were blown away 20-8 in a gale and a fortnight later England were in storming form again, thumping France 31-10 with two tries by Tony Underwood and one by Jeremy Guscott, the boot of Rob Andrew doing the rest. In Cardiff, England's pack dominated in a 23-9 beating in which Dean Richards, with 41 England appearances and six for the Lions, broke the world record for a No. 8. England rounded off their Grand Slam with a 24-12 win over the Scots at Twickenham, a slightly flat ending somewhat soured by the ever-voluble Brian Moore complaining about the negative tactics of the Scots.

England were playing the more expansive game required to make significant advances in the World Cup. Jack Rowell promised his team would 'hit the ground running' in South Africa. They hit the ground sure enough, but the most enduring image of the most memorable festival in the history of the game is that of England players on the ground as they were trampled underfoot by the extraordinary Jonah Lomu.

England travelled to South Africa in hope as well as expectation. The style in which they had won the Grand Slam had impressed even their most grudging opponents. Their pack had a real steeliness and behind them Rob Andrew had reinvented his kicking style under the tutelage of the coach Dave Alred. Andrew had kicked 12 out of 12 against Canada the previous December and was continuing to pass milestones. Outside him, Will Carling and Jeremy Guscott were continuing their productive partnership and with the Underwood brothers there was plenty of try-scoring potential to be

50 Greatest Players

JASON LEONARD Prop

Clubs: Saracens, Harlequins

Debut: v Argentina, 28 July 1990

No. of Caps: 103 **No. of Points:** 5

After England hooker Brian Moore had stood shoulder to shoulder with his new loose-head prop Jason Leonard for 80 minutes in Buenos Aires in 1990, he said: 'It was patently obvious that he's going to be an outstanding player.'

Leonard was, at 21, the youngest prop to play for England since Nick Drake-Lee (in 1963). Yet even in those relatively carefree days at the start of the 1990s, when players enjoyed a few beers after a match and went back on Monday mornings to their jobs outside rugby, it was clear that England had found a genuine grafter who would take some moving in the front row. He went on to become the first Englishman to win 100 caps for his country and is the world's most-capped forward.

His dedication to training and fitness and discipline in adhering to a strict diet regimen have enabled Leonard to stay at the top of his game during a decade that has seen the demands on leading players change beyond all recognition. Throughout it all, moreover, he has been the one constant in England's equation. Four times he featured in Grand Slam sides (1991, 1992, 1995 and 2003), making him the first player for 75 years (and only the fourth all-time in the history of the championship) to achieve such a distinction.

unleashed. Jack Rowell believed that he could take England's play to another level and by the time the tournament rolled around his team were 3-1 to win the Webb Ellis trophy.

Once the tournament began it was evident that it was going to be nothing like the low-key affair in Britain and France four years earlier. Commercialism was rampant and all vestiges of amateurism had disappeared. Francois Pienaar was appearing in television adverts plugging a restaurant chain and even the staid old BBC was exploiting the laughable 'Old Farts' affair. Before England's meeting with Argentina, Radio 5 Live coverage was advertised with a slogan that carried a picture of Will Carling. 'Silent but Deadly' it sniggered. It soon got serious and England's tag of pool favourites looked a little premature in the early stage victories over

Brian Moore attempts to hand off Australia's Willie Ofahengaue in England's dramatic World Cup quarter-final victory in Cape Town.

Argentina and Italy. England were relieved just to escape with victory over the Pumas whose pack contained Paul Ackford's nemesis Federico Mendez. England beat Argentina 24-18 but only thanks to the boot of Rob Andrew, Argentina scoring both tries.

The 27-20 win over Italy with the Underwoods scoring a try each was also less than convincing. Only in the 44-22 win over Western Samoa, with Dean Richards restored to the side, did England really hit their straps. It seemed that, more than anyone, Richards was a totem England could not do without. The policeman was not a modern streamlined back-rower like Francois Pienaar or an extravagantly gifted player like the All Black Zinzan Brooke. He appeared to shamble around the field but the ball often seemed attracted to him like a magnet. When Richards was around England powered forwards; when he was not around, opposition packs tended to rest easier.

The victories set England up with a quarter-final meeting with the world champions Australia in Cape Town, an epic remembered for Rob Andrew's 45-metre injury-time drop goal that gave England a dramatic 25-22 victory. It was one year to the day that Andrew had looked a forlorn figure at Newlands as England had been humbled by the Springboks and the win was treated at home with euphoric headlines. The Cape Town victory was an emotionally charged affair which England deserved to win and they fancied their chances the following week of returning to Newlands to see off the challenge of the All Blacks. Not for the last time, though, was Jonah Lomu, the huge Tonga-born wing, to terrorise England.

Rhinoceros in Ballet Shoes

Lomu, described in the rugby press variously and with black humour as 'a cross between Michael Jordan and K2' and 'a rhinoceros in ballet shoes', was a nightmare made flesh for opposition defences. When Lomu got into his stride he was almost impossible to bring down with a conventional tackle. Jack Rowell said he was not going to make special arrangements to stop Lomu and, in truth, admitting they were particularly concerned would have betrayed a weakness. England hoped their pack could deprive Lomu of the ball and that their own backs could create some mayhem of their own. Marking the left-wing was Tony Underwood. It was to be no contest. Within a minute Lomu had walked over Underwood and Mike Catt to score the first of his four tries. Within 12 minutes the All Blacks were 15-0 up. England rallied in the second half with some defiant and often brilliant back play but they were beaten 45-29. That England got within 16 points of New Zealand was something of a travesty. But in their history New Zealand had never been close to conceding 45 points.

England's nemesis Jonah Lomu passes Tony Underwood to score the first New Zealand try in the semi-final in Cape Town. The All Blacks won 45-29.

After the game Will Carling declared that Lomu was a freak talent and hoped that he would soon go away. The problem for England was that Lomu was not the only exceptional talent in a team that included the brilliant Frank Bunce at centre, Christian Cullen at full-back and Zinzan Brooke who almost casually dropped a long-range drop goal. Amazingly, the All Black coach Laurie Mains revealed that Lomu had nearly not been picked for the squad because he was too raw.

After a dull third-place play-off against France in Pretoria – this consolation game is always flat by definition – England were on their way home. South Africa memorably won the 1995 World Cup with a 15-12 win over the All Blacks in Johannesburg with another famous drop goal in extra-time by their fly-half Joel Stransky. The Underwoods briefly cashed in by appearing as Jonah Lomu's victims in a Pizza Hut advert, but England's chances of dining at rugby's top table had been thwarted. Francois Pienaar appeared in an iconic photo being handed the World Cup by Nelson Mandela wearing a Springbok shirt. The Rainbow Nation had its crock of gold. Rugby union would never be the same again and before the summer was out the amateur game had collapsed completely.

Death of Amateurism

On 23 June 1995, the eve of the World Cup final, Rupert Murdoch agreed to pay $550 million for the rights to broadcast the new Tri-Nations tournament between South Africa, New Zealand and Australia, the three winners of the World Cup. Players would be contracted. At the end of August, in Paris, the International Board declared that amateurism was dead. A summer that had begun with the very English Whitehall farce of old farts and men in blazers had ended with rugby union at the very top becoming an open sport. It was the burning of rugby's vanities and the day that the dusty Corinthian baggage of the Edwardian era was consigned to the depths of the wardrobe. In England there was a very swift and painful culture shift.

The Rugby Football Union announced there would be a one-year moratorium on professionalism until it could be administered. The obvious problem was who was going to pay players, who would be contracted and how much would they earn. But in the north-east Sir John Hall ignored the moratorium as Newcastle United took over the city's rugby club Gosforth. It became Newcastle Gosforth and a new club was formed with the football club owning three-quarters of the shares and Newcastle Gosforth the rest. The club began recruiting heavily with the England fly-half Rob Andrew at the forefront. Andrew took his Wasps colleagues Dean Ryan, Steve Bates and Nick Popplewell to the north-east and soon other businessmen followed Hall's example in underwriting rugby's domestic revolution, Chris Wright at Wasps, Nigel Wray at Saracens, Andrew Brownsword at Bath and Ashley Levett at Richmond. The new investors began to put players under contract and instigated a long-running dispute with Twickenham that lasted for almost the rest of the decade over who had first call on the services of the leading players. It was a dispute that would overshadow the remaining two years of the era of Jack Rowell and be a major distraction in his attempt to revive England's fortunes after the traumas of the World Cup.

50 Greatest Players

MARTIN JOHNSON Lock

Club: Leicester

Debut: v France, 16 January 1993

No. of Caps: 76 **No. of Points:** 10

Martin Johnson is England's most-capped lock, having overtaken the record of the man he replaced at late notice to make his Test debut against France in 1993, Wade Dooley. For strength of character and sheer physical power, it is doubtful whether English rugby will find his like again.

Johnson quickly became a fixture in the England packs under first Geoff Cooke and then Jack Rowell, forming with Martin Bayfield the engine-room of the pack that laid the foundations of the 1995 Grand Slam. Strong and imperturbable, Johnson was the solid backbone of the scrum and an effective rucker and mauler who revelled in the frolics of the loose.

In 1997 he led the Lions to a series victory in South Africa, but it wasn't until Lawrence Dallaglio was stripped of the captaincy in the spring of 1999 that Johnson became Clive Woodward's regular captain in the field.

He led his country to eight consecutive wins in 2000-01, but his absence from the Grand Slam showdown in Dublin in 2001 was the telling factor in England's abject defeat. Still, his finest hour was to come back in Dublin two years later in 2003, when Woodward's side, with Johnson at the helm for the 30th time, finally achieved its Holy Grail, the Six Nations Grand Slam.

Brian Moore had called it a day and England's key men Rob Andrew, Dean Richards and Rory Underwood would soon be joining him in international retirement. But Rowell continued to be cursed by the Springboks who came to Twickenham in the autumn as world champions and beat England convincingly 24-14. Damian Hopley had replaced Tony Underwood on the right wing, Bristol's hooker Mark Regan stepped into Moore's berth and there was a return at open-side flanker for Andy Robinson. But the experimental England side were undone by errors and the power of the Springbok front five. Mike Catt's pre-match assertion that his countryman Francois Pienaar was an 'average player' only served to wind up the visitors. The day was to have been a celebration of a revamped Twickenham but, like Catt's remark, the day backfired.

There was more to cheer in the next game, though, a 27-9 win against Western Samoa under the new Twickenham floodlights, helping lift the gloom of defeats by the year's World Cup finalists. England fielded two new half-backs in the Northampton pair Matt Dawson and Paul Grayson, while the young Wasps flanker Lawrence Dallaglio, who had toured South Africa in 1994 and was already captain of his club, also made his first Test start. Dallaglio had made a name for himself alongside Dawson in England's unexpected win at the World Sevens tournament in Scotland in 1993. In his early playing days, he had found himself in demand by Italy, the land of his father Vincenzo, but turned down overtures from the Milan club. Dallaglio's early life had been touched by tragedy. His sister Francesca had drowned when the *Marchioness* pleasure craft, packed with revellers, collided with a gravel barge in the Thames in August 1989 and his mother Eileen spent the next seven years leading a campaign for compensation. As a student at Kingston University Dallaglio lived on a houseboat on the river at Strawberry Vale to help cope with the tragedy. On a clear day he could see the West Stand of Twickenham and he vowed one day to play there for England. He scored a try against the Samoans, a heart-warming moment on a dank December afternoon.

With Jonah Lomu and Francois Pienaar on the other side of the equator, England, the Grand Slam champions, could contemplate more glories in their own backyard in 1996. They won the Triple Crown and finished as champions but their slam disappeared in their first match, a trip to Paris where a drop goal from the 20-year-old Toulouse centre Thomas Castaignede in the final minute had condemned England to a heartbreaking defeat. Both sides were rebuilding but the French looked the more vibrant side that year and were laying the foundations of a team that would win Grand Slams in 1997 and 1998.

Going Backwards

England roused themselves to see off Wales 21-15 at Twickenham, Scotland 18-9 at Murrayfield and Ireland 28-15 at Twickenham. But they scored only three tries in the entire tournament, leaving their best until last against the Irish when the new wing Jon Sleightholme crossed the line after a smart dummy run by Jeremy Guscott. But this unadventurous rugby was not going to challenge southern hemisphere supremacy. England were going backwards and the most enduring image of the tournament was the sight of the recalled Dean Richards controlling every scrum and line-out at Murrayfield. Richards' recall, along with the debut of the Newcastle lock Garath Archer, were successful but short-term measures by Rowell.

And even the championship win was muted. After half an hour of the final match Will Carling tore ankle ligaments and was carried off the field on a stretcher, hobbling up the steps to the royal box later to collect the trophy. A week before the Ireland game Carling, who at the start of the season had been under intense media scrutiny for his relationship with the Princess of Wales, announced that his 66th England match would be his last as captain. He had been in charge for 59 of those games, winning 44, but it was no secret that he and Rowell did not get on. Carling wanted no fanfares. He simply could not see himself leading England in another World Cup. 'Eight

50 Greatest Players

NEIL BACK Flanker

Club: Leicester

Debut: v Scotland, 5 February 1994

No. of Caps: 59 **No. of Points:** 73

'Too small for international rugby,' they said when 5 foot 9 inch Neil Back began to make the headlines with his all-action support play in the Leicester club sides of the early 1990s. Yet what the blond flanker lacked in inches he more than made up for in courage, stamina and determination.

He personified perpetual motion on the pitch, making him very difficult to ignore. Even so, he had a stuttering start to his Test career in the mid-1990s and didn't become an automatic choice in the England No. 7 shirt until the autumn of 1997, when Clive Woodward took up the reins as chief coach.

Back was always within a five-metre radius of the ball and a deadly finisher close to the goal-line, as was demonstrated in a World Cup qualifying match in November 1998 when he scored four tries against Holland – the first England forward to achieve the feat since George Burton did so against Wales in 1881.

Indeed, he has made a habit of creating pieces of rugby history for himself. In 2000 against Italy in Rome he became the first England forward to drop a goal in a Test match and he is his country's leading forward try-scorer.

Back, a loyal servant throughout the 'near-miss' years 1999-2002, was doubly rewarded for his efforts in England's recent record run. Twice he was awarded the captaincy as the side marched to 13 successive victories, though arguably the honour that meant most to him was the elusive Grand Slam secured in Dublin in late March, nine years on from his Test debut.

years is a long time and it saps a bit of your energy and after a bloody good run of which I'm immensely proud it is obviously time to move on and time for the England team to move on.' Rowell was at least generous in his tribute: 'England rugby will now be like Trafalgar Square without Nelson.'

Rowell or Carling?

The gulf, though, between the captain and coach had widened to a chasm. Carling was peeved that he was not involved in team selection, as he had been under Cooke, and Rowell had become frustrated that the players were not assimilating his notions of how to play. Under Geoff Cooke, England were simply told how to play. Rowell's strategy was one of collective responsibility. As he had done at Bath, he would suggest a general plan and hope the players made it work. There were private divisions in the England camp and either Carling or Rowell had to go. Rather surprisingly, it was the most successful captain in English history who chose to walk.

Rowell's choice of a successor was also a surprise. The leading candidates were Lawrence Dallaglio, who in his first international season had shown impressive maturity, the warrior prop Jason Leonard and the No. 8 Ben Clarke. Instead Rowell chose a player who had always suffered with the 'third man' tag. During the era of Carling and Jeremy Guscott, Phil de Glanville, the Bath centre, had sat on so many England benches he was in danger of getting splinters. Nevertheless, de Glanville had a good relationship with Rowell and had struck up a winning one at Bath with Guscott. The only problem was Will Carling was playing on and Rowell was faced with the dilemma of which of his established centres he must drop.

De Glanville began his job at the end of an autumn of bitter acrimony between the leading English clubs and Twickenham over the issue of money and delegated power. In September the entire England squad, barring the Coventry prop Rob Hardwick who played his club rugby in the second division, boycotted a training camp at Bisham Abbey. An uneasy truce followed but Rowell's tenure as coach continued to be overshadowed by political events off the field. In November Phil de Glanville led England for the first time in a 54-21 win over Italy. The new captain played alongside Carling – Guscott, amid much head scratching, was left out. He did, however, come back for a thoroughly ordinary 20-18 win the following month against Argentina but only because of an injury to de Glanville. Jason Leonard captained the side and scored the only try.

On the eve of the 1997 Five Nations, rumours were circulating that Jack Rowell may be sacked. It was an unhappy time, but de Glanville led his team

50 Greatest Players

LAWRENCE DALLAGLIO Flanker/No. 8

Club: Wasps

Debut: v South Africa, 18 November 1995

No. of Caps: 58 **No. of Points:** 65

It was the constructive and forthright play that he brought to England's 1993 Rugby World Cup Sevens triumph that catapulted Lawrence Dallaglio into the rugby limelight. Having almost achieved a full set of England representative honours, he subsequently broke into the England squad after the 1995 Rugby World Cup.

He proved such an outstanding loose forward that he quickly became the player England could not afford to drop. After Phil de Glanville relinquished his brief hold on the captaincy in succession to Will Carling, Dallaglio was given the skipper's armband when Clive Woodward entered the scene in November 1997. Dallaglio went on to lead his country 14 times before Martin Johnson took over the captaincy against Australia in June 1999. During his time at the helm England enjoyed a Triple Crown season in 1998 and later the same year brought to an end South Africa's world record-equalling run of 17 successive Test victories.

A long-term shoulder injury and a knee injury that brought a premature end to his Lions tour in Australia in 2001 disrupted his progress. But in 2003, after starting the championship campaign on the bench against France, he found new reserves of strength and determination to reclaim his place alongside Neil Back and Richard Hill in a back-row that has played together more times at Test level than any other international trio. Dallaglio showed he was back to his best in Dublin, where he scored the opening try of the winner-takes-all Grand Slam showdown with Ireland.

to a resounding 41-13 victory over Scotland with the young Wasps scrum-half Andy Gomarsall marking his championship debut with a try. It was Scotland's worst defeat in the championship since 1910 and Carling played brilliantly. Ireland were also cut to pieces, England winning 46-6 in Dublin with some of their most devastating rugby in years. It was also Ireland's worst defeat in the championship and England were cutting loose. But the wheels came off the chariot against the French at Twickenham, England surrendering a 14-point lead before losing 23-20.

The final match in Cardiff was a valedictory one for Will Carling and for Rob Andrew who came on the field late in the game to replace Mike Catt.

Jeremy Guscott makes an impression as a substitute in the 34-13 win over Wales in 1997.

England won 34-13 with Jeremy Guscott also coming on as a substitute and showing England supporters what they had been missing. Guscott was to star in the Lions series victory in South Africa that summer, scoring a memorable late drop goal to clinch the second Test in Durban. Leaving him out of the England team when he was in some of the best form of his life made no sense. The retirement of Will Carling at least allowed Guscott a smooth passage back into the England side. Carling, who won 72 caps, had become the first real English star of rugby union, recognised by people with no interest in the sport. Rowell was spared the agony of dropping Carling and the manager and Phil de Glanville were able to go on a relatively successful and happy tour of Argentina in the summer while Will Greenwood, the centre who had been groomed as Carling's successor, travelled with Guscott on the Lions tour.

In South Africa the Lions were led by Martin Johnson, a man the coaches Ian McGeechan and Jim Telfer hoped would lead by example in the intimidating arenas of that land. Jack Rowell resigned before the end of the summer when his contract was to run out. In the professional era England needed a full-time coach and a captain who would be sure of his place in the side.

Chapter Nine: 1997-2003
Grand Affairs

At first the new-look England set-up in the autumn of 1997, the first of the professional era, looked like a gathering of England's 1980 Grand Slam old boys. Behind the scenes were Bill Beaumont, the new chairman of playing at the Rugby Football Union, and his deputy was Fran Cotton, a successful manager of the Lions that summer. Roger Uttley, who had resigned after the World Cup final six years earlier, returned as manager and the new coach was Clive Woodward, the England and Lions centre of the early 1980s.

England coach Clive Woodward watches as his team lose to New Zealand in the 1999 World Cup.

Woodward became the 12th England coach and he appointed New Zealander John Mitchell, who had made a name for himself as coach at Sale, as his assistant. Mitchell's elevation as the first imported coach showed that rugby was now business and crossed boundaries, although there was still some unease at the prospect of a New Zealander preparing an England team to face the All Blacks. The same disquiet was to follow Graham Henry's appointment as first Wales coach and then coach of the 2001 Lions. Henry was accepted in Wales as long as his side was successful and Woodward knew that Mitchell would be too. It was an early sign of Woodward's radical thinking. A few weeks into his tenure Woodward also picked Phil Larder, the former Great Britain rugby league coach, as part of the new Twickenham coaching team. Clearly this really was going to be different.

Woodward had had spells coaching Henley and London Irish and had briefly been at Bath as assistant to Andy Robinson. He admitted he lacked experience at the highest level. 'I suppose it's like picking a 19-year-old to play for England,' he said. Woodward's first task was to appoint a new captain. The obvious choice may have been Martin Johnson who had just led the Lions to an historic series victory in South Africa. But Woodward avoided the obvious. He chose the 25-year-old Lawrence Dallaglio who had toured South Africa and the previous year led Wasps to the league title. Dallaglio was a ruthless competitor as well as he was handsome, articulate and media-savvy and like Will Carling would be a good ambassador for the sport. It was the populist choice that would raise the public profile of the England team after the rather sour stand-off between previous coach and former captain.

Wacky Selection

Woodward and Dallaglio were given a start that must have been planned by someone with a wicked sense of humour. On four successive weekends in November and December, England would face Australia, New Zealand, South Africa and New Zealand again. Woodward reacted with a slightly wacky first selection. There were new caps for backs including Will Greenwood, whose Lions trip that summer had been cut short by a horrific injury when he was knocked cold against Orange Free State, the Sale wing David Rees and the Bath full-back Matt Perry. These were straightforward choices but the selection of the Wasps prop Will Green and a Bath hooker Andy Long, who had barely a handful of first-team appearances at Woodward's old club, raised eyebrows. England drew 15-15 with the Wallabies, but it was a flat occasion with the Australians scoring the only two tries through George Gregan and Ben Tune and Mike Catt replying with five penalties. Andy Long lasted half the match and spent the rest of the season leading the England Under-21 team.

Twickenham wanted to take the England team to the provinces and Old Trafford was selected for the venue for the first of the All Black Tests. It was another highly charged affair, Leicester's spiky hooker Richard Cockerill replacing Andy Long and earning a kind of notoriety before the match began. Cockerill had watched videos of the Ireland team walking towards the challenge of the New Zealanders' pre-match haka war-dance and decided it would be a good idea to do the same. Cockerill saw that the All Black flanker Josh Kronfeld had put his scrum-cap on the halfway line and he kicked it away before he led the England team into the faces of the All Blacks as they were performing their dance. The confrontation set the tone for the match in which Martin Johnson punched the All Blacks captain Justin Marshall and was cited and banned for the next match against the Springboks. England lost 25-8 but played better than in drawing against the Wallabies. Afterwards they did a lap of honour. They claimed it was to thank the Manchester crowd for showing up. The All Blacks were in crowing form and said laps of honours were not for losers, and for good measure the All Blacks coach John Hart claimed Cockerill's actions were a 'disgrace'.

Woodward's new England were in a fix. They now had a small matter of a Test against the world champion Springboks who had just slaughtered the Grand Slam champions France 52-10 in Paris. Woodward knew he had to ring the changes to keep some semblance of a team together to face the All Blacks the following week. Danny Grewcock had to replace Johnson, the Wasps centre Nick Greenstock and the successful Lion John Bentley were brought in to bolster the back division and Darren Garforth, the experienced Leicester tight-head prop came into the front row. England were beaten 29-11 with Greenstock scoring a try but their defeat was put into perspective a week later when the Springboks put 62 points past Scotland.

Glorious Abandon

'Men in Black Part 2' was an epic. England made more changes including restoring Paul Grayson to fly-half and the game at Twickenham finished 26-26. England played with glorious abandon, scoring tries through David Rees, Richard Hill and Lawrence Dallaglio. At one stage they led 20-3 before the All Blacks hauled themselves back into the match with tries by Andrew Mehrtens and Walter Little. Grayson's late penalty was eventually needed to prevent a defeat which would have been unjustified. Woodward called it an 'outstanding one-off performance' while England supporters hoped it wasn't. The All Blacks may have been tired after a year of almost non-stop rugby but the match was one of the greatest internationals ever seen at Twickenham and a total contrast to the limp draw that had begun Woodward's reign a month earlier. Woodward had also backed the right hunch with his discovery of a new full-back in the 20-year-old Matt Perry who shared a flat in Bath with Andy Long. But whereas Long went hastily back into the relative obscurity of club rugby and never really held down the first-team place at his club, Perry, with only 11 league games behind him before his selection against the Australians, made the position his own.

It was Woodward's next surprise selection in the new year, though, that was to have the more lasting impact on the England team. A few months before the new coach had taken the helm, an England Schools side had prevented France from winning a junior version of the Grand Slam with a 20-10 win over the visitors at Twickenham. Watching the game from the stands it was possible to see the match as an international in miniature with both teams conforming to national stereotypes. England had a big, ball-winning pack with two beefy locks in Andrew Sheridan and Steve Borthwick. Both were to earn full caps before long as was the full-back Iain Balshaw, a sinewy runner with the looks of senior international Nick Beal. But it was the England No. 10, a late replacement from a Hampshire school, who really caught the eye as a younger version of Rob Andrew. Jonny Wilkinson controlled the game, kicking his goals with a minimum of fuss. An old head on young shoulders. Less than 12 months later Wilkinson came on as a replacement for Mike Catt with two minutes remaining of England's 35-17 win over Ireland. He was 18 years 314 days old, the youngest full England international since another fly-half Colin Laird of Harlequins played against Wales in 1927 at 18 years and 134 days. Laird won ten caps, but Jonny Wilkinson was obviously going to win a lot more. Wilkinson became the new phenomenon, the professional rugby player who went straight from school into this new career. His former schoolteacher Steve Bates took Wilkinson to the north-east where Bates was helping coach Newcastle. Wilkinson came under the wing of his mentor Rob Andrew and in his first full season helped the club to the English league title.

Meanwhile the optimism generated by the electrifying draw against the All Blacks lasted only two months by which time England had flopped again in Paris, beaten 24-17 by France. Woodward admitted that the scoreline rather flattered England. All week the pitch at the new Stade de France pitch had been frozen and only English pitch experts saved the game. On the day England froze but they went on to rack up a record 146 points in the championship. A rather worrying gulf was opening in the Five Nations with England beating Wales 60-26 in their next match, a record score for the championship and a record aggregate. England scored eight tries, the only blemish being the citing of the Gloucester prop Cornishman Phil Vickery for foul play on his debut. England won 34-20 on a Sunday in Edinburgh much to the disgust of the some of the more religious locals who staged a Sabbath protest before Ireland were trounced and Wilkinson made his cameo role.

England had won a Triple Crown in Woodward's first championship year, but the real honour once more went across the English Channel with France romping to a second successive Grand Slam with a 51-0 trouncing of Wales at Wembley, a new record win in the championship. Woodward knew that

The English front row (left to right): Darren Garforth, Richard Cockerill and Jason Leonard line up against Scotland in 1998.

he would be judged on Grand Slams and was confident it would not be long before France would no longer be Europe's top dogs.

But the road to hell is paved with good intentions and England were about to experience their time in purgatory. The struggle for power between the club owners and the Rugby Football Union continued to provide an unhappy backdrop. The controversial chairman of the RFU's management board Cliff Brittle continued to be at loggerheads with the clubs for most of the season, but in May of 1998 the Mayfair agreement was announced, a kind of peace treaty in which the principle of a release period for players was enshrined. It also made a major concession to the clubs to agree to play through international weekends the following season. But the clubs, uncertain whether there would be relegation and promotion or whether English clubs would be in Europe the following season, had demanded that the bulk of their players should remain at home that summer instead of embarking on another gruelling tour of the southern hemisphere. A Test against the Australians would be followed by two against the All Blacks followed by a trip to Cape Town to meet the Springboks. Woodward had to name 17 uncapped players in his squad. The chairman of the Australian union Dick McGruther tastelessly called it the 'biggest English sell-out since Gallipoli'.

Fireworks

The pre-match fireworks at Brisbane's Suncorp Stadium were nothing compared to what the Wallabies had in store. Australia scored 11 tries in a 76-0 rout. England, led by the Saracens No. 8 Tony Diprose, had collapsed in the biggest defeat in a match between senior members of the International Board.

On the so-called 'Tour from Hell' it is difficult to pinpoint the worst depths of despair plumbed by England. In Dunedin, a fortnight later, the All Blacks won 64-22. At least this time, the raw England were competitive. Their lock Danny Grewcock, though, became only the third Englishman to be sent off when he was dismissed after half an hour for kicking the All Blacks hooker Anton Oliver on the back of the head when a scrum collapsed. Grewcock was banned for five weeks. Later that night Richard Cockerill, who had scored a try but had been roundly booed for his antics at Old Trafford the previous year, had a brawl in the street with his old adversary Norm Hewitt.

50 Greatest Players

WILL GREENWOOD Centre

Clubs: Leicester, Harlequins

Debut: v Australia, 15 November 1997

No. of Caps: 40 **No. of Points:** 125

When Clive Woodward became England's chief coach in 1997 he named five new caps in his inaugural side for a Test against Australia. Five and a half years and several Grand Slam misses later, when England finally secured the elusive Slam for Woodward with a sublime performance in Ireland, the only survivor of Woodward's new bloods to hold his place until Dublin 2003 was Will Greenwood, the Leicester and Harlequins centre.

Greenwood's strong running and solid tackling in the England three-quarter line that dominated the championship season in 2003 stood out like a beacon. Yet for years he had shown all the subtle skills in attack to supplement his power game. He was the Six Nations Championship's leading try-scorer in both 2001 and 2002, and England's joint leading try getter in the 2003 campaign when his try early in the second-half at Cardiff secured victory for his side after a tricky first half.

Rugby certainly courses freely through Greenwood's blood: his father Dick was an England captain in the 1960s and later coached the national side.

Clive Woodward had returned home because of the death of his father and was back in England when news of the brawl hit the back pages. Woodward was furious with his hooker but persisted in playing him for another year, eventually dropping Cockerill when he criticised his selection policy in the 1999 World Cup.

England went on to Auckland where they were beaten 40-10 in the second Test with the Gloucester locks Dave Sims and Rob Fidler playing defiantly. In a Cape Town mudbath, England were beaten 18-0 by the Springboks. England's Test performances actually improved during the tour, but in truth the only way was up after the Brisbane nightmare. Needless to say they lost all seven games on their tour.

Some of the tourists, such as Dominic Chapman, a young Richmond wing who had scored freely in domestic rugby, were never heard of again. Chapman gave up full-time rugby soon afterwards. Others like Jonny Wilkinson and Lewis Moody, the Leicester flanker, were to prosper later while the tour captain Matt Dawson somehow enhanced his reputation. The midweek captain Tony Diprose was brave and wholehearted, particularly in a heavy pounding by a New Zealand Maori side. But Diprose, a gifted footballer, was never able to get his international career back on track. The fear for Woodward was that the tour had merely served to expose northern hemisphere rugby. It may have been England's reserves out there in Brisbane but what did it say about northern standards if England conceded 76 points four months after running up 60 points against Wales?

Bitter Pill

Clive Woodward swallowed the bitter pill of the tour and began to prepare for the following year's World Cup in Britain, France and Ireland. The coach asked to be judged on the World Cup but even the qualifiers were not without worries. England easily dispatched the amateurs of the Netherlands with a record 110-0 win in Huddersfield. It was by far England's biggest ever win, the 16 tries were the most they had scored in a Test and Neil Back became the first English forward to score four tries in a match since George Burton against Wales in 1881. But later that month against Italy at the McAlpine Stadium, England were lucky to escape with a 23-15 win with Italy's scrum-half Alessandro Troncon having what looked like a fair try disallowed.

By now England and Australia were meeting annually for the Cook Cup and Lawrence Dallaglio returned from injury to lead England against the Wallabies at Twickenham. England lost by a solitary point through four penalties by Australia's captain and lock John Eales. The game wiped out memories of Brisbane but defeat was hard to take. South Africa then came to Twickenham on the back of 17 successive wins. Nick Mallett's Springboks were the best side in the world in 1998 and one more win would break New Zealand's run of 17 victories in a row. England played some superb rugby and won 13-7 with a try from Jeremy Guscott. Woodward at last was building a team that could cross the divide between the northern and the southern hemisphere where the Super-12 competition seemed to be producing fitter, more competitive international sides.

First, though, Woodward's side had to nail down a Grand Slam. And so began a shaggy dog story that England supporters would find increasingly tiresome as the years rolled on. Four of them to be precise. For the next four years England lost one match per year in a championship which in 2000 became the Six Nations with the arrival of Italy. In 1999 the tournament began with England having been thrown out over a TV contract dispute. They were reinstated, but began the tournament nervously with a 24-21 win over Scotland. Jonny Wilkinson, 19 years old but maturing rapidly after his trip down under, landed all his four kicks at goal. Tim Rodber, now in the second row, scored a try and Dan Luger added another. But after a bright beginning England faded. England were well in control, though, in Dublin, winning 27-15. Wilkinson was also in prime form against France, the teenager kicking all of England's 21 points in the 21-10 win, and equalling a Five Nations penalty record.

Martin Johnson wins line-out ball for England against South Africa at Twickenham in 1998.

Inevitable Slam?

A win in their final game over Wales would clinch what looked like an inevitable slam. The match on 11 April 1999 was at Wembley, Wales's temporary home while the Millennium Stadium was rising from the rubble of the Arms Park in time for the autumn World Cup. Wales, under their new coach, the New Zealander Graham Henry, were improving after their disastrous 1998 but England were expected to win comfortably. England had two new caps in the Sale three-quarters Steve Hanley and the former rugby league international Barrie-Jon Mather. The game was, along with England's 1990 defeat at Murrayfield, the most memorable climax to the tournament. The last ever Five Nations game had a vicious sting in the tail. England were in the lead until injury-time when, after Lawrence Dallaglio had opted to kick for touch instead of giving Wilkinson what should have been a winning penalty, Wales surged back down the field. Scott Gibbs then broke five tackles to score a try which Neil Jenkins still had to convert for victory. Jenkins did and Wales had won 32-31 and Scotland took the last championship of the millennium. Dallaglio castigated himself for his error but the England captain was about to suffer an even bigger fall from grace.

In the week that English football found itself on a high with Manchester United completing a treble by winning the European Cup in dramatic fashion, Chelsea supporter Lawrence Dallaglio scored a spectacular own-goal when he appeared on the front page of the *News of the World*.

Dallaglio Trapped

The newspaper had trapped Dallaglio into saying he had taken and supplied recreational drugs and that there had been drug-taking on the 1997 Lions tour. Two days after the allegations the England captain appeared at a Twickenham press conference, denying almost everything bar the fact that he had dabbled in drugs in his teens. There was more sorrow than shock among the rugby press among with whom Dallaglio was popular. There was a general sympathy amongst the hacks for the tragedy that he had endured as a teenager following the death of his sister. But these were different times for rugby; it was now big business and it could not afford a sullied reputation.

Clive Woodward stood by his captain who resigned and Martin Johnson took over as skipper. Johnson was not comfortable in the media spotlight and his uncompromising play on the field had attracted controversy, but he had great stature as a player and would lead England by example. The Leicester lock's first job was to lead England in the Centenary Test in Sydney that summer. It was the 500th England cap international and a crowd of 81,006 watched the celebrating Wallabies win 22-15.

By the autumn Lawrence Dallaglio was back in the white shirt of England. In public he was more subdued but on the field he was playing with a new

50 Greatest Players

RICHARD HILL Flanker/No. 8

Club: Saracens

Debut: v Scotland, 1 February 1997

No. of Caps: 59 **No. of Points:** 55

Over the years, national selectors have been notoriously fickle about their choice of back-row players. Stars invariably shine for a season before passing meteor-like from the Test firmament. In Richard Hill, however, England's selectors found a flanker whose brilliant talents year in, year out were impossible to ignore.

Hill had the remarkable achievement of appearing for his country at every level, spanning Schools 16- and 18-Groups, Colts, Students Under-21s, Under-21s, Students, Emerging Players, the A team and Sevens before he finally began his senior Test career with nine caps in 1997. He launched his international run by scoring tries against Ireland and Wales in his first championship season before injury and surgery disrupted his development. That he appeared in all 12 of England's full cap matches in the 1999 World Cup year was testimony to his powers of endurance, and he remained an automatic choice in the back-row up to the 2003 World Cup.

Together with Back and Dallaglio he formed a back-row that played more times in combination than any other international trio at this level. Versatile enough to practise any of the back-row roles, Hill's all-round playing skills and uncanny powers of anticipation were important elements of England's 2003 Grand Slam success.

verve. He was made man-of-the-match in a World Cup warm-up against Canada and England were convinced, with their pool matches at Twickenham, that they could go one better than when Will Carling's team stumbled in the final eight years earlier. Once again Jonah Lomu and New Zealand would be the major stumbling block. The All Blacks, led by the No. 8 Taine Randell, did not look quite the force that they were in 1995. The brilliant pairing of Bunce and Little had gone, as had the driven hooker Sean Fitzpatrick, but Lomu was still there and they were the favourites to win the competition.

First up were Italy who England casually dismissed 67-7 with an eight-try blitz at Twickenham. Italy were about to enter the new Six Nations and the defeat, coupled with a 101-3 reverse at Huddersfield when the All Blacks ran in 14 tries, showed how a worrying gap was opening up in the professional era between the major and the aspiring rugby nations.

Lawrence Dallaglio jumps at a line-out as England meet New Zealand at Twickenham in the 1999 World Cup.

The All Blacks were fired up with their usual righteous anger with England when the teams met on 9 October. England competed well but when Lomu was given the ball on the left-hand touchline on the hour there was only one result. The giant wing broke English tackles as if they were no more than dead wood in an autumn gale. It was the decisive try. England tried to get back in the game and Phil de Glanville crashed into the padding on the posts for a marvellous try of his own, a sweet moment for the Bath centre following his vicious raking by the All Blacks in 1993, but England were beaten 30-16. That meant they would travel to Paris in the quarter-finals for a probable meeting with the Springboks. England's passage to Paris was straightforward but painful. Tonga threatened them with mayhem, but they were a disorganised rabble and were beaten 101-10 with England running in 13 tries while their prop Ngalu Taufo'ou was sent off. In another Polynesian challenge at Twickenham, Fiji proved much more worthy opponents, going down 45-24, but they gave England plenty of bruises to rub on their way to Paris. England were running in tries, but Woodward still could not decide who to start at fly-half. Paul Grayson started against the Tongans, Jonny Wilkinson against Fiji and Woodward still did not seem to know who his frontline No. 10 was when England reached Paris.

Woodward began the quarter-final with Grayson and brought Wilkinson on early in the second half. By then South Africa's fly-half Jannie de Beer had landed five drop goals, including three in 14 minutes after the break. That coupled with an early disputed try by Joost van der Westhuizen dumped England out of the World Cup. South Africa won 44-21. It was an inglorious exit. While Australia won the World Cup for the second time in a muted final in Cardiff, the real drama had been in the second semi-final at Twickenham where France recovered from 14 points down to beat the All Blacks 43-31 in the greatest game in the history of the competition.

Clive Woodward had always asked to be judged on the World Cup and *The Times* duly ran a strident campaign to get rid of him. As the century ended, the southern hemisphere nations seemed to be pulling away. One school of thought believed that too many imported players were coming into the English club game and that the development of English players was being hampered. Jonny Wilkinson was the exception to this rule, but if foreign stars such as Joel Stransky were holding down places it followed that homegrown fly-halves were not being allowed to flourish.

After the World Cup, Jean-Claude Skrela, the coach of runners-up France, resigned as did John Hart, following New Zealand's fourth place. But Clive Woodward stayed put into the next century. The 1999 World Cup campaign cost England some £8 million and for that they reached the quarter-finals with the coach failing to decide who should play in pivotal positions. Still, the comfort blanket of the Six Nations was coming up and England looked set for their first Grand Slam for five years when they trounced Ireland 50-18 at Twickenham, won 15-9 in Paris, cut loose against Wales with a 46-12 win at Twickenham and at Rome's Stadio Flaminio took advantage of Italian ill-discipline to win 59-12.

Thumping Tackle

The win in Paris was notable in that England finished the game with 13 men after Simon Shaw and Austin Healey had been sent to the sin-bin. Jonny Wilkinson made one thumping tackle on Emile Ntamack that was much photographed. But England were without their injured totem Martin Johnson during the campaign. Matt Dawson had taken over as captain but in the final game of the season England were rudderless at Murrayfield when, on a dreadful wet Sunday, they were submerged, going down 19-13 to the Scots after they had looked secure with an early Lawrence Dallaglio try. Duncan Hodge scored a try in the second half and it was his kicks that condemned England to defeat. England had played some expansive rugby but had lacked leadership when it mattered and, against the Scots, they didn't really deserve to win.

Woodward's team had been outwitted in Edinburgh, but the coach was convinced they could recover for a summer trip to South Africa. Johnson was back to lead the side and England lost a Test in Pretoria 18-13 that they would and should have won had Tim Stimpson not been controversially tackled just before he touched down for a try. But in Bloemfontein, England deservedly won 27-22 with Wilkinson kicking all their points. England played with real conviction and their defence in the second Test was unyielding. The key factor was the return of Johnson, the tour's outstanding player, while Wilkinson's self-assurance was growing with every game.

The second Test win in South Africa, England's first victory against one of the southern hemisphere big three on their own patch for six years, began a run of 11 successive victories – including a heart-stopping win over the Wallabies in November that came thanks to Dan Luger's try deep into injury-time. The video referee was called to judge on the try by the match referee André Watson and England sneaked home 22-19.

Joy was not exactly unconfined that month, however. The England players almost went on strike over the issue of intellectual property rights or the use of players' images. The RFU had sold these to sponsors but the players claimed they were not theirs to sell. The RFU also wanted players' pay to be more performance-related. The players objected, claiming that had Luger's try, for example, been disallowed they would have lost but their effort to win could not have been greater. The players decided to shelve their disagreements until after the Australia game, arguing that Twickenham would have be more sympathetic to them if they beat the world champions. In a secret ballot the players voted to withdraw their labour for the meeting with Argentina a week later.

Foot and Mouth

The matter was sorted out within 24 hours but Clive Woodward was disappointed. Argentina were beaten 19-0 with a try for Ben Cohen but it was a laboured victory that suggested England were still working to rule. The Springboks were beaten again at Twickenham a week later, 25-17, with a try by Will Greenwood. Jonny Wilkinson kicked seven out of seven and England marched into the 2001 Six Nations convinced that it would be third time lucky in their quest for a Grand Slam. They had been defeated first by hubris, then by the weather and now it was foot-and-mouth disease. No one knows what would have happened if England had been able to complete their Six Nations campaign in 2001. They touched new heights in overcoming Wales 44-15 in Cardiff, swamping Italy 80-23, the biggest score and biggest margin ever in the competition, and in beating Scotland 43-3 and France 48-19. But the foot-and-mouth disease that had spread virulently around Britain meant that Ireland could not finish their campaign. Their final three fixtures were postponed until the following autumn when they lost 32-10 to Scotland but thumped Wales 36-6 in Cardiff.

England were already assured of the championship when they travelled to Dublin for a final fixture in this 'hangover' Six Nations. But the summer Lions tour to Australia had deprived England of the services of key forwards Phil Vickery, Lawrence Dallaglio and Martin Johnson, and Matt Dawson returned as captain. Keith Wood's Ireland team won 20-14 with Wood plunging over from a line-out for a first-half try. Austin Healey came on as a substitute to score a try in the second half but Peter Stringer's tap tackle prevented Dan Luger from scoring what could have been a winning try. The 11-match winning run came to a shuddering halt and any hangovers belonged to Ireland's supporters.

England were, though, pushing the boundaries. Woodward, whose job title changed from coach to manager to head coach, introduced the former Wigan rugby league wing Jason Robinson into his team with devastating results in 2001. Robinson, who had played for Bath in the mid-1990s alongside another rugby league player Henry Paul, had an often devastating running style, cutting unorthodox angles through defences. Woodward played him on the wing and at full-back but it was on the wing that he made the biggest impact on the Lions tour. He scored four tries against the amateurs of Romania in a 134-0 win at Twickenham in November 2001 and two more in the opening quarter in England's first match of the 2002 Six Nations at Murrayfield. He scored again in Paris but France beat England 20-15 to at least prevent England from blowing a Grand Slam in their last game. Ex-Kiwi rugby league star Henry Paul made a debut as a substitute, but Jonny Wilkinson was subdued by the French flanker Serge Betsen. Fifty points against Wales secured the Triple Crown but the Grand Slam went to Bernard Laporte's disciplined French side.

The year 2002, though, continued to be a triumph for England. In June a shadow team travelled to Argentina for a Test in Buenos Aires. Lawrence Dallaglio was due to be captain after recovering from a knee injury which cut short his 2001 Lions trip. It completed the rehabilitation of Dallaglio, but he pulled out of the tour at the last minute after injuring his elbow and Phil Vickery took a youthful squad to play at the Velez Sarsfield. The Pumas had beaten Grand Slam champions France a week earlier but England's youthful side drowned out the boos of the crowd with a quite emphatic display, winning 26-18. Considering that England had only Vickery, Ben Kay and Steve Thompson from the pack that finished the Six Nations it was a win against the odds. In many ways it was the most impressive win of Clive

Woodward's reign and showed that England's strength in depth was not a fanciful notion. The contrast between this youthful side and the one that travelled to Australia four summers earlier could not have been greater.

And neither could the contrast between the autumn Tests that followed and those that began the Woodward era be any greater. In 1997 the three southern hemisphere superpowers were too much for England on successive weekends. In 2002 New Zealand, Australia and South Africa played on successive weekends at Twickenham and England won the lot. New Zealand went down 31-28 with Cohen scoring and saving the game with a big tackle on Ben Blair, Australia were beaten 32-31 with a dramatic late try by Ben Cohen, and the Springbok team that had come to Twickenham hell bent on intimidation were trounced 53-3.

It was a glorious fortnight. But Clive Woodward had described England's failure to nail down a Grand Slam as 'the monkey on our back' and by the time the 2003 Six Nations campaign rolled round the monkey had, after those failures at Wembley, Murrayfield and Lansdowne Road, mutated into King Kong. The 2003 Six Nations was to have a higher profile than in recent years. England's autumn wins over the southern hemisphere big three had heightened expectations to fever pitch and behind the scenes the BBC had regained the television rights to screen the competition. This was important for the English team and all their Six Nations opponents. Research had

England's Ben Cohen, here tackled by New Zealand's Marty Holah, was a thorn in the All Blacks' side at Twickenham in 2002.

shown that giving the contract to Sky to broadcast Twickenham matches six years earlier meant that England's new generation, players like Jonny Wilkinson and Will Greenwood, were not as recognisable as the likes of Carling and Rob Andrew a decade earlier. Now a terrestrial television audience ten times the size that had watched Woodward's team beat the Tri-Nations was going to watch their latest assault on European rugby's holy grail.

Twenty-one Successive Home Victories

It would not be easy despite England playing three of their five matches at home. France had won the Grand Slam in 2002 and in a comprehensive win over the South Africans and a 20-20 draw against the All Blacks the previous

50 Greatest Players

JONNY WILKINSON Fly-half/Centre

Club: Newcastle

Debut: v Ireland, 4 April 1998

No. of Caps: 45 **No. of Points:** 686

The player who above all typified the professionalism and determination of the 2003 Grand Slam side was Jonny Wilkinson.

Arguably the finest all-round fly-half in world rugby, the deadly accurate place-kicker's name dominates international records – most points by a player in a championship season (89 in 2001), holder of the individual match record (35 v Italy in 2001), and the leading points scorer in the history of English Test rugby (686).

But it was Wilkinson's readiness to put his body on the line that surpassed his brilliant kicking and tactical direction in 2003. In match after match in the championship he put in the big-hitting tackles that demoralise opponents and inspire forwards. Simon Barnes of *The Times* wrote after the match in Dublin: 'You wondered if Wilkinson wore a No. 10 to show how many of him there were on the pitch. Head on, at full speed from behind, fast men, big men – it all came as one. With perfect technique he slammed them all to the ground. He knocked the stuffing out of them.'

Wilkinson won the first of his 45 caps at the age of 18 years 314 days as a replacement wing for Mike Catt against Ireland in 1998, making him the youngest England cap since 1927. He spent a season playing at centre before becoming England's first-choice at fly-half for the World Cup in 1999.

autumn had shown they were growing in stature under their coach Bernard Laporte. They would be first up at Twickenham. The last hurdle would also be tricky. The Irish were threatening to break the Anglo-French stranglehold. During the autumn they had triumphantly beaten the world champions Australia in a dank Dublin. Under their inspirational new captain Brian O'Driscoll, but still without the front-row totem Keith Wood, whose try had ripped the 2001 Grand Slam from England's grasp, Ireland were England's opponents in Dublin on the last day of the championship, Sunday 30 March.

Again, though, the ravages of an English club winter were taking their toll. England were without two frontline props, the Gloucester pair Phil Vickery and Trevor Woodman, while Austin Healey was to miss the entire tournament with an Achilles injury. The build-up to England's crucial first game against the French was dominated by two stories both involving props. France's South African born Pieter de Villiers had failed a drugs test following a club match that December for Stade Francais against Harlequins in Paris. He was to miss the entire tournament. On a happier note Jason Leonard, the world's most capped international forward, was to make his 100th appearance against France, a remarkable record for a man working on rugby's coalface.

For England, though, there was shattering news on the eve of the French game. Leonard's Harlequins club-mate, the 21-year-old scrum-half Nick Duncombe, had been warm-weather training in Lanzarote when he was suddenly taken ill and died as the result of blood poisoning. Duncombe had made his two England appearances in the previous championship. The England players had been told of his death the night before the France game and the news was made public on the morning of the match, stunning Twickenham. Duncombe had recovered from a broken neck in an England Under-18 group game three years earlier and, among a crop of excellent scrum-halves, it was considered that he may have been potentially the best.

Duncombe's death cast a pall over the France game. England won 25-17, Jason Robinson slicing through during their best period of the game, the third quarter, but they conceded two late tries and only the poor kicking of France's fly-half Gerald Merceron preserved England's slender lead. The Sale fly-half Charlie Hodgson was selected in the centre to take the pressure off Jonny Wilkinson. It was thought that using Hodgson in this five-eighth role would fox the French flanker Serge Betsen whose close-marking of Wilkinson had been so instrumental in France's win in Paris a year earlier. The move was only a qualified success while Leonard hobbled off early in the game, the victim of a hamstring injury. Normally a win over the Grand Slam champions would be just the kick-start any team needed but the muted victory beneath the shadow of Duncombe's death gave Woodward's men little reason to celebrate, especially with a trip to Cardiff to come. That match was only seven days away in a restructured tournament that left players little time to draw breath let alone recover from bumps and bruises.

The Welsh had just lost in Rome to Italy with a display that was tepid by even Wales's low standards. If England could beat France without playing well, what would they do to a Welsh team on its knees? The answer was nothing to worry Ireland unduly. England, retaining the Wilkinson-Hodgson midfield axis, won comfortably 26-9 but Wales, under a new captain, the veteran hooker Jonathan Humphreys, were defiant. Second-half tries from Will Greenwood and the replacement Joe Worsley were enough but had the Welsh centre Mark Taylor not spurned a first-half overlap the score could have been close.

Ireland had hit their straps with thumping wins in Edinburgh and Rome, while England badly needed the scrum-half Matt Dawson to grab the reins. Martin Johnson had picked up a strain and was to be replaced as captain by Jonny Wilkinson for the visit of Italy. Injuries were taking their toll and Jason Robinson, ineffective in attack at full-back in the first two matches, joined the walking wounded and was replaced by Josh Lewsey, who had shown good form for Wasps during the winter. When Lewsey blazed through for two tries in a glorious period of attacking rugby in the first quarter, England were soon 33 points to the good and a repeat of the 80 points they had racked up against the Italians two years earlier looked within their range. It was not to be. England spent most of the rest of the match on the back foot. Twickenham had not quite expected a lesson in the art of defensive play but it got one. Italy under their new coach John Kirwan were now better organised, fitter and better disciplined. They scored a try through Mirco Bergamasco that was richly deserved, but it was cancelled out by a late effort from Dan Luger. England won 40-5 but they were only really playing in fits and starts.

England's 2003 Grand Slam try scorer Mike Tindall finds another gap in the Ireland defence.

Still, they had the enormous comfort of knowing that Scotland,

50 Greatest Players

JASON ROBINSON Wing/Full-back

Club: Sale

Debut: v Italy, 17 February 2001

No. of Caps: 20 **No. of Points:** 55

The most successful league convert to 'Go South' has been the former Wigan and Great Britain wing, Jason Robinson. Soon after the union code went professional in 1995, Robinson enjoyed a short run with Bath, then the most successful club side in the English union game. But it was when he finally switched to Sale in November 2000 that Robinson excited the game's critics and was fast-tracked by Clive Woodward into the England set-up.

Robinson was the outstanding Lions tourist on the visit to Australia that summer. He returned to make his first England start in the Grand Slam failure in Dublin in October 2001, after which he was successfully switched to full-back. Many union diehards, however, maintained that the outstanding skills that stood out during his glittering league career were better suited to the three-quarter line than at full-back. Indeed, when Josh Lewsey established himself in the No. 15 jersey while Robinson was briefly injured during the 2003 championship season, Clive Woodward so desperately wanted Robinson back in the side that he restored him to the wing.

There, Robinson's ability to mesmerise opponents with his change of pace and direction made him a potent strike force close to the line. The real benefit of the transition was seen when, operating in the centre, he scored two spectacular tries in the 40-9 demolition of Scotland on the way to the 2003 Grand Slam.

their next opponents at Twickenham, had not won there for two decades. Johnson returned as captain and the 40-9 rout was England's 21st successive victory at home. Jason Robinson was moved to the right wing to accommodate Lewsey and his two second-half tries, one from long-range, the other from close-range, put a gloss on the score. England were finding their best form at last, while Ireland won almost apologetically at Cardiff with an injury-time drop goal from Ronan O'Gara. For only the sixth time in the history of the championship two teams, both going for the Grand Slam, were meeting each other on the last day of the competition. The outcome was a thumb to the nose of those who had suggested that

England celebrate their comprehensive 2003 Grand Slam win over Ireland.

England and France were the only worthy teams in the tournament and should always meet on its last day.

England crossed the Irish Sea five days after the Scottish win on an ocean of hype. In the newspapers were miles of column inches about Ireland's only other Grand Slam in 1948 and at every opportunity there were mentions of how Woodward's teams had stumbled at their final Grand Slam hurdles. Matt Dawson, who had led England in their 2001 Dublin defeat, played despite 13 stitches in a head wound. But, apart from the long-term injuries to Phil Vickery and Austin Healey, England were by now at full strength and on a perfect spring day the ghosts of the past were laid to rest. England demolished Ireland 42-6. Martin Johnson created a bit of a diplomatic incident when he refused to move his team alongside the red carpet before the match and Johnson's tacit message was that his team was not going to concede ground.

England produced a potent forward performance, Lawrence Dallaglio combining well with Matt Dawson for an early try, Jonny Wilkinson keeping England ahead with two drop-kicks and four tries after the break from three-quarters, two from Will Greenwood, one from Mike Tindall and one from replacement Dan Luger ending Ireland's own unbeaten run of ten victories. England had won the first Grand Slam of Woodward's era and when it mattered they had done so in the grandest manner possible.

Many critics thought England were being too bold that summer when they travelled down under to take on the All Blacks and Australia on successive

Great Matches

SIX NATIONS CHAMPIONSHIP **Lansdowne Road, Dublin, 30 March 2003**
Attendance: 45,000

Ireland 6 **England 42**

At last Clive Woodward had a Grand Slam to celebrate. Five times in five attempts his England side had failed in one crucial championship game, three times at the final hurdle. But in Dublin in front of a packed audience and in the final championship match before the 2003 World Cup, Woodward's men achieved their holy grail.

Each side was unbeaten to add to the tension and excitement of the occasion. For an hour there was little to choose between the sides as Ireland, with the advantage of fervent home backing, relied on David Humphreys and a lively pack to keep their hopes of victory alive. Jonny Wilkinson was an outstanding general behind an immense eight that slowly but surely subdued and conquered their opponents. Wilkinson, who gave a master-class in kicking and tackling, was named the man of the match.

In the last quarter England were so comfortably the better side and so sure of their tactical strategy that they brushed Ireland aside with a tide of tries. Forwards and backs interacted with precision to score four times in an impressive display that gave notice of England's high stock ahead of the World Cup in Australia.

Ireland: G.E.A. Murphy; J.P. Bishop, B.G. O'Driscoll (captain), K.M. Maggs, D.A. Hickie; D.G. Humphreys, P.A. Stringer; M.J. Horan, J.S. Byrne, J.J. Hayes, G.W. Longwell, M.E. O'Kelly, V.C.P. Costello, A.G. Foley, K.D. Gleeson. Substitutions: P.J. O'Connell for Longwell; R.J.R. O'Gara for Humphreys; A. Quinlan for Costello; J.M. Fitzpatrick for Horan; G.T. Dempsey for O'Driscoll
Scorer: Penalty Goal Humphreys **Drop Goal** Humphreys

England: O.J. Lewsey; J. Robinson, W.J.H. Greenwood, M.J. Tindall, B.C. Cohen; J.P. Wilkinson, M.J.S. Dawson; G.C. Rowntree, S. Thompson, J. Leonard, M.O. Johnson (captain), B.J. Kay, R.A. Hill, L.B.N. Dallaglio, N.A. Back. Substitutions: J.P.R. Worsley for Hill; K.P.P. Bracken for Dawson; T.J. Woodman for Rowntree; D.J. Grewcock for Kay; P.J. Grayson for Wilkinson; D.D. Luger for Tindall
Scorers: Tries Greenwood 2, Dallaglio, Tindall, Luger **Conversions** Wilkinson 3, Grayson **Penalty Goal** Wilkinson **Drop Goals** Wilkinson 2

Referee: J.I. Kaplan (South Africa)

weekends for World Cup warm-ups in Wellington and Melbourne. Instead Woodward's Grand Slam champions continuted to break records. A 15-13 triumph over New Zealand and an emphatic 25-14 win over the Wallabies under the roof at the Colonial Stadium took England's winning run to 13 matches, a sequence never bettered.

It is impossible to compare teams from different eras, especially in a game like rugby union which has changed beyond recognition in the 132 years since Freddie Stokes took his pioneering 20-a-side team to face Scotland in Edinburgh on that long cold train journey in 1871. Even comparing Martin Johnson's professional team of 2003 with Bill Beaumont's gifted amateurs of 1980 would be futile. Both won Grand Slams, but the tactics, team preparations and the laws of the game itself are as different as chalk and cheese. What is perhaps beyond dispute, though, is that the 2002-03 season was the most successful in England's history, three wins, over New Zealand, Australia and South Africa on successive autumn weekends followed by a Grand Slam of 173 points and 18 tries.

What is also undisputed in the story of England is that the national rugby union team carries a lot of historical baggage. Because England has a larger player-base than the other nations and because Twickenham is not just a ground but a huge bureaucracy at the forefront of the running of the sport, everybody wants to cut them down to size. All Black fly-half Andrew Mehrtens, before the meeting with England in 2002, called the English 'arrogant' although he later said his comments were directed at the team's supporters rather than the players themselves. This theme was developed before the 2003 Six Nations by the France No. 8 Imanol Harinordoquy: 'Every time I played against English teams in my youth I found it extremely unpleasant. They are so chauvinistic and arrogant. I despise them as much as they despise everybody else. And as long as we beat England I wouldn't mind if we lost every other game in the Six Nations.'

Similarly, Will Carling's 1990 team did not just have to face 15 Scottish players. They faced a nation seething with indignation about the poll tax which saw Carling's team, bizarrely, as the embodiment of swanky establishment England. When England travel to Dublin, a crowd fuelled on Guinness and Jamesons blame the England rugby team for everything from the potato famine to the Black-and-Tans while in Wales the annual meeting with the English has always roused extreme passions. England's detractors claim that its national rugby team represents stolid, dull, yeoman virtues. But there is a sort of beauty in a rolling maul and all good teams rely on a ball-winning pack. The Welsh teams of the golden era of the 1970s were as much about tough forwards doing the hard-yards as brilliant backs. Clive Woodward's England side, though, in the professional era aspired to 15-man rugby at a high velocity that was as entertaining as anything the world's leading nations offered. And while their opponents may not like England, the national team under Woodward had never felt better about itself than it did on that spring day in Dublin in 2003, a day when England, at the end of the season in which they had won eight successive games, were rated the best side in the world, and played like it.

ENGLAND

STATISTICS

The England Directory

Rugby Football Union

- Founded 1871

Honours

- Rugby World Cup runners-up 1991
- Grand Slam winners 1913, 1914, 1921, 1923, 1924, 1928, 1957, 1980, 1991, 1992, 1995, 2003
- Triple Crown winners 1883, 1884, 1892, 1913, 1914, 1921, 1923, 1924, 1928, 1934, 1937, 1954, 1957, 1960, 1980, 1991, 1992, 1995, 1996, 1997, 1998, 2002, 2003
- International Championship winners (outright) 1883, 1884, 1892, 1910, 1913, 1914, 1921, 1923, 1924, 1928, 1930, 1934, 1937, 1953, 1957, 1958, 1963, 1980, 1991, 1992, 1995, 1996, 2000, 2001, 2003

  (shared) 1886, 1890, 1912, 1920, 1932, 1939, 1947, 1954, 1960, 1973
- International record (cap matches only)

  OVERALL P544 W290 D48 L206
  v Argentina P11 W8 D1 L2
  v Australia P28 W11 D1 L16
  v Canada P5 W5 D0 L0
  v Fiji P4 W4 D0 L0
  v France P80 W44 D7 L29
  v Holland P1 W1 D0 L0
  v Ireland P116 W69 D8 L39
  v Italy P9 W9 D0 L0
  v Japan P1 W1 D0 L0
  v New Zealand P25 W6 D1 L18
  v NZ Natives P1 W1 D0 L0
  v RFU President's XV P1 W0 D0 L1
  v Romania P4 W4 D0 L0
  v Samoa P2 W2 D0 L0
  v Scotland P120 W63 D17 L40
  v South Africa P22 W9 D1 L12
  v Tonga P1 W1 D0 L0
  v Wales P109 W48 D12 L49
  v United States P4 W4 D0 L0

Top Tens

- CAPS

  Jason Leonard 103
  Rory Underwood 85
  Martin Johnson 76
  Will Carling 72
  Rob Andrew 71
  Jeremy Guscott 65
  Brian Moore 64
  Neil Back 59
  Richard Hill 59
  Lawrence Dallaglio 58
  Peter Winterbottom 58
- POINTS SCORERS

  Jonny Wilkinson 686
  Rob Andrew 396
  Paul Grayson 314
  Jonathan Webb 296
  Dusty Hare 240
  Rory Underwood 210
  Simon Hodgkinson 203
  Jeremy Guscott 143
  Bob Hiller 138
  Mike Catt 128
- HIGHEST SCORES

  134-0 v Romania 2001
  110-0 v Holland 1998
  106-8 v United States 1999
  101-10 v Tonga 1999
  80-23 v Italy 2001
  67-7 v Italy 1999
  60-7 v Japan 1987
  60-19 v Canada 1994
  60-26 v Wales 1998
  59-12 v Italy 2000
  59-20 v Canada 2001
- HEAVIEST DEFEATS

  0-76 v Australia 1998
  22-64 v New Zealand 1998
  10-40 v New Zealand 1998
  15-42 v New Zealand 1985
  6-33 v Scotland 1986
  9-35 v South Africa 1984
  0-25 v Wales 1905
  12-37 v France 1972
  15-40 v Australia 1991
  3-27 v Wales 1979

50 Greatest Players

John Griffiths makes his choice of the 50 greatest players who have appeared for England. It is a selection based on their performances, achievements and commitment to the national side. This list is not intended to be definitive. Not many fans would agree on exactly the same choice of the greatest players ever to have donned an England rugby shirt.

No. 1 Jason Leonard (Prop) – Caps: 103 Points: 5. Dedication kept Leonard at the top of his game during a decade that saw the demands on leading players change beyond all recognition (see page 149).

No. 2 Jonny Wilkinson (Fly-half/Centre/Wing) – Caps: 45 Points: 686. The player who above all typified the professionalism and determination of the 2003 Grand Slam side (see page 174).

Jonny Wilkinson is England's leading international points scorer.

No. 3 Rob Andrew (Fly-half/Full-back) – Caps: 71 Points: 396. Evolved into the tactical controller who showed vision in England's honour-laden seasons of the 1990s (see page 135).

No. 4 W.J.A. 'Dave' Davies (Fly-half) – Caps: 22 Points: 24. English rugby's guiding genius behind the packs of the pre- and post-Great War era (see page 36).

No. 5 Martin Johnson (Lock) – Caps: 76 Points: 10. Strong and imperturbable, he has been the backbone of the scrum for a decade and a rallying captain during Woodward's years as manager (see page 153).

No. 6 Wavell Wakefield (Forward) – Caps: 31 Points: 18. A forward of immense power and tremendous pace, Wakefield was dominant personality of English rugby during its Golden Era in the 1920s (see page 34).

No. 7 Rory Underwood (Wing) – Caps: 85 Points: 210. With his surge of pace Underwood was the player who turned matches in England's favour during the successful early 1990s (see page 141).

No. 8 Jeremy Guscott (Centre) – Caps: 65 Points: 143. His inventiveness and silky skills placed him planes above his worldwide rivals in the outside centre position in the 1990s (see page 147).

No. 9 Bill Beaumont (Lock) – Caps: 34 Points: 0. The British Bulldog from Fylde and Lancashire was responsible for England's rugby revival in 1980. He had stepped in as leader in 1978 but quickly showed his knack for player management (see page 100).

No. 10 Will Carling (Centre) – Caps: 72 Points: 54. Carling worked closely with both Geoff Cooke and Jack Rowell to engender in his sides a collective responsibility to adhere to game plans worked out at squad training (see page 142).

No. 11 Brian Moore (Hooker) – Caps: 64 Points: 4. Hooker whose mental steel and all-round skills epitomised the new breed of England forward in the late 1980s (see page 116).

No. 12 Jeff Butterfield (Centre) – Caps: 28 Points: 15. A natural sportsman who had the vision to straighten a three-quarter attack but could also tackle opponents to a standstill (see page 64).

No. 13 Adrian Stoop (Fly-half) – Caps: 15 Points: 6. Stoop's name became synonymous with Twickenham. The exciting brand of open rugby he advocated was the catalyst for a sea-change in the fortunes of the England side (see page 24).

No. 14 Cyril Lowe (Wing) – Caps: 25 Points: 58. Lowe was England's deadliest finisher before Rory Underwood. His eight tries in the 1914 Five Nations have never been surpassed in the history of the International Championship (see page 32).

No. 15 Peter Wheeler (Hooker) – Caps: 41 Points: 0. Wheeler's polished contributions as a fast-striking right-footed hooker in the tight was invaluable to the side's 1980 Grand Slam (see page 102).

No. 16 Paul Ackford (Lock) – Caps: 22 Points: 4. Always one to rise to the big occasion, Ackford's untiring energy as the winner of line-out possession helped lay the foundations for the 1991 Grand Slam (see page 123).

Paul Ackford prepares to win more line-out ball in the England cause.

No. 17 Wade Dooley (Lock) – Caps: 55 Points: 12. A healthy competitive edge carried him to the middle-of-the-line-out position during the golden years of the Carling Era (see page 112).

No. 18 Richard Hill (Flanker/No. 8) – Caps: 59 Points: 55. The flanker whose brilliant talents have been impossible to ignore. Hill was versatile enough to play anywhere the back-row (see page 168).

No. 19 Ronald Poulton (Wing/Centre) – Caps: 17 Points: 28. Poulton scored four tries against France in 1914 setting an England Five Nations Championship record that still stands today (see page 29).

No. 20 John Pullin (Hooker) – Caps: 42 Points: 3. The outstanding far-foot striker of the ball in the front-rows of the late 1960s and early 1970s and first captain to lead England to victories over each of the Tri Nations (see page 82).

No. 21 Eric Evans (Prop/Hooker) – Caps: 30 Points: 15. Evans set high standards as captain, forging England into a formidable unit that from 1956 to 1958 lost only twice (see page 57).

No. 22 Dickie Jeeps (Scrum-half) – Caps: 24 Points: 0. England's inspiring captain from 1960 to 1962 gave immaculate service from the scrum, tackled resolutely and shrugged off the heavy attention he received from flankers (see page 72).

No. 23 Richard Sharp (Fly-half) – Caps: 14 Points: 26. Sharp was the destroyer whose adventurous running and bold breaks brought a breath of fresh air to the England side of the early 1960s (see page 75).

No. 24 Budge Rogers (Flanker) – Caps: 34 Points: 9. England's most dynamic open-side flanker during the 1960s. Captained his country and ended a distinguished international career by breaking Wavell Wakefield's long-standing cap record (see page 76).

No. 25 Peter Winterbottom (Flanker) – Caps: 58 Points: 13. Winterbottom made flattening opponents with vigorous tackles an art form and possessed immense upper body strength which was put to good use (see page 107).

No. 26 Cecil Kershaw (Scrum-half) – Caps: 16 Points: 6. Kershaw was the epitome of the attacking scrum half. He linked cleverly with the back row and posed all manner of problems for defences (see page 37).

No. 27 Ronald Cove-Smith (Forward) – Caps: 29 Points: 3. A studious player who was a firm believer in Wakefield's philosophy that forwards should pack down in fixed positions at scrums (see page 39).

No. 28 Tom Voyce (Flanker) – Caps: 27 Points: 15. A key element in Wakefield's theory of specialist scrum positions, Voyce was a flanker with safe hands and an uncanny sense of position (see page 40).

No. 29 David Duckham (Centre/Wing) – Caps: 36 Points: 36. Strongly built and a fast runner who could leave defenders standing with his electric sidestep, Duckham was the most powerful three-quarter of the early 1970s (see page 87).

No. 30 Alex Obolensky (Wing) – Caps: 4 Points: 6. He set no special records, only appearing four times for England. Yet his deeds against New Zealand in 1936 made him a household name (see page 46).

No. 31 Bernard Gadney (Scrum-half) – Caps: 14 Points: 3. Gadney emerged as the outstanding scrum half of the early 1930s, a player ideally suited to bear the pressures of the times (see page 48).

No. 32 Neil Back (Flanker) – Caps: 59 Points: 73. What the blond flanker lacked in inches he more than made up for in determination. Back personified perpetual-motion on the pitch (see page 155).

No. 33 Lawrence Dallaglio (Flanker/No. 8) – Caps: 58 Points: 65. A versatile loose forward who quickly became indispensable to the England cause working with Neil Back and Richard Hill in a record-breaking back-row (see page 157).

No. 34 Peter Jackson (Wing) – Caps: 20 Points: 18. Jackson was an unorthodox wing to whom beating players came instinctively. His unpredictability, however, sometimes bamboozled his own colleagues (see page 59).

No. 35 Fran Cotton (Prop) – Caps: 31 Points: 4. He had the ideal temperament for front-row operations and brought his expertise to the subdue-and-exploit approach used during the 1980 Grand Slam season (see page 94).

No. 36 Lennard Stokes (Full back/Three-quarter) – Caps: 12 Points: 17 conversions and two drop goals (before scoring by points was introduced). England's first rugby superstar. Stokes was a household name in the original 20-a-side as well as 15-a-side formations (see page 15).

No. 37 Roger Uttley (Lock/No. 8/Flanker) – Caps: 23 Points: 8. Uttley's high work-rate and ball-winning capacity made him an automatic choice. His high octane performances were a particular feature of the 1980 Grand Slam wins (see page 98).

No. 38 Dean Richards (No. 8) – Caps: 48 Points: 24. A tower of strength at the back of the pack, the hallmark of the player was his stamina and undying support for his colleagues (see page 126).

No. 39 Will Greenwood (Centre) – Caps: 40 Points: 125. Unquestionably a product of the Woodward reign, Greenwood's subtle powers in attack have stood out like a beacon among his all-round skills (see page 164).

No. 40 Tony Neary (Flanker) – Caps: 43 Points: 19. What set Neary apart from the run-of-the-mill flankers was his willingness to become involved at the breakdown and his effectiveness recycling ball at the mauls (see page 90).

No. 41 Andy Ripley (No. 8) – Caps: 24 Points: 8. On the hoof he was the England player who more than any other put the fear of God into would-be tacklers during his 24-cap career (see page 88).

No. 42 Edward Temple Gurdon (Forward) – Caps: 16 Points 1 try (before scoring by points was introduced). Gurdon was the forward who through his outstanding technique lorded it over all opponents in the early years of international rugby (see page 20).

No. 43 Charles Pillman (Forward) – Caps: 18 Points: 26. Credited with developing wing forward play, Pillman was the anchorman in four of England's championship-winning packs before the Great War (see page 28).

No. 44 Norman 'Nim' Hall (Full-back/Fly-half) – Caps: 17 Points: 39. Hall was the backbone of the England side for the best part of nine post-war seasons, leading the side a then record-equalling 13 times (see page 54).

No. 45 Jason Robinson (Wing/Full-back) – Caps: 20 Points: 55. Robinson's ability to mesmerise opponents with his change of pace and direction made him England's most potent strike force close to the line (see page 177).

No. 46 Norman Wodehouse (Forward) – Caps: 14 Points: 6. Quite the best leader of his day, Wodehouse became in 1913 the first player to lead England to the Grand Slam (see page 30).

No. 47 Bev Risman (Fly-half/Centre) – Caps: 8 Points: 8. Few English fly-halves cultivated more finesse than Bev Risman whose flawless basic skills enabled him to create scoring opportunities for his threequarters (see page 69).

No. 48 Malcolm Phillips (Centre/Wing) – Caps: 25 Points: 15. An unsung hero whose direct running and determined bursts created openings for vital tries in the honours-laden seasons of 1958, 1960 and 1963 (see page 70).

No. 49 Peter Robbins (Flanker) – Caps: 19 Points: 0. A flanker who tackled like a thunderbolt and covered the ground with lightning pace in the packs that dominated the Five Nations in 1957, 1958 and 1960 (see page 67).

No. 50 Carl Aarvold (Centre/Wing) – Caps: 16 Points: 12. Aarvold, with his graceful, long-raking stride in the centre of the three-quarter line, was the youngster the Twickenham crowds warmed to in the 1928 Grand Slam (see page 42).

Nim Hall led England on 13 occasions in the 1950s.

In the 1920s Carl Aarvold was the darling of the Twickenham crowd.

Results and Tables 1871-2003

Team line-ups are given in blocks to show clearly, in any formation from 20- to 15-a-side, the full-backs, three-quarters, halves and forwards in that order. Where possible three-quarters are given from wing to wing, the fly-half precedes the scrum-half, and forwards are listed from front-row to back-row. Specialisation has not always existed, so it is only since the 1920s that the familiar prop/hooker/prop/lock/lock/flanker/No. 8/flanker formation is given with any certainty.

It should be noted that until 1875 international matches were decided by a majority of goals, but from 1876 the try-count was employed to decide a match when teams were level on goals. Scoring by points was not introduced until the late 1880s, a try scoring one point, a conversion two and a dropped goal three. Various experiments were made until 1890-91 when the International Board system was adopted to make scoring uniform in international matches. Since 1890-91, official scoring values have been as follows:

	Try (T)	Conversion (C)	Drop Goal (DG)	Penalty Goal (PG)	Goal from Mark (GM)
1891	1	2	3	2	3
1892 to 1893	2	3	4	3	4
1894 to 1905	3	2	4	3	4
1906 to 1948	3	2	4	3	3
1949 to 1971	3	2	3	3	3
1972 to 1977	4	2	3	3	3
1978 to 1992	4	2	3	3	Void
1993 to date	5	2	3	3	Void

The penalty goal did not become a scoring device until 1891 and the goal from a mark ceased to exist when the Free Kick clause entered the Law Book in 1977-78. Traditionally a converted try has been referred to as a goal (G). Penalty tries (‡), where appropriate, are credited to players.

The symbol (†) is used to indicate a new cap and (*) shows the player captaining the side. Replacements were sanctioned in 1968-69. Full replacements are denoted using numerical indices (3) and temporary substitutes are shown with lettered indices (a).

The International Championship began as a four-nations tournament in 1883. England first met France in 1906 and the championship became five nations in 1910, but reverted to four between 1932 and 1939 when the French were temporarily excluded. Italy became full championship members in 2000, making it a six nations tournament.

England's Tests against overseas sides began in 1889 but only matches against the former Dominions – New Zealand, Australia and South Africa – were recognised as official cap games before 1981, when the International Board ruled that their senior members could award official caps against whom they liked.

The Rugby World Cup was first played in Australia and New Zealand in 1987.

These statistics are correct up to 31 July 2003.

1871-74

Friendlies

v SCOTLAND

LOST
Scotland: 1G 1T
England: 1T
Raeburn Place, 27 Mar 1871

† A. Lyon
† A.G. Guillemard
† R.R. Osborne

† W. MacLaren

† F. Tobin
† J.E. Bentley
† J.F. Green

*† F. Stokes
† C.W. Sherrard
† B.H. Burns
† C.A. Crompton
† A. Davenport
† J.M. Dugdale
† A.S. Gibson
† H.J.C. Turner
† R.H. Birkett 1T
† J.H. Luscombe
† A. St. G. Hamersley
† J.H. Clayton
† D.P. Turner

v SCOTLAND

WON
England: 1G 1DG 2T
Scotland: 1DG
Kennington Oval, 5 Feb 1872

A.G. Guillemard
† W.O. Moberley
† F.W. Mills

† H. Freeman 1DG

† S. Finney 1T
J.E. Bentley
† P. Wilkinson

* F. Stokes
C.W. Sherrard
† T. Batson
† F.W. Isherwood 1C
† W.W. Pinching
† J.A. Body
† J.E.H. Mackinlay
† J.A. Bush
† F.B.G. d'Aguilar 1T
† F.I. Currey
A. St. G. Hamersley 1T
† F. Luscombe
D.P. Turner

v SCOTLAND

DRAWN
Scotland: Nil
England: Nil
Glasgow, 3 Mar 1873

† C.H.R. Vanderspar
† S. Morse
F.W. Mills

H. Freeman

S. Finney
† C.W. Boyle

† W.R.B. Fletcher
* F. Stokes
† H.A. Lawrence
J.A. Bush
† C.H. Rickards
† E.R. Still
J.A. Body
J.E.H. Mackinlay
† E.C. Cheston
† M.W. Marshall
† H. Marsh
A. St. G. Hamersley
F. Luscombe
D.P. Turner

v SCOTLAND

WON
England: 1DG
Scotland: 1T
Kennington Oval, 23 Feb 1874

† M.J. Brooks
† J.M. Batten

H. Freeman 1DG

† W.H. Milton
S. Morse
† W.E. Collins

† J.S.M. Genth
† E. Kewley
H.A. Lawrence
T. Batson
† W.F.H. Stafford
† H.A. Bryden
† C.W. Crosse
† S. Parker
E.C. Cheston
M.W. Marshall
† F.L. Cunliffe
* A. St. G. Hamersley
† R. Walker
D.P. Turner

FACT FILE

- Until 1877, international matches were played between teams of 20 players.
- Players' preparations for big matches were amusing. John Clayton, following selection for the 1871 match, trained hard for a month before the game, running four miles with a large Newfoundland dog to make the pace every morning in the dark before breakfast. As was then the custom for rugby players, Clayton adhered to a diet of underdone beef and beer.

1874-76

Friendlies

v IRELAND

WON
England: 1G 1DG 1T
Ireland: Nil
Kennington Oval, 15 Feb 1875

† A.W. Pearson 1C
† L. Stokes

W.H. Milton

W.E. Collins
† E.H. Nash 1DG
† A.T. Michell 1T

* H.A. Lawrence
† F.R. Adams
† W.H.H. Hutchinson
T. Batson
† E.C. Fraser
† H.J. Graham
C.W. Crosse
J.E.H. MacKinlay
E.C. Cheston 1T
M.W. Marshall
† E.S. Perrott
F. Luscombe
R. Walker
D.P. Turner

v SCOTLAND

DRAWN
Scotland: Nil
England: Nil
Raeburn Place, 8 Mar 1875

A.W. Pearson
† L.H. Birkett

S. Morse

W.E. Collins
† W.A.D. Evanson
A.T. Michell

* H.A. Lawrence
F.R. Adams
W.R.B. Fletcher
J.A. Bush
R.H. Birkett
H.J. Graham
† J.E. Paul
S. Parker
E.C. Cheston
M.W. Marshall
E. Kewley
F. Luscombe
J.S.M. Genth
D.P. Turner

v IRELAND

WON
Ireland: Nil
England: 1G 1T
Leinster C.G., 13 Dec 1875

† S.H.M. Login
A.W. Pearson 1C

† C.R. Gunner
A.T. Michell

† C.W.H. Clark 1T
W.E. Collins

† E.B. Turner
† E.E. Marriott
W.H.H. Hutchinson
J.A. Bush
† C.C. Bryden
H.J. Graham
† J.D.G. Graham
† J. Brewer
† W. Greg
M.W. Marshall
E. Kewley 1T
* F. Luscombe
† C.L. Verelst
† A.J. Bulteel

v SCOTLAND

WON
England: 1G 1T
Scotland: Nil
Kennington Oval, 6 Mar 1876

† A.H. Heath
A.W. Pearson

R.H. Birkett
† J.S. Tetley
L. Stokes 1C

W.E. Collins 1T
† W.C. Hutchinson

F.R. Adams
E.C. Cheston
J.A. Bush
† G.R. Turner
H.J. Graham
† F.H. Lee 1T
† W.C.W. Rawlinson
W. Greg
M.W. Marshall
E. Kewley
* F. Luscombe
R. Walker
† W.H. Hunt

FACT FILE

- England completed the 20-a-side era with an unbeaten run through 1875 and 1876.
- England had capped 86 players in the first eight matches, and 19 of these appeared three or more times. Dawson Turner, Francis Luscombe and Murray Marshall played in six of the games, more than any of their contemporaries.

1876-78

Friendlies

v IRELAND

WON
England: 2G 2T
Ireland: Nil
Kennington Oval, 5 Feb 1877

L.H. Birkett
L. Stokes 2C

† A.N. Hornby 1T
R.H. Birkett

W.C. Hutchinson 2T
† P.L.A. Price

* E. Kewley
F.R. Adams 1T
† R.H. Fowler
M.W. Marshall
† G. Harrison
W.H. Hunt
† C.J.C. Touzel
F.H. Lee
E.B. Turner

v SCOTLAND

LOST
Scotland: 1DG
England: Nil
Raeburn Place, 5 Mar 1877

L.H. Birkett
A.W. Pearson

A.N. Hornby
L. Stokes

W.A.D. Evanson
P.L.A. Price

* E. Kewley
† H.W.T. Garnett
† R. Todd
M.W. Marshall
G. Harrison
W.H. Hunt
C.J.C. Touzel
C.C. Bryden
† A.F. Law

v SCOTLAND

DRAWN
England: Nil
Scotland: Nil
Kennington Oval, 4 Mar 1878

† H.E. Kayll
A.W. Pearson

A.N. Hornby
L. Stokes

W.A.D. Evanson
P.L.A. Price

* E. Kewley
F.R. Adams
† F.D. Fowler
M.W. Marshall
† J.M. Biggs
† G.F. Vernon
† G.T. Thomson
† E.T. Gurdon
† H. Fowler

v IRELAND

WON
Ireland: Nil
England: 2G 1T
Lansdowne Road, 11 Mar 1878

† W.J. Penny 1T
A.W. Pearson 2C

A.N. Hornby
† H.J. Enthoven

† A.H. Jackson
† J.L. Bell

† H.P. Gardner 1T
C.L. Verelst
† T. Blatherwick
* M.W. Marshall
† A. Budd
G.F. Vernon
W.H. Hunt
† E.F. Dawson
E.B. Turner 1T

FACT FILE

- The reduction of players to 15-a-side marked the beginning of modern rugby. Forwards were now found in packs restricted to between eight and ten players, with the result that there were eight fewer men in scrums and mauls; furthermore, the dimensions of the pitch had become settled at around 120 yards by 80 – considerably wider than in the early internationals.
- Albert Hornby was the prominent English back of this period. Later he was to win distinction as captain of both the England cricket and rugby sides.

1878-80

Friendlies

v SCOTLAND

DRAWN
Scotland: 1DG
England: 1G
Raeburn Place, 10 Mar 1879

W.J. Penny
† H. Huth
L. Stokes 1C
W.A.D. Evanson
† H.H. Taylor
† H.H. Springman
† S. Neame
* F.R. Adams
F.D. Fowler
A. Budd
G. Harrison
† G.W. Burton 1T
† H.C. Rowley
R. Walker
† N.F. McLeod

v IRELAND

WON
England: 2G 1DG 2T
Ireland: Nil
Kennington Oval, 24 Mar 1879

W.J. Penny
W.A.D. Evanson 1T
L. Stokes 1DG 2C
† H.T. Twynam 1T
† W.E. Openshaw
† H.D. Bateson
S. Neame
* F.R. Adams 1T
J.M. Biggs
A. Budd
G. Harrison
G.W. Burton
H.C. Rowley 1T
E.T. Gurdon
N.F. McLeod

v IRELAND

WON
Ireland: 1T
England: 1G 1T
Lansdowne Road, 30 Jan 1880

† T.W. Fry
A.N. Hornby
* L. Stokes 1C
† R. Hunt
H.T. Twynam
A.H. Jackson
S. Neame
† C. Gurdon
† B. Kilner
G.F. Vernon
† E. Woodhead
† S.S. Ellis 1T
H.C. Rowley
† E.T. Markendale 1T
† J.W. Schofield

v SCOTLAND

WON
England: 2G 3T
Scotland: 1G
Manchester, 28 Feb 1880

T.W. Fry 1T
† C.H. Sawyer
* L. Stokes 2C
† R.T. Finch
H.H. Taylor 2T
† C.H. Coates
S. Neame
C. Gurdon
† C. Phillips
G.F. Vernon
G. Harrison
G.W. Burton 1T
H.C. Rowley
E.T. Gurdon 1T
R. Walker

FACT FILE

- England were the early experts in the 15-man game, and between 1878 and 1882 not a game was lost, and no side was fielded without either Albert Hornby or Lennard Stokes among the backs.
- Stokes retired in 1881 as holder of the England cap record (with 12). Incredibly, his 17 conversions in internationals remained an English record for more than a hundred years.

1880-82

Friendlies

v IRELAND

WON
England: 2G 2T
Ireland: Nil
Manchester, 5 Feb 1881

A.N. Hornby

C.H. Sawyer **1T**
* L. Stokes **2C**

† W.R. Richardson
H.H. Taylor **3T**

† J.I. Ward
† C.W.L. Fernandes
C. Gurdon
C. Phillips
G.F. Vernon
† J.J. Ravenscroft
G.W. Burton
H.C. Rowley
E.T. Gurdon
† W.W. Hewitt

v WALES

WON
England: 7G 6T 1DG
Wales: Nil
Blackheath, 19 Feb 1881

T.W. Fry

R. Hunt **1DG 1T 1C**
* L. Stokes **6C**

H.T. Twynam **1T**
H.H. Taylor **1T**

† C.P. Wilson
C.W.L. Fernandes **1T**
C. Gurdon
A. Budd **1T**
† H. Vassall **3T**
H. Fowler
G.W. Burton **4T**
H.C. Rowley **1T**
E.T. Gurdon
W.W. Hewitt

v SCOTLAND

DRAWN
Scotland: IG 1T
England: 1DG 1T
Raeburn Place, 19 Mar 1881

A.N. Hornby

R. Hunt
* L. Stokes **1DG**

H.C. Rowley **1T**
† F.T. Wright

C.H. Coates
C.W.L. Fernandes
C. Gurdon
A. Budd
H. Vassall
H. Fowler
G.W. Burton
W.W. Hewitt
E.T. Gurdon
C. Phillips

v IRELAND

DRAWN
England: 2T
Ireland: 2T
Lansdowne Road, 6 Feb 1882

A.N. Hornby

† W.N. Bolton **1T**
† E. Beswick
R. Hunt **1T**

H.T. Twynam
H.C. Rowley

J.J. Ward
* C. Gurdon
† B.B. Middleton
H. Vassall
† H.G. Fuller
† J.T. Hunt
G.T. Thomson
† A. Spurling
W.W. Hewitt

v SCOTLAND

LOST
England: Nil
Scotland: 2T
Manchester, 4 Mar 1882

* A.N. Hornby

W.N. Bolton
E. Beswick

† J.H. Payne
H.H. Taylor

C.H. Coates
† W.M. Tatham
C. Gurdon
† P.A. Newton
H. Vassall
H.G. Fuller
J.T. Hunt
G.T. Thomson
E.T. Gurdon
H.C. Rowley

FACT FILE

- Disappointing crowds of around 4,000 had led the RFU to staging matches in the North of England, and England opened their matches of 1881 at Manchester

1882-83

Four Nations Championship

v WALES

WON
Wales: Nil
England: 2G 4T
St Helens, 16 Dec 1882

† A.S. Taylor

W.N. Bolton 1T
† A.M. Evanson 2C
† C.G. Wade 3T

J.H. Payne
† Al. Rotherham

W.M. Tatham
† R.S. Kindersley
† C.S. Wooldridge
H. Vassall
H.G. Fuller
† R.S.F. Henderson 1T
G.T. Thomson 1T
* E.T. Gurdon
† G. Standing

v IRELAND

WON
England: 1G 3T
Ireland: 1T
Manchester, 5 Feb 1883

A.S. Taylor

W.N. Bolton 1T
A.M. Evanson 1C
C.G. Wade 1T

JH. Payne
H.T. Twynam 1T

W.M. Tatham 1T
G. Standing
C.S. Wooldridge
B.B. Middleton
H.G. Fuller
† R.M. Pattisson
G.T. Thomson
* E.T. Gurdon
† E.J. Moore

v SCOTLAND

WON
Scotland: 1T
England: 2T
Raeburn Place, 3 Mar 1883

† H.B. Tristram

W.N. Bolton 1T
A.M. Evanson
C.G. Wade

J.H. Payne
Al. Rotherham 1T

W.M. Tatham
C. Gurdon
C.S. Wooldridge
R.S.F. Henderson
H.G. Fuller
R.M. Pattisson
G.T. Thomson
* E.T. Gurdon
E.J. Moore

FACT FILE

- England met the three other Home Countries in 1883, to establish a new but unofficial championship. And by winning each of the matches, they became first holders of the mythical Triple Crown

FINAL TABLE

	P	W	D	L	Pts
England	**3**	**3**	**0**	**0**	**6**
Scotland	3	2	0	1	4
Ireland	2	0	0	2	0
Wales	2	0	0	2	0

Ireland and Wales did not meet

1884 England XV against Scotland. Temple Gurdon's side lines up at Blackheath before winning back-to-back Triple Crowns.

1883-84

Four Nations Championship

v WALES

WON
England: 1G 2T
Wales: 1G
Leeds, 5 Jan 1884

H.B. Tristram

W.N. Bolton 1C
† C.E. Chapman
C.G. Wade 1T

H.T. Twynam 1T
Al. Rotherham 1T

W.M. Tatham
C. Gurdon
C.S. Wooldridge
R.S.F. Henderson
H.G. Fuller
J.T. Hunt
† E.L. Strong
* E.T. Gurdon
† C.J.B. Marriott

v IRELAND

WON
Ireland: Nil
England: 1G
Lansdowne Road, 4 Feb 1884

† C.H. Sample 1C

W.N. Bolton 1T
† H. Wigglesworth
† H. Fallas

J.H. Payne
H.T. Twynam

W.M. Tatham
† A. Wood
C.S. Wooldridge
† A. Teggin
† H. Bell
E.L. Strong
G.T. Thomson
* E.T. Gurdon
C.J.B. Marriott

v SCOTLAND

WON
England: 1G
Scotland: 1T
Blackheath, 1 Mar 1884

H.B. Tristram

W.N. Bolton 1C
A.M. Evanson
C.G. Wade

H.T. Twynam
Al. Rotherham

W.M. Tatham
C. Gurdon
C.S. Wooldridge
R.S.F. Henderson
R.S. Kindersley 1T
E.L. Strong
G.T. Thomson
* E.T. Gurdon
C.J.B. Marriott

FACT FILE

- England continued to dominate the Home Countries in 1884, again securing the Triple Crown.
- The match against Wales was the first international staged in Leeds.

FINAL TABLE

	P	W	D	L	Pts
England	**3**	**3**	**0**	**0**	**6**
Scotland	3	2	0	1	4
Wales	3	1	0	2	2
Ireland	3	0	0	3	0

1884-85

Four Nations Championship

v WALES

WON
Wales: 1G 1T
England: 1G 4T
St Helens, 3 Jan 1885

H.B. Tristram

† J.J. Hawcridge 1T
† A.E. Stoddart
C.G. Wade 1T

J.H. Payne 1C
Al. Rotherham

† E.D. Court
R.S. Kindersley 1T
R.S.F. Henderson
A. Teggin 1T
G. Harrison
† H.J. Ryall 1T
† F. Moss
* E.T. Gurdon
† A.T. Kemble

v IRELAND

WON
England: 2T
Ireland: 1T
Manchester, 7 Feb 1885

C.H. Sample

J.J. Hawcridge 1T
A.E. Stoddart
W.N. Bolton 1T

J.H. Payne
Al. Rotherham

† C.H. Horley
C. Gurdon
C.S. Woolridge
G.T. Thomson
G. Harrison
H.J. Ryall
F. Moss
* E.T. Gurdon
A.T. Kemble

FACT FILE

- Although England remained unbeaten in 1885 and 1886, Scotland twice denied them the Triple Crown. There was no game between the nations in 1885, and the match of 1886, in which Temple Gurdon led England for the last time, ended in a scoreless draw.

FINAL TABLE

	P	W	D	L	Pts
England	**2**	**2**	**0**	**0**	**4**
Scotland	2	1	1	0	3
Wales	2	0	1	1	1
Ireland	2	0	0	2	0

Ireland and Wales did not meet; Scotland and England did not meet

Left: *Charles Gurdon*

Right: *Gregory Wade*

Bottom right: *Wilfred Bolton*

1885-86

Four Nations Championship

v WALES

WON
England: 1GM 2T
Wales: 1G
Blackheath, 2 Jan 1886

A.S. Taylor

A.E. Stoddart 1GM
† R. Robertshaw
C.G. Wade 1T

† F. Bonsor
Al. Rotherham

† R.E. Inglis
C. Gurdon
† G.L. Jeffery
† C.H. Elliot
† W.G. Clibborn
† P.F. Hancock
F. Moss
† E. Wilkinson 1T
* C.J.B. Marriott

v IRELAND

WON
Ireland: Nil
England: 1T
Lansdowne Road, 6 Feb 1886

A.S. Taylor

A.E. Stoddart
R. Robertshaw
C.G. Wade

F. Bonsor
Al. Rotherham

R.E. Inglis
C. Gurdon
G.L. Jeffery
A. Teggin
W.G. Clibborn
P.F. Hancock
† N. Spurling
E. Wilkinson 1T
* C.J.B. Marriott

v SCOTLAND

DRAWN
Scotland: Nil
England: Nil
Raeburn Place, 13 Mar 1886

C.H. Sample

A.E. Stoddart
R. Robertshaw
† E.B. Brutton

F. Bonsor
Al. Rotherham

R.E. Inglis
C. Gurdon
G.L. Jeffery
A. Teggin
W.G. Clibborn
E. Wilkinson
N. Spurling
* E.T. Gurdon
C.J.B. Marriott

FACT FILE

- Andrew Stoddart, later a noted cricketer, gained the distinction of scoring England's first goal from a mark with his kick in the 1886 match against Wales.

FINAL TABLE

	P	W	D	L	Pts
Scotland	3	2	1	0	5
England	**3**	**2**	**1**	**0**	**5**
Wales	2	0	0	2	0
Ireland	2	0	0	2	0

Ireland and Wales did not meet

1886-89

Four Nations Championship

v WALES

DRAWN
Wales: Nil
England: Nil
Stradey Park, 8 Jan 1887

† S. Roberts

† J. Le Fleming
R. Robertshaw
† R.E. Lockwood

F. Bonsor
* Al. Rotherham

† J.L. Hickson
† R.L. Seddon
G.L. Jeffery
† H.C. Baker
W.G. Clibborn
E. Wilkinson
N. Spurling
† J.H. Dewhurst
† C.R. Cleveland

v IRELAND

LOST
Ireland: 2G
England: Nil
Lansdowne Road, 5 Feb 1887

S. Roberts

W.N. Bolton
† A. St. L. Fagan
R.E. Lockwood

† M.T. Scott
* Al. Rotherham

J.L. Hickson
R.L. Seddon
G.L. Jeffery
A. Teggin
W.G. Clibborn
A.T. Kemble
† F.E. Pease
J.H. Dewhurst
C.J.B. Marriott

v SCOTLAND

DRAWN
England: 1T
Scotland: 1T
Manchester, 5 Mar 1887

H.B. Tristram

W.N. Bolton
R. Robertshaw
R.E. Lockwood

F. Bonsor
* Al. Rotherham

J.L. Hickson
R.L. Seddon
G.L. Jeffery 1T
A. Teggin
W.G. Clibborn
E. Wilkinson
H.H. Springman
J.H. Dewhurst
C.R. Cleveland

Tour Match

v MAORIS

WON
England: 1G 4T
Maoris: Nil
Blackheath, 16 Feb 1889

† A.V. Royle

† J.W. Sutcliffe 1C 1T
A.E. Stoddart 1T
R.E. Lockwood

† W.M. Scott
* F. Bonsor

† F. Evershed 1T
† D. Jowett
† C. Anderton
† H.J. Wilkinson
† H. Bedford 2T
† W. Yiend
† J.W. Cave
† F. Lowrie
† A. Robinson

FACT FILE

- The RFU's refusal to accept the conditions for a proposed International Board meant that England did not play the other Home Countries in 1888 or 1889. There was a match in 1889, however, against the colourful New Zealand Native side, and England, with a pack of nine new caps, mostly Northerners too, overcame the strong challenge of the Natives in an entertaining match.

FINAL TABLE

	P	W	D	L	Pts
Scotland	3	2	1	0	5
Wales	3	1	1	1	3
Ireland	3	1	0	2	2
England	**3**	**0**	**2**	**1**	**2**

1889-90

Four Nations Championship

v WALES

LOST 0-1
England: Nil
Wales: 1T
Dewsbury, 15 Feb 1890

† W.G. Mitchell

† P.H. Morrison
* A.E. Stoddart
† J. Valentine

† J. Wright
† F.H. Fox

F. Evershed
J.L. Hickson
† S.M.J. Woods
† R.T.D. Budworth
† J.H. Rogers
P.F. Hancock
J.H. Dewhurst
F. Lowrie
A. Robinson

v SCOTLAND

WON 6-0
Scotland: Nil
England: 1G 1T
Raeburn Place, 1 Mar 1890

W.G. Mitchell

P.H. Morrison
† R.L. Aston
† J.W. Dyson 1T

M.T. Scott
F.H. Fox

F. Evershed 1T
* J.L. Hickson
S.M.J. Woods
† J. Toothill
J.H. Rogers
D. Jowett 1C
H. Bedford
† E. Holmes
A. Robinson

v IRELAND

WON 3-0
England: 3T
Ireland: Nil
Blackheath, 15 Mar 1890

W.G. Mitchell

P.H. Morrison 1T
R.L. Aston
* A.E. Stoddart 1T

M.T. Scott
† F.W. Spence

F. Evershed
J.L. Hickson
S.M.J. Woods
J. Toothill
J.H. Rogers 1T
D. Jowett
H. Bedford
E. Holmes
A. Robinson

FACT FILE

- With the international dispute happily settled, England resumed their home matches at Dewsbury where defeat was suffered at the hands of Wales for the first time.
- England recovered to regain a share in the championship title, thanks to wins over Scotland and Ireland.
- Andrew Stoddart followed Albert Hornby as a rugby player who captained England at both rugby football and cricket.

FINAL TABLE

	P	W	D	L	Pts
England	**3**	**2**	**0**	**1**	**4**
Scotland	3	2	0	1	4
Wales	3	1	1	1	3
Ireland	3	0	1	2	1

1890-91

Four Nations Championship

v WALES

WON 7-3
Wales: 1G
England: 2G 1T
Newport, 3 Jan 1891

W.G. Mitchell

† P. Christopherson 2T
*† F.H.R. Alderson 2C
R.E. Lockwood

† W.R.M. Leake
† J. Berry

† E.G.H. North
† T. Kent
S.M.J. Woods
J. Toothill
† W.E. Bromet
D. Jowett
R.T.D. Budworth 1T
† J. Richards
† R.P. Wilson

v IRELAND

WON 9-0
Ireland: Nil
England: 2G 3T
Lansdowne Road, 7 Feb 1891

W.G. Mitchell

P.H. Morrison
* F.H.R. Alderson
R.E. Lockwood 2C 2T

W.R.M. Leake
J. Berry

E.G.H. North
T. Kent
S.M.J. Woods
J. Toothill 1T
W.E. Bromet
D. Jowett
† L.J. Percival
J. Richards
R.P. Wilson 2T

v SCOTLAND

LOST 3-9
England: 1G
Scotland: 2G 1DG
Richmond, 7 Mar 1891

W.G. Mitchell

P. Christopherson
* F.H.R. Alderson 1C
R.E. Lockwood 1T

W.R.M. Leake
J. Berry

E.G.H. North
T. Kent
S.M.J. Woods
† E. Bonham-Carter
J.H. Rogers
D. Jowett
R.T.D. Budworth
J. Richards
R.P. Wilson

FACT FILE

- Frederic Alderson, a product of the Hartlepool Rovers, was appointed captain on his international debut and contributed two fine conversions in the match with Wales.

FINAL TABLE

	P	W	D	L	F	A	Pts
Scotland	3	3	0	0	38	3	6
England	**3**	**2**	**0**	**1**	**19**	**12**	**4**
Wales	3	1	0	2	9	26	2
Ireland	3	0	0	3	4	29	0

1891-92

Four Nations Championship

v WALES

WON 17-0
England: 3G 1T
Wales: Nil
Blackheath, 2 Jan 1892

† W.B. Thomson

† G.C. Hubbard 1T
* F.H.R. Alderson 1C 1T
R.E. Lockwood 2C

† C. Emmott
† A. Briggs

F. Evershed 1T
T. Kent
† A. Allport
J. Toothill
W.E. Bromet
W. Yiend
† J. Pyke
† W. Nichol 1T
† E. Bullough

v IRELAND

WON 7-0
England: 1G 1T
Ireland: Nil
Manchester, 6 Feb 1892

† S. Houghton

G.C. Hubbard
† J. Marsh
R.E. Lockwood

† E.W. Taylor
A. Briggs

F. Evershed 1T
T. Kent
* S.M.J. Woods 1C
J. Toothill
W.E. Bromet
W. Yiend
L.J. Percival 1T
† A. Ashworth
E. Bullough

v SCOTLAND

WON 5-0
Scotland: Nil
England: 1G
Raeburn Place, 5 Mar 1892

† T. Coop

J.W. Dyson
* F.H.R. Alderson
R.E. Lockwood 1C

† H. Varley
A. Briggs

F. Evershed
T. Kent
S.M.J. Woods
J. Toothill
W.E. Bromet 1T
W. Yiend
† H. Bradshaw
W. Nichol
E. Bullough

FACT FILE

- This was England's *annus mirabilis*. The Triple Crown was regained, and a 17-0 win over Wales, followed by victories over the Irish and Scots, made England undisputed champions in a season in which they did not concede a point.

FINAL TABLE

	P	W	D	L	F	A	Pts
England	**3**	**3**	**0**	**0**	**29**	**0**	**6**
Scotland	3	2	0	1	9	7	4
Ireland	3	1	0	2	9	9	2
Wales	3	0	0	3	2	33	0

1892-93

Four Nations Championship

v WALES

LOST 11-12
Wales: 1G 1PG 2T
England: 1G 3T
Cardiff Arms Park, 7 Jan 1893

† E. Field

* A.E. Stoddart 1C
F.H.R. Alderson
R.E. Lockwood

† H. Marshall 3T
† R.F. de Winton

F. Evershed
† J.H. Greenwell
S.M.J. Woods
J. Toothill
W.E. Bromet
† F.C. Lohden 1T
H. Bradshaw
† T. Broadley
† P. Maud

v IRELAND

WON 4-0
Ireland: Nil
England: 2T
Lansdowne Road, 4 Feb 1893

E. Field

J.W. Dyson
R.E. Lockwood
† T. Nicholson

E.W. Taylor 1T
† H. Duckett

F. Evershed
J.H. Greenwell
* S.M.J. Woods
J. Toothill
W.E. Bromet
W. Yiend
H. Bradshaw 1T
A. Allport
P. Maud

v SCOTLAND

LOST 0-8
England: Nil
Scotland: 2DG
Leeds, 4 Mar 1893

W.G. Mitchell

* A.E. Stoddart
J.W. Dyson
† F.P. Jones

† C.M. Wells
H. Duckett

F. Evershed
† F. Soane
† J.J. Robinson
J. Toothill
W.E. Bromet
W. Yiend
H. Bradshaw
T. Broadley
L.J. Percival

FACT FILE

- Howard Marshall, half-back against Wales, had the peculiar distinction of scoring three tries in his one and only international appearance.

FINAL TABLE

	P	W	D	L	F	A	Pts
Wales	3	3	0	0	23	11	6
Scotland	3	1	1	1	8	9	3
England	**3**	**1**	**0**	**2**	**15**	**20**	**2**
Ireland	3	0	1	2	0	6	1

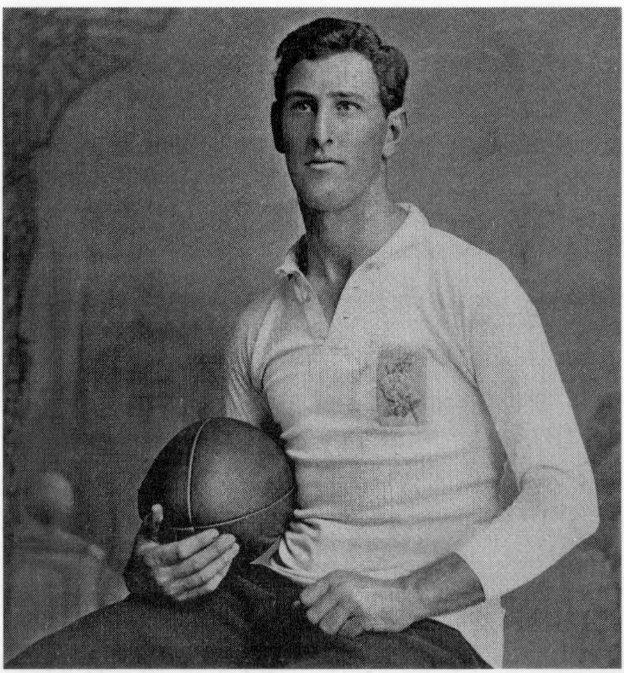

Sammy Woods played both rugby and cricket for England.

1893-94

Four Nations Championship

v WALES

WON 24-3
England: 4G 1GM
Wales: 1T
Birkenhead, 6 Jan 1894

† J.F. Byrne

† F. Firth
† C.A. Hooper
† S. Morfitt 1T
* R.E. Lockwood 1T 3C

C.M. Wells
E.W. Taylor 1GM 1T 1C

F. Soane
† J. Hall
J. Toothill
† H. Speed
† W.E. Tucker
H. Bradshaw 1T
T. Broadley
A. Allport

v IRELAND

LOST 5-7
England: 1G
Ireland: 1DG 1T
Blackheath, 3 Feb 1894

J.F. Byrne

F. Firth
C.A. Hooper
S. Morfitt
* R.E. Lockwood 1T

† R. Wood
E.W. Taylor 1C

F. Soane
J. Hall
J. Toothill
H. Speed
W.E. Tucker
H. Bradshaw
T. Broadley
A. Allport

v SCOTLAND

LOST 0-6
Scotland: 2T
England: Nil
Raeburn Place, 17 Mar 1894

J.F. Byrne

F. Firth
C.A. Hooper
S. Morfitt
† W.J. Jackson

C.M. Wells
* E.W. Taylor

F. Soane
J. Hall
† W. Walton
H. Speed
† A.E. Elliott
H. Bradshaw
T. Broadley
A. Allport

FACT FILE

- England adopted the Welsh example of playing four three-quarters for 1894.

FINAL TABLE

	P	W	D	L	F	A	Pts
Ireland	3	3	0	0	15	5	6
England	**3**	**1**	**0**	**2**	**29**	**16**	**2**
Wales	3	1	0	2	10	27	2
Scotland	3	1	0	2	6	12	2

1894-95

Four Nations Championship

v WALES

WON 14-6
Wales: 2T
England: 1G 3T
St Helens, 5 Jan 1895

† H. Ward

† J.H.C. Fegan
W.B. Thomson 1T
† F.A. Leslie-Jones 1T
† E.M. Baker

† R.H.B. Cattell
E.W. Taylor

† G.M. Carey 1T
* S.M.J. Woods 1T
† H.W. Finlinson
W.E. Bromet
W.E. Tucker
† F. Mitchell 1C
† F.O. Poole
† C. Thomas

v IRELAND

WON 6-3
Ireland: 1T
England: 2T
Lansdowne Road, 2 Feb 1895

J.F. Byrne

J.H.C. Fegan 1T
W.B. Thomson
F.A. Leslie-Jones
E.M. Baker

R.H.B. Cattell
E.W. Taylor

G.M. Carey
* S.M.J. Woods
H.W. Finlinson
W.E. Bromet
W.E. Tucker
F. Mitchell
F.O. Poole
C. Thomas 1T

v SCOTLAND

LOST 3-6
England: 1PG
Scotland: 1PG 1T
Richmond, 9 Mar 1895

J.F. Byrne 1PG

J.H.C. Fegan
W.B. Thomson
† T.H. Dobson
E.M. Baker

R.H.B. Cattell
E.W. Taylor

G.M. Carey
* S.M.J. Woods
H.W. Finlinson
W.E. Bromet
W.E. Tucker
F. Mitchell
F.O. Poole
C. Thomas

FACT FILE

- Fred Byrne, the full-back, landed England's first penalty goal in an international in the game against Scotland.

FINAL TABLE

	P	W	D	L	F	A	Pts
Scotland	3	3	0	0	17	7	6
England	**3**	**2**	**0**	**1**	**23**	**15**	**4**
Wales	3	1	0	2	15	22	2
Ireland	3	0	0	3	6	17	0

1895-96

Four Nations Championship

v WALES

WON 25-0
England: 2G 5T
Wales: Nil
Blackheath, 4 Jan 1896

S. Houghton

S. Morfitt 2T
J. Valentine 1C
E.M. Baker
† E.F. Fookes 2T

R.H.B. Cattell 2T
* E.W. Taylor 1C

G.M. Carey
† J. Pinch
† A. Starks
† L.F. Giblin
† J. Rhodes
F. Mitchell 1T
† J.W. Ward
† W. Whiteley

v IRELAND

LOST 4-10
England: 1DG
Ireland: 2G
Leeds, 1 Feb 1896

J.F. Byrne 1DG

S. Morfitt
J. Valentine
E.M. Baker
E.F. Fookes

R.H.B. Cattell
* E.W. Taylor

G.M. Carey
J. Pinch
A. Starks
L.F. Giblin
J. Rhodes
F. Mitchell
J.W. Ward
W.E. Bromet

v SCOTLAND

LOST 0-11
Scotland: 1G 2T
England: Nil
Glasgow, 14 Mar 1896

† R.W. Poole

S. Morfitt
J. Valentine
E.M. Baker
E.F. Fookes

R.H.B. Cattell
C.M. Wells

† G.E. Hughes
† J.H. Barron
† E. Knowles
H. Speed
J. Rhodes
* F. Mitchell
J.W. Ward
T. Broadley

FACT FILE

- Professionalism in any form had been outlawed by the RFU at their meeting in September 1895, and by-laws were adopted to govern the structure of the game. These laws affected the administration of the game in the north and the result was a breakaway and formation of a Northern Union – later the Rugby League.
- England had to wait until 1910 before winning the championship.

FINAL TABLE

	P	W	D	L	F	A	Pts
Ireland	3	2	1	0	18	8	5
Scotland	3	1	1	1	11	6	3
England	**3**	**1**	**0**	**2**	**29**	**21**	**2**
Wales	3	1	0	2	10	33	2

1896-97

Four Nations Championship

v WALES

LOST 0-11
Wales: 1G 2T
England: Nil
Newport, 9 Jan 1897

J.F. Byrne

† F.A. Byrne
† T. Fletcher
E.M. Baker
E.F. Fookes

C.M. Wells
* E.W. Taylor

† F. Jacob
J.H. Barron
† P.J. Ebdon
† R.F. Oakes
† W.B. Stoddart
† F.M. Stout
† W. Ashford
† R.H. Mangles

v IRELAND

LOST 9-13
Ireland: 1GM 3T
England: 2PG 1T
Lansdowne Road, 6 Feb 1897

J.F. Byrne 2PG

† G.C. Robinson 1T
† W.L. Bunting
† J.T. Taylor
E.F. Fookes

† S. Northmore
* E.W. Taylor

F. Jacob
J.H. Barron
P.J. Ebdon
R.F. Oakes
W.B. Stoddart
F.M. Stout
W. Ashford
R.H. Mangles

v SCOTLAND

WON 12-3
England: 1G 1DG 1T
Scotland: 1T
Manchester, 13 Mar 1897

J.F. Byrne 1C, 1DG

G.C. Robinson 1T
W.L. Bunting
† O.G. Mackie
E.F. Fookes 1T

C.M. Wells
* E.W. Taylor

F. Jacob
J. Pinch
E. Knowles
R.F. Oakes
W.B. Stoddart
† H.W. Dudgeon
L.F. Giblin
† Jas Davidson

FACT FILE

- For the match with Wales to open the 1897 season, fewer than half the England team were from the powerful North. There were 25 players used in the three matches, with 16 new caps awarded.
- The win over Scotland brought the Calcutta Cup to England for the first time for four years. Scotland had been so confident of victory that they had not brought the Calcutta Cup to Manchester.

FINAL TABLE

	P	W	D	L	F	A	Pts
England	**3**	**1**	**0**	**2**	**21**	**27**	**2**
Ireland	2	1	0	1	16	17	2
Wales	1	1	0	0	11	0	2
Scotland	2	1	0	1	11	15	2

CHAMPIONSHIP UNRESOLVED
Wales did not meet Ireland or Scotland

1897-98

Four Nations Championship

v IRELAND

LOST 6-9
England: 1PG 1T
Ireland: 1PG 2T
Richmond, 5 Feb 1898

* J.F. Byrne 1PG

G.C. Robinson 1T
W.L. Bunting
O.G. Mackie
E.F. Fookes

† H. Myers
† P.G. Jacob

F. Jacob
† R. Pierce
† F. Shaw
R.F. Oakes
H.W. Dudgeon
F.M. Stout
† J.H. Blacklock
† C.E. Wilson

v SCOTLAND

DRAWN 3-3
Scotland: 1T
England: 1T
Powderhall, 12 Mar 1898

* J.F. Byrne

† P.W. Stout
W.L. Bunting
† P.M.R. Royds 1T
† W.N. Pilkington

† G.T. Unwin
† Ar. Rotherham

F. Jacob
† J.F. Shaw
† H.E. Ramsden
R.F. Oakes
H.W. Dudgeon
F.M. Stout
W. Ashford
Jas Davidson

v WALES

WON 14-7
England: 1G 3T
Wales: 1DG 1T
Blackheath, 2 Apr 1898

* J.F. Byrne 1C

P.W. Stout 1T
W.L. Bunting
P.M.R. Royds
E.F. Fookes 2T

† R. O'H. Livesay
Ar. Rotherham

F. Jacob
J.F. Shaw
H.E. Ramsden
R.F. Oakes
H.W. Dudgeon
F.M. Stout 1T
W. Ashford
Jas Davidson

FACT FILE

- The Welsh match, played in April at Blackheath, was to be England's last victory over the Principality for 12 years.
As one historian reviewing the 1898 season subsequently wrote, 'English rugby was in a bad state, but worse was in store'.

FINAL TABLE

	P	W	D	L	F	A	Pts
England	**3**	**1**	**1**	**1**	**23**	**19**	**3**
Scotland	2	1	1	0	11	3	3
Wales	2	1	0	1	18	17	2
Ireland	3	1	0	2	12	25	2

CHAMPIONSHIP UNRESOLVED
Wales and Scotland did not meet

1898-99

Four Nations Championship

v WALES

LOST 3-26
Wales: 4G 2T
England: 1T
St Helens, 7 Jan 1899

† H.T. Gamlin

G.C. Robinson 1T
P.W. Stout
P.M.R. Royds
† R. Forrest

R. O'H. Livesay
* Ar. Rotherham

F. Jacob
† G.R. Gibson
† J. Daniell
R.F. Oakes
H.W. Dudgeon
† W. Mortimer
† Jos Davidson
† C.H. Harper

v IRELAND

LOST 0-6
Ireland: 1PG 1T
England: Nil
Lansdowne Road, 4 Feb 1899

J.F. Byrne

† S. Anderson
P.W. Stout
J.T. Taylor
E.F. Fookes

E.W. Taylor
* Ar. Rotherham

F. Jacob
† J.H. Shooter
† A.J.L. Darby
C. Thomas
H.W. Dudgeon
F.M. Stout
J.H. Blacklock
Jas Davidson

v SCOTLAND

LOST 0-5
England: Nil
Scotland: 1G
Blackheath, 11 Mar 1899

H.T. Gamlin

† J.C. Matters
P.W. Stout
W.L. Bunting
E.F. Fookes

† R.O. Schwarz
* Ar. Rotherham

† R.F.A. Hobbs
J.H. Shooter
† A.O. Dowson
R.F. Oakes
H.W. Dudgeon
F.M. Stout
Jos Davidson
Jas Davidson

FACT FILE

- The critics were hard on the England packs of 1899: former player Arthur Budd called them a 'rustic collection' and *The Times* referred to the northern element in the pack as 'delinquents'. For the first time England lost all three matches, and only one try was scored during the season.

FINAL TABLE

	P	W	D	L	F	A	Pts
Ireland	3	3	0	0	18	3	6
Scotland	3	2	0	1	29	19	4
Wales	3	1	0	2	36	27	2
England	**3**	**0**	**0**	**3**	**3**	**37**	**0**

1899-1900

Four Nations Championship

v WALES

LOST 3-13
Wales: 2G 1PG
England: 1T
Gloucester, 6 Jan 1900

H.T. Gamlin

† S.F. Coopper
† G.W. Gordon-Smith
† A.T. Brettargh
† E.T. Nicholson **1T**

* R.H.B. Cattell
† G.H. Marsden

† J. Baxter
† A. Cockerham
† J.W. Jarman
† C.T. Scott
† F.J. Bell
† R.W. Bell
† S. Reynolds
† W. Cobby

v IRELAND

WON 15-4
England: 1G 1DG 2T
Ireland: 1DG
Richmond, 3 Feb 1900

H.T. Gamlin

G.C. Robinson **2T**
G.W. Gordon-Smith **1DG 1T**
J.T. Taylor
E.T. Nicholson

† J.C. Marquis
G.H. Marsden

J. Baxter
J.H. Shooter
* J. Daniell
C.T. Scott
† H. Alexander **1C**
R.W. Bell
S. Reynolds
† A.F. Todd

v SCOTLAND

DRAWN 0-0
Scotland: Nil
England: Nil
Inverleith, 10 Mar 1900

H.T. Gamlin

G.C. Robinson
G.W. Gordon-Smith
W.L. Bunting
R. Forrest

J.C. Marquis
G.H. Marsden

J. Baxter
J.H. Shooter
* J. Daniell
† A.F.C.C. Luxmoore
H. Alexander
R.W. Bell
S. Reynolds
A.F. Todd

FACT FILE

- England introduced 13 new caps for the start of the 1900 season. Two of the men, Sidney Coopper and James Baxter, were to serve various RFU committees for many years. Baxter became Chairman of the England selection committee, and Coopper served the RFU as secretary from 1924 to 1947.

FINAL TABLE

	P	W	D	L	F	A	Pts
Wales	3	3	0	0	28	6	6
England	**3**	**1**	**1**	**1**	**18**	**17**	**3**
Scotland	3	0	2	1	3	12	2
Ireland	3	0	1	2	4	18	1

1900-01

Four Nations Championship

v WALES

LOST 0-13
Wales: 2G 1T
England: Nil
Cardiff Arms Park, 5 Jan 1901

† J.W. Sagar

† C. Smith
† E.J. Vivyan
* J.T. Taylor
† E.W. Elliot

R.O. Schwarz
† E.J. Walton

† A. O'Neill
† D. Graham
A.F.C.C. Luxmoore
C.T. Scott
H. Alexander
† N.C. Fletcher
† C.O.P. Gibson
† E.W. Roberts

v IRELAND

LOST 6-10
Ireland: 2G
England: 1PG 1T
Lansdowne Road, 9 Feb 1901

J.W. Sagar

G.C. Robinson 1T
* W.L. Bunting
J.T. Taylor
E.W. Elliot

R.O. Schwarz
E.J. Walton

A. O'Neill
† R.D. Wood
† C. Hall
C.T. Scott
H. Alexander 1PG
N.C. Fletcher
S. Reynolds
E.W. Roberts

v SCOTLAND

LOST 3-18
England: 1T
Scotland: 3G 1T
Blackheath, 9 Mar 1901

H.T. Gamlin

G.C. Robinson 1T
* W.L. Bunting
† N.S. Cox
E.W. Elliot

† B. Oughtred
† P.D. Kendall

A. O'Neill
G.R. Gibson
C. Hall
† H.T.F. Weston
H. Alexander
N.C. Fletcher
† C.S. Edgar
† B.C. Hartley

FACT FILE

- England used 28 players in 1901, when the improvement shown in the previous season was not maintained.
- Herbert Gamlin was the outstanding English full-back of the era and enhanced his reputation with an impressive display against Scotland. He was a tall and powerful player with a strong tackle which offered no hope of escape to its victim.

FINAL TABLE

	P	W	D	L	F	A	Pts
Scotland	3	3	0	0	45	16	6
Wales	3	2	0	1	31	27	4
Ireland	3	1	0	2	24	25	2
England	**3**	**0**	**0**	**3**	**9**	**41**	**0**

1901-02

Four Nations Championship

v WALES

LOST 8-9
England: 1G 1T
Wales: 1PG 2T
Blackheath, 11 Jan 1902

H.T. Gamlin

† P.L. Nicholas
† J.E. Raphael
J.T. Taylor
S.F. Coopper

B. Oughtred
P.D. Kendall

† G. Fraser
J.J. Robinson 1T
† T.H. Willcocks
† L.R. Tosswill
* H. Alexander 1C
† D.D. Dobson 1T
† J. Jewitt
† S.G. Williams

v IRELAND

WON 6-3
England: 2T
Ireland: 1T
Leicester, 8 Feb 1902

H.T. Gamlin

R. Forrest
J.E. Raphael
J.T. Taylor
S.F. Coopper 1T

B. Oughtred
E.J. Walton

G. Fraser
J.J. Robinson
* J. Daniell
L.R. Tosswill
H. Alexander
D.D. Dobson
† P.F. Hardwick
S.G. Williams 1T

v SCOTLAND

WON 6-3
Scotland: 1T
England: 2T
Inverleith, 15 Mar 1902

H.T. Gamlin

R. Forrest
J.E. Raphael
J.T. Taylor 1T
† T. Simpson

B. Oughtred
E.J. Walton

G. Fraser
J.J. Robinson
* J. Daniell
L.R. Tosswill
B.C. Hartley
D.D. Dobson
P.F. Hardwick
S.G. Williams 1T

John Daniell led this England team to their first win on Scottish soil in ten years at Inverleith in 1902.

FACT FILE

- Only the antics of the Welsh scrum-half allowed Wales to poach victory in the dying moments of the match. Oughtred was lured into an offside tackle at a scrummage near the English posts and Wales converted the resulting penalty to win by a point.

FINAL TABLE

	P	W	D	L	F	A	Pts
Wales	3	3	0	0	38	13	6
England	**3**	**2**	**0**	**1**	**20**	**15**	**4**
Ireland	3	1	0	2	8	21	2
Scotland	3	0	0	3	8	25	0

1902-03

Four Nations Championship

v WALES

LOST 5-21
Wales: 3G 2T
England: 1G
St Helens, 10 Jan 1903

H.T. Gamlin

† J.H. Miles
J.T. Taylor 1C
† R.H. Spooner
T. Simpson

* B. Oughtred
† F.C. Hulme

G. Fraser
R.D. Wood
† V.H. Cartwright
R.F.A. Hobbs
† R. Bradley
D.D. Dobson 1T
P.F. Hardwick
† J. Duthie

v IRELAND

LOST 0-6
Ireland: 1PG 1T
England: Nil
Lansdowne Road, 14 Feb 1903

H.T. Gamlin

R. Forrest
J.T. Taylor
A.T. Brettargh
T. Simpson

* B. Oughtred
F.C. Hulme

G. Fraser
R.D. Wood
V.H. Cartwright
† W.G. Heppell
† B.A. Hill
D.D. Dobson
P.F. Hardwick
S.G. Williams

v SCOTLAND

LOST 6-10
England: 2T
Scotland: 1DG 2T
Richmond, 21 Mar 1903

H.T. Gamlin

T. Simpson
† E.I.M. Barrett
A.T. Brettargh
R. Forrest 1T

† W.V. Butcher
* P.D. Kendall

N.C. Fletcher
R. Pierce
V.H. Cartwright
F.M. Stout
B.A. Hill
D.D. Dobson 1T
P.F. Hardwick
S.G. Williams

FACT FILE

- Three defeats from three matches was again England's miserable return in 1903. Selection was fickle with 26 players taking part.
- Forward Denys Dobson was one of three to play throughout the season. He had the misfortune to be gored by a charging rhinoceros in 1916, whilst serving as a Colonial Officer in Nyasaland. There is a legend that his former schoolmaster, hearing of Dobson's demise, stated that he had always had a weak hand-off.

FINAL TABLE

	P	W	D	L	F	A	Pts
Scotland	3	3	0	0	19	6	6
Wales	3	2	0	1	39	11	4
Ireland	3	1	0	2	6	21	2
England	**3**	**0**	**0**	**3**	**11**	**37**	**0**

1903-04

Four Nations Championship

v WALES

DRAWN 14-14
England: 1G 1PG 2T
Wales: 2G 1GM
Leicester, 9 Jan 1904

H.T. Gamlin 1PG

E.J. Vivyan
A.T. Brettargh 1T
† E.W. Dillon
E.W. Elliot 2T

† P.S. Hancock
W.V. Butcher

† G.H. Keeton
† J.G. Milton
V.H. Cartwright
* F.M. Stout 1C
B.A. Hill
† N.J. Moore
P.F. Hardwick
† C.J. Newbold

v IRELAND

WON 19-0
England: 2G 3T
Ireland: Nil
Blackheath, 13 Feb 1904

H.T. Gamlin

E.J. Vivyan 2T, 2C
A.T. Brettargh
E.W. Dillon
T. Simpson 1T

P.S. Hancock
W.V. Butcher

G.H. Keeton
J.G. Milton
* J. Daniell
F.M. Stout
B.A. Hill
N.J. Moore 2T
P.F. Hardwick
C.J. Newbold

v SCOTLAND

LOST 3-6
Scotland: 2T
England: 1T
Inverleith, 19 Mar 1904

H.T. Gamlin

E.J. Vivyan 1T
A.T. Brettargh
E.W. Dillon
T. Simpson

P.S. Hancock
W.V. Butcher

G.H. Keeton
J.G. Milton
* J. Daniell
F.M. Stout
V.H. Cartwright
N.J. Moore
P.F. Hardwick
C.J. Newbold

FACT FILE

- The season of 1904 was England's best for many years.
- John Daniell, in his last season in the side, returned to skipper the team to a big win over Ireland. Daniell was to become an influential RFU Committee member, and his shrewd sporting judgment was a valuable asset to England rugby and cricket selectors for many years.

FINAL TABLE

	P	W	D	L	F	A	Pts
Scotland	3	2	0	1	28	27	4
Wales	3	1	1	1	47	31	3
England	**3**	**1**	**1**	**1**	**36**	**20**	**3**
Ireland	3	1	0	2	17	50	2

1904-05

Four Nations Championship

v WALES

LOST 0-25
Wales: 2G 5T
England: Nil
Cardiff Arms Park, 14 Jan 1905

† S.H. Irvin

† F.H. Palmer
J.E. Raphael
E.W. Dillon
S.F. Coopper

W.V. Butcher
F.C. Hulme

† T.A. Gibson
† W.L.Y. Rogers
V.H. Cartwright
* F.M. Stout
B.A. Hill
† W.T.C. Cave
† J.L. Mathias
C.J. Newbold

v IRELAND

LOST 3-17
Ireland: 1G 4T
England: 1T
Cork, 11 Feb 1905

† C.F. Stanger-Leathes

T. Simpson
† H.E. Shewring
A.T. Brettargh
S.F. Coopper 1T

W.V. Butcher
F.C. Hulme

† J. Green
W.L.Y. Rogers
V.H. Cartwright
* F.M. Stout
† G. Vickery
† W.M. Grylls
J.L. Mathias
C.J. Newbold

v SCOTLAND

LOST 0-8
England: Nil
Scotland: 1G 1T
Richmond, 18 Mar 1905

J.T. Taylor

T. Simpson
J.E. Raphael
A.T. Brettargh
S.F. Coopper

† A.D. Stoop
W.V. Butcher

T.A. Gibson
J.G. Milton
V.H. Cartwright
* F.M. Stout
† S.H. Osborne
† C.E.L. Hammond
J.L. Mathias
C.J. Newbold

FACT FILE

- For the match against Ireland at Cork, it was noted that the team travelled from Dublin to Cork in third-class railway compartments. The RFU were severely criticised for their travel arrangements in the press, one leading critic, writing later, stating that the journey was a byword for discomfort and lack of organisation.

FINAL TABLE

	P	W	D	L	F	A	Pts
Wales	3	3	0	0	41	6	6
Ireland	3	2	0	1	31	18	4
Scotland	3	1	0	2	16	17	2
England	**3**	**0**	**0**	**3**	**3**	**50**	**0**

1905-06

Tour Match

v NEW ZEALAND

LOST 0-15
England: Nil
NZ: 5T
Crystal Palace, 2 Dec 1905

† E.J. Jackett

† H.M. Imrie
† R.E. Godfray
H.E. Shewring
† A.E. Hind

J.E. Raphael
† D.R. Gent
† J. Braithwaite

† G. Summerscales
* V.H. Cartwright
† R.F. Russell
B.A. Hill
C.E.L. Hammond
J.L. Mathias
E.W. Roberts

Four Nations Championship

v WALES

LOST 3-16
England: 1T
Wales: 2G 2T
Richmond, 13 Jan 1906

E.J. Jackett

A.E. Hind
J.E. Raphael
H.E. Shewring
† A. Hudson 1T

D.R. Gent
† R.A. Jago

† G.E.B. Dobbs
† H.A. Hodges
* V.H. Cartwright
† T.S. Kelly
† A.L. Kewney
C.E.L. Hammond
† W.A. Mills
E.W. Roberts

v IRELAND

LOST 6-16
England: 2T
Ireland: 2G 2T
Leicester, 10 Feb 1906

E.J. Jackett

† J.E. Hutchinson
† J.R.P. Sandford
† C.H. Milton
A. Hudson

D.R. Gent
R.A. Jago 1T

G.E.B. Dobbs
H.A. Hodges
* V.H. Cartwright
T.S. Kelly
A.L. Kewney
C.E.L. Hammond
W.A. Mills 1T
E.W. Roberts

v SCOTLAND

WON 9-3
Scotland: 1T
England: 3T
Inverleith, 17 Mar 1906

E.J. Jackett

J.E. Raphael 1T
H.E. Shewring
† J.G.G. Birkett
T. Simpson 1T

† J. Peters
A.D. Stoop

J. Green
† R. Dibble
* V.H. Cartwright
T.S. Kelly
A.L. Kewney
C.E.L. Hammond
W.A. Mills 1T
† C.H. Shaw

Friendly

v FRANCE

WON 35-8
France: 1G 1T
England: 4G 5T
Parc des Princes, 22 Mar 1906

E.J. Jackett

J.E. Raphael
H.E. Shewring
J.G.G. Birkett
A. Hudson 4T

J. Peters 1T
A.D. Stoop 1T

J. Green
R. Dibble
* V.H. Cartwright 4C
T.S. Kelly
A.L. Kewney 1T
C.E.L. Hammond
W.A. Mills 1T
† T.B. Hogarth 1T

FACT FILE

- Two new opponents were added to the fixture list for 1905-06, England losing at the Crystal Palace to the First All Blacks from New Zealand, and winning, at the end of the season, the first international played against France.

FINAL TABLE

	P	W	D	L	F	A	Pts
Wales	3	2	0	1	31	17	4
Ireland	3	2	0	1	33	25	4
Scotland	3	1	0	2	19	24	2
England	**3**	**1**	**0**	**2**	**18**	**35**	**2**

1906-07

Tour Match

v SOUTH AFRICA

DRAWN 3-3
England: 1T
SA: 1T
Crystal Palace, 8 Dec 1906

E.J. Jackett

† F.G. Brooks 1T
H.E. Shewring
J.G.G. Birkett
T. Simpson

A.D. Stoop
R.A. Jago

J. Green
R. Dibble
* V.H. Cartwright
T.S. Kelly
B.A. Hill
† A. Alcock
W.A. Mills
C.H. Shaw

Friendly

v FRANCE

WON 41-13
England: 5G 1DG 4T
France: 2G 1PG
Richmond, 5 Jan 1907

† H. Lee

† T.B. Batchelor
H.E. Shewring 1T
J.G.G. Birkett 1DG, 1T
† D. Lambert 5T

A.D. Stoop
† T.G. Wedge

J. Green
† F.J.V. Hopley
† W.M.B. Nanson 1T
T.S. Kelly
* B.A. Hill 5C
† L.A.N. Slocock 1T
W.A. Mills
C.H. Shaw

Four Nations Championship

v WALES

LOST 0-22
Wales: 2G 4T
England: Nil
St Helens, 12 Jan 1907

E.J. Jackett

† F.S. Scott
H.E. Shewring
J.G.G. Birkett
S.F. Coopper

A.D. Stoop
R.A. Jago

J. Green
F.J.V. Hopley
W.M.B. Nanson
T.S. Kelly
* B.A. Hill
L.A.N. Slocock
W.A. Mills
C.H. Shaw

v IRELAND

LOST 9-17
Ireland: 1G 1GM 3T
England: 1PG 2T
Lansdowne Road, 9 Feb 1907

E.J. Jackett

† W.C. Wilson
H.E. Shewring
† A.S. Pickering 1PG
H.M. Imrie 1T

J. Peters
R.A. Jago

* J. Green
J.G. Milton
† G. Leather
T.S. Kelly
S.G. Williams
L.A.N. Slocock 1T
W.A. Mills
C.H. Shaw

v SCOTLAND

LOST 3-8
England: 1T
Scotland: 1G 1T
Blackheath, 16 Mar 1907

E.J. Jackett

W.C. Wilson
H.E. Shewring
J.G.G. Birkett
† A.W. Newton

J. Peters 1T
† S.P. Start

J. Green
† G.D. Roberts
* E.W. Roberts
T.S. Kelly
S.G. Williams
L.A.N. Slocock
W.A. Mills
C.H. Shaw

FACT FILE

- England made a promising start this season, holding the First Springboks to a draw on a boggy pitch at Crystal Palace.
- There is an interesting tale in connection with the selection of the side to meet the South Africans. It is believed that Arnold Alcock, a medical student at Guy's, won his cap owing to a clerical error, and at the expense of Lancelot Slocock, who appeared later in the season.

FINAL TABLE

	P	W	D	L	F	A	Pts
Scotland	3	3	0	0	29	9	6
Wales	3	2	0	1	54	6	4
Ireland	3	1	0	2	20	53	2
England	**3**	**0**	**0**	**3**	**12**	**47**	**0**

1907-08

Friendly

v FRANCE

WON **19-0**
France: Nil
England: 2G 3T
Stade Colombes, 1 Jan 1908

† A.E. Wood

D. Lambert 1T
J.G.G. Birkett 1T
† W.N. Lapage 1T
A. Hudson

† G.V. Portus 1T
† H.J.H. Sibree

† E.L. Chambers
† F. Boylen
* T.S. Kelly
G.D. Roberts 2C
L.A.N. Slocock
R. Dibble
W.A. Mills 1T
† H. Havelock

Four Nations Championship

v WALES

LOST **18-28**
Wales: 3G 1DG 1PG 2T
England: 3G 1T
Bristol City AFC, 18 Jan 1908

A.E. Wood 2C

D. Lambert
* J.G.G. Birkett 2T
W.N. Lapage 1T
A. Hudson

J. Peters
† R.H. Williamson 1T

† R. Gilbert
F. Boylen
C.E.L. Hammond
G.D. Roberts 1C
L.A.N. Slocock
R. Dibble
W.A. Mills
H. Havelock

v IRELAND

WON **13-3**
England: 2G 1T
Ireland: 1PG
Richmond, 8 Feb 1908

A.E. Wood 2C

W.N. Lapage
J.G.G. Birkett
† H.H. Vassall
A. Hudson 2T

G.V. Portus
R.H. Williamson 1T

R. Gilbert
F. Boylen
* C.E.L. Hammond
T.S. Kelly
L.A.N. Slocock
R. Dibble
F.J.V. Hopley
H. Havelock

v SCOTLAND

LOST **10-16**
Scotland: 1G 2DG 1T
England: 2G
Inverleith, 21 Mar 1908

† G.H. D'OLyon

D. Lambert 2C
J.G.G. Birkett 1T
W.N. Lapage
A. Hudson

† J. Davey
R.H. Williamson

R. Gilbert
F. Boylen
† T. Woods
T.S. Kelly
* L.A.N. Slocock 1T
R. Dibble
† W.L. Oldham
† F.B. Watson

FACT FILE

- An easy win over the French in Paris was followed by England's only international to be staged at Bristol. On a foggy, damp afternoon, Wales won a match in which both XVs frequently disappeared from sight.

FINAL TABLE

	P	W	D	L	F	A	Pts
Wales	3	3	0	0	45	28	6
England	**3**	**1**	**0**	**2**	**41**	**47**	**2**
Scotland	3	1	0	2	32	32	2
Ireland	3	1	0	2	24	35	2

1908-09

Tour Match

v AUSTRALIA

LOST 3-9
England: 1T
Australia: 3T
Blackheath, 9 Jan 1909

* G.H. D'OLyon

† E.R. Mobbs 1T
† F.N. Tarr
† E.W. Assinder
† B.B. Bennetts

† A.H. Ashcroft
R.H. Williamson

† J.G. Cooper
R. Dibble
A.L. Kewney
† S.H. Penny
† A.D. Warrington-Morris
† F.P. Knight
† P.J. Down
W.L. Oldham

Four Nations Championship

v WALES

LOST 0-8
Wales: 1G 1T
England: Nil
Cardiff Arms Park, 16 Jan 1909

E.J. Jackett

E.R. Mobbs
F.N. Tarr
E.W. Assinder
B.B. Bennetts

T.G. Wedge
J. Davey

J.G. Cooper
* R. Dibble
A.L. Kewney
† W.A. Johns
A.D. Warrington-Morris
† E.D. Ibbitson
† F.G. Handford
† H. Archer

Friendly

v FRANCE

WON 22-0
England: 2G 4T
France: Nil
Leicester, 30 Jan 1909

E.J. Jackett 2C

E.R. Mobbs 1T
F.N. Tarr 2T
† R.W. Poulton
T. Simpson 1T

† F. Hutchinson 1T
R.H. Williamson

† C.A. Bolton
* R. Dibble
A.L. Kewney
W.A. Johns 1T
A.D. Warrington-Morris
E.D. Ibbitson
F.G. Handford
H. Archer

Four Nations Championship

v IRELAND

WON 11-5
Ireland: 1G
England: 1G 2T
Lansdowne Road, 13 Feb 1909

E.J. Jackett

† A.C. Palmer 1C 2T
† C.C.G. Wright
R.W. Poulton
E.R. Mobbs 1T

F. Hutchinson
H.J.H. Sibree

† H.J.S. Morton
* R. Dibble
A.L. Kewney
W.A. Johns
† A.J. Wilson
E.D. Ibbitson
F.G. Handford
H. Archer

v SCOTLAND

LOST 8-18
England: 1G 1T
Scotland: 3G 1T
Richmond, 20 Mar 1909

E.J. Jackett

A.C. Palmer 1C
C.C.G. Wright
R.W. Poulton
E.R. Mobbs 1T

F. Hutchinson
H.J.H. Sibree

H.J.S. Morton
* R. Dibble
A.L. Kewney
W.A. Johns
† H.C. Harrison
E.D. Ibbitson
F.G. Handford
F.B. Watson 1T

FACT FILE

- The find of the season was Edgar Mobbs, who played in all five matches and scored tries in four. Surprisingly, he only appeared for England on two further occasions, but he was a fine sportsman, outstanding three-quarter, and a brave soldier who died in action at Zillebeke in 1917.
- Due to a delay in the building of stands at Twickenham, the RFU was obliged to stage the Scotland match at Richmond, the last international played at the Athletic Ground.

FINAL TABLE

	P	W	D	L	F	A	Pts
Wales	3	3	0	0	31	8	6
Scotland	3	2	0	1	30	16	4
England	**3**	**1**	**0**	**2**	**19**	**31**	**2**
Ireland	3	0	0	3	13	38	0

1909-10

Five Nations Championship

v WALES

WON 11-6
England: 1G 1PG 1T
Wales: 2T
Twickenham, 15 Jan 1910

† W.R. Johnston

† F.E. Chapman 1T 1PG 1C
† B. Solomon 1T
J.G.G. Birkett
R.W. Poulton

* A.D. Stoop
D.R. Gent

H.J.S. Morton
E.L. Chambers
† H. Berry
W.A. Johns
† L. Haigh
† L.E. Barrington-Ward
† D.F. Smith
† C.H. Pillman

v IRELAND

DRAWN 0-0
England: Nil
Ireland: Nil
Twickenham, 12 Feb 1910

W.R. Johnston

F.E. Chapman
† L.W. Hayward
J.G.G. Birkett
E.R. Mobbs

* A.D. Stoop
D.R. Gent

H.J.S. Morton
E.L. Chambers
H. Berry
W.A. Johns
L. Haigh
L.E. Barrington-Ward
D.F. Smith
C.H. Pillman

v FRANCE

WON 11-3
France: 1T
England: 1G 2T
Parc des Princes, 3 Mar 1910

† C.S. Williams

F.E. Chapman 1C
† A.A. Adams
A. Hudson 2T
* E.R. Mobbs

† H. Coverdale
† A.L.H. Gotley

† N.A. Wodehouse
† J.A.S. Ritson
H. Berry 1T
W.A. Johns
† E.S. Scorfield
L.E. Barrington-Ward
† R.H.M. Hands
C.H. Pillman

v SCOTLAND

WON 14-5
Scotland: 1G
England: 1G 3T
Inverleith, 19 Mar 1910

W.R. Johnston

F.E. Chapman 1C
† F.M. Stoop
* J.G.G. Birkett 2T
† P.W. Lawrie

A.D. Stoop
A.L.H. Gotley

R. Dibble
J.A.S. Ritson 1T
H. Berry 1T
† G.R. Hind
L. Haigh
L.E. Barrington-Ward
R.H.M. Hands
C.H. Pillman

FACT FILE

- The championship title returned to England at last in 1910, the season in which Twickenham was first opened. The grounds had been acquired by the RFU in 1908 for £5,573 and there was a sensational start to the international there against Wales, England scoring from the kick-off. Their subsequent victory was the first against Wales since 1898.

FINAL TABLE

	P	W	D	L	F	A	Pts
England	**4**	**3**	**1**	**0**	**36**	**14**	**7**
Wales	4	3	0	1	88	28	6
Scotland	4	2	0	2	46	28	4
Ireland	4	1	1	2	11	36	3
France	4	0	0	4	20	95	0

1910-11

Five Nations Championship

v WALES

LOST 11-15
Wales: 1PG 4T
England: 1G 2T
St Helen's, 21 Jan 1911

† S.H. Williams

† A.D. Roberts 1T
† J.A. Scholfield 1T
* J.G.G. Birkett
D. Lambert 1C

A.D. Stoop
A.L.H. Gotley

R. Dibble
N.A. Wodehouse
A.L. Kewney 1T
† J.A. King
† W.E. Mann
L. Haigh
† L.G. Brown
C.H. Pillman

v FRANCE

WON 37-0
England: 5G 2PG 2T
France: Nil
Twickenham, 28 Jan 1911

S.H. Williams

A.D. Roberts
F.M. Stoop
* J.G.G. Birkett
D. Lambert 2T 2PG 5C

A.D. Stoop 1T
A.L.H. Gotley

R. Dibble
N.A. Wodehouse 1T
A.L. Kewney
J.A. King
W.E. Mann 1T
L. Haigh
L.G. Brown
C.H. Pillman 2T

v IRELAND

LOST 0-3
Ireland: 1T
England: Nil
Lansdowne Road, 11 Feb 1911

S.H. Williams

A.D. Roberts
F.M. Stoop
* J.G.G. Birkett
D. Lambert

A.D. Stoop
A.L.H. Gotley

G.R. Hind
N.A. Wodehouse
A.L. Kewney
J.A. King
W.E. Mann
L. Haigh
L.G. Brown
C.H. Pillman

v SCOTAND

WON 13-8
England: 2G 1T
Scotland: 1G 1T
Twickenham, 18 Mar 1911

S.H. Williams

A.D. Roberts
R.W. Poulton
J.G.G. Birkett 1T
P.W. Lawrie 1T

A.D. Stoop
* A.L.H. Gotley

R. Dibble
N.A. Wodehouse 1T
A.L. Kewney
J.A. King
† R.O. Lagden 2C
L. Haigh
L.G. Brown
C.H. Pillman

FACT FILE

- The biggest win of the season was over France, and Douglas Lambert, who had registered five tries against them in 1907, notched 22 points to create a record for points in an England international match. He kicked five conversions, two penalties and touched-down two tries.

FINAL TABLE

	P	W	D	L	F	A	Pts
Wales	4	4	0	0	78	21	8
Ireland	4	3	0	1	44	31	6
England	**4**	**2**	**0**	**2**	**61**	**26**	**4**
France	4	1	0	3	21	92	2
Scotland	4	0	0	4	43	77	0

1911-12

Five Nations Championship

v WALES

WON 8-0
England: 1G 1T
Wales: Nil
Twickenham, 20 Jan 1912

W.R. Johnston

F.E. Chapman 1C
R.W. Poulton
J.G.G. Birkett
† H. Brougham 1T

A.D. Stoop
† J.A. Pym 1T

* R. Dibble
N.A. Wodehouse
† A.H. MacIlwaine
J.A. King
† J.H. Eddison
† R.C. Stafford
† D. Holland
C.H. Pillman

v IRELAND

WON 15-0
England: 5T
Ireland: Nil
Twickenham, 10 Feb 1912

W.R. Johnston

A.D. Roberts 2T
R.W. Poulton 1T
J.G.G. Birkett 1T
H. Brougham 1T

H. Coverdale
J.A. Pym

* R. Dibble
N.A. Wodehouse
A.H. MacIlwaine
J.A. King
J.H. Eddison
R.C. Stafford
D. Holland
A.L. Kewney

v SCOTLAND

LOST 3-8
Scotland: 1G 1T
England: 1T
Inverleith, 16 Mar 1912

W.R. Johnston

A.D. Roberts
R.W. Poulton
J.G.G. Birkett
H. Brougham

A.D. Stoop
J.A. Pym

* R. Dibble
N.A. Wodehouse
A.H. MacIlwaine
J.A. King
J.H. Eddison
R.C. Stafford
D. Holland 1T
A.L. Kewney

v FRANCE

WON 18-8
France: 1G 1T
England: 1G 1DG 3T
Parc des Princes, 8 Apr 1912

W.R. Johnston

A.D. Roberts 1T
† M.E. Neale
J.G.G. Birkett 1T
H. Brougham 1T

H. Coverdale 1DG
J.A. Pym

J.A.S. Ritson
* N.A. Wodehouse
A.H. MacIlwaine
† W.B. Hynes
J.H. Eddison 1T
R.C. Stafford
† J.E. Greenwood
C.H. Pillman 1C

FACT FILE

- Dick Stafford, a teenager who played in all four matches this season, died of spinal cancer before the end of the year.

FINAL TABLE

	P	W	D	L	F	A	Pts
England	**4**	**3**	**0**	**1**	**44**	**16**	**6**
Ireland	4	3	0	1	33	34	6
Scotland	4	2	0	2	53	37	4
Wales	4	2	0	2	40	34	4
France	4	0	0	4	25	74	0

1912-13

Tour Match

v SOUTH AFRICA

LOST 3-9
England: 1T
SA: 2PG 1T
Twickenham, 4 Jan 1913

W.R. Johnston

† C.N. Lowe
F.M. Stoop
R.W.Poulton 1T
† V.H.M. Coates

† W.J.A. Davies
† W.I. Cheesman

J.A.S. Ritson
* N.A. Wodehouse
† S.E.J. Smart
J.A. King
L.G. Brown
A.L. Kewney
J.E. Greenwood
C.H. Pillman

Five Nations Championship

v WALES

WON 12-0
Wales: Nil
England: 1G 1DG 1T
Cardiff Arms Park, 18 Jan 1913

W.R. Johnston

C.N. Lowe
† F.E. Steinthal
R.W. Poulton 1DG
V.H.M. Coates 1T

W.J.A. Davies
W.I. Cheesman

J.A.S. Ritson
* N.A. Wodehouse
S.E.J. Smart
J.A. King
L.G. Brown
† G. Ward
J.E. Greenwood 1C
C.H. Pillman 1T

v FRANCE

WON 20-0
England: 1G 5T
France: Nil
Twickenham, 25 Jan 1913

W.R. Johnston

C.N. Lowe
F.E. Steinthal
R.W. Poulton 1T
V.H.M. Coates 3T

W.J.A. Davies
W.I. Cheesman

J.A.S. Ritson
* N.A. Wodehouse
S.E.J. Smart
J.A. King
L.G. Brown
G. Ward
J.E. Greenwood 1C
C.H. Pillman 2T

v IRELAND

WON 15-4
Ireland: 1DG
England: 1PG 4T
Lansdowne Road, 8 Feb 1913

W.R. Johnston

C.N. Lowe
† A.J. Dingle
R.W. Poulton
V.H.M. Coates 2T

W.J.A. Davies
W.I. Cheesman

J.A.S. Ritson 1T
* N.A. Wodehouse
S.E.J. Smart
J.A. King
L.G. Brown
† A.E. Kitching
J.E. Greenwood 1PG
C.H. Pillman 1T

v SCOTLAND

WON 3-0
England: 1T
Scotland: Nil
Twickenham, 15 Mar 1913

W.R. Johnston

C.N. Lowe
F.N. Tarr
R.W. Poulton
V.H.M. Coates

W.J.A. Davies
† F.E. Oakeley

J.A.S. Ritson
* N.A. Wodehouse
S.E.J. Smart
J.A. King
L.G. Brown 1T
G. Ward
J.E. Greenwood
C.H. Pillman

FACT FILE

- 1913 marks the true beginning of England's golden era in rugby football, an era which spanned the decade to 1924. Yet the run started with a defeat against the Second Springboks in an epic match best remembered for the cork-screwing runs of the brilliant English centre, Ronnie Poulton.
- The team was changed little for the Grand Slam, which started with England's first ever win at Cardiff.

FINAL TABLE

	P	W	D	L	F	A	Pts
England	**4**	**4**	**0**	**0**	**50**	**4**	**8**
Wales	4	3	0	1	35	33	6
Scotland	4	2	0	2	50	28	4
Ireland	4	1	0	3	55	60	2
France	4	0	0	4	11	76	0

1913-14

Five Nations Championship

v WALES

WON 10-9
England: 2G
Wales: 1G 1DG
Twickenham, 17 Jan 1914

W.R. Johnston

C.N. Lowe
F.E. Chapman 2C
* R.W. Poulton
† J.H.D. Watson

† F.M. Taylor
† G.W. Wood

† J. Brunton
† A.G. Bull
S.E.J. Smart
† A.F. Maynard
L.G. Brown 1T
G. Ward
J.E. Greenwood
C.H. Pillman 1T

v IRELAND

WON 17-12
England: 1G 4T
Ireland: 1DG 1G 1T
Twickenham, 14 Feb 1914

W.R. Johnston

C.N. Lowe 2T
F.E. Chapman 1C
* R.W. Poulton
A.D. Roberts 1T

W.J.A. Davies 1T
F.E. Oakeley

J. Brunton
H.C. Harrison
S.E.J. Smart
A.F. Maynard
L.G. Brown
G. Ward
† A.L. Harrison
C.H. Pillman 1T

v SCOTLAND

WON 16-15
Scotland: 1G 1DG 2T
England: 2G 2T
Inverleith, 21 Mar 1914

W.R. Johnston

C.N. Lowe 3T
J.H.D. Watson
* R.W. Poulton 1T
A.J. Dingle

W.J.A. Davies
F.E. Oakeley

J. Brunton
H.C. Harrison 2C
S.E.J. Smart
A.F. Maynard
L.G. Brown
G. Ward
J.E. Greenwood
C.H. Pillman

v FRANCE

WON 39-13
France: 2G 1T
England: 6G 3T
Stades Colombes, 13 Apr 1914

W.R. Johnston

C.N. Lowe 3T
J.H.D. Watson 1T
* R.W. Poulton 4T
A.J. Dingle

W.J.A. Davies 1T
F.E. Oakeley

† F. Le S. Stone
H.C. Harrison
S.E.J. Smart
† R.L. Pillman
L.G. Brown
A.L. Harrison
J.E. Greenwood 6C
† A.R.V. Sykes

FACT FILE

- The Triple Crown, championship and Grand Slam were again won by England in 1914.

FINAL TABLE

	P	W	D	L	F	A	Pts
England	**4**	**4**	**0**	**0**	**82**	**49**	**8**
Wales	4	3	0	1	75	18	6
Ireland	4	2	0	2	29	34	4
Scotland	3	0	0	3	20	46	0
France	3	0	0	3	19	78	0

Scotland and France did not meet

1919-20

Five Nations Championship

v WALES

LOST 5-19
Wales: 1G 2DG 1PG 1T
England: 1G
St Helen's, 17 Jan 1920

† B.S. Cumberlege

C.N. Lowe
† E.D.G. Hammett
† J.A. Krige
† H.L.V. Day 1T 1C

H. Coverdale
† C.A. Kershaw

S.E.J. Smart
† J.R. Morgan
† W.H.G. Wright
† G. Holford
† L.P.B. Merriam
† F.W. Mellish
† W.W. Wakefield
* J.E. Greenwood

v FRANCE

WON 8-3
England: 1G 1PG
France: 1T
Twickenham, 31 Jan 1920

† H. Millett

C.N. Lowe
E.D.G. Hammett
† A.M. Smallwood
† W.M. Lowry

W.J.A. Davies 1T
C.A. Kershaw

† F. Taylor
† G.S. Conway
W.H.G. Wright
G. Holford
L.P.B. Merriam
F.W. Mellish
W.W. Wakefield
* J.E. Greenwood 1PG 1C

v IRELAND

WON 14-11
Ireland: 1G 1PG 1T
England: 1G 3T
Lansdowne Road, 14 Feb 1920

B.S. Cumberlege

C.N. Lowe 1T
† E. Myers 1T
A.M. Smallwood
† S.W. Harris

W.J.A. Davies
C.A. Kershaw

F. Taylor
G.S. Conway
S.E.J. Smart
A.H. MacIlwaine
† A.T. Voyce
F.W. Mellish 1T
W.W. Wakefield 1T
* J.E. Greenwood 1C

v SCOTLAND

WON 13-4
England: 2G 1T
Scotland: 1DG
Twickenham, 20 Mar 1920

B.S. Cumberlege

C.N. Lowe 1T
E. Myers
E.D.G. Hammett
S.W. Harris 1T

W.J.A. Davies
C.A. Kershaw 1T

S.E.J. Smart
G.S. Conway
† T. Woods
† A.F. Blakiston
A.T. Voyce
F.W. Mellish
W.W. Wakefield
* J.E. Greenwood 2C

FACT FILE

- Wilfrid Lowry of Birkenhead Park had a rare experience at Swansea. He was actually photographed as a member of the team, only to be replaced at the last minute by Harold Day. The selectors felt that conditions were more suited to Day's style. Fortunately, Lowry did win his cap later in the season against France.

FINAL TABLE

	P	W	D	L	F	A	Pts
Wales	4	3	0	1	58	23	6
Scotland	4	3	0	1	37	18	6
England	**4**	**3**	**0**	**1**	**40**	**37**	**6**
France	4	1	0	3	23	26	2
Ireland	4	0	0	4	22	76	0

1920-21

Five Nations Championship

v WALES

WON 18-3
England: 1G 1DG 3T
Wales: 1T
Twickenham, 15 Jan 1921

B.S. Cumberlege

C.N. Lowe **1T**
E. Myers
E.D.G. Hammett **1C**
A.M. Smallwood **2T**

* W.J.A. Davies **1DG**
C.A. Kershaw **1T**

L.G. Brown
A.F. Blakiston
T. Woods
† R. Edwards
W.W. Wakefield
A.T. Voyce
F.W. Mellish
† E.R. Gardner

v IRELAND

WON 15-0
England: 1G 1DG 2T
Ireland: Nil
Twickenham, 12 Feb 1921

B.S. Cumberlege **1C**

C.N. Lowe **1DG 1T**
E. Myers
E.D.G. Hammett
A.M. Smallwood

* W.J.A. Davies
C.A. Kershaw

L.G. Brown **1T**
A.F. Blakiston **1T**
T. Woods
R. Edwards
W.W. Wakefield
A.T. Voyce
F.W. Mellish
E.R. Gardner

v SCOTLAND

WON 18-0
Scotland: Nil
England: 3G 1T
Inverleith, 19 Mar 1921

B.S. Cumberlege

C.N. Lowe
A.M. Smallwood
E.D.G. Hammett **3C**
† Q.E.M.A. King **1T**

* W.J.A. Davies
C.A. Kershaw

L.G. Brown **1T**
A.F. Blakiston
T. Woods **1T**
R. Edwards **1T**
W.W. Wakefield
A.T. Voyce
† R. Cove-Smith
E.R. Gardner

v FRANCE

WON 10-6
France: 2PG
England: 2G
Stade Colombes, 28 Mar 1921

B.S. Cumberlege

C.N. Lowe **1T**
† L.J. Corbett
E.D.G. Hammett **2C**
A.M. Smallwood

* W.J.A. Davies
C.A. Kershaw

L.G. Brown
A.F. Blakiston **1T**
T. Woods
R. Edwards
W.W. Wakefield
A.T. Voyce
R. Cove-Smith
G.S. Conway

FACT FILE

- The events of 1921 showed that England had recovered more quickly from the war than other Home Nations. The Grand Slam was won without difficulty and the XV was virtually unchanged during the season.

FINAL TABLE

	P	W	D	L	F	A	Pts
England	**4**	**4**	**0**	**0**	**61**	**9**	**8**
France	4	2	0	2	33	32	4
Wales	4	2	0	2	29	36	4
Scotland	4	1	0	3	22	38	2
Ireland	4	1	0	3	19	49	2

1921-22

Five Nations Championship

v WALES

LOST 6-28
Wales: 2G 6T
England: 2T
Cardiff Arms Park, 21 Jan 1922

B.S. Cumberlege

C.N. Lowe 1T
E. Myers
E.D.G. Hammett
H.L.V. Day 1T

† V.G. Davies
C.A. Kershaw

E.R. Gardner
† J.S. Tucker
* L.G. Brown
G.S. Conway
R. Edwards
A.T. Voyce
W.W. Wakefield
A.F. Blakiston

v IRELAND

WON 12-3
Ireland: 1T
England: 4T
Lansdowne Road, 11 Feb 1922

† R.C.W. Pickles

C.N. Lowe 1T
E. Myers
† M.S. Bradby
A.M. Smallwood 1T

* W.J.A. Davies
C.A. Kershaw

G.S. Conway
E.R. Gardner 1T
† R.F.H. Duncan
R. Cove-Smith
† J.E. Maxwell-Hyslop 1T
A.T. Voyce
W.W. Wakefield
† H.L. Price

v FRANCE

DRAWN 11-11
England: 1G 2PG
France: 1G 2T
Twickenham, 25 Feb 1922

R.C.W. Pickles

C.N. Lowe
E. Myers
M.S. Bradby
H.L.V. Day 1C 2PG

* W.J.A. Davies
C.A. Kershaw

G.S. Conway
E.R. Gardner
R.F.H. Duncan
R. Cove-Smith
J.E. Maxwell-Hyslop
A.T. Voyce 1T
W.W. Wakefield
R. Edwards

v SCOTLAND

WON 11-5
England: 1G 2T
Scotland: 1G
Twickenham, 18 Mar 1922

† J.A. Middleton

C.N. Lowe 2T
E. Myers
A.M. Smallwood
† I.J. Pitman

* W.J.A. Davies 1T
C.A. Kershaw

G.S. Conway 1C
† P.B. William-Powlett
R.F.H. Duncan
R. Cove-Smith
J.E. Maxwell-Hyslop
A.T. Voyce
W.W. Wakefield
H.L. Price

FACT FILE

- There was a lucky escape for England at Twickenham against France. The French were leading 11-6 in the closing minutes of the match when Harold Day was called upon to attempt a long penalty kick. His kick drifted across the face of the goal and Tom Voyce, following up rapidly as always, scored. Day converted to give England a draw and preserve the Twickenham ground record – England having avoided defeat in all championship matches there since 1910.

FINAL TABLE

	P	W	D	L	F	A	Pts
Wales	4	3	1	0	59	23	7
England	**4**	**2**	**1**	**1**	**40**	**47**	**5**
Scotland	4	1	2	1	23	26	4
France	4	0	2	2	20	33	2
Ireland	4	1	0	3	19	32	2

1922-23

Five Nations Championship

v WALES

WON 7-3
England: 1DG 1T
Wales: 1T
Twickenham, 20 Jan 1923

† F. Gilbert

C.N. Lowe
E. Myers
L.J. Corbett
A.M. Smallwood **1DG**

* W.J.A. Davies
C.A. Kershaw

E.R. Gardner
R. Edwards
† W.G.E. Luddington
W.W. Wakefield
R. Cove-Smith
A.T. Voyce
G.S. Conway
H.L. Price **1T**

v IRELAND

WON 23-5
England: 2G 1DG 3T
Ireland: 1G
Leicester, 10 Feb 1923

F. Gilbert

C.N. Lowe **1T**
E. Myers
L.J. Corbett **1T**
A.M. Smallwood **1T**

* W.J.A. Davies **1DG**
C.A. Kershaw

E.R. Gardner
† F.W. Sanders
W.G.E. Luddington
W.W. Wakefield
R. Cove-Smith
A.T. Voyce **1T**
G.S. Conway **2C**
H.L. Price **1T**

v SCOTLAND

WON 8-6
Scotland: 2T
England: 1G 1T
Inverleith, 17 Mar 1923

† T.E. Holliday

C.N. Lowe
E. Myers
† H.M. Locke
A.M. Smallwood **1T**

* W.J.A. Davies
C.A. Kershaw

E.R. Gardner
F.W. Sanders
W.G.E. Luddington **1C**
W.W. Wakefield
R. Cove-Smith
A.T. Voyce **1T**
G.S. Conway
A.F. Blakiston

v FRANCE

WON 12-3
France: 1PG
England: 1G 1DG 1T
Stade Colombes, 2 Apr 1923

T.E. Holliday

C.N. Lowe
E. Myers
H.M. Locke
A.M. Smallwood

* W.J.A. Davies **1DG**
C.A. Kershaw

E.R. Gardner
F.W. Sanders
W.G.E. Luddington **1C**
W.W. Wakefield **1T**
R. Cove-Smith
A.T. Voyce
G.S. Conway **1T**
A.F. Blakiston

FACT FILE

- The Grand Slam of 1923 was the final flourish for three of England's most famous players. Cecil Kershaw and 'Dave' Davies, the Navy halves, retired, and Cyril Lowe, the classic right wing, played the last of his 25 consecutive matches – setting a new record for England.
- In the Paris match, Davies, on his honeymoon too, dropped a goal with virtually his last kick as an international.

FINAL TABLE

	P	W	D	L	F	A	Pts
England	**4**	**4**	**0**	**0**	**50**	**17**	**8**
Scotland	4	3	0	1	46	22	6
Wales	4	1	0	3	31	31	2
France	4	1	0	3	28	52	2
Ireland	4	1	0	3	21	54	2

1923-24

Five Nations Championship

v WALES

WON **17-9**
Wales: 3T
England: 1G 4T
St Helen's, 19 Jan 1924

† B.S. Chantrill

† H.C. Catcheside **2T**
L.J. Corbett
H.M. Locke **1T**
† H.P. Jacob **1T**

E. Myers **1T**
† A.T. Young

R. Edwards
† A. Robson
W.G.E. Luddington
R. Cove-Smith
* W.W. Wakefield
A.F. Blakiston
G.S. Conway **1C**
A.T. Voyce

v IRELAND

WON **14-3**
Ireland: 1T
England: 1G 3T
Ravenhill, 9 Feb 1924

B.S. Chantrill

H.C. Catcheside **2T**
L.J. Corbett **1T**
H.P. Jacob
† R.H. Hamilton-Wickes **1T**

E. Myers
A.T. Young

† C.K.T. Faithfull
A. Robson
W.G.E. Luddington
R. Cove-Smith
* W.W. Wakefield
A.F. Blakiston
G.S. Conway **1C**
A.T. Voyce

v FRANCE

WON **19-7**
England: 2G 3T
France: 1DG 1T
Twickenham, 23 Feb1924

B.S. Chantrill

H.C. Catcheside **1T**
L.J. Corbett
H.M. Locke
H.P. Jacob **3T**

E. Myers
A.T. Young **1T**

R. Edwards
A. Robson
W.G.E. Luddington
R. Cove-Smith
* W.W. Wakefield
A.F. Blakiston
G.S. Conway **2C**
A.T. Voyce

v SCOTLAND

WON **19-0**
England: 3G 1DG
Scotland: Nil
Twickenham, 15 Mar 1924

B.S. Chantrill

H.C. Catcheside **1T**
L.J. Corbett
H.M. Locke
H.P. Jacob

E. Myers **1T 1DG**
A.T. Young

R. Edwards
A. Robson
W.G.E. Luddington
R. Cove-Smith
* W.W. Wakefield **1T**
A.F. Blakiston
G.S. Conway **3C**
A.T. Voyce

FACT FILE

- Despite the retirements of leading players, Wavell Wakefield led England to another Grand Slam in 1924.
- The match in Belfast remains England's only visit to the North of Ireland for an international.

FINAL TABLE

	P	W	D	L	F	A	Pts
England	**4**	**4**	**0**	**0**	**69**	**19**	**8**
Scotland	4	2	0	2	58	49	4
Ireland	4	2	0	2	30	37	4
Wales	4	1	0	3	39	71	2
France	4	1	0	3	25	45	2

1924-25

Tour Match

v NEW ZEALAND

LOST 11-17
England: 1G 1PG 1T
NZ: 1G 1PG 3T
Twickenham, 3 Jan 1925

† J.W. Brough

R.H. Hamilton-Wickes
V.G. Davies
L.J. Corbett **1PG**
† J.C. Gibbs

† H.J. Kittermaster **1T**
A.T. Young

R. Edwards
J.S. Tucker
† R.J. Hillard
* W.W. Wakefield
R. Cove-Smith **1T**
A.F. Blakiston
G.S. Conway **1C**
A.T. Voyce

Five Nations Championship

v WALES

WON 12-6
England: 1PG 3T
Wales: 2T
Twickenham, 17 Jan 1925

J.W. Brough

R.H. Hamilton-Wickes **1T**
H.M. Locke
L.J. Corbett
J.C. Gibbs

H.J. Kittermaster **1T**
† E.J. Massey

R. Cove-Smith
J.S. Tucker
† R. Armstrong **1PG**
A.F. Blakiston
W.G.E. Luddington
† H.G. Periton
* W.W. Wakefield
A.T. Voyce **1T**

v IRELAND

DRAWN 6-6
England: 2T
Ireland: 2T
Twickenham, 14 Feb 1925

T.E.Holliday

R.H.Hamilton-Wickes
H.M.Locke
L.J.Corbett
A.M.Smallwood **2T**

H.J.Kittermaster
E.J.Massey

R.Cove-Smith
J.S.Tucker
† R.G.Lawson
† R.R.F.MacLennan
W.G.E.Luddington
A.F.Blakiston
* W.W.Wakefield
A.T.Voyce

v SCOTLAND

LOST 11-14
Scotland: 2G 1DG
England: 1G 1PG 1T
Murrayfield, 21 Mar 1925

T.E. Holliday

R.H. Hamilton-Wickes **1T**
H.M. Locke
L.J. Corbett
A.M. Smallwood

E. Myers
E.J. Massey

R. Cove-Smith
J.S. Tucker
† D.C. Cumming
R.R.F. MacLennan
W.G.E. Luddington **1PG 1C**
A.F. Blakiston
* W.W. Wakefield **1T**
A.T. Voyce

v FRANCE

WON 13-11
France: 1G 2T
England: 2G 1GM
Stade Colombes, 13 Apr 1925

T.E. Holliday

R.H. Hamilton-Wickes **1T**
H.M. Locke
L.J. Corbett
† S.G.U. Considine

E. Myers
A.T. Young

R. Cove-Smith
J.S. Tucker
D.C. Cumming
R.R.F. MacLennan
W.G.E. Luddington **1GM 2C**
A.F. Blakiston
* W.W. Wakefield **1T**
A.T. Voyce

FACT FILE

- A record Twickenham attendance of 60,000 watched a fascinating match between the All Blacks, in their last match of an unbeaten tour, and England, the reigning Home Champions. The New Zealanders went out to a 14-point lead before Wakefield inspired his men to make a grand recovery and earn considerable honour in a brave defeat.

FINAL TABLE

	P	W	D	L	F	A	Pts
Scotland	4	4	0	0	77	37	8
Ireland	4	2	1	1	42	26	5
England	**4**	**2**	**1**	**1**	**42**	**37**	**5**
Wales	4	1	0	3	34	60	2
France	4	0	0	4	23	58	0

1925-26

Five Nations Championship

v WALES

DRAWN 3-3
Wales: 1T
England: 1T
Cardiff Arms Park, 16 Jan 1926

H.C. Catcheside

† H.C. Burton
† A.R. Aslett
† T.E.S. Francis
R.H. Hamilton-Wickes

H.J. Kittermaster
† J.R.B. Worton

† R.J. Hanvey
J.S. Tucker
† E. Stanbury
A. Robson
W.G.E. Luddington
H.G. Periton
* W.W. Wakefield 1T
A.T. Voyce

v IRELAND

LOST 15-19
Ireland: 2G 1PG 2T
England: 3G
Lansdowne Road, 13 Feb 1926

H.C. Catcheside

R.H. Hamilton-Wickes
A.R. Aslett
T.E.S. Francis 3C
† Sir T.G. Devitt

H.J. Kittermaster
A.T. Young 1T

R.J. Hanvey
J.S. Tucker
E. Stanbury
† L.W. Haslett 1T
† W.E. Tucker
H.G. Periton 1T
* W.W. Wakefield
A.T. Voyce

v FRANCE

WON 11-0
England: 1G 2T
France: Nil
Twickenham, 27 Feb 1926

T.E. Holliday

Sir T.G. Devitt
A.R. Aslett 2T
T.E.S. Francis 1C
J.C. Gibbs

H.J. Kittermaster 1T
A.T. Young

R.J. Hanvey
J.S. Tucker
C.K.T. Faithfull
L.W. Haslett
† J.W.G. Webb
H.G. Periton
* W.W. Wakefield
A.T. Voyce

v SCOTLAND

LOST 9-17
England: 3T
Scotland: 2G 1DG 1T
Twickenham, 20 Mar 1926

T.E. Holliday

R.H. Hamilton-Wickes
A.R. Aslett
T.E.S. Francis
H.L.V. Day

H.J. Kittermaster
A.T. Young

R.J. Hanvey
J.S. Tucker 1T
C.K.T. Faithfull
E. Stanbury
J.W.G. Webb 1T
H.G. Periton
* W.W. Wakefield
A.T. Voyce 1T

FACT FILE

- The King was present to see Scotland become the first country to win a championship match at Twickenham.

FINAL TABLE

	P	W	D	L	F	A	Pts
Scotland	4	3	0	1	45	23	6
Ireland	4	3	0	1	41	26	6
Wales	4	2	1	1	26	24	5
England	**4**	**1**	**1**	**2**	**38**	**39**	**3**
France	4	0	0	4	11	49	0

1926-27

Five Nations Championship

v WALES

WON 11-9
England: 1G 1GM 1PG
Wales: 1PG 2T
Twickenham, 15 Jan 1927

† K.A. Sellar

R.H. Hamilton-Wickes
* L.J. Corbett 1GM 1T
H.M. Locke
J.C. Gibbs

† H.C.C. Laird
J.R.B. Worton

E. Stanbury 1C 1PG
J.S. Tucker
R. Cove-Smith
G.S. Conway
† K.J. Stark
H.G. Periton
† T. Coulson
† J. Hanley

v IRELAND

WON 8-6
England: 1G 1T
Ireland: 1PG 1T
Twickenham, 12 Feb 1927

K.A. Sellar

H.C. Catcheside
* L.J. Corbett
H.M. Locke
J.C. Gibbs 1T

H.C.C. Laird 1T
A.T. Young

E. Stanbury 1C
J.S. Tucker
R. Cove-Smith
† D.E. Law
K.J. Stark
H.G. Periton
† W.C.T. Eyres
† P.H. Davies

v SCOTLAND

LOST 13-21
Scotland: 1G 1DG 4T
England: 2G 1PG
Murrayfield, 19 Mar 1927

K.A. Sellar

H.C. Catcheside
* L.J. Corbett
H.M. Locke
J.C. Gibbs 1T

H.C.C. Laird 1T
A.T. Young

E. Stanbury 1C
J.S. Tucker
R. Cove-Smith
† W.E. Pratten
K.J. Stark 1PG 1C
H.G. Periton
W.W. Wakefield
J. Hanley

v FRANCE

LOST 0-3
France: 1T
England: Nil
Stade Colombes, 2 Apr 1927

† J.N.S. Wallens

† W. Alexander
* L.J. Corbett
† R.A. Buckingham
J.C. Gibbs

† C.C. Bishop
A.T. Young

E. Stanbury
J.S. Tucker
R. Cove-Smith
W.E. Pratten
K.J. Stark
H.G. Periton
W.W. Wakefield
J. Hanley

FACT FILE

- In the Welsh match Colin Laird became England's youngest player, aged just 18 years and 134 days.

FINAL TABLE

	P	W	D	L	F	A	Pts
Scotland	4	3	0	1	49	25	6
Ireland	4	3	0	1	39	20	6
England	**4**	**2**	**0**	**2**	**32**	**39**	**4**
Wales	4	1	0	3	43	42	2
France	4	1	0	3	19	56	2

1927-28

Tour Match

v NEW SOUTH WALES

WON 18-11
England: 3G 1T
NSW: 1G 2T
Twickenham, 7 Jan 1928

K.A. Sellar

† W.J. Taylor 1T
† C.D. Aarvold
† J.V. Richardson 3C
Sir T.G. Devitt

H.C.C. Laird 1T
A.T. Young

E. Stanbury
J.S. Tucker 1T
* R. Cove-Smith
† D. Turquand-Young
K.J. Stark
† T.M. Lawson
T. Coulson
H.G. Periton 1T

Five Nations Championship

v WALES

WON 10-8
Wales: 1G 1T
England: 2G
St Helen's, 21 Jan 1928

K.A. Sellar

W.J. Taylor 1T
C.D. Aarvold
J.V. Richardson 2C
Sir T.G. Devitt

H.C.C. Laird 1T
A.T. Young

E. Stanbury
J.S. Tucker
* R. Cove-Smith
D. Turquand-Young
K.J. Stark
T.M. Lawson
T. Coulson
J. Hanley

v IRELAND

WON 7-6
Ireland: 2T
England: 1DG 1T
Lansdowne Road, 11 Feb 1928

K.A.Sellar

W.J.Taylor
C.D.Aarvold
J.V.Richardson 1DG, 1T
† G.V.Palmer

H.C.C.Laird
A.T.Young

E.Stanbury
J.S.Tucker
† R.H.W.Sparks
* R.Cove-Smith
K.J.Stark
H.G.Periton
† F.D.Prentice
J.Hanley

v FRANCE

WON 18-8
England: 3G 1T
France: 1G 1T
Twickenham, 25 Feb 1928

K.A. Sellar

W.J. Taylor
C.D. Aarvold
J.V. Richardson 3C
G.V. Palmer 2T

H.C.C. Laird
A.T. Young

E. Stanbury
J.S. Tucker
R.H.W. Sparks
* R. Cove-Smith
K.J. Stark
H.G. Periton 2T
F.D. Prentice
J. Hanley

v SCOTLAND

WON 6-0
England: 2T
Scotland: Nil
Twickenham, 17 Mar 1928

† T.W. Brown

W.J. Taylor
C.D. Aarvold
J.V. Richardson
G.V. Palmer

H.C.C. Laird 1T
A.T. Young

E. Stanbury
J.S. Tucker
R.H.W. Sparks
* R. Cove-Smith
K. J.Stark
H.G. Periton
F.D. Prentice
J. Hanley 1T

FACT FILE

- England, with a young back division prepared to play open rugby, enjoyed a triumphant season, recording five wins in five matches for the first time in their history.

FINAL TABLE

	P	W	D	L	F	A	Pts
England	**4**	**4**	**0**	**0**	**41**	**22**	**8**
Ireland	4	3	0	1	44	30	6
Wales	4	1	0	3	34	31	2
France	4	1	0	3	30	48	2
Scotland	4	1	0	3	20	38	2

1928-29

Five Nations Championship

v WALES

WON 8-3
England: 1G 1T
Wales: 1T
Twickenham, 19 Jan 1929

T.W. Brown

† R.W. Smeddle
C.D. Aarvold
† G.M. Sladen
† G.S. Wilson 1C

H.C.C. Laird
† H. Whitley

E. Stanbury
J.S. Tucker
† R.T. Foulds
* R. Cove-Smith
† J.W.R. Swayne
H.G. Periton
R.H.W. Sparks
† H. Wilkinson 2T

v IRELAND

LOST 5-6
England: 1G
Ireland: 2T
Twickenham, 9 Feb 1929

T.W. Brown

R.W. Smeddle 1T
C.D. Aarvold
G.M. Sladen
G.S. Wilson 1C

H.C.C. Laird
A.T. Young

E. Stanbury
J.S. Tucker
R.T. Foulds
* R. Cove-Smith
D. Turquand-Young
H.G. Periton
R.H.W. Sparks
H. Wilkinson

v SCOTLAND

LOST 6-12
Scotland: 4T
England: 2T
Murrayfield, 16 Mar 1929

T.W. Brown

R.W. Smeddle
A.R. Aslett
G.M. Sladen
† A.L. Novis 1T

† S.S.C. Meikle 1T
† E.E. Richards

E. Stanbury
† T. Harris
† H. Rew
J.W.G. Webb
D. Turquand-Young
* H.G. Periton
R.H.W. Sparks
H. Wilkinson

v FRANCE

WON 16-6
France: 2T
England: 2G 2T
Stade Colombes, 1 Apr 1929

T.W. Brown

C.D. Aarvold 2T
A.R. Aslett
A.L. Novis
† J.S.R. Reeve

† R.S. Spong
E.E. Richards

E. Stanbury 2C
J.S. Tucker
H. Rew
† S.A. Martindale
D. Turquand-Young
* H.G. Periton 1T
† C.H.A. Gummer 1T
† E. Coley

FACT FILE

- Tom Brown of Bristol was the only member of the back division to retain his place. In November 1933 he joined Broughton Rangers rugby league team for a considerable sum, regretted his decision immediately after and returned his cheque. The RFU refused to reinstate him.

FINAL TABLE

	P	W	D	L	F	A	Pts
Scotland	4	3	0	1	41	30	6
Wales	4	2	1	1	30	23	5
Ireland	4	2	1	1	24	26	5
England	**4**	**2**	**0**	**2**	**35**	**27**	**4**
France	4	0	0	4	12	36	0

1929-30

Five Nations Championship

v WALES

WON 11-3
Wales: 1T
England: 1G 1PG 1T
Cardiff Arms Park, 18 Jan 1930

† J.G. Askew

A.L. Novis
† F.W.S. Malir
† M. Robson
J.S.R. Reeve 2T

R.S. Spong
† W.H. Sobey

† D.A. Kendrew
J.S. Tucker
† A.H. Bateson
† B.H. Black 1PG 1C
† J.W. Forrest
W.E. Tucker
† P.D. Howard
* H.G. Periton

v IRELAND

LOST 3-4
Ireland: 1DG
England: 1T
Lansdowne Road, 8 Feb 1930

J.G. Askew

A.L. Novis 1T
F.W.S. Malir
M. Robson
J.S.R. Reeve

R.S. Spong
† A. Key

D.A. Kendrew
J.S. Tucker
A.H. Bateson
B.H. Black
J.W. Forrest
W.E. Tucker
P.D. Howard
* H.G. Periton

v FRANCE

WON 11-5
England: 1G 2T
France: 1G
Twickenham, 22 Feb 1930

J.G. Askew

J.S.R. Reeve 1T
A.L. Novis
M. Robson 1T
H.P. Jacob

R.S. Spong
W.H. Sobey

H. Rew
* J.S. Tucker
A.H. Bateson
B.H. Black 1C
J.W. Forrest
H. Wilkinson
P.D. Howard
H.G. Periton 1T

v SCOTLAND

DRAWN 0-0
England: Nil
Scotland: Nil
Twickenham, 15 Mar 1930

† J.C. Hubbard

† C.C. Tanner
F.W.S. Malir
M. Robson
J.S.R. Reeve

R.S. Spong
W.H. Sobey

H. Rew
* J.S. Tucker
A.H. Bateson
B.H. Black
J.W. Forrest
† P.W.P. Brook
P.D. Howard
H.G. Periton

FACT FILE

- Sam Tucker made a frantic dash by aeroplane across the Bristol Channel on the morning of the Cardiff match to lead a young and relatively inexperienced pack. England's victory was their first at the Arms Park since 1913, and only their second since the first visit back in 1893.

FINAL TABLE

	P	W	D	L	F	A	Pts
England	**4**	**2**	**1**	**1**	**25**	**12**	**5**
Wales	4	2	0	2	35	30	4
Ireland	4	2	0	2	25	31	4
France	4	2	0	2	17	25	4
Scotland	4	1	1	2	26	30	3

1930-31

Five Nations Championship

v WALES

DRAWN 11-11
England: 1G 2PG
Wales: 1G 1GM 1T
Twickenham, 17 Jan 1931

† L.L. Bedford

J.S.R. Reeve
† D.W. Burland 1T 1C
† M.A. McCanlis
C.D. Aarvold

† T.J.M. Barrington
† E.B. Pope

H. Rew
* J.S. Tucker
† M.S. Bonaventura
B.H. Black 2PG
J.W. Forrest
† D.H. Swayne
P.D. Howard
† R.F. Davey

v IRELAND

LOST 5-6
England: 1G
Ireland: 1PG 1T
Twickenham, 14 Feb 1931

L.L. Bedford

J.S.R. Reeve
D.W. Burland
M.A. McCanlis
† A.C. Harrison

T.J.M. Barrington
† G.J. Dean

† P.C. Hordern
R.H.W. Sparks
† G.G. Gregory
B.H. Black 1T 1C
J.W. Forrest
* P.D. Howard
† E.H. Harding
† P.E. Dunkley

v SCOTLAND

LOST 19-28
Scotland: 5G 1T
England: 2G 1PG 2T
Murrayfield, 21 Mar 1931

† E.C.P. Whiteley

J.S.R. Reeve 2T
† J.A. Tallent 2T
* C.D. Aarvold
A.C. Harrison

† T.C. Knowles
E.B. Pope

R.H.W. Sparks
G.G. Gregory
H. Rew
B.H. Black 2C 1PG
J.W. Forrest
P.C. Hordern
P.D. Howard
P.E. Dunkley

v FRANCE

LOST 13-14
France: 2DG 2T
England: 2G 1T
Stade Colombes, 6 Apr 1931

E.C.P. Whiteley

R.W. Smeddle 1T
J.A. Tallent 1T
D.W. Burland 1T
* C.D. Aarvold

R.S. Spong
E.B. Pope

R.H.W. Sparks
G.G. Gregory
H. Rew
B.H. Black 1C
J.W. Forrest 1C
P.C. Hordern
P.D. Howard
P.W.P. Brook

FACT FILE

- Lack of penetration in midfield and an inexperienced pack hampered England this season, and for the first time since the French had become regular opponents, not a single match of the four played was won.

FINAL TABLE

	P	W	D	L	F	A	Pts
Wales	4	3	1	0	74	25	7
Scotland	4	2	0	2	47	44	4
France	4	2	0	2	24	44	4
Ireland	4	2	0	2	17	28	4
England	**4**	**0**	**1**	**3**	**38**	**59**	**1**

1931-32

Tour Match

v SOUTH AFRICA

LOST 0-7
England: Nil
SA: 1DG 1T
Twickenham, 2 Jan 1932

† R.J. Barr

C.C. Tanner
J.A. Tallent
† R.A. Gerrard
* C.D. Aarvold

R.S. Spong
W.H. Sobey

† A.D. Carpenter
† D.J. Norman
G.G. Gregory
† C.S.H. Webb
† R.G.S. Hobbs
† L.E. Saxby
† A.J. Rowley
† J.M. Hodgson

Four Nations Championship

v WALES

LOST 5-12
Wales: 1G 1DG 1PG
England: 1G
St Helen's, 16 Jan 1932

R.J. Barr 1C

C.C. Tanner
R.A. Gerrard
J.A. Tallent
* C.D. Aarvold

R.S. Spong
W.H. Sobey

† N.L. Evans
D.J. Norman
G.G. Gregory
C.S.H. Webb
R.G.S. Hobbs
L.E. Saxby
E. Coley 1T
J.M. Hodgson

v IRELAND

WON 11-8
Ireland: 1G 1PG
England: 1G 2PG
Lansdowne Road, 13 Feb 1932

R.J. Barr

C.C. Tanner
D.W. Burland 1T 1C 2PG
R.A. Gerrard
* C.D. Aarvold

† W. Elliot
† B.C. Gadney

N.L. Evans
† R.S. Roberts
G.G. Gregory
C.S.H. Webb
R.G.S. Hobbs
† A. Vaughan-Jones
T. Harris
J.M. Hodgson

v SCOTLAND

WON 16-3
England: 2G 2T
Scotland: 1T
Twickenham, 19 Mar 1932

T.W. Brown

C.C. Tanner 1T
D.W. Burland 2C
R.A. Gerrard
* C.D. Aarvold 2T

W. Elliot
B.C. Gadney

N.L. Evans
G.G. Gregory
† R.J. Longland
C.S.H. Webb
R.G.S. Hobbs
A. Vaughan-Jones
B.H. Black 1T
J.M. Hodgson

FACT FILE

- Ray Longland made his debut this season. He won 19 caps during the 1930s, ranking as the outstanding English prop of the decade. But for the war and the banishment of the French he would surely have set a new England cap record.

FINAL TABLE

	P	W	D	L	F	A	Pts
Ireland	3	2	0	1	40	29	4
Wales	3	2	0	1	28	17	4
England	**3**	**2**	**0**	**1**	**32**	**23**	**4**
Scotland	3	0	0	3	11	42	0

1932-33

Four Nations Championship

v WALES

LOST 3-7
England: 1T
Wales: 1DG 1T
Twickenham, 21 Jan 1933

T.W. Brown

† L.A. Booth
D.W. Burland
R.A. Gerrard
* C.D. Aarvold

W. Elliot 1T
A. Key

N.L. Evans
G.G. Gregory
R.J. Longland
C.S.H. Webb
† A.D.S. Roncoroni
A. Vaughan-Jones
B.H. Black
† R. Bolton

v IRELAND

WON 17-6
England: 1G 4T
Ireland: 1PG 1T
Twickenham, 11 Feb 1933

T.W. Brown

L.A. Booth 1T
D.W. Burland
R.A. Gerrard
* A.L. Novis 2T

W. Elliot
B.C.Gadney 1T

N.L. Evans
G.G. Gregory
D.A. Kendrew 1C
C.S.H. Webb
A.D.S. Roncoroni
† W.H. Weston
† C.L. Troop
† E.H. Sadler 1T

v SCOTLAND

LOST 0-3
Scotland: 1T
England: Nil
Murrayfield, 18 Mar 1933

T.W. Brown

L.A. Booth
D.W. Burland
R.A. Gerrard
* A.L. Novis

W. Elliot
B.C. Gadney

R.J. Longland
G.G. Gregory
D.A. Kendrew
C.S.H. Webb
A.D.S. Roncoroni
W.H. Weston
C.L. Troop
E.H. Sadler

FACT FILE

- England lacked the speed and cleverness to press for the title in 1933. Poor backing-up deprived them of a win over a young Welsh side at Twickenham.
- It was the first time (and at the tenth attempt) that Wales had won at Twickenham.

FINAL TABLE

	P	W	D	L	F	A	Pts
Scotland	3	3	0	0	22	9	6
Ireland	3	1	0	2	22	30	2
England	**3**	**1**	**0**	**2**	**20**	**16**	**2**
Wales	3	1	0	2	15	24	2

1933-34

Four Nations Championship

v WALES

WON 9-0
Wales: Nil
England: 3T
Cardiff Arms Park, 20 Jan 1934

† H.G. Owen-Smith

† A.L. Warr 1T
† P. Cranmer
R.A. Gerrard
† G.W.C. Meikle 2T

W. Elliot
* B.C. Gadney

R.J. Longland
G.G. Gregory
H. Rew
† J.C. Wright
† J. Dicks
J.M. Hodgson
P.C. Hordern
† H.A. Fry

v IRELAND

WON 13-3
Ireland: 1T
England: 2G 1T
Lansdowne Road, 10 Feb 1934

H.G. Owen-Smith

A.L. Warr
P. Cranmer
R.A. Gerrard
G.W.C. Meikle 1T

W. Elliot
* B.C. Gadney

R.J. Longland
G.G. Gregory 2C
H. Rew
J.W. Forrest
J. Dicks
W.H. Weston
J.M. Hodgson
H.A. Fry 2T

v SCOTLAND

WON 6-3
England: 2T
Scotland: 1T
Twickenham, 17 Mar 1934

H.G. Owen-Smith

L.A. Booth 1T
P. Cranmer
R.A. Gerrard
G.W.C. Meikle 1T

† C.F. Slow
* B.C. Gadney

R.J. Longland
G.G. Gregory
H. Rew
J.W. Forrest
J. Dicks
W.H. Weston
D.A. Kendrew
H.A. Fry

Allan Clarke, on his debut, beats Harry Truman of Wales during a line-out at Twickenham in 1935.

FACT FILE

- This was England's year. After routing the Welsh pack at Cardiff, England were clearly the better side in Dublin after an anxious opening quarter, and defeated Scotland (though not without some desperately narrow squeaks in the closing stages) to take the Triple Crown for the first time since 1928.

FINAL TABLE

	P	W	D	L	F	A	Pts
England	**3**	**3**	**0**	**0**	**28**	**6**	**6**
Wales	3	2	0	1	26	15	4
Scotland	3	1	0	2	25	28	2
Ireland	3	0	0	3	12	42	0

1934-35

Four Nations Championship

v WALES

DRAWN 3-3
England: 1PG
Wales: 1T
Twickenham, 19 Jan 1935

† H. Boughton **1PG**

L.A. Booth
P. Cranmer
† J. Heaton
† R. Leyland

† P.L. Candler
† J.L. Giles

R.J. Longland
† E.S. Nicholson
* D.A. Kendrew
† A.J. Clarke
J. Dicks
† A.G. Cridlan
† D.T. Kemp
W.H. Weston

v IRELAND

WON 14-3
England: 1G 3PG
Ireland: 1T
Twickenham, 9 Feb 1935

H. Boughton **3PG 1C**

L.A. Booth
J. Heaton
R. Leyland
P. Cranmer

J.A. Tallent
J.L. Giles **1T**

R.J. Longland
E.S. Nicholson
* D.A. Kendrew
A.J. Clarke
J. Dicks
A.G. Cridlan
† A.T. Payne
W.H. Weston

v SCOTLAND

LOST 7-10
Scotland: 2G
England: 1DG 1T
Murrayfield, 16 Mar 1935

H. Boughton

L.A. Booth **1T**
P. Cranmer **1DG**
J. Heaton
R. Leyland

† J.R. Auty
* B.C. Gadney

R.J. Longland
E.S. Nicholson
C.S.H. Webb
A.J. Clarke
J. Dicks
A.G. Cridlan
A.T. Payne
W.H. Weston

FACT FILE

- England were saved from the wooden spoon in 1935 by the kicking of Harold Boughton. His penalty tied the match with Wales and his four successful goal kicks against the Irish proved the difference between the sides.
- Only one try was scored by an English three-quarter during the season: the worst return since 1905.

FINAL TABLE

	P	W	D	L	F	A	Pts
Ireland	3	2	0	1	24	22	4
England	**3**	**1**	**1**	**1**	**24**	**16**	**3**
Wales	3	1	1	1	16	18	3
Scotland	3	1	0	2	21	29	2

1935-36

Tour Match

v NEW ZEALAND

WON 13-0
England: 1DG 3T
NZ: Nil
Twickenham, 4 Jan 1936

H.G. Owen-Smith

† A. Obolensky 2T
R.A. Gerrard
P. Cranmer 1DG
† H.S. Sever 1T

P.L. Candler
* B.C. Gadney

R.J. Longland
E.S. Nicholson
D.A. Kendrew
A.J. Clarke
C.S.H. Webb
W.H. Weston
P.E. Dunkley
† E.A. Hamilton-Hill

Four Nations Championship

v WALES

DRAWN 0-0
Wales: Nil
England: Nil
St Helen's, 18 Jan 1936

H.G. Owen-Smith

A. Obolensky
R.A. Gerrard
P. Cranmer
H.S. Sever

P.L. Candler
* B.C. Gadney

R.J. Longland
E.S. Nicholson
D.A. Kendrew
A.J. Clarke
C.S.H. Webb
W.H. Weston
P.E. Dunkley
E.A. Hamilton-Hill

v IRELAND

LOST 3-6
Ireland: 2T
England: 1T
Lansdowne Road, 8 Feb 1936

H.G. Owen-Smith

A. Obolensky
R.A. Gerrard
P. Cranmer
H.S. Sever 1T

P.L. Candler
* B.C. Gadney

R.J. Longland
D.A. Kendrew
† H.F. Wheatley
A.J. Clarke
C.S.H. Webb
J.M. Hodgson
P.E. Dunkley
E.A. Hamilton-Hill

v SCOTLAND

WON 9-8
England: 3T
Scotland: 1G 1PG
Twickenham, 21 Mar 1936

H.G. Owen-Smith

A. Obolensky
R.A. Gerrard
P. Cranmer 1T
H.S. Sever

P.L. Candler 1T
* B.C. Gadney

R.J. Longland
† H.B. Toft
J. Dicks
P.E. Dunkley
C.S.H. Webb
W.H. Weston
P.W.P. Brook
R. Bolton 1T

FACT FILE

- In 1936 a young Russian prince named Alex Obolensky earned eternal fame with two spectacular tries as a crowd of 73,000 saw the All Blacks beaten by a solid pack. It is a pecularity of rugby history that Obolensky should create such a name for himself and yet play in only four international matches. Obolensky continued playing club rugby until he was killed in a flying training accident in Norfolk in March 1940. But his tries against the All Blacks will never be forgotten.

FINAL TABLE

	P	W	D	L	F	A	Pts
Wales	3	2	1	0	16	3	5
Ireland	3	2	0	1	16	10	4
England	**3**	**1**	**1**	**1**	**12**	**14**	**3**
Scotland	3	0	0	3	15	32	0

1936-37

Four Nations Championship

v WALES

WON 4-3
England: 1DG
Wales: 1T
Twickenham, 16 Jan 1937

* H.G.Owen-Smith

† A.G. Butler
P.L. Candler
P. Cranmer
H.S. Sever 1DG

† T.A. Kemp
J.L. Giles

R.J. Longland
H.B. Toft
† R.E. Prescott
† A. Wheatley
† T.F. Huskisson
W.H. Weston
† D.L.K. Milman
† D.A. Campbell

v IRELAND

WON 9-8
England: 1PG 2T
Ireland: 1G 1T
Twickenham, 13 Feb 1937

* H.G.Owen-Smith

A.G. Butler 1T
P.L. Candler
P. Cranmer 1PG
H.S. Sever 1T

T.A. Kemp
J.L. Giles

R.J. Longland
H.B. Toft
R.E. Prescott
A. Wheatley
T.F. Huskisson
W.H. Weston
J. Dicks
D.A. Campbell

v SCOTLAND

WON 6-3
Scotland: 1PG
England: 2T
Murrayfield, 20 Mar 1937

* H.G. Owen-Smith

† E.J. Unwin 1T
P.L. Candler
P. Cranmer
H.S. Sever 1T

† F.J. Reynolds
B.C. Gadney

R.J. Longland
H.B. Toft
H.F. Wheatley
A. Wheatley
T.F. Huskisson
W.H. Weston
† J.G. Cook
R. Bolton

FACT FILE

- England regained the Triple Crown in 1937, cheerful full-back and former South African Test cricketer 'Tuppy' Owen-Smith leading the side to three narrow victories. The pack was the best in the championship and Toft proved to be the most skilful hooker in British rugby this season.

FINAL TABLE

	P	W	D	L	F	A	Pts
England	**3**	**3**	**0**	**0**	**19**	**14**	**6**
Ireland	3	2	0	1	24	16	4
Scotland	3	1	0	2	20	23	2
Wales	3	0	0	3	12	22	0

1937-38

Four Nations Championship

v WALES

LOST 8-14
Wales: 1G 2PG 1T
England: 1G 1T
Cardiff Arms Park, 15 Jan 1938

† H.D. Freakes 1C

E.J. Unwin
* P. Cranmer
† B.E. Nicholson
H.S. Sever 1T

P.L. Candler 1T
B.C. Gadney

R.J. Longland
H.B. Toft
H.F. Wheatley
A. Wheatley
T.F. Huskisson
W.H. Weston
D.L.K. Milman
R. Bolton

v IRELAND

WON 36-14
Ireland: 1G 3T
England: 6G 1PG 1T
Lansdowne Road, 12 Feb 1938

† G.W. Parker 6C 1PG

E.J. Unwin 1T
* P. Cranmer
B.E. Nicholson 1T
H.S. Sever

F.J. Reynolds 1T
J.L. Giles 1T

R.J. Longland
H.B. Toft
R.E. Prescott 1T
† R.M. Marshall 1T
T.F. Huskisson
W.H. Weston
D.L.K. Milman
R. Bolton 1T

v SCOTLAND

LOST 16-21
England: 1DG 3PG 1T
Scotland: 2PG 5T
Twickenham, 19 Mar 1938

G.W. Parker 3PG

E.J. Unwin 1T
P. Cranmer
P.L. Candler
H.S. Sever

F.J. Reynolds 1DG
J.L. Giles

R.J. Longland
* H.B. Toft
H.F. Wheatley
R.M. Marshall
A. Wheatley
W.H. Weston
D.L.K. Milman
† A.A. Brown

FACT FILE

- England's score of 36 points against Ireland was their highest in an international between the wars, and Grahame Parker's six conversions equalled the England match record.

FINAL TABLE

	P	W	D	L	F	A	Pts
Scotland	3	3	0	0	52	36	6
Wales	3	2	0	1	31	21	4
England	**3**	**1**	**0**	**2**	**60**	**49**	**2**
Ireland	3	0	0	3	33	70	0

1938-39

Four Nations Championship

v WALES

WON 3-0
England: 1T
Wales: Nil
Twickenham, 21 Jan 1939

H.D. Freakes

† R.H. Guest
J. Heaton
† G.E. Hancock
† R.S.L. Carr

† G.A. Walker
† P. Cooke

R.E. Prescott
* H.B. Toft
† D.E. Teden 1T
T.F. Huskisson
H.F. Wheatley
† J.T.W. Berry
R.M. Marshall
† J.K. Watkins

v IRELAND

LOST 0-5
England: Nil
Ireland: 1G
Twickenham, 11 Feb 1939

H.D. Freakes

R.H. Guest
J. Heaton
G.E. Hancock
R.S.L. Carr

G.A. Walker
P. Cooke

R.E. Prescott
* H.B. Toft
D.E. Teden
T.F. Huskisson
H.F. Wheatley
J.T.W. Berry
R.M. Marshall
J.K. Watkins

v SCOTLAND

WON 9-6
Scotland: 2T
England: 3PG
Murrayfield, 18 Mar 1939

† E.I. Parsons

R.H. Guest
J. Heaton 3PG
G.E. Hancock
R.S.L. Carr

T.A. Kemp
† J. Ellis

R.E. Prescott
* H.B. Toft
D.E. Teden
T.F. Huskisson
H.F. Wheatley
J.T.W. Berry
R.M. Marshall
J.K. Watkins

FACT FILE

- In the last full international played before the war, England won a dour struggle at Murrayfield, thanks to some magnificent place-kicking by Jack Heaton. His three penalties equalled the England record. After the war Heaton returned to captain England.

FINAL TABLE

	P	W	D	L	F	A	Pts
Wales	3	2	0	1	18	6	4
Ireland	3	2	0	1	17	10	4
England	**3**	**2**	**0**	**1**	**12**	**11**	**4**
Scotland	3	0	0	3	12	32	0

1946-47

Five Nations Championship

v WALES

WON 9-6
Wales: 2T
England: 1G 1DG
Cardiff Arms Park, 18 Jan 1947

† A. Gray 1C

R.H. Guest
† N.O. Bennett
† E.K. Scott
† D.W. Swarbrick

† N.M. Hall 1DG
† W.K.T. Moore

† G.A. Kelly
† A.P. Henderson
† H.W. Walker
†* J. Mycock
† S.V. Perry
† M.R. Steele-Bodger
† B.H. Travers
† D.F. White 1T

v IRELAND

LOST 0-22
Ireland: 2G 1PG 3T
England: Nil
Lansdowne Road, 8 Feb 1947

A. Gray

R.H. Guest
J. Heaton
† M.P. Donnelly
D.W. Swarbrick

N.M. Hall
W.K.T. Moore

G.A. Kelly
A.P. Henderson
H.W. Walker
* J. Mycock
S.V. Perry
M.R. Steele-Bodger
B.H. Travers
D.F. White

v SCOTLAND

WON 24-5
England: 4G 1DG
Scotland: 1G
Twickenham, 15 Mar 1947

A. Gray

† C.B. Holmes 1T
N.O. Bennett 1T
* J. Heaton 4C
R.H. Guest 1T

N.M. Hall 1DG
† J.O. Newton-Thompson

G.A. Kelly
A.P. Henderson 1T
H.W. Walker
J. Mycock
† J. George
M.R. Steele-Bodger
† R.H.G. Weighill
D.F. White

v FRANCE

WON 6-3
England: 2T
France: 1PG
Twickenham, 19 Apr 1947

† S.C. Newman

D.W. Swarbrick
N.O. Bennett
* J. Heaton
R.H. Guest 1T

N.M. Hall
J.O. Newton-Thompson

† G.A. Gibbs
A.P. Henderson
H.W. Walker
J. Mycock
J. George
M.R. Steele-Bodger
R.H.G. Weighill
† V.G. Roberts 1T

FACT FILE

- Full internationals resumed in 1947, with England sharing the championship with Wales.
- A drop-goal by 'Nim' Hall, one of a noted St Mary's Hospital trio, robbed Wales of the lead in the second half to set up England's fourth win at Cardiff.

FINAL TABLE

	P	W	D	L	F	A	Pts
Wales	4	3	0	1	37	17	6
England	**4**	**3**	**0**	**1**	**39**	**36**	**6**
Ireland	4	2	0	2	33	18	4
France	4	2	0	2	23	20	4
Scotland	4	0	0	4	16	57	0

1947-48

Tour Match

v AUSTRALIA

LOST 0-11
England: Nil
Australia: 1G 2T
Twickenham, 3 Jan 1948

S.C. Newman

R.H. Guest
N.O. Bennett
* E.K. Scott
D.W. Swarbrick

T.A. Kemp
† R.J.P. Madge

† E. Evans
† J.H. Keeling
H.W. Walker
J. Mycock
S.V. Perry
M.R. Steele-Bodger
† D.B. Vaughan
B.H. Travers

Five Nations Championship

v WALES

DRAWN 3-3
England: 1PG
Wales: 1T
Twickenham, 17 Jan 1948

S.C. Newman 1PG

R.H. Guest
N.O. Bennett
E.K. Scott
D.W. Swarbrick

* T.A. Kemp
R.J.P. Madge

G.A. Kelly
J.H. Keeling
H.W. Walker
† H.F. Luya
S.V. Perry
M.R. Steele-Bodger
D.B. Vaughan
B.H. Travers

v IRELAND

LOST 10-11
England: 2G
Ireland: 1G 2T
Twickenham, 14 Feb 1948

† R. Uren 2C

R.H. Guest 2T
N.O. Bennett
* E.K. Scott
C.B. Holmes

† I. Preece
R.J.P. Madge

G.A. Gibbs
A.P. Henderson
H.W. Walker
H.F. Luya
S.V. Perry
M.R. Steele-Bodger
D.B. Vaughan
D.F. White

v SCOTLAND

LOST 3-6
Scotland: 2T
England: 1PG
Murrayfield, 20 Mar 1948

R. Uren 1PG

R.H. Guest
N.O. Bennett
* E.K. Scott
† M.F. Turner

I. Preece
R.J.P. Madge

† T.W. Price
A.P. Henderson
H.W. Walker
H.F. Luya
S.V. Perry
M.R. Steele-Bodger
R.H.G. Weighill
D.B. Vaughan

v FRANCE

LOST 0-15
France: 1G 1DG 2T
England: Nil
Stade Colombes, 29 Mar 1948

R. Uren

M.F. Turner
† L.B. Cannell
† A.C. Towell
C.B. Holmes

I. Preece
† P.W. Sykes

T.W. Price
A.P. Henderson
H.W. Walker
H.F. Luya
S.V. Perry
M.R. Steele-Bodger
* R.H. G.Weighill
D.F. White

FACT FILE

- England finished this season without winning a match and thus fell from joint champions to holders of the wooden spoon. But the huge post-war interest in rugby can be measured from the fact that more than 70,000 crowded into Twickenham for England's home matches, despite the team's lack of success on the field.

FINAL TABLE

	P	W	D	L	F	A	Pts
Ireland	4	4	0	0	36	19	8
France	4	2	0	2	40	25	4
Scotland	4	2	0	2	15	31	4
Wales	4	1	1	2	23	20	3
England	**4**	**0**	**1**	**3**	**16**	**35**	**1**

1948-49

Five Nations Championship

v WALES

LOST 3-9
Wales: 3T
England: 1DG
Cardiff Arms Park, 15 Jan 1949

† W.B. Holmes

† J.A. Gregory
L.B. Cannell
† C.B. van Ryneveld
† T. Danby

* N.M. Hall 1DG
† G. Rimmer

T.W. Price
A.P. Henderson
† M.J. Berridge
H.F. Luya
† G.R.D. 'A Hosking
† E.L. Horsfall
† B. Braithwaite-Exley
V.G. Roberts

v IRELAND

LOST 5-14
Ireland: 1G 2PG 1T
England: 1G
Lansdowne Road, 12 Feb 1949

W.B. Holmes 1C

D.W. Swarbrick
L.B. Cannell
C.B. van Ryneveld 1T
† R.D. Kennedy

* N.M. Hall
G. Rimmer

T.W. Price
A.P. Henderson
M.J. Berridge
J. George
G.R.D. 'A Hosking
D.B. Vaughan
† J.M. Kendall-Carpenter
V.G. Roberts

v FRANCE

WON 8-3
England: 1G 1DG
France: 1DG
Twickenham, 26 Feb 1949

W.B. Holmes 1C

R.H. Guest
L.B. Cannell 1T
C.B. van Ryneveld
R.D. Kennedy

* I. Preece 1DG
W.K.T. Moore

T.W. Price
† J.H. Steeds
J.M. Kendall-Carpenter
† J.R.C. Matthews
G.R.D. 'A Hosking
B.H. Travers
D.B. Vaughan
V.G. Roberts

v SCOTLAND

WON 19-3
England: 2G 3T
Scotland: 1PG
Twickenham, 19 Mar 1949

W.B. Holmes

R.H. Guest 1T
L.B. Cannell
C.B. van Ryneveld 2T
R.D. Kennedy 1T

* I. Preece
W.K.T. Moore

T.W. Price
J.H. Steeds
J.M. Kendall-Carpenter
J.R.C. Matthews
G.R.D. 'A Hosking 1T
B.H. Travers 2C
D.B. Vaughan
V.G. Roberts

FACT FILE

- During the season 26 players were used and 13 new caps were recognised. Among the new players was Clive van Ryneveld, a South African Test cricketer and scholar at Oxford. His two tries against Scotland were marvellous spectacles.

FINAL TABLE

	P	W	D	L	F	A	Pts
Ireland	4	3	0	1	41	24	6
England	**4**	**2**	**0**	**2**	**35**	**29**	**4**
France	4	2	0	2	24	28	4
Scotland	4	2	0	2	20	37	4
Wales	4	1	0	3	17	19	2

1949-50

Five Nations Championship

v WALES

LOST 5-11
England: 1G
Wales: 1G 1PG 1T
Twickenham, 21 Jan 1950

† M.B. Hofmeyr 1C

† J.V. Smith 1T
† B. Boobbyer
L.B. Cannell
† I.J. Botting

* I. Preece
G. Rimmer

J.M. Kendall-Carpenter
E. Evans
† W.A. Holmes
G.R.D. 'A Hosking
† H.A. Jones
† H.D. Small
D.B. Vaughan
† J.J. Cain

v IRELAND

WON 3-0
England: 1T
Ireland: Nil
Twickenham, 11 Feb 1950

R. Uren

J.V. Smith
B. Boobbyer
L.B. Cannell
I.J. Botting

* I. Preece
W.K.T. Moore

J.M. Kendall-Carpenter
J.H. Steeds
W.A. Holmes
J.R.C. Matthews
H.A. Jones
H.D. Small
† S.J. Adkins
V.G. Roberts 1T

v FRANCE

LOST 3-6
France: 2T
England: 1T
Stade Colombes, 25 Feb 1950

M.B. Hofmeyr

J.V. Smith 1T
B. Boobbyer
L.B. Cannell
† J.P. Hyde

* I. Preece
W.K.T. Moore

J.M. Kendall-Carpenter
J.H. Steeds
W.A. Holmes
J.R.C. Matthews
H.A. Jones
H.D. Small
S.J. Adkins
V.G. Roberts

v SCOTLAND

LOST 11-13
Scotland: 2G 1T
England: 1G 1PG 1T
Murrayfield, 18 Mar 1950

M.B. Hofmeyr 1PG 1C

J.V. Smith 2T
B. Boobbyer
L.B. Cannell
J.P. Hyde

* I. Preece
W.K.T. Moore

† J.L. Baume
J.H. Steeds
W.A. Holmes
J.R.C. Matthews
S.J. Adkins
H.D. Small
J.M. Kendall-Carpenter
V.G. Roberts

FACT FILE

- Controversy was aroused in 1950 by the unusual number of Dominion players – mostly South African but including one All Black – who played for England. The RFU's attitude to leading players from overseas was that such players should be accepted as 'one of us' while the man was a resident in England.

FINAL TABLE

	P	W	D	L	F	A	Pts
Wales	4	4	0	0	50	8	8
Scotland	4	2	0	2	21	49	4
Ireland	4	1	1	2	27	12	3
France	4	1	1	2	14	35	3
England	**4**	**1**	**0**	**3**	**22**	**30**	**2**

1950-51

Five Nations Championship

v WALES

LOST 5-23
Wales: 4G 1T
England: 1G
St Helen's, 20 Jan 1951

† E.N. Hewitt 1C

† C.G. Woodruff
† L.F.L. Oakley
B. Boobbyer
† V.R. Tindall

I. Preece
G. Rimmer

† R.V. Stirling
† T. Smith
W.A. Holmes
† D.T. Wilkins
† J.T. Bartlett
* V.G. Roberts
† P.B.C. Moore
† G.C. Rittson-Thomas 1T

v IRELAND

LOST 0-3
Ireland: 1PG
England: Nil
Lansdowne Road, 10 Feb 1951

E.N. Hewitt

C.G. Woodruff
I. Preece
† J.M. Williams
V.R. Tindall

† E.M.P. Hardy
G. Rimmer

R.V. Stirling
E. Evans
W.A. Holmes
D.T. Wilkins
† B.A. Neale
V.G. Roberts
* J.M. Kendall-Carpenter
G.C. Rittson-Thomas

v FRANCE

LOST 3-11
England: 1T
France: 1G 1DG 1T
Twickenham, 24 Feb 1951

E.N. Hewitt

C.G. Woodruff
I. Preece
B. Boobbyer 1T
V.R. Tindall

E.M.P. Hardy
G. Rimmer

R.V. Stirling
E. Evans
W.A. Holmes
D.T. Wilkins
B.A. Neale
V.G. Roberts
* J.M. Kendall-Carpenter
G.C. Rittson-Thomas

v SCOTLAND

WON 5-3
England: 1G
Scotland: 1T
Twickenham, 17 Mar 1951

† W.G. Hook 1C

C.G. Woodruff
A.C. Towell
J.M. Williams
V.R. Tindall

E.M.P. Hardy
† D.W. Shuttleworth

R.V. Stirling
E. Evans
W.A. Holmes
D.T. Wilkins
B.A. Neale
V.G. Roberts
* J.M. Kendall-Carpenter
D.F. White 1T

FACT FILE

- England found themselves at the bottom of the championship again in 1951. After a heavy defeat at Swansea – England's last international in that city – there was only the consolation of a home win against Scotland in their last match of the season.

FINAL TABLE

	P	W	D	L	F	A	Pts
Ireland	4	3	1	0	21	16	7
France	4	3	0	1	41	27	6
Wales	4	1	1	2	29	35	3
Scotland	4	1	0	3	39	25	2
England	**4**	**1**	**0**	**3**	**13**	**40**	**2**

1951-52

Tour Match

v SOUTH AFRICA

LOST 3-8
England: 1T
SA: 1G 1PG
Twickenham, 5 Jan 1952

W.G. Hook

† J.E. Woodward
† A.E. Agar
L.B. Cannell
† C.E. Winn 1T

* N.M. Hall
G. Rimmer

W.A. Holmes
E. Evans
R.V. Stirling
J.R.C. Matthews
D.T. Wilkins
D.F. White
J.M. Kendall-Carpenter
† A.O. Lewis

Five Nations Championship

v WALES

LOST 6-8
England: 2T
Wales: 1G 1T
Twickenham, 19 Jan 1952

W.G. Hook

J.E. Woodward 1T
A.E. Agar 1T
L.B. Cannell
C.E. Winn

* N.M. Hall
G. Rimmer

† E. Woodgate
E. Evans
R.V. Stirling
J.R.C. Matthews
D.T. Wilkins
D.F. White
J.M. Kendall-Carpenter
A.O. Lewis

v SCOTLAND

WON 19-3
Scotland: 1T
England: 2G 1DG 2T
Murrayfield, 15 Mar 1952

† P.J. Collins

J.E. Woodward 1T
A.E. Agar 1DG
B. Boobbyer
C.E. Winn 1T

* N.M. Hall 2C
P.W. Sykes

W.A. Holmes
E. Evans 1T
R.V. Stirling
J.R.C. Matthews
D.T. Wilkins
D.F. White
J.M. Kendall-Carpenter 1T
A.O. Lewis

v IRELAND

WON 3-0
England: 1T
Ireland: Nil
Twickenham, 29 Mar 1952

P.J. Collins

C.E. Winn
A.E. Agar
B. Boobbyer 1T
† R.C. Bazley

* N.M. Hall
P.W. Sykes

W.A. Holmes
E. Evans
R.V. Stirling
J.R.C. Matthews
D.T. Wilkins
D.F. White
J.M. Kendall-Carpenter
A.O. Lewis

v FRANCE

WON 6-3
France: 1T
England: 2PG
Stade Colombes, 5 Apr 1952

P.J. Collins

C.E. Winn
A.E. Agar
B. Boobbyer
R.C. Bazley

* N.M. Hall 2PG
P.W. Sykes

W.A. Holmes
E. Evans
R.V. Stirling
J.R.C. Matthews
D.T. Wilkins
D.F. White
J.M. Kendall-Carpenter
A.O. Lewis

FACT FILE

- Eric Evans was reaching the height of his powers as one of the best technical hookers in the British Isles and he was worthily supported by Wally Holmes and Bob Stirling as props. The 3-4-1 formation was now generally in use in international matches, and England's eighth man, John Kendall-Carpenter, was the outstanding example of the new back-row player.

FINAL TABLE

	P	W	D	L	F	A	Pts
Wales	4	4	0	0	42	14	8
England	**4**	**3**	**0**	**1**	**34**	**14**	**6**
Ireland	4	2	0	2	26	33	4
France	4	1	0	3	29	37	2
Scotland	4	0	0	4	22	55	0

1952-53

Five Nations Championship

v WALES

WON 8-3
Wales: 1PG
England: 1G 1PG
Cardiff Arms Park, 17 Jan 1953

* N.M. Hall 1C

J.E. Woodward 1PG
A.E. Agar
L.B. Cannell 1T
R.C. Bazley

† M. Regan
P.W. Sykes

W.A. Holmes
† N.A. Labuschagne
R.V. Stirling
S.J. Adkins
D.T. Wilkins
D.F. White
J.M. Kendall-Carpenter
A.O. Lewis

v IRELAND

DRAWN 9-9
Ireland: 2PG 1T
England: 2PG 1T
Lansdowne Road, 14 Feb 1953

* N.M. Hall 2PG

J.E. Woodward
A.E. Agar
L.B. Cannell
R.C. Bazley

M. Regan
P.W. Sykes

W.A. Holmes
E. Evans 1T
R.V. Stirling
S.J. Adkins
D.T. Wilkins
D.F. White
J.M. Kendall-Carpenter
A.O. Lewis

v FRANCE

WON 11-0
England: 1G 2T
France: Nil
Twickenham, 28 Feb 1953

* N.M. Hall 1C

J.E. Woodward 1T
† J. Butterfield 1T
L.B. Cannell
R.C. Bazley

M. Regan
P.W. Sykes

W.A. Holmes
E. Evans 1T
R.V. Stirling
S.J. Adkins
D.T. Wilkins
† D.S. Wilson
J.M. Kendall-Carpenter
A.O. Lewis

v SCOTLAND

WON 26-8
England: 4G 2T
Scotland: 1G 1T
Twickenham, 21 Mar 1953

* N.M. Hall 4C

J.E. Woodward 1T
J. Butterfield 1T
† W.P.C. Davies
R.C. Bazley 2T

M. Regan
D.W. Shuttleworth

W.A. Holmes
E. Evans
R.V. Stirling 1T
S.J. Adkins 1T
D.T. Wilkins
D.F. White
J.M. Kendall-Carpenter
A.O. Lewis

FACT FILE

- England captured the title in 1953, their first outright championship since 1937.
- The introduction of Phil Davies and Jeff Butterfield, two splendid all-round centres, made England the most complete side of the championship.

FINAL TABLE

	P	W	D	L	F	A	Pts
England	**4**	**3**	**1**	**0**	**54**	**20**	**7**
Wales	4	3	0	1	26	14	6
Ireland	4	2	1	1	54	25	5
France	4	1	0	3	17	38	2
Scotland	4	0	0	4	21	75	0

1953-54

Five Nations Championship

v WALES

WON 9-6
England: 3T
Wales: 1PG 1T
Twickenham, 16 Jan 1954

† I. King

J.E. Woodward 2T
† J.P. Quinn
J. Butterfield
C.E. Winn 1T

M. Regan
G. Rimmer

† D.L. Sanders
E. Evans
* R.V. Stirling
† P.D. Young
† P.G. Yarranton
D.S. Wilson
J.M. Kendall-Carpenter
† R. Higgins

Tour Match

v NEW ZEALAND

LOST 0-5
England: Nil
NZ: 1G
Twickenham, 30 Jan 1954

I. King

J.E. Woodward
J.P. Quinn
J. Butterfield
W.P.C. Davies

M. Regan
G. Rimmer

D.L. Sanders
E. Evans
* R.V. Stirling
P.D. Young
P.G. Yarranton
D.S. Wilson
J.M. Kendall-Carpenter
R. Higgins

Five Nations Championship

v IRELAND

WON 14-3
England: 1G 1PG 2T
Ireland: 1PG
Twickenham, 13 Feb 1954

I. King 1PG 1C

J.E. Woodward
J.P. Quinn
J. Butterfield 1T
W.P.C. Davies

M. Regan 1T
G. Rimmer

D.L. Sanders
E. Evans
* R.V. Stirling
P.D. Young
P.G. Yarranton
D.S. Wilson 1T
J.M. Kendall-Carpenter
R. Higgins

v SCOTLAND

WON 13-3
Scotland: 1T
England: 2G 1T
Murrayfield, 20 Mar 1954

† N. Gibbs 2C

J.E. Woodward
J.P. Quinn
J. Butterfield
C.E. Winn

M. Regan
G. Rimmer

D.L. Sanders
† E. Robinson
* R.V. Stirling
P.D. Young 1T
† J.F. Bance
D.S. Wilson 2T
† V.H. Leadbetter
R. Higgins

v FRANCE

LOST 3-11
France: 1G 1DG 1T
England: 1T
Stade Colombes, 10 Apr 1954

N. Gibbs

J.E. Woodward
J.P. Quinn
J. Butterfield
C.E. Winn

M. Regan
† J.E. Williams

D.L. Sanders
E. Evans
* R.V. Stirling
P.D. Young
V.H. Leadbetter
D.S. Wilson 1T
J.M. Kendall-Carpenter
A.O. Lewis

FACT FILE

- Huge crowds for earlier Welsh visits to Twickenham had compelled the RFU to make the 1954 game between the nations the first all-ticket international at headquarters.

FINAL TABLE

	P	W	D	L	F	A	Pts
Wales	4	3	0	1	52	34	6
England	**4**	**3**	**0**	**1**	**39**	**23**	**6**
France	4	3	0	1	35	22	6
Ireland	4	1	0	3	18	34	2
Scotland	4	0	0	4	6	37	0

1954-55

Five Nations Championship

v WALES

LOST 0-3
Wales: 1PG
England: Nil
Cardiff Arms Park, 22 Jan 1955

* N.M. Hall

J.E. Woodward
J. Butterfield
W.P.C. Davies
R.C. Bazley

† D.G.S. Baker
J.E. Williams

† D. St. G. Hazell
N.A. Labuschagne
† G.W.D. Hastings
P.D. Young
† J.H. Hancock
† P.H. Ryan
† P.J. Taylor
R. Higgins

v IRELAND

DRAWN 6-6
Ireland: 1PG 1T
England: 2T
Lansdowne Road, 12 Feb 1955

* N.M. Hall

J.E. Woodward
J. Butterfield 1T
W.P.C. Davies
R.C. Bazley

D.G.S. Baker
J.E. Williams

D. St. G. Hazell
N.A. Labuschagne
G.W.D. Hastings 1T
P.D. Young
J.H. Hancock
P.H. Ryan
P.J. Taylor
R. Higgins

v FRANCE

LOST 9-16
England: 2PG 1T
France: 2G 2DG
Twickenham, 26 Feb 1955

† H. Scott

† F.D. Sykes
J. Butterfield
W.P.C. Davies
R.C. Bazley

D.G.S. Baker
J.E. Williams

D. St. G. Hazell 2PG
N.A. Labuschagne
G.W.D. Hastings
* P.D. Young
P.G. Yarranton
D.S. Wilson
† I.D.S. Beer
R. Higgins 1T

v SCOTLAND

WON 9-6
England: 1PG 2T
Scotland: 1PG 1T
Twickenham, 19 Mar 1955

† N.S.D. Estcourt

F.D. Sykes 1T
J. Butterfield
W.P.C. Davies
R.C. Bazley

D.G.S. Baker
J.E. Williams

D. St. G. Hazell 1PG
N.A. Labuschagne
G.W.D. Hastings
* P.D. Young
P.G. Yarranton
D.S. Wilson
I.D.S. Beer 1T
R. Higgins

FACT FILE

- Six new caps (including five in the forwards) made the trip to Cardiff in the middle of January, only to find the game postponed through heavy snow. The same side eventually played a week later, this time in such wet conditions that the pitch resembled a morass.

FINAL TABLE

	P	W	D	L	F	A	Pts
Wales	4	3	0	1	48	28	6
France	4	3	0	1	47	28	6
Scotland	4	2	0	2	32	35	4
England	**4**	**1**	**1**	**2**	**24**	**31**	**3**
Ireland	4	0	1	3	15	44	1

1955-56

Five Nations Championship

v WALES

LOST 3-8
England: 1PG
Wales: 1G 1T
Twickenham, 21 Jan 1956

† D.F. Allison 1PG

† P.B. Jackson
J. Butterfield
W.P.C. Davies
† P.H. Thompson

† M.J.K. Smith
† R.E.G. Jeeps

D.L. Sanders
* E. Evans
† C.R. Jacobs
† J.D. Currie
† R.W.D. Marques
† P.G.D. Robbins
† A. Ashcroft
V.G. Roberts

v IRELAND

WON 20-0
England: 1G 3PG 2T
Ireland: Nil
Twickenham, 11 Feb 1956

D.F. Allison 1PG

P.B. Jackson 1T
J. Butterfield 1T
L.B. Cannell
P.H. Thompson

M. Regan
J.E. Williams

D.L. Sanders
* E. Evans 1T
C.R. Jacobs
J.D. Currie 2PG 1C
R.W.D. Marques
P.G.D. Robbins
A. Ashcroft
V.G. Roberts

v SCOTLAND

WON 11-6
Scotland: 1PG 1T
England: 1G 2PG
Murrayfield, 17 Mar 1956

D.F. Allison

J.E. Woodward
J. Butterfield
L.B. Cannell
P.H. Thompson

M. Regan
J.E. Williams 1T

D.L. Sanders
* E. Evans
C.R. Jacobs
J.D. Currie 2PG 1C
R.W.D. Marques
P.G.D. Robbins
A. Ashcroft
V.G. Roberts

v FRANCE

LOST 9-14
France: 1G 2PG 1T
England: 2PG 1T
Stade Colombes, 14 Apr 1956

D.F. Allison 2PG

P.B. Jackson
J. Butterfield
L.B. Cannell
P.H. Thompson 1T

M. Regan
J.E. Williams

D.L. Sanders
* E. Evans
C.R. Jacobs
J.D. Currie
R.W.D. Marques
P.G.D. Robbins
A. Ashcroft
V.G. Roberts

FACT FILE

- There were ten new caps under a new captain, Eric Evans of Sale, for the opening game of 1956.
- The pack, it will be noted, was unchanged during the season.
- John Currie and David Marques began a long second-row partnership that was to last for five seasons. Their 22 appearances in tandem became a record partnership for England.

FINAL TABLE

	P	W	D	L	F	A	Pts
Wales	4	3	0	1	25	20	6
England	**4**	**2**	**0**	**2**	**43**	**28**	**4**
Ireland	4	2	0	2	33	47	4
France	4	2	0	2	31	34	4
Scotland	4	1	0	3	31	34	2

1956-57

Five Nations Championship

v WALES

WON 3-0
Wales: Nil
England: 1PG
Cardiff Arms Park, 19 Jan 1957

D.F. Allison 1PG

P.B. Jackson
J. Butterfield
L.B. Cannell
P.H. Thompson

† R.M. Bartlett
R.E.G. Jeeps

C.R. Jacobs
* E. Evans
G.W.D. Hastings
J.D. Currie
R.W.D. Marques
P.G.D. Robbins
A. Ashcroft
R. Higgins

v IRELAND

WON 6-0
Ireland: Nil
England: 1PG 1T
Lansdowne Road, 9 Feb 1957

† R. Challis 1PG

P.B. Jackson 1T
J. Butterfield
L.B. Cannell
P.H. Thompson

R.M. Bartlett
R.E.G. Jeeps

C.R. Jacobs
* E. Evans
G.W.D. Hastings
J.D. Currie
R.W.D. Marques
P.G.D. Robbins
A. Ashcroft
R. Higgins

v FRANCE

WON 9-5
England: 3T
France: 1G
Twickenham, 23 Feb 1957

R. Challis

P.B. Jackson 2T
J. Butterfield
W.P.C. Davies
P.H. Thompson

R.M. Bartlett
R.E.G. Jeeps

C.R. Jacobs
* E. Evans 1T
G.W.D. Hastings
J.D. Currie
R.W.D. Marques
P.G.D. Robbins
A. Ashcroft
R. Higgins

v SCOTLAND

WON 16-3
England: 2G 1PG 1T
Scotland: 1PG
Twickenham, 16 Mar 1957

R. Challis 1PG 2C

P.B. Jackson
J. Butterfield
W.P.C. Davies 1T
P.H. Thompson 1T

R.M. Bartlett
R.E.G. Jeeps

C.R. Jacobs
* E. Evans
G.W.D. Hastings
J.D. Currie
R.W.D. Marques
P.G.D. Robbins
A. Ashcroft
R. Higgins 1T

FACT FILE

- Against Scotland, England played with assurance and their forwards took complete control in the tight and loose. The result was a comfortable victory which secured the Triple Crown and Grand Slam – England's first since 1928.

FINAL TABLE

	P	W	D	L	F	A	Pts
England	**4**	**4**	**0**	**0**	**34**	**8**	**8**
Wales	4	2	0	2	31	30	4
Scotland	4	2	0	2	21	21	4
Ireland	4	2	0	2	21	27	4
France	4	0	0	4	24	45	0

1957-58

Five Nations Championship

v WALES

DRAWN 3-3
England: 1T
Wales: 1PG
Twickenham, 18 Jan 1958

D.F. Allison

P.B. Jackson
J. Butterfield
W.P.C. Davies
P.H. Thompson 1T

† J.P. Horrocks-Taylor
R.E.G. Jeeps

G.W.D. Hastings
* E. Evans
C.R. Jacobs
J.D. Currie
R.W.D. Marques
P.G.D. Robbins
A. Ashcroft
† R.E. Syrett

Tour Match

v AUSTRALIA

WON 9-6
England: 2T 1PG
Australia: 1PG 1DG
Twickenham, 1 Feb 1958

† J.G.G. Hetherington 1PG

P.B. Jackson 1T
J. Butterfield
† M.S. Phillips 1T
P.H. Thompson

J.P. Horrocks-Taylor
R.E.G. Jeeps

G.W.D. Hastings
* E. Evans
C.R. Jacobs
J.D. Currie
R.W.D. Marques
P.G.D. Robbins
A. Ashcroft
R.E. Syrett

Five Nations Championship

v IRELAND

WON 6-0
England: 1PG 1T
Ireland: Nil
Twickenham, 8 Feb 1958

J.G.G. Hetherington 1PG

† J.R.C. Young
J. Butterfield
M.S. Phillips
P.H. Thompson

R.M. Bartlett
R.E.G. Jeeps

G.W.D. Hastings
* E. Evans
C.R. Jacobs
J.D. Currie
R.W.D. Marques
P.G.D. Robbins
A. Ashcroft 1T
R.E. Syrett

v FRANCE

WON 14-0
France: Nil
England: 1G 1PG 2T
Stade Colombes, 1 Mar 1958

† J.S.M. Scott

P.B. Jackson 1T
J. Butterfield
M.S. Phillips
P.H. Thompson 2T

R.M. Bartlett
R.E.G. Jeeps

G.W.D. Hastings 1PG 1C
* E. Evans
C.R. Jacobs
J.D. Currie
R.W.D. Marques
† A.J. Herbert
A. Ashcroft
R.E. Syrett

v SCOTLAND

DRAWN 3-3
Scotland: 1PG
England: 1PG
Murrayfield, 15 Mar 1958

D.F. Allison

P.B. Jackson
J. Butterfield
M.S. Phillips
P.H. Thompson

R.M. Bartlett
R.E.G. Jeeps

G.W.D. Hastings 1PG
* E. Evans
C.R. Jacobs
J.D. Currie
R.W.D. Marques
P.G.D. Robbins
A. Ashcroft
A.J. Herbert

FACT FILE

- England gained their first post-war victory over a Dominion side when they beat Australia. In the closing minutes with the scores level, Peter Jackson set off on a run which ended with a dive in the corner for a try.
- A disappointing draw at Murrayfield brought Eric Evans' England career to an end. His 30 appearances stood as a figure exceeded only by Wavell Wakefield.

FINAL TABLE

	P	W	D	L	F	A	Pts
England	**4**	**2**	**2**	**0**	**26**	**6**	**6**
Wales	4	2	1	1	26	28	5
France	4	2	0	2	36	37	4
Scotland	4	1	1	2	23	32	3
Ireland	4	1	0	3	24	32	2

1958-59

Five Nations Championship

v WALES

LOST 0-5
Wales: 1G
England: Nil
Cardiff Arms Park, 17 Jan 1959

J.G.G. Hetherington

P.B. Jackson
M.S. Phillips
* J. Butterfield
P.H. Thompson

† A.B.W. Risman
† S.R. Smith

† L.H. Webb
† J.A.S. Wackett
† G.J. Bendon
J.D. Currie
R.W.D. Marques
A.J. Herbert
† B.J. Wightman
R. Higgins

v IRELAND

WON 3-0
Ireland: Nil
England: 1PG
Lansdowne Road, 14 Feb 1959

J.G.G. Hetherington

P.B. Jackson
M.S. Phillips
* J. Butterfield
P.H. Thompson

A.B.W. Risman **1PG**
R.E.G. Jeeps

L.H. Webb
J.A.S. Wackett
G.J. Bendon
J.D. Currie
R.W.D. Marques
A.J. Herbert
A. Ashcroft
† J.W. Clements

v FRANCE

DRAWN 3-3
England: 1PG
France: 1PG
Twickenham, 28 Feb 1959

J.G.G. Hetherington **1PG**

P.B. Jackson
M.S. Phillips
* J. Butterfield
P.H. Thompson

A.B.W. Risman
S.R. Smith

L.H. Webb
† H.O. Godwin
G.J. Bendon
J.D. Currie
R.W.D. Marques
A.J. Herbert
A. Ashcroft
J.W. Clements

v SCOTLAND

DRAWN 3-3
England: 1PG
Scotland: 1PG
Twickenham, 21 Mar 1959

J.G.G. Hetherington

P.B. Jackson
M.S. Phillips
* J. Butterfield
P.H. Thompson

A.B.W. Risman **1PG**
S.R. Smith

L.H. Webb
H.O. Godwin
G.J. Bendon
J.D. Currie
R.W.D. Marques
A.J. Herbert
A. Ashcroft
J.W. Clements

FACT FILE

- England failed to score a single try in 1959, yet only lost one of their four matches.

FINAL TABLE

	P	W	D	L	F	A	Pts
France	4	2	1	1	28	15	5
Ireland	4	2	0	2	23	19	4
Wales	4	2	0	2	21	23	4
England	**4**	**1**	**2**	**1**	**9**	**11**	**4**
Scotland	4	1	1	2	12	25	3

1959-60

Five Nations Championship

v WALES

WON 14-6
England: 1G 2PG 1T
Wales: 2PG
Twickenham, 16 Jan 1960

† D. Rutherford 2PG 1C

J.R.C. Young
M.S. Phillips
† M.P. Weston
† J. Roberts 2T

† R.A.W. Sharp
* R.E.G. Jeeps

C.R. Jacobs
† S.A.M. Hodgson
† P.T. Wright
R.W.D. Marques
J.D. Currie
P.G.D. Robbins
† W.G.D. Morgan
R.E. Syrett

v IRELAND

WON 8-5
England: 1G 1DG
Ireland: 1G
Twickenham, 13 Feb 1960

D. Rutherford 1C

J.R.C. Young
M.S. Phillips
M.P. Weston
J. Roberts

R.A.W. Sharp 1DG
* R.E.G. Jeeps

C.R. Jacobs
S.A.M. Hodgson
P.T. Wright
R.W.D. Marques 1T
J.D. Currie
P.G.D. Robbins
W.G.D. Morgan
R.E. Syrett

v FRANCE

DRAWN 3-3
France: 1PG
England: 1T
Stade Colombes, 27 Feb 1960

D. Rutherford

J.R.C. Young
M.S. Phillips
M.P. Weston 1T
J. Roberts

R.A.W. Sharp
* R.E.G. Jeeps

C.R. Jacobs
S.A.M. Hodgson
P.T. Wright
R.W.D. Marques
J.D. Currie
P.G.D. Robbins
W.G.D. Morgan
R.E. Syrett

v SCOTLAND

WON 21-12
Scotland: 3PG 1T
England: 3G 1DG 1PG
Murrayfield, 19 Mar 1960

D. Rutherford 1PG 3C

J.R.C. Young 1T
M.S. Phillips
M.P. Weston
J. Roberts 1T

R.A.W. Sharp 1DG
* R.E.G. Jeeps

C.R. Jacobs
S.A.M. Hodgson
P.T. Wright
R.W.D. Marques
J.D. Currie
P.G.D. Robbins
W.G.D. Morgan
R.E. Syrett 1T

FACT FILE

- The England side, for the first time in its history, was unchanged throughout the season.
- The Triple Crown was secured after victory at Murrayfield where England's total of 21 points was their highest international score since 1953.

FINAL TABLE

	P	W	D	L	F	A	Pts
France	4	3	1	0	55	28	7
England	**4**	**3**	**1**	**0**	**46**	**26**	**7**
Wales	4	2	0	2	32	39	4
Scotland	4	1	0	3	29	47	2
Ireland	4	0	0	4	25	47	0

1960-61

Tour Match

v SOUTH AFRICA

LOST 0-5
England: Nil
SA: 1G
Twickenham, 7 Jan 1961

D. Rutherford

J.R.C. Young
† W.M. Patterson
M.P. Weston
J. Roberts

A.B.W. Risman
* R.E.G. Jeeps

C.R. Jacobs
S.A.M. Hodgson
P.T. Wright
R.W.D. Marques
J.D. Currie
P.G.D. Robbins
W.G.D. Morgan
† L.I. Rimmer

Five Nations Championship

v WALES

LOST 3-6
Wales: 2T
England: 1T
Cardiff Arms Park, 21 Jan 1961

† M.N. Gavins

J.R.C. Young 1T
M.S. Phillips
M.P. Weston
J. Roberts

A.B.W. Risman
* R.E.G. Jeeps

C.R. Jacobs
S.A.M. Hodgson
P.T. Wright
R.W.D. Marques
† R.J. French
P.G.D. Robbins
W.G.D. Morgan
L.I. Rimmer

v IRELAND

LOST 8-11
Ireland: 1G 2PG
England: 1G 1T
Lansdowne Road, 11 Feb 1961

† J.G. Willcox

J.R.C. Young
A.B.W. Risman 1C
M.P. Weston
J. Roberts 1T

R.A.W. Sharp
* R.E.G. Jeeps

C.R. Jacobs
E. Robinson
P.T. Wright
† J. Price
R.J. French
† D.P. Rogers 1T
W.G.D. Morgan
L.I. Rimmer

v FRANCE

DRAWN 5-5
England: 1G
France: 1G
Twickenham, 25 Feb 1961

J.G. Willcox 1C

J.R.C. Young
A.B.W. Risman
M.P. Weston
J. Roberts

R.A.W. Sharp
* R.E.G. Jeeps

C.R. Jacobs
E. Robinson
P.T. Wright
† V.S.J. Harding 1T
R.J. French
D.P. Rogers
W.G.D. Morgan
L.I. Rimmer

v SCOTLAND

WON 6-0
England: 1PG 1T
Scotland: Nil
Twickenham, 18 Mar 1961

J.G. Willcox

P.B. Jackson
W.M. Patterson
M.P. Weston
J. Roberts 1T

J.P. Horrocks-Taylor 1PG
* R.E.G. Jeeps

C.R. Jacobs
E. Robinson
P.T. Wright
V.S.J. Harding
R.J. French
D.P. Rogers
W.G.D. Morgan
L.I. Rimmer

FACT FILE

- During the season the selectors were criticised over their inability to decide which player, Bev Risman or Richard Sharp, was better equipped to spearhead the English attack from fly-half. As a compromise they had used both players, preferring Risman as a centre, but with little effect.

FINAL TABLE

	P	W	D	L	F	A	Pts
France	4	3	1	0	39	14	7
Wales	4	2	0	2	21	14	4
Scotland	4	2	0	2	19	25	4
England	**4**	**1**	**1**	**2**	**22**	**22**	**3**
Ireland	4	1	0	3	22	48	2

1961-62

Five Nations Championship

v WALES

DRAWN 0-0
England: Nil
Wales: Nil
Twickenham, 20 Jan 1962

J.G. Willcox

† A.M. Underwood
† M.R. Wade
M.P. Weston
J. Roberts

R.A.W. Sharp
* R.E.G. Jeeps

† P.E. Judd
S.A.M. Hodgson
P.T. Wright
V.S.J. Harding
J.D. Currie
D.P. Rogers
P.J. Taylor
R.E. Syrett

v IRELAND

WON 16-0
England: 2G 1PG 1T
Ireland: Nil
Twickenham, 10 Feb 1962

J.G. Willcox

A.M. Underwood
M.R. Wade 1T
M.P. Weston
J. Roberts 1T

R.A.W. Sharp 1PG 1T 2C
* R.E.G. Jeeps

P.E. Judd
S.A.M. Hodgson
P.T. Wright
V.S.J. Harding
J.D. Currie
D.P. Rogers
P.J. Taylor
R.E. Syrett

v FRANCE

LOST 0-13
France: 2G 1T
England: Nil
Stade Colombes, 24 Feb 1962

J.G. Willcox

A.M. Underwood
M.R. Wade
M.P. Weston
J. Roberts

R.A.W. Sharp
* R.E.G. Jeeps

P.E. Judd
S.A.M. Hodgson
P.T. Wright
V.S.J. Harding
J.D. Currie
D.P. Rogers
P.J. Taylor
R.E. Syrett

v SCOTLAND

DRAWN 3-3
Scotland: 1PG
England: 1PG
Murrayfield, 17 Mar 1962

J.G. Willcox 1PG

† A.C.B. Hurst
A.M. Underwood
† J.M. Dee
J. Roberts

J.P. Horrocks-Taylor
* R.E.G. Jeeps

P.E. Judd
S.A.M. Hodgson
P.T. Wright
V.S.J. Harding
† T.A. Pargetter
P.G.D. Robbins
P.J. Taylor
† S.J. Purdy

FACT FILE

- England returned a disappointing record in 1962. There was a scoreless draw against Wales – the first between the sides since 1936 – and an uninspiring drawn game at Murrayfield where both sides scored a penalty goal (the third 3-3 draw in the series since 1958).

FINAL TABLE

	P	W	D	L	F	A	Pts
France	4	3	0	1	35	6	6
Scotland	4	2	1	1	34	23	5
England	**4**	**1**	**2**	**1**	**19**	**16**	**4**
Wales	4	1	2	1	9	11	4
Ireland	4	0	1	3	9	50	1

1962-63

Five Nations Championship

v WALES

WON 13-6
Wales: 1PG 1T
England: 2G 1DG
Cardiff Arms Park, 19 Jan 1963

J.G. Willcox

P.B. Jackson
M.S. Phillips 1T
M.P. Weston
J. Roberts

* R.A.W. Sharp 2C 1DG
† S.J.S. Clarke

† N.J. Drake-Lee
† J.D. Thorne
† B.A. Dovey
† A.M. Davis
† J.E. Owen 1T
D.P. Rogers
B.J. Wightman
† D.C. Manley

v IRELAND

DRAWN 0-0
Ireland: Nil
England: Nil
Lansdowne Road, 9 Feb 1963

J.G. Willcox

P.B. Jackson
M.S. Phillips
M.P. Weston
J. Roberts

* R.A.W. Sharp
S.J.S. Clarke

N.J. Drake-Lee
J.D. Thorne
B.A. Dovey
A.M.Davis
J.E. Owen
D.P. Rogers
B.J. Wightman
D.C. Manley

v FRANCE

WON 6-5
England: 2PG
France: 1G
Twickenham, 23 Feb 1963

J.G. Willcox 2PG

P.B. Jackson
M.S. Phillips
M.P. Weston
J. Roberts

* R.A.W. Sharp
S.J.S. Clarke

N.J. Drake-Lee
J.D. Thorne
† K.J. Wilson
T.A. Pargetter
J.E. Owen
D.P. Rogers
† D.G. Perry
D.C. Manley

v SCOTLAND

WON 10-8
England: 2G
Scotland: 1G 1DG
Twickenham, 16 Mar 1963

J.G. Willcox 2C

P.B. Jackson
M.S. Phillips
M.P. Weston
J. Roberts

* R.A.W. Sharp 1T
S.J.S. Clarke

N.J. Drake-Lee 1T
H.O. Godwin
P.E. Judd
A.M. Davis
J.E. Owen
D.P. Rogers
D.G. Perry
D.C. Manley

FACT FILE

- England fielded an experimental side for their opening match of 1963. Seven new caps were in a XV which gained England's seventh win at Cardiff.
- Richard Sharp made a captain's effort to snatch the Calcutta Cup and the championship late in the Scottish game. With the help of three audacious dummies the Cornishman squeezed through a narrow opening in the Scottish defence for a try which John Willcox converted.

FINAL TABLE

	P	W	D	L	F	A	Pts
England	**4**	**3**	**1**	**0**	**29**	**19**	**7**
France	4	2	0	2	40	25	4
Scotland	4	2	0	2	22	22	4
Ireland	4	1	1	2	19	33	3
Wales	4	1	0	3	21	32	2

Tour Match

1st v NEW ZEALAND

LOST 11-21
NZ: 3G 1DG 1PG
England: 1G 2PG
Auckland, 25 May 1963

† R.W. Hosen 2PG 1C

† J.M. Ranson 1T
M.S. Phillips
* M.P. Weston
J.M. Dee

J.P. Horrocks-Taylor
S.J.S. Clarke

C.R. Jacobs
H.O. Godwin
P.E. Judd
T.A. Pargetter
A.M. Davis
D.P. Rogers
D.G. Perry
† V.R. Marriott

1962-63 continued

Tour Matches

2ND v NEW ZEALAND

LOST 6-9
NZ: 1GM 2T
England: 1PG 1T
Christchurch, 1 June 1963

R.W. Hosen 1PG

J.M. Ranson
M.S. Phillips 1T
* M.P. Weston
F.D. Sykes

J.P. Horrocks-Taylor
S.J.S. Clarke

C.R. Jacobs
H.O. Godwin
P.E. Judd
D.G. Perry
A.M. Davis
D.P. Rogers
B.J. Wightman
V.R. Marriott

v AUSTRALIA

LOST 9-18
Australia: 3G 1T
England: 3T
Sydney, 4 June 1963

R.W. Hosen

F.D. Sykes
M.S. Phillips 1T
* M.P. Weston
J.M. Ranson

J.P. Horrocks-Taylor
S.J.S. Clarke 1T

C.R. Jacobs
H.O. Godwin 1T
P.E. Judd
D.G. Perry
J.E. Owen
D.P. Rogers
B.J. Wightman
V.R. Marriott

FACT FILE

- England were not at full strength when they carried out their first tour to Australasia in the summer of 1963. Mike Weston was captain of a side which became the first Home Union to tour down under.

Richard Sharp leaves Pierre Lacroix floundering at Twickenham in 1963.

1963-64

Tour Match

v NEW ZEALAND

LOST 0-14
England: Nil
NZ: 1G 2PG 1T
Twickenham, 4 Jan 1964

* J.G. Willcox

M.S. Phillips
M.P. Weston
† R.D. Sangwin
J. Roberts

J.P. Horrocks-Taylor
S.J.S. Clarke

P.E. Judd
H.O. Godwin
N.J. Drake-Lee
A.M. Davis
J.E. Owen
D.P. Rogers
D.G. Perry
V.R. Marriott

Five Nations Championship

v WALES

DRAWN 6-6
England: 2T
Wales: 2T
Twickenham, 18 Jan 1964

* J.G. Willcox

M.S. Phillips
M.P. Weston
R.D. Sangwin
J.M. Ranson 1T

J.P. Horrocks-Taylor
S.J.S. Clarke

C.R. Jacobs
S.A.M. Hodgson
N.J. Drake-Lee
A.M. Davis
† R.E. Rowell
D.P. Rogers
D.G. Perry 1T
† P.J. Ford

v IRELAND

LOST 5-18
England: 1G
Ireland: 3G 1T
Twickenham, 8 Feb 1964

* J.G. Willcox 1C

A.M. Underwood
M.S. Phillips
M.P. Weston
J.M. Ranson

† T.J. Brophy
S.J.S. Clarke

C.R. Jacobs
H.O. Godwin
N.J. Drake-Lee
A.M. Davis
† C.M. Payne
D.P. Rogers 1T
D.G. Perry
P.J. Ford

v FRANCE

WON 6-3
France: 1T
England: 1PG 1T
Stade Colombes, 22 Feb 1964

J.G. Willcox

R.W. Hosen 1PG
M.S. Phillips 1T
M.P. Weston
J.M. Ranson

T.J. Brophy
S.R. Smith

* C.R. Jacobs
H.O. Godwin
† D.F.B. Wrench
A.M. Davis
C.M. Payne
D.P. Rogers
† T.G.A.H. Peart
P.J. Ford

v SCOTLAND

LOST 6-15
Scotland: 3G
England: 1PG 1T
Murrayfield, 21 Mar 1964

J.G. Willcox

R.W. Hosen 1PG
M.S. Phillips
M.P. Weston
J.M. Ranson

T.J. Brophy
S.R. Smith

* C.R. Jacobs
H.O. Godwin
D.F.B. Wrench
A.M. Davis
C.M. Payne
D.P. Rogers 1T
T.G.A.H. Peart
P.J. Ford

FACT FILE

- England's defeat against New Zealand by 14 points at Twickenham was their worst result at the ground since the inaugural match of 1910.

FINAL TABLE

	P	W	D	L	F	A	Pts
Wales	4	2	2	0	43	26	6
Scotland	4	3	0	1	34	20	6
France	4	1	1	2	41	33	3
England	**4**	**1**	**1**	**2**	**23**	**42**	**3**
Ireland	4	1	0	3	33	53	2

1964-65

Five Nations Championship

v WALES

LOST 3-14
Wales: 1G 1DG 2T
England: 1PG
Cardiff Arms Park, 16 Jan 1965

D. Rutherford 1PG

† E.L. Rudd
† D.W.A. Rosser
† G.P. Frankcom
† C.P. Simpson

T.J. Brophy
J.E. Williams

† A.L. Horton
† S.B. Richards
N.J. Drake-Lee
J.E. Owen
R.E. Rowell
D.P. Rogers
* D.G. Perry
† N. Silk

v IRELAND

LOST 0-5
Ireland: 1G
England: Nil
Lansdowne Road, 13 Feb 1965

D. Rutherford

E.L. Rudd
D.W.A. Rosser
G.P. Frankcom
† P.W. Cook

T.J. Brophy
S.J.S. Clarke

A.L. Horton
S.B. Richards
P.E. Judd
J.E. Owen
C.M. Payne
D.P. Rogers
* D.G. Perry
N. Silk

v FRANCE

WON 9-6
England: 2PG 1T
France: 1PG 1T
Twickenham, 27 Feb 1965

D. Rutherford 2PG

† A.W. Hancock
D.W.A. Rosser
G.P. Frankcom
P.W. Cook

M.P. Weston
S.J.S. Clarke

A.L. Horton
S.B. Richards
P.E. Judd
J.E. Owen
C.M. Payne 1T
D.P. Rogers
* D.G. Perry
N. Silk

v SCOTLAND

DRAWN 3-3
England: 1T
Scotland: 1DG
Twickenham, 20 Mar 1965

D. Rutherford

E.L. Rudd
D.W.A. Rosser
G.P. Frankcom
A.W. Hancock 1T

M.P. Weston
S.J.S. Clarke

A.L. Horton
S.B. Richards
P.E. Judd
J.E. Owen
C.M. Payne
D.P. Rogers
* D.G. Perry
N. Silk

FACT FILE

- HM the Queen was present at Twickenham to watch Andy Hancock deny the Scots victory with a last-minute try. Scotland led 3-0 in the dying minutes of the match when Weston threw a pass to Hancock on the left and near touch. The Northampton wing made the longest run for a try ever seen in an international match.

FINAL TABLE

	P	W	D	L	F	A	Pts
Wales	4	3	0	1	55	45	6
France	4	2	1	1	47	33	5
Ireland	4	2	1	1	32	23	5
England	**4**	**1**	**1**	**2**	**15**	**28**	**3**
Scotland	4	0	1	3	29	49	1

1965-66

Five Nations Championship

v WALES

LOST 6-11
England: 1PG 1T
Wales: 1G 2PG
Twickenham, 15 Jan 1966

D. Rutherford 1PG

E.L. Rudd
† T.G. Arthur
D.W.A. Rosser
† K.F. Savage

T.J. Brophy
† J. Spencer

P.E. Judd
† J.V. Pullin
† D.L. Powell
C.M. Payne
A.M. Davis
* D.P. Rogers
D.G. Perry 1T
† R.B. Taylor

v IRELAND

DRAWN 6-6
England: 1PG 1T
Ireland: 1PG 1T
Twickenham, 12 Feb 1966

D. Rutherford 1PG

E.L. Rudd
T.G. Arthur
† C.W. McFadyean
K.F. Savage

T.J. Brophy
† R.C. Ashby

P.E. Judd
† W.T. Treadwell
D.L. Powell
C.M. Payne
J.E. Owen
* D.P. Rogers
D.G. Perry
† J.R.H. Greenwood 1T

v FRANCE

LOST 0-13
France: 2G 1T
England: Nil
Stade Colombes, 26 Feb 1966

D. Rutherford

K.F. Savage
† R.D. Hearn
C.W. McFadyean
A.W. Hancock

T.J. Brophy
R.C. Ashby

P.E. Judd
W.T. Treadwell
A.L. Horton
C.M. Payne
J.E. Owen
* D.P. Rogers
D.G. Perry
J.R.H. Greenwood

v SCOTLAND

LOST 3-6
Scotland: 1PG 1T
England: 1DG
Murrayfield, 19 Mar 1966

D. Rutherford

E.L. Rudd
R.D. Hearn
C.W. McFadyean 1DG
K.F. Savage

M.P. Weston
† T.C. Wintle

P.E. Judd
W.T. Treadwell
A.L. Horton
C.M. Payne
J.E. Owen
* D.P. Rogers
† G.A. Sherriff
J.R.H. Greenwood

FACT FILE

- Three defeats and a draw left England floundering at the bottom of the championship in 1966 with only one point out of eight – their worst return in the competition since 1948. Altogether 26 players were used, including 13 new caps and three different scrum-halves.

FINAL TABLE

	P	W	D	L	F	A	Pts
Wales	4	3	0	1	34	26	6
France	4	2	1	1	35	18	5
Scotland	4	2	1	1	23	17	5
Ireland	4	1	1	2	24	34	3
England	**4**	**0**	**1**	**3**	**15**	**36**	**1**

1966-67

Tour Match

v AUSTRALIA

LOST 11-23
England: 1G 2PG
Australia: 1G 3DG 2PG 1T
Twickenham, 7 Jan 1967

R.W. Hosen **2PG 1C**

† P.B. Glover
C.W. McFadyean
† C.R. Jennins
K.F. Savage

* R.A.W. Sharp
R.C. Ashby **1T**

P.E. Judd
S.B. Richards
† M.J. Coulman
A.M. Davis
† P.J. Larter
D.P. Rogers
G.A. Sherriff
J.R.H. Greenwood

Five Nations Championship

v IRELAND

WON 8-3
Ireland: 1PG
England: 1G 1PG
Lansdowne Road, 11 Feb 1967

R.W. Hosen **1PG 1C**

K.F. Savage
R.D. Hearn
C.R. Jennins
C.W. McFadyean **1T**

† J.F. Finlan
† R.D.A. Pickering

* P.E. Judd
S.B. Richards
M.J. Coulman
† J. Barton
† D.E.J. Watt
† D.M. Rollitt
† J.N. Pallant
R.B. Taylor

v FRANCE

LOST 12-16
England: 3PG 1DG
France: 2G 1DG 1PG
Twickenham, 25 Feb 1967

R.W. Hosen **3PG**

K.F. Savage
R.D. Hearn
C.R. Jennins
C.W. McFadyean

J.F. Finlan **1DG**
R.D.A. Pickering

* P.E. Judd
S.B. Richards
M.J. Coulman
J. Barton
D.E.J. Watt
D.M. Rollitt
J.N. Pallant
R.B. Taylor

v SCOTLAND

WON 27-14
England: 3G 2PG 1DG 1T
Scotland: 1G 2PG 1T
Twickenham, 18 Mar 1967

R.W. Hosen **2PG 3C**

K.F. Savage
R.D. Hearn
C.W. McFadyean **2T**
† R.E. Webb **1T**

J.F. Finlan **1DG**
R.D.A. Pickering

* P.E. Judd
S.B. Richards
M.J. Coulman
J.N. Pallant
D.E.J. Watt
D.P. Rogers
D.M. Rollitt
R.B. Taylor **1T**

v WALES

LOST 21-34
Wales: 5G 2PG 1DG
England: 4PG 3T
Cardiff Arms Park, 15 Apr 1967

R.W. Hosen **4PG**

K.F. Savage **1T**
R.D. Hearn
C.W. McFadyean
R.E. Webb

J.F. Finlan
R.D.A. Pickering

* P.E. Judd
S.B. Richards
M.J. Coulman
J. Barton **2T**
D.E.J. Watt
D.P. Rogers
D.M. Rollitt
R.B. Taylor

FACT FILE

- Roger Hosen's total of points for the season was 46, a new English record.

FINAL TABLE

	P	W	D	L	F	A	Pts
France	4	3	0	1	55	41	6
England	**4**	**2**	**0**	**2**	**68**	**67**	**4**
Scotland	4	2	0	2	37	45	4
Ireland	4	2	0	2	17	22	4
Wales	4	1	0	3	53	55	2

1967-68

Tour Match

v NEW ZEALAND

LOST 11-23
England: 1G 1PG 1T
NZ: 4G 1T
Twickenham, 4 Nov 1967

D. Rutherford **1C**

K.F. Savage
C.W. McFadyean
† R.H. Lloyd **2T**
R.E. Webb

J.F. Finlan
† W.J. Gittings

A.L. Horton
H.O. Godwin
* P.E. Judd
P.J. Larter **1PG**
J.E. Owen
D.P. Rogers
G.A. Sherriff
R.B. Taylor

Five Nations Championship

v WALES

DRAWN 11-11
England: 1G 1PG 1T
Wales: 1G 1DG 1T
Twickenham, 20 Jan 1968

† R. Hiller **1PG 1C**

† D.H. Prout
* C.W. McFadyean **1T**
R.H. Lloyd
K. F. Savage

J.F. Finlan
† B.W. Redwood **1T**

† B.W. Keen
J.V. Pullin
M.J. Coulman
† M.J. Parsons
P.J. Larter
† B.R. West
† D.J. Gay
† P.J. Bell

v IRELAND

DRAWN 9-9
England: 2PG 1DG
Ireland: 3PG
Twickenham, 10 Feb 1968

R. Hiller **2PG**

D.H. Prout
* C.W. McFadyean
R.H. Lloyd
R.E. Webb

J.F. Finlan **1DG**
B.W. Redwood

B.W. Keen
J.V. Pullin
M.J. Coulman
M.J. Parsons
P.J. Larter
B.R. West
D.J. Gay
P.J. Bell

v FRANCE

LOST 9-14
France: 1G 1PG 2DG
England: 1DG 2PG
Stade Colombes, 24 Feb 1968

R. Hiller **2PG**

K.F. Savage
† T.J. Brooke
R.H. Lloyd
R.E. Webb

* M.P. Weston **1DG**
R.D.A. Pickering

B.W. Keen
J.V. Pullin
M.J. Coulman
M.J. Parsons
P.J. Larter
B.R. West
D.J. Gay
P.J. Bell

v SCOTLAND

WON 8-6
Scotland: 1PG 1DG
England: 1G 1PG
Murrayfield, 16 Mar 1968

R. Hiller **1C 1PG**

K.F. Savage
T.J. Brooke
R.H. Lloyd
R.E. Webb

* M.P. Weston
R.D.A. Pickering

B.W. Keen
J.V. Pullin
M.J. Coulman **1T**
M.J. Parsons
P.J. Larter
B.R. West
D.J. Gay
P.J. Bell

FACT FILE

- Bob Hiller entered international rugby against the Welsh. He was to play 19 times at full-back and score 138 points for England, records which stood for a decade until overhauled by the Leicester full-back, Dusty Hare.

FINAL TABLE

	P	W	D	L	F	A	Pts
France	4	4	0	0	52	30	8
Ireland	4	2	1	1	38	37	5
England	**4**	**1**	**2**	**1**	**37**	**40**	**4**
Wales	4	1	1	2	31	34	3
Scotland	4	0	0	4	18	35	0

1968-69

Five Nations Championship

v IRELAND

LOST 15-17
Ireland: 1G 2PG 1DG 1T
England: 4PG 1T
Lansdowne Road, 8 Feb 1969

R. Hiller 4PG

† K.J. Fielding
† J.S. Spencer
† D.J. Duckham 1T
R.E. Webb

J.F. Finlan
T.C. Wintle

D.L. Powell
J.V. Pullin
† K.E. Fairbrother
P.J. Larter
† N.E. Horton
D.P. Rogers
D.M. Rollitt
* J.R.H. Greenwood

v FRANCE

WON 22-8
England: 2G 3PG 1T
France: 1G 1DG
Twickenham, 22 Feb 1969

R. Hiller 3PG 2C

K.J. Fielding 1T
J.S. Spencer
D.J. Duckham
R.E. Webb 1T

J.F. Finlan
T.C. Wintle

D.L. Powell
J.V. Pullin
K.E. Fairbrother
P.J. Larter
N.E. Horton
* D.P. Rogers
D.M. Rollitt 1T
R.B. Taylor

v SCOTLAND

WON 8-3
England: 1G 1T
Scotland: 1PG
Twickenham, 15 Mar 1969

R. Hiller 1C

K.J. Fielding [1]
J.S. Spencer
D.J. Duckham 2T
R.E. Webb

J.F. Finlan
T.C. Wintle

D.L. Powell
J.V. Pullin
K.E. Fairbrother
P.J. Larter
N.E. Horton
* D.P. Rogers
D.M. Rollitt
R.B. Taylor

1 Rep by † T.J. Dalton

v WALES

LOST 9-30
Wales: 3G 2PG 1DG 2T
England: 3PG
Cardiff Arms Park, 12 Apr 1969

R. Hiller 3PG

† K.C. Plummer
J.S. Spencer
D.J. Duckham
R.E. Webb

J.F. Finlan
T.C. Wintle

D.L. Powell
J.V. Pullin
K.E. Fairbrother
P.J. Larter
N.E. Horton
* D.P. Rogers
D.M. Rollitt
R.B. Taylor

FACT FILE

- The finale of the season, at Cardiff in April, resulted in an overwhelming defeat by Wales. Although the scores were level at half-time (3-3), Wales coasted to a win by 21 points in the second half, registering their biggest win over England since 1922.

FINAL TABLE

	P	W	D	L	F	A	Pts
Wales	4	3	1	0	79	31	7
Ireland	4	3	0	1	61	48	6
England	**4**	**2**	**0**	**2**	**54**	**58**	**4**
Scotland	4	1	0	3	12	44	2
France	4	0	1	3	28	53	1

1969-70

Tour Match

v SOUTH AFRICA

WON 11-8
England: 1G 1PG 1T
SA: 1G 1PG
Twickenham, 20 Dec 1969

* R. Hiller[1] 1PG 1C

K.J. Fielding
J.S. Spencer
D.J. Duckham
† P.M. Hale

† I.R. Shackleton
† N.C. Starmer-Smith

† C.B. Stevens
J.V. Pullin 1T
K.E. Fairbrother
A.M. Davis
P.J. Larter 1T
B.R. West
R.B. Taylor
† A.L. Bucknall

1 Rep by † C.S. Wardlow

Five Nations Championship

v IRELAND

WON 9-3
England: 2DG 1T
Ireland: 1PG
Twickenham, 14 Feb 1970

* R. Hiller 2DG

K.J. Fielding
J.S. Spencer
D.J. Duckham
P.M. Hale

I.R. Shackleton 1T
N.C. Starmer-Smith

C.B. Stevens
J.V. Pullin
K.E. Fairbrother
A.M. Davis
P.J. Larter
B.R. West
R.B. Taylor
A.L. Bucknall

v WALES

LOST 13-17
England: 2G 1PG
Wales: 1G 1DG 3T
Twickenham, 28 Feb 1970

* R. Hiller 1PG 2C

† M.J. Novak 1T
J.S. Spencer
D.J. Duckham 1T
P.M. Hale

I.R. Shackleton
N.C. Starmer-Smith

C.B. Stevens
J.V. Pullin
K.E. Fairbrother
A.M. Davis
P.J. Larter
B.R. West
R.B. Taylor
A.L. Bucknall

v SCOTLAND

LOST 5-14
Scotland: 1G 2PG 1T
England: 1G
Murrayfield, 21 Mar 1970

* R. Hiller 1C

M.J. Novak
J.S. Spencer 1T
D.J. Duckham
† M.P. Bulpitt

I.R. Shackleton
N.C. Starmer-Smith

C.B. Stevens
J.V. Pullin
K.E. Fairbrother
A.M. Davis
P.J. Larter
B.R. West[1]
R.B. Taylor
A.L. Bucknall

1 Rep by † B.K. Jackson

v FRANCE

LOST 13-35
France: 4G 2DG 1PG 2T
England: 2G 1PG
Stade Colombes, 18 Apr 1970

† A.M. Jorden 2C 1PG

K.J. Fielding
J.S. Spencer 1T
D.J. Duckham
M.J. Novak

J.F. Finlan
N.C. Starmer-Smith

B.K. Jackson
J.V. Pullin
K.E. Fairbrother
† M.M. Leadbetter
P.J. Larter
* R.B. Taylor 1T
† G.F. Redmond
A.L. Bucknall

FACT FILE

- In 1969-70 England adopted a squad system for the first time, naming 30 players for the Springbok encounter. The result was England's first win over the South Africans.

FINAL TABLE

	P	W	D	L	F	A	Pts
France	4	3	0	1	60	33	6
Wales	4	3	0	1	46	42	6
Ireland	4	2	0	2	33	28	4
Scotland	4	1	0	3	43	50	2
England	**4**	**1**	**0**	**3**	**40**	**69**	**2**

1970-71

Five Nations Championship

v WALES

LOST 6-22
Wales: 2G 2DG 1PG 1T
England: 1PG 1T
Cardiff Arms Park, 16 Jan 1971

† P.A. Rossborough 1PG

† J.P.A.G. Janion
C.S. Wardlow
J.S. Spencer
D.J. Duckham

† I.D. Wright
† J.J. Page

D.L. Powell
J.V. Pullin
K.E. Fairbrother
P.J. Larter
† B.F. Ninnes
* A.L. Bucknall
† R.C. Hannaford 1T
† A. Neary

v IRELAND

WON 9-6
Ireland: 2T
England: 3PG
Lansdowne Road, 13 Feb 1971

R. Hiller 3PG

J.P.A.G. Janion
* J.S. Spencer
C.S. Wardlow
D.J. Duckham

I.D. Wright
J.J. Page

D.L. Powell
J.V. Pullin
K.E. Fairbrother
P.J. Larter
N.E. Horton
A.L. Bucknall
R.C. Hannaford
A. Neary

v FRANCE

DRAWN 14-14
England: 1G 3PG
France: 1G 1PG 1DG 1T
Twickenham, 27 Feb 1971

* R. Hiller 3PG 1C 1T

J.P.A.G. Janion
C.S. Wardlow
D.J. Duckham
P.B. Glover

I.D. Wright
J.J. Page

D.L. Powell
J.V. Pullin
K.E. Fairbrother
P.J. Larter
N.E. Horton
A.L. Bucknall
R.C. Hannaford
A. Neary

1st v SCOTLAND

LOST 15-16
England: 3PG 2T
Scotland: 2G 1DG 1T
Twickenham, 20 Mar 1971

R. Hiller 1T 3PG

J.P.A.G. Janion
C.S. Wardlow [1]
* J.S. Spencer
D.J. Duckham

† A.R. Cowman
J.J. Page

D.L. Powell
J.V. Pullin
† F.E. Cotton
P.J. Larter
N.E. Horton
A.L. Bucknall
R.B. Taylor
A. Neary 1T

1 Rep by I.D. Wright

FACT FILE

- Seldom has England been so thoroughly outclassed as they were in their centenary season, 1971. Two special celebration matches added to the usual round of championship matches, but only one game was won.
- Bob Hiller was the only English player to emerge from the season with credit. He scored 49 points for the season, a new England record, and became the first full-back to score three tries at Twickenham in one season.

FINAL TABLE

	P	W	D	L	F	A	Pts
Wales	4	4	0	0	73	38	8
France	4	1	2	1	41	40	4
England	**4**	**1**	**1**	**2**	**44**	**58**	**3**
Ireland	4	1	1	2	41	46	3
Scotland	4	1	0	3	47	64	2

1970-71 continued

Centenary Matches

2nd v SCOTLAND

LOST 6-26
Scotland: 4G 1PG 1T
England: 1DG 1PG
Murrayfield, 27 Mar 1971

R. Hiller **1PG**

J.P.A.G. Janion
C.S. Wardlow
* J.S. Spencer
D.J. Duckham

A.R. Cowman **1DG**
N.C. Starmer-Smith

D.L. Powell
J.V. Pullin
F.E. Cotton
P.J. Larter
† C.W. Ralston
A.L. Bucknall
R.B. Taylor
A. Neary

v RFU PRESIDENT'S XV

LOST 11-28
England: 1G 2PG
RFU President's XV: 5G 1T
Twickenham, 17 Apr 1971

R. Hiller **1C 2PG 1T**

J.P.A.G. Janion
* J.S. Spencer
D.J. Duckham
P.B. Glover

A.R. Cowman
N.C. Starmer-Smith

C.B. Stevens
J.V. Pullin
F.E. Cotton
P.J. Larter
C.W. Ralston
† R.N. Creed
† P.J. Dixon
A. Neary

1971-72

Five Nations Championship

v WALES

LOST 3-12
England: 1PG
Wales: 1G 2PG
Twickenham, 15 Jan 1972

* R. Hiller **1PG**

J.P.A.G. Janion
† M.C. Beese
D.J. Duckham
K.J. Fielding

† A.G.B. Old
† J.G. Webster

C.B. Stevens
J.V. Pullin
† M.A. Burton
† A. Brinn
C.W. Ralston
P.J. Dixon
† A.G. Ripley
A. Neary

v IRELAND

LOST 12-16
England: 1G 2PG
Ireland: 1G 1T 1PG 1DG
Twickenham, 12 Feb 1972

* R. Hiller **2PG 1C**

K.J. Fielding
M.C. Beese
D.J. Duckham
R.E. Webb

A.G.B. Old
J.G. Webster

C.B. Stevens
J.V. Pullin
M.A. Burton
A. Brinn
C.W. Ralston **1T**
P.J. Dixon
A.G. Ripley
A. Neary

v FRANCE

LOST 12-37
France: 5G 1PG 1T
England: 1G 2PG
Stade Colombes, 26 Feb 1972

† P.M. Knight

K.J. Fielding
M.C. Beese **1T**
D.J. Duckham
R.E. Webb

A.G.B. Old **2PG 1C**
† L.E. Weston

C.B. Stevens
J.V. Pullin
M.A. Burton
J. Barton
C.W. Ralston
* P.J. Dixon
A.G. Ripley
A. Neary[1]

1 Rep by † N.O. Martin

1971-72 continued

Five Nations Championship

v SCOTLAND

LOST 9-23
Scotland: 4PG 1DG 2T
England: 3PG
Murrayfield, 18 Mar 1972

P.M. Knight

K.J. Fielding
J.P.A.G. Janion
† G.W. Evans
D.J. Duckham

A.G.B. Old **3PG**
L.E. Weston

C.B. Stevens
J.V. Pullin
M.A. Burton
A. Brinn
C.W. Ralston
* P.J. Dixon
A.G. Ripley
A. Neary

Tour Match

v SOUTH AFRICA

WON 18-9
SA: 3PG
England: 1G 4PG
Johannesburg, 3 June 1972

† S.A. Doble **4PG 1C**

P.M. Knight
† P.S. Preece
J.P.A.G. Janion
† A.J. Morley **1T**

A.G.B. Old
J.G. Webster

C.B. Stevens
* J.V. Pullin
M.A. Burton
P.J. Larter
C.W. Ralston
† J.A. Watkins
A.G. Ripley
A. Neary

FACT FILE

- For the first time ever, England lost all four of their matches in the international championship.
- England toured South Africa during the summer under the captaincy of John Pullin. England ended an unbeaten tour with a convincing victory over the mighty Springboks.

FINAL TABLE

	P	W	D	L	F	A	Pts
Wales	3	3	0	0	67	21	6
Scotland	3	2	0	1	55	53	4
Ireland	2	2	0	0	30	21	4
France	4	1	0	3	61	66	2
England	**4**	**0**	**0**	**4**	**36**	**88**	**0**

CHAMPIONSHIP UNRESOLVED
Ireland did not meet Wales or Scotland

1972-73

Tour Match

v NEW ZEALAND

LOST 0-9
England: Nil
NZ: 1G 1DG
Twickenham, 6 Jan 1973

S.A. Doble

A.J. Morley
† P.J. Warfield
P.S. Preece
D.J. Duckham

J.F. Finlan
J.G. Webster

C.B. Stevens
* J.V. Pullin
† W.F. Anderson
P.J. Larter
C.W. Ralston
J.A. Watkins
A.G. Ripley
A. Neary

Five Nations Championship

v WALES

LOST 9-25
Wales: 1G 4T 1PG
England: 1DG 2PG
Cardiff Arms Park, 20 Jan 1973

S.A. Doble **2PG**

A.J. Morley
P.J. Warfield [1]
P.S. Preece
D.J. Duckham

A.R. Cowman **1DG**
J.G. Webster

C.B. Stevens
* J.V. Pullin
F.E. Cotton
P.J. Larter
C.W. Ralston
J.A. Watkins
A.G. Ripley
A. Neary

1 Rep by G.W. Evans

v IRELAND

LOST 9-18
Ireland: 2G 1DG 1PG
England: 1G 1PG
Lansdowne Road, 10 Feb 1973

A.M. Jorden **1C 1PG**

A.J. Morley
P.J. Warfield
P.S. Preece
D.J. Duckham

A.R. Cowman
† S.J. Smith

C.B. Stevens
* J.V. Pullin
F.E. Cotton
† R.M. Uttley
C.W. Ralston
P.J. Dixon
A.G. Ripley
A. Neary **1T**

1972-73 continued

Five Nations Championship

v FRANCE

WON 14-6
England: 2T 2PG
France: 1G
Twickenham, 24 Feb 1973

A.M. Jorden 2PG

† P.J. Squires
G.W. Evans
P.S. Preece
D.J. Duckham 2T

† M.J. Cooper
S.J. Smith

C.B. Stevens
* J.V. Pullin
F.E. Cotton
R.M. Uttley
C.W. Ralston
P.J. Dixon
A.G. Ripley
A. Neary

v SCOTLAND

WON 20-13
England: 2G 2T
Scotland: 1G 1PG 1T
Twickenham, 17 Mar 1973

A.M. Jorden 2C

P.J. Squires 1T
G.W. Evans 1T
P.S. Preece
D.J. Duckham

M.J. Cooper
S.J. Smith

C.B. Stevens
* J.V. Pullin
F.E. Cotton
R.M. Uttley
C.W. Ralston
P.J. Dixon 2T
A.G. Ripley
A. Neary

FACT FILE

- The first win in the championship for two years was against the French, and England's swift, determined pack outplayed the visitors. The names of 'Stack' Stevens, John Pullin, Fran Cotton, Roger Uttley and Chris Ralston were to become regular entries in the English programmes for several seasons, and the back-row of Peter Dixon, Tony Neary and Andy Ripley created a record by playing together 12 times in all.

FINAL TABLE

	P	W	D	L	F	A	Pts
Wales	4	2	0	2	53	43	4
Ireland	4	2	0	2	50	48	4
France	4	2	0	2	38	36	4
Scotland	4	2	0	2	55	59	4
England	**4**	**2**	**0**	**2**	**52**	**62**	**4**

1973-74

Tour Matches

v NEW ZEALAND

WON 16-10
NZ: 1G 1T
England: 2G 1T
Auckland, 15 Sep 1973

P.A. Rossborough 2C

P.J. Squires 1T
G.W. Evans [1]
P.S. Preece
D.J. Duckham

A.G. B.Old
J.G. Webster

C.B. Stevens 1T
* J.V. Pullin
F.E. Cotton
R.M. Uttley
C.W. Ralston
J.A. Watkins
A.G. Ripley
A. Neary 1T

1 Rep by M.J. Cooper

v AUSTRALIA

WON 20-3
England: 1G 2PG 2T
Australia: 1PG
Twickenham, 17 Nov 1973

P.A. Rossborough 2PG 1C

P.J. Squires
J.P.A.G. Janion
† D. Roughley
D.J. Duckham

A.G.B. Old 1T
S.J. Smith

C.B. Stevens
* J.V. Pullin
F.E. Cotton
R.M. Uttley
C.W. Ralston
J.A. Watkins
A.G. Ripley 1T
A. Neary 1T

Five Nations Championship

v SCOTLAND

LOST 14-16
Scotland: 1G 2PG 1T
England: 1DG 1PG 2T
Murrayfield, 2 Feb 1974

P.A. Rossborough 1DG

P.J. Squires
D. Roughley
G.W. Evans
D.J. Duckham

A.G.B. Old 1PG
J.G. Webster

C.B. Stevens
* J.V. Pullin
F.E. Cotton 1T
N.E. Horton
C.W. Ralston
P.J. Dixon
A.G. Ripley
A. Neary 1T

1973-74 continued

Five Nations Championship

v IRELAND

LOST **21-26**
England: 1G 5PG
Ireland: 2G 2T 1DG 1PG
Twickenham, 16 Feb 1974

P.A. Rossborough

P.J. Squires **1T**
D. Roughley
G.W. Evans
D.J. Duckham

A.G.B. Old **1C 5PG**
S.J. Smith

C.B. Stevens
* J.V. Pullin
F.E. Cotton
R.M. Uttley
C.W. Ralston
P.J. Dixon
A.G. Ripley
A. Neary

v FRANCE

DRAWN **12-12**
France: 1G 1PG 1DG
England: 1G 1PG 1DG
Parc des Princes, 2 Mar 1974

A.M. Jorden

P.J. Squires
† K. Smith
G.W. Evans **1DG**
D.J. Duckham **1T**

A.G.B. Old **1C 1PG**
S.J. Smith

C.B. Stevens
* J.V. Pullin
M.A. Burton
R.M. Uttley
C.W. Ralston
P.J. Dixon
A.G. Ripley
A. Neary

v WALES

WON **16-12**
England: 1G 2PG 1T
Wales: 1G 2PG
Twickenham, 16 Mar 1974

† W.H. Hare

P.J. Squires
K. Smith
G.W. Evans
D.J. Duckham **1T**

A.G.B. Old **2PG 1C**
J.G. Webster

C.B. Stevens
* J.V. Pullin
M.A. Burton
R.M. Uttley
C.W. Ralston
P.J. Dixon
A.G. Ripley **1T**
A. Neary

FACT FILE

- John Pullin set a remarkable record: by leading England to victory in the only Test of the autumn tour to New Zealand, and by captaining the side to a win over Australia in November, he became the first international captain in history to win Tests against all three dominion nations.
- Andy Ripley went on to become England's most-capped No. 8, playing 24 times.

FINAL TABLE

	P	W	D	L	F	A	Pts
Ireland	4	2	1	1	50	45	5
Wales	4	1	2	1	43	41	4
France	4	1	2	1	43	53	4
Scotland	4	2	0	2	41	35	4
England	**4**	**1**	**1**	**2**	**63**	**66**	**3**

1974-75

Five Nations Championship

v IRELAND

LOST 9-12
Ireland: 2G
England: 1G 1DG
Lansdowne Road, 18 Jan 1975

P.A. Rossborough

P.J. Squires
P.J. Warfield
P.S. Preece
D.J. Duckham

A.G.B. Old **1C 1DG**
J.G. Webster

C.B. Stevens **1T**
J.V. Pullin
* F.E. Cotton
† W.B. Beaumont
C.W. Ralston
P.J. Dixon
A.G. Ripley
A. Neary

v FRANCE

LOST 20-27
England: 4PG 2T
France: 4G 1PG
Twickenham, 1 Feb 1975

P.A. Rossborough **1T 4PG**

P.J. Squires
P.J. Warfield
P.S. Preece
D.J. Duckham **1T**

M.J. Cooper
J.G. Webster

C.B. Stevens
† P.J. Wheeler
* F.E. Cotton
R.M. Uttley
C.W. Ralston
J.A. Watkins
A.G. Ripley
A. Neary

v WALES

LOST 4-20
Wales: 1G 2PG 2T
England: 1T
Cardiff Arms Park, 15 Feb 1975

A.M. Jorden

P.J. Squires
K. Smith
P.S. Preece
D.J. Duckham

M.J. Cooper
J.G. Webster [1]

C.B. Stevens
P.J. Wheeler [2]
* F.E. Cotton
N.E. Horton **1T**
C.W. Ralston
J.A. Watkins
R.M. Uttley
A. Neary

1 Rep by S.J. Smith
2 Rep by J.V. Pullin

v SCOTLAND

WON 7-6
England: 1PG 1T
Scotland: 2PG
Twickenham, 15 Mar 1975

A.M. Jorden

P.J. Squires
P.J. Warfield
K. Smith
A.J. Morley **1T**

† W.N. Bennett **1PG**
J.J. Page

C.B. Stevens
J.V. Pullin
M.A. Burton
R.M. Uttley
C.W. Ralston
D.M. Rollitt
A.G. Ripley
* A. Neary

FACT FILE

- England started the season with a new coach in John Burgess, a new skipper in Fran Cotton, and a positive attitude which made them favourites to win the championship. However, their failure to play the open attacking rugby which had been a feature of the final trial, and a series of dreadful defensive lapses, left them clutching the wooden spoon for the third season in four.

FINAL TABLE

	P	W	D	L	F	A	Pts
Wales	4	3	0	1	87	30	6
Ireland	4	2	0	2	54	67	4
France	4	2	0	2	53	79	4
Scotland	4	2	0	2	47	40	4
England	**4**	**1**	**0**	**3**	**40**	**65**	**2**

1974-75 continued

Tour Matches

1st v AUSTRALIA

LOST 9-16
Australia: 2PG 2DG 1T
England: 1G 1PG
Sydney C.G., 24 May 1975

† P.E. Butler **1PG 1C**

P.J. Squires **1T**
J.P.A.G. Janion
† A.W. Maxwell
A.J. Morley

W.N. Bennett [1]
† P.J. Kingston

† B.G. Nelmes
J.V. Pullin
M.A. Burton
† N.D. Mantell
R.M. Uttley
D.M. Rollitt
A.G. Ripley
* A. Neary [2]

1 Rep by † A.J. Wordsworth
2 Rep by W.B. Beaumont

2nd v AUSTRALIA

LOST 21-30
Australia: 2G 2PG 3T
England: 2G 3PG
Brisbane, 31 May 1975

† A.J. Hignell

P.J. Squires **1T**
J.P.A.G. Janion
P.S. Preece
A.J. Morley

A.G.B. Old **2C 3PG**
P.J. Kingston

B.G. Nelmes
* J.V. Pullin
M.A. Burton
† R.M. Wilkinson
W.B. Beaumont
D.M. Rollitt
A.G. Ripley
R.M. Uttley **1T**

FACT FILE

- The second of the Tests was marred by an unprecedented outburst of thuggery at the start of the match. Mike Burton, having been reprimanded for butting an opponent, was given his marching orders in the second minute of the game for a late tackle. He thus became the first English player to be sent off in an international.

1975-76

Tour Match

v AUSTRALIA

WON 23-6
England: 1G 3PG 2T
Australia: 2PG
Twickenham, 3 Jan 1976

A.J. Hignell **3PG 1C**

P.J. Squires
A.W. Maxwell
† B.J. Corless **1T**
D.J. Duckham **1T**

M.J. Cooper
† M.S. Lampkowski **1T**

M.A. Burton
P.J. Wheeler
F.E. Cotton
W.B. Beaumont
R.M. Wilkinson
† M. Keyworth
A.G. Ripley
* A. Neary

Five Nations Championship

v WALES

LOST 9-21
England: 3PG
Wales: 3G 1PG
Twickenham, 17 Jan 1976

A.J. Hignell **3PG**

P.J. Squires [1]
A.W. Maxwell
† D.A. Cooke
D.J. Duckham

M.J. Cooper
M.S. Lampkowski

M.A. Burton
P.J. Wheeler
F.E. Cotton
W.B. Beaumont
R.M. Wilkinson
M. Keyworth
A.G. Ripley
* A. Neary

1 Rep by P.S. Preece

v SCOTLAND

LOST 12-22
Scotland: 2G 2PG 1T
England: 1G 2PG
Murrayfield, 21 Feb 1976

A.J. Hignell

K.C. Plummer
A.W. Maxwell [1] **1T**
D.A. Cooke
D.J. Duckham [2]

A.G.B. Old **1C 2PG**
M.S. Lampkowski

M.A. Burton
P.J. Wheeler
F.E. Cotton
W.B. Beaumont
R.M. Wilkinson
M. Keyworth
A.G. Ripley
* A. Neary

1 Rep by W.N. Bennett
2 Rep by † D.M. Wyatt

1975-76 continued

Five Nations Championship

v IRELAND

LOST 12-13
England: 4PG
Ireland: 2PG 1DG 1T
Twickenham, 6 Mar 1976

A.J. Hignell [1]

K.C. Plummer
A.W. Maxwell
D.A. Cooke
† M.A.C. Slemen

A.G.B. Old **4PG**
M.S. Lampkowski

M.A. Burton
P.J. Wheeler
F.E. Cotton
W.B. Beaumont
R.M. Wilkinson
M. Keyworth
† G.J. Adey
* A. Neary

1 Rep by B.J. Corless

v FRANCE

LOST 9-30
France: 3G 3T
England: 1G 1PG
Parc des Princes, 20 Mar 1976

P.E. Butler **1C 1PG**

K.C. Plummer
A.W. Maxwell
D.A. Cooke
M.A.C. Slemen

† C.G. Williams
S.J. Smith

M.A. Burton
J.V. Pullin
F.E. Cotton
W.B. Beaumont
R.M. Wilkinson
P.J. Dixon **1T**
G.J. Adey
* A. Neary

FACT FILE

- A new coach prepared the team for the opening match of 1976, Peter Colston. After a convincing victory over Australia, all four matches were lost in the Home Internationals for only the second time and just one player, Andy Maxwell, kept his place among the backs during the season.

FINAL TABLE

	P	W	D	L	F	A	Pts
Wales	4	4	0	0	102	37	8
France	4	3	0	1	82	37	6
Scotland	4	2	0	2	49	59	4
Ireland	4	1	0	3	31	87	2
England	**4**	**0**	**0**	**4**	**42**	**86**	**0**

Andy Ripley breaks from the back of the scrum against France at Twickenham in 1975.

1976-77

Five Nations Championship

v SCOTLAND

WON 26-6
England: 2G 2PG 2T
Scotland: 2PG
Twickenham, 15 Jan 1977

A.J. Hignell **2PG 2C**

P.J. Squires
B.J. Corless
† C.P. Kent **1T**
M.A.C. Slemen **1T**

M.J. Cooper
† M. Young **1T**

† R.J. Cowling
P.J. Wheeler
F.E. Cotton
W.B. Beaumont
N.E. Horton
P.J. Dixon
* R.M. Uttley **1T**
† M. Rafter

v IRELAND

WON 4-0
Ireland: Nil
England: 1T
Lansdowne Road, 5 Feb 1977

A.J. Hignell

P.J. Squires
B.J. Corless
C.P. Kent
M.A.C. Slemen

M.J. Cooper **1T**
M. Young

R.J. Cowling
P.J. Wheeler
F.E. Cotton
W.B. Beaumont
N.E. Horton
P.J. Dixon
* R.M. Uttley
A. Neary

v FRANCE

LOST 3-4
England: 1PG
France: 1T
Twickenham, 19 Feb 1977

A.J. Hignell **1PG**

P.J. Squires
B.J. Corless
C.P. Kent
M.A.C. Slemen

M.J. Cooper
M. Young [1]

R.J. Cowling
P.J. Wheeler
F.E. Cotton
W.B. Beaumont
N.E. Horton
P.J. Dixon
* R.M. Uttley
M. Rafter

1 Rep by S.J. Smith

v WALES

LOST 9-14
Wales: 2PG 2T
England: 3PG
Cardiff Arms Park, 5 Mar 1977

A.J. Hignell **3PG**

P.J. Squires
B.J. Corless
C.P. Kent
M.A.C. Slemen

M.J. Cooper
M. Young

R.J. Cowling
P.J. Wheeler
F.E. Cotton
W.B. Beaumont
N.E. Horton
P.J. Dixon
* R.M. Uttley
M. Rafter

FACT FILE

- The same team was picked for each match, although Mike Rafter was forced to withdraw for the Irish game, Tony Neary replacing him. In a brave attempt to win the Triple Crown at Cardiff, England eventually lost – but by only five points.

FINAL TABLE

	P	W	D	L	F	A	Pts
France	4	4	0	0	58	21	8
Wales	4	3	0	1	66	43	6
England	**4**	**2**	**0**	**2**	**42**	**24**	**4**
Scotland	4	1	0	3	39	85	2
Ireland	4	0	0	4	33	65	0

1977-78

Five Nations Championship

v FRANCE

LOST 6-15
France: 2G 1PG
England: 2DG
Park des Princes, 21 Jan 1978

W.H. Hare

P.J. Squires
B.J. Corless
A.W. Maxwell [1]
M.A.C. Slemen

A.G.B. Old **2DG**
M. Young

R.J. Cowling
P.J. Wheeler
M.A. Burton
* W.B. Beaumont
N.E. Horton
P.J. Dixon [2]
† J.P. Scott
M. Rafter

1 Rep by C.P. Kent
2 Rep by A. Neary

v WALES

LOST 6-9
England: 2PG
Wales: 3PG
Twickenham, 4 Feb 1978

A.J. Hignell **2PG**

P.J. Squires
B.J. Corless
† P.W. Dodge
M.A.C. Slemen

† J.P. Horton
M. Young

B.G. Nelmes
P.J. Wheeler
M.A. Burton
* W.B. Beaumont
N.E. Horton
† R.J. Mordell
J.P. Scott
M. Rafter

v SCOTLAND

WON 15-0
Scotland: Nil
England: 2G 1PG
Murrayfield, 4 Mar 1978

† D.W.N. Caplan

P.J. Squires **1T**
B.J. Corless
P.W. Dodge **1PG**
M.A.C. Slemen

J.P. Horton
M. Young **2C**

B.G. Nelmes **1T**
P.J. Wheeler
F.E. Cotton
* W.B. Beaumont
† M.J. Colclough
P.J. Dixon
J.P. Scott
M. Rafter

v IRELAND

WON 15-9
England: 2G 1PG
Ireland: 1DG 2PG
Twickenham, 18 Mar 1978

D.W.N. Caplan

P.J. Squires
B.J. Corless
P.W. Dodge
M.A.C. Slemen **1T**

J.P. Horton
M. Young **1PG 2C**

B.G. Nelmes
P.J. Wheeler
F.E. Cotton
* W.B. Beaumont
M.J. Colclough
P.J. Dixon **1T**
J.P. Scott
M. Rafter

FACT FILE

- England's win in Scotland was their first at Murrayfield for ten years.
- Bill Beaumont went on to become England's most popular captain since the 1920s. In an admirable career he led England on 21 occasions and gained 11 victories as captain – new records for his nation.

FINAL TABLE

	P	W	D	L	F	A	Pts
Wales	4	4	0	0	67	43	8
France	4	3	0	1	51	47	6
England	**4**	**2**	**0**	**2**	**42**	**33**	**4**
Ireland	4	1	0	3	46	54	2
Scotland	4	0	0	4	39	68	0

1978-79

Tour Match

v NEW ZEALAND

LOST 6-16
England: 1DG 1PG
NZ: 1G 2PG 1T
Twickenham, 25 Nov 1978

W.H. Hare 1DG 1PG

P.J. Squires
† A.M. Bond
P.W. Dodge
M.A.C. Slemen

J.P. Horton
M. Young

R.J. Cowling
P.J. Wheeler
B.G. Nelmes
* W.B. Beaumont
J.P. Scott
P.J. Dixon
R.M. Uttley
M. Rafter

Five Nations Championship

v SCOTLAND

DRAWN 7-7
England: 1PG 1T
Scotland: 1PG 1T
Twickenham, 3 Feb 1979

A.J. Hignell

P.J. Squires
A.M. Bond
P.W. Dodge
M.A.C. Slemen 1T

W.N. Bennett 1PG
M. Young

R.J. Cowling
P.J. Wheeler
† G.S. Pearce
W.B. Beaumont
N.E. Horton
A. Neary
* R.M. Uttley [1]
M. Rafter

1 Rep by J.P. Scott

v IRELAND

LOST 7-12
Ireland: 1G 1PG 1DG
England: 1PG 1T
Lansdowne Road, 17 Feb 1979

A.J. Hignell

P.J. Squires
A.M. Bond
P.W. Dodge
M.A.C. Slemen

W.N. Bennett 1PG 1T
P.J. Kingston

R.J. Cowling
P.J. Wheeler
G.S. Pearce
* W.B. Beaumont
N.E. Horton
A. Neary
J.P. Scott
M. Rafter

v FRANCE

WON 7-6
England: 1PG 1T
France: 1G
Twickenham, 3 Mar 1979

A.J. Hignell

P.J. Squires
† R.M. Cardus
P.W. Dodge
M.A.C. Slemen

W.N. Bennett 1PG 1T
P.J. Kingston

† C.E. Smart
P.J. Wheeler
G.S. Pearce
* W.B. Beaumont
N.E. Horton
A. Neary
J.P. Scott
M. Rafter

v WALES

LOST 3-27
Wales: 2G 1DG 3T
England: 1PG
Cardiff Arms Park, 17 Mar 1979

A.J. Hignell

P.J. Squires
R.M. Cardus
P.W. Dodge
M.A.C. Slemen

W.N. Bennett 1PG
P.J. Kingston

C.E. Smart
P.J. Wheeler
G.S. Pearce
* W.B. Beaumont
N.E. Horton
A. Neary
J.P. Scott
M. Rafter

FACT FILE

- Neil Bennett became the only England player to date capped direct from the London Welsh club.

FINAL TABLE

	P	W	D	L	F	A	Pts
Wales	4	3	0	1	83	51	6
France	4	2	1	1	50	46	5
Ireland	4	1	2	1	53	51	4
England	**4**	**1**	**1**	**2**	**24**	**52**	**3**
Scotland	4	0	2	2	48	58	2

1979-80

Tour Match

v NEW ZEALAND

LOST 9-10
England: 3PG
NZ: 2PG 1T
Twickenham, 24 Nov 1979

W.H. Hare 3PG

† J. Carleton
A.M. Bond
† N.J. Preston
M.A.C. Slemen

† L. Cusworth
S.J. Smith

C.E. Smart
P.J. Wheeler
F.E. Cotton
* W.B. Beaumont
M.J. Colclough
A. Neary
J.P. Scott
M. Rafter

Five Nations Championship

v IRELAND

WON 24-9
England: 3G 2PG
Ireland: 3PG
Twickenham, 19 Jan 1980

W.H. Hare 3C 2PG

J. Carleton
A.M. Bond [1]
N.J. Preston
M.A.C. Slemen 1T

J.P. Horton
S.J. Smith 1T

F.E. Cotton
P.J. Wheeler
† P.J. Blakeway
* W.B. Beaumont
N.E. Horton
R.M. Uttley
J.P. Scott 1T
A. Neary

1 Rep by † C.R. Woodward

v FRANCE

WON 17-13
France: 1G 1PG 1T
England: 1PG 2DG 2T
Parc des Princes, 2 Feb 1980

W.H. Hare 1PG

J. Carleton 1T
C.R. Woodward
N.J. Preston 1T
M.A.C. Slemen

J.P. Horton 2DG
S.J. Smith

F.E. Cotton
P.J. Wheeler
P.J. Blakeway
* W.B. Beaumont
M.J. Colclough
R.M. Uttley
J.P. Scott
A. Neary

v WALES

WON 9-8
England: 3PG
Wales: 2T
Twickenham, 16 Feb 1980

W.H. Hare 3PG

J. Carleton
C.R. Woodward
P.W. Dodge
M.A.C. Slemen

J.P. Horton
S.J. Smith

F.E. Cotton
P.J. Wheeler
P.J. Blakeway
* W.B. Beaumont
M.J. Colclough
R.M. Uttley [1]
J.P. Scott
A. Neary

1 Rep by M. Rafter

v SCOTLAND

WON 30-18
Scotland: 2G 2PG
England: 2G 2PG 3T
Murrayfield, 15 Mar 1980

W.H. Hare 2PG 2C

J. Carleton 3T
C.R. Woodward
P.W. Dodge
M.A.C. Slemen 1T

J.P. Horton
S.J. Smith 1T

F.E. Cotton
P.J. Wheeler
P.J. Blakeway
* W.B. Beaumont
M.J. Colclough
R.M. Uttley
J.P. Scott
A. Neary

FACT FILE

- 1980 was England's season. The side gained the Grand Slam for the first time since 1957, the Triple Crown was lifted for the first time since 1960, and the championship title was England's first outright success for 17 years.
- Against the Scots, John Carleton became the first England player since 1924 to score three tries in an international.

FINAL TABLE

	P	W	D	L	F	A	Pts
England	**4**	**4**	**0**	**0**	**80**	**48**	**8**
Ireland	4	2	0	2	70	65	4
Wales	4	2	0	2	50	45	4
Scotland	4	1	0	3	61	83	2
France	4	1	0	3	55	75	2

1980-81

Five Nations Championship

v WALES

LOST 19-21
Wales: 1G 4PG 1DG
England: 5PG 1T
Cardiff Arms Park, 17 Jan 1981

W.H. Hare **5PG 1T**

J. Carleton
C.R. Woodward
P.W. Dodge
M.A.C. Slemen

J.P. Horton
S.J. Smith

F.E. Cotton [1]
P.J. Wheeler
P.J. Blakeway
* W.B. Beaumont
M.J. Colclough
M. Rafter
J.P. Scott
† D.H. Cooke

1 Rep by † A. Sheppard

v SCOTLAND

WON 23-17
England: 1G 3PG 2T
Scotland: 1G 1PG 2T
Twickenham, 21 Feb 1981

W.H. Hare **3PG 1C**

J. Carleton
C.R. Woodward **1T**
P.W. Dodge
M.A.C. Slemen **1T**

† G.H. Davies **1T**
S.J. Smith

C.E. Smart
P.J. Wheeler
P.J. Blakeway
* W.B. Beaumont
M.J. Colclough
† N.C. Jeavons [1]
J.P. Scott
D.H. Cooke

1 Rep by † R. Hesford

v IRELAND

WON 10-6
Ireland: 2DG
England: 1G 1T
Lansdowne Road, 7 Mar 1981

† W.M.H. Rose **1T 1C**

J. Carleton
C.R. Woodward
P.W. Dodge **1T**
M.A.C. Slemen

G.H. Davies
S.J. Smith

C.E. Smart
P.J. Wheeler
P.J. Blakeway [1]
* W.B. Beaumont
M.J. Colclough
N.C. Jeavons
J.P. Scott
D.H. Cooke

1 Rep by † G.A.F. Sargent

v FRANCE

LOST 12-16
England: 4PG
France: 1G 2DG 1T
Twickenham, 21 Mar 1981

W.M.H. Rose **4PG**

J. Carleton
C.R. Woodward
P.W. Dodge
M.A.C. Slemen

G.H. Davies
S.J. Smith

C.E. Smart
P.J. Wheeler
P.J. Blakeway
* W.B. Beaumont
M.J. Colclough
N.C. Jeavons
J.P. Scott
D.H. Cooke

FACT FILE

- France were winners at Twickenham thanks to a try which strictly should never have been awarded. The French scored from a quick throw-in, but whereas the law prescribes that only the ball that went into touch may be retrieved by the players for the throw, France took their chance with a ball supplied by a bystander.

FINAL TABLE

	P	W	D	L	F	A	Pts
France	4	4	0	0	70	49	8
England	**4**	**2**	**0**	**2**	**64**	**60**	**4**
Scotland	4	2	0	2	51	54	4
Wales	4	2	0	2	51	61	4
Ireland	4	0	0	4	36	48	0

1980-81

Tour Matches

1st v ARGENTINA

DRAWN 19-19
Argentina: 1G 2DG 1PG 1T
England: 2G 1PG 1T
Buenos Aires, 30 May 1981

W.M.H. Rose 1PG 2C

J. Carleton
P.W. Dodge
C.R. Woodward 2T
† A.H. Swift

G.H. Davies 1T
S.J. Smith

C.E. Smart
† S.G.F. Mills
G.S. Pearce
* W.B. Beaumont
† J.H. Fidler
N.C. Jeavons
J.P. Scott
M. Rafter

2nd v ARGENTINA

WON 12-6
Argentina: 1G
England: 1G 2PG
Buenos Aires, 6 June 1981

W.H. Hare 2PG 1C

J. Carleton
P.W. Dodge
C.R. Woodward
A.H. Swift

G.H. Davies 1T
S.J. Smith

C.E. Smart
S.G.F. Mills
G.S. Pearce
* W.B. Beaumont
J.H. Fidler
N.C. Jeavons
J.P. Scott
M. Rafter

FACT FILE

- England became the first of the Home Countries to take advantage of a new International Board ruling to the effect that members may award full caps for games against non-IB countries. Caps were awarded for the matches against Argentina.

1981-82

Tour Match

v AUSTRALIA

WON 15-11
England: 1G 3PG
Australia: 1PG 2T
Twickenham, 2 Jan 1982

W.M.H. Rose 3PG

J. Carleton
C.R. Woodward
P.W. Dodge 1C
M.A.C. Slemen 1

G.H. Davies
S.J. Smith

C.E. Smart
P.J. Wheeer
G.S. Pearce
* W.B. Beaumont
M.J. Colclough
N.C. Jeavons 1T
R. Hesford
† P.J. Winterbottom

1 Rep by † N.C. Stringer

Five Nations Championship

v SCOTLAND

DRAWN 9-9
Scotland: 1DG 2PG
England: 3PG
Murrayfield, 16 Jan 1982

W.M.H. Rose 1PG

J. Carleton
C.R. Woodward
P.W. Dodge 2PG
M.A.C. Slemen

G.H. Davies
S.J. Smith

C.E. Smart
P.J. Wheeer
G.S. Pearce
* W.B. Beaumont
M.J. Colclough
N.C. Jeavons
R. Hesford
P.J. Winterbottom

v IRELAND

LOST 15-16
England: 1G 3PG
Ireland: 1G 2PG 1T
Twickenham, 6 Feb 1982

W.M.H. Rose 3PG 1C

J. Carleton
C.R. Woodward
A.M. Bond
M.A.C. Slemen 1T

G.H. Davies
* S.J. Smith

C.E. Smart
P.J. Wheeer
P.J. Blakeway
† J.P. Syddall
M.J. Colclough
N.C. Jeavons
J.P. Scott
P.J. Winterbottom

1981-82 continued

Five Nations Championship

v FRANCE

WON 27-15
France: 1G 1DG 2PG
England: 2G 5PG
Parc des Princes, 20 Feb 1982

W.H. Hare 5PG 2C

J. Carleton 1T
C.R. Woodward 1T
P.W. Dodge
M.A.C. Slemen

L. Cusworth
* S.J. Smith

C.E. Smart
P.J. Wheeer
P.J. Blakeway
† S. Bainbridge
M.J. Colclough
N.C. Jeavons [1]
J.P. Scott
P.J. Winterbottom

1 Rep by R. Hesford

v WALES

WON 17-7
England: 3PG 2T
Wales: 1DG 1T
Twickenham, 6 Mar 1982

W.H. Hare 3PG

J. Carleton 1T
C.R. Woodward
P.W. Dodge
M.A.C. Slemen 1T

L. Cusworth
* S.J. Smith

C.E. Smart
P.J. Wheeer
P.J. Blakeway
M.J. Colclough
S. Bainbridge
N.C. Jeavons
J.P. Scott
P.J. Winterbottom

FACT FILE

- Bill Beaumont played his last international in January, against the Scots. He was injured leading Lancashire to the County Championship just before the Irish match. Acting on medical advice, he subsequently retired from the game.

FINAL TABLE

	P	W	D	L	F	A	Pts
Ireland	4	3	0	1	66	61	6
Scotland	4	2	1	1	71	55	5
England	**4**	**2**	**1**	**1**	**68**	**47**	**5**
Wales	4	1	0	3	59	83	2
France	4	1	0	3	56	74	2

1982-83

Five Nations Championship

v FRANCE

LOST 15-19
England: 4PG 1DG
France: 2G 1PG 1T
Twickenham, 15 Jan 1983

W.H. Hare 4PG

J. Carleton
G.H. Davies
P.W. Dodge
A.H. Swift

L. Cusworth 1DG
* S.J. Smith

C.E. Smart
P.J. Wheeer
G.S. Pearce
M.J. Colclough [1]
S. Bainbridge
N.C. Jeavons
J.P. Scott
P.J. Winterbottom

1 Rep by R. Hesford

v WALES

DRAWN 13-13
Wales: 2PG 1DG 1T
England: 2PG 1DG 1T
Cardiff Arms Park, 5 Feb 1983

W.H. Hare 2PG

J. Carleton 1T
G.H. Davies
P.W. Dodge
A.H. Swift

L. Cusworth 1DG
* S.J. Smith

C.E. Smart
S.G.F. Mills
G.S. Pearce
† S.B. Boyle
S. Bainbridge
N.C. Jeavons
J.P. Scott
P.J. Winterbottom

v SCOTLAND

LOST 12-22
England: 3PG 1DG
Scotland: 1G 3PG 1DG 1T
Twickenham, 5 Mar 1983

W.H. Hare 3PG

J. Carleton
G.H. Davies
P.W. Dodge
A.H. Swift

J.P. Horton 1DG
S.J. Smith

C.E. Smart
P.J. Wheeler
G.S. Pearce
S.B. Boyle
S. Bainbridge
N.C. Jeavons
* J.P. Scott
P.J. Winterbottom

1982-83 continued

Five Nations Championship

v IRELAND

LOST 15-25
Ireland: 1G 5PG 1T
England: 5PG
Lansdowne Road, 19 Mar 1983

W.H. Hare **5PG**

J. Carleton
C.R. Woodward
P.W. Dodge
† D.M. Trick

J.P. Horton
† N.G. Youngs

C.E. Smart
P.J. Wheeler
G.S. Pearce
S.B. Boyle
S. Bainbridge
N.C. Jeavons
* J.P. Scott
P.J. Winterbottom

FACT FILE

- Mike Davis ended his reign as England coach, having seen the side to a Grand Slam at the start of his tenure. Speaking philosophically during this wooden spoon season, he remarked: 'I have turned wine into water.'

FINAL TABLE

	P	W	D	L	F	A	Pts
France	4	3	0	1	70	61	6
Ireland	4	3	0	1	71	67	6
Wales	4	2	1	1	64	53	5
Scotland	4	1	0	3	65	65	2
England	**4**	**0**	**1**	**3**	**55**	**79**	**1**

1983-84

Tour Match

v NEW ZEALAND

WON 15-9
England: 1G 3PG
NZ: 1G 1PG
Twickenham, 19 Nov 1983

W.H. Hare **3PG 1C**

J. Carleton [1]
C.R. Woodward
P.W. Dodge
M.A.C. Slemen

L. Cusworth
N.G. Youngs

† C. White
* P.J. Wheeler
G.S. Pearce
M.J. Colclough **1T**
S. Bainbridge
† P.D. Simpson
J.P. Scott
P.J. Winterbottom

1 Rep by N.C. Stringer

Five Nations Championship

v SCOTLAND

LOST 6-18
Scotland: 2G 2PG
England: 2PG
Murrayfield, 4 Feb 1984

W.H. Hare **2PG**

J. Carleton
G.H. Davies
C.R. Woodward
M.A.C. Slemen

L. Cusworth
N.G. Youngs

C. White
* P.J. Wheeler
G.S. Pearce
M.J. Colclough
S. Bainbridge
P.D. Simpson
J.P. Scott
P.J. Winterbottom [1]

1 Rep by † J.P. Hall

v IRELAND

WON 12-9
England: 3PG 1DG
Ireland: 3PG
Twickenham, 18 Feb 1984

W.H. Hare **3PG**

J. Carleton
† B. Barley
C.R. Woodward
† R. Underwood

L. Cusworth **1DG**
N.G. Youngs

C. White [1]
* P.J. Wheeler
P.J. Blakeway
M.J. Colclough
S. Bainbridge
J.P. Hall
J.P. Scott
D.H. Cooke

1 Rep by † S. Redfern

1983-84 continued

Five Nations Championship

v FRANCE

LOST 18-32
France: 3G 1PG 1DG 2T
England: 2G 2PG
Parc des Princes, 3 Mar 1984

W.H.Hare 2C 1T 2PG

J. Carleton
C.R. Woodward
B. Barley
R. Underwood 1T

L. Cusworth
N.G. Youngs

C. White
* P.J. Wheeler
P.J. Blakeway
M.J. Colclough
S. Bainbridge
J.P. Hall
J.P. Scott
P.J. Winterbottom

v WALES

LOST 15-24
England: 5PG
Wales: 1G 4PG 2DG
Twickenham, 17 Mar 1984

W.H. Hare 5PG

J. Carleton
B. Barley
C.R. Woodward
R. Underwood

L. Cusworth
N.G. Youngs

† P.A.G. Rendall
* P.J. Wheeler
P.J. Blakeway
M.J. Colclough
S. Bainbridge
† A.F. Dun
J.P. Scott
P.J. Winterbottom

Tour Matches

1st v SOUTH AFRICA

LOST 15-33
SA: 3G 5PG
England: 4PG 1DG
Port Elizabeth, 2 Jun 1984

W.H. Hare 4PG

† M.D. Bailey[1]
† J.A. Palmer
G.H. Davies
D.M. Trick

J.P. Horton 1DG
† R.J. Hill

† M. Preedy
S.G.F. Mills
P.J. Blakeway
* J.P. Scott
J.H. Fidler
J.P. Hall
† C.J.S. Butcher
P.J. Winterbottom

1 Rep by N.C. Stringer

2nd v SOUTH AFRICA

LOST 9-35
SA: 4G 1PG 2T
England: 3PG
Johannesburg, 9 Jun 1984

W.H. Hare 3PG

M.D. Bailey
J.A. Palmer
G.H. Davies
A.H. Swift

J.P. Horton
R.J. Hill

P.A.G. Rendall
† S.E. Brain
G.S. Pearce
* J.P. Scott
J.H. Fidler
J.P. Hall[1]
C.J.S. Butcher
P.J. Winterbottom

1 Rep by † G.W. Rees

FACT FILE

- England began the season under new management. Former internationals Derek Morgan and Dick Greenwood took over as chairman of the selectors and coach respectively, and for Peter Wheeler, in his final season of international rugby, there was the honour of the captaincy. The new men celebrated their new partnership with a famous win over the All Blacks, England's first against them at Twickenham since 1936.

FINAL TABLE

	P	W	D	L	F	A	Pts
Scotland	4	4	0	0	86	36	8
France	4	3	0	1	90	67	6
Wales	4	2	0	2	67	60	4
England	**4**	**1**	**0**	**3**	**51**	**83**	**2**
Ireland	4	0	0	4	39	87	0

1984-85

Tour Match

v AUSTRALIA

LOST 3-19
England: 1PG
Australia: 2G 1PG 1T
Twickenham, 3 Nov 1984

N.C. Stringer

J. Carleton
† R.A.P. Lozowski
B. Barley
R. Underwood

† S. Barnes 1PG
*† N.D. Melville

† G.J. Chilcott
S.G.F. Mills [1]
G.S. Pearce
J.P. Syddall
† N.C. Redman
J.P. Hall
C.J.S. Butcher
G.W. Rees

1 Rep by S.E. Brain

Friendly

v ROMANIA

WON 22-15
England: 4PG 2DG 1T
Romania: 5PG
Twickenham, 5 Jan 1985

N.C. Stringer [1]

† S.T. Smith 1T
† K.G. Simms [2]
* P.W. Dodge
R. Underwood

† C.R. Andrew 2DG 4PG
† R.M. Harding

P.J. Blakeway
S.E. Brain
G.S. Pearce
† J. Orwin
† W.A. Dooley
J.P. Hall
R. Hesford
D.H. Cooke

1 Rep by S. Barnes
2 Rep by G.H. Davies

Five Nations Championship

v FRANCE

DRAWN 9-9
England: 1DG 2PG
France: 3DG
Twickenham, 2 Feb 1985

† C.R. Martin

S.T. Smith
K.G. Simms
* P.W. Dodge
R. Underwood

C.R. Andrew 1DG 2PG
R.M. Harding

P.J. Blakeway
S.E. Brain
G.S. Pearce
J. Orwin
W.A. Dooley
J.P. Hall [1]
R. Hesford
D.H. Cooke

1 Rep by † M.C. Teague

Five Nations Championship

v SCOTLAND

WON 10-7
England: 2PG 1T
Scotland: 1PG 1T
Twickenham, 16 Mar 1985

C.R. Martin

S.T. Smith 1T
K.G. Simms
* P.W. Dodge
R. Underwood

C.R. Andrew 2PG
R.M. Harding

P.J. Blakeway
S.E. Brain
G.S. Pearce
J. Orwin
W.A. Dooley
J.P. Hall
R. Hesford
D.H. Cooke

v IRELAND

LOST 10-13
Ireland: 1DG 2PG 1T
England: 2PG 1T
Lansdowne Road, 30 Mar 1985

C.R. Martin

S.T. Smith
K.G. Simms
* P.W. Dodge
R. Underwood 1T

C.R. Andrew 2PG
N.D. Melville [1]

P.J. Blakeway
S.E. Brain
G.S. Pearce
J. Orwin
W.A. Dooley
J.P. Hall
R. Hesford
D.H. Cooke

1 Rep by R.J. Hill

v WALES

LOST 15-24
Wales: 2G 3PG 1DG
England: 1G 2PG 1DG
Cardiff Arms Park, 20 Apr 1985

C.R. Martin

S.T. Smith 1T
K.G. Simms
* P.W. Dodge
R. Underwood

C.R. Andrew 2PG 1DG 1C
N.D. Melville

A. Sheppard
S.E. Brain
G.S. Pearce
J. Orwin
W.A. Dooley
J.P. Hall
R. Hesford
D.H. Cooke

1984-85 continued

Tour Matches

1st v NEW ZEALAND

LOST **13-18**
NZ: 6PG
England: 1G 1T 1PG
Christchurch, 1 Jun 1985

G.H. Davies

S.T. Smith
* P.W. Dodge
† J.L.B. Salmon
† M.E. Harrison **1T**

S. Barnes **1PG 1C**
N.D. Melville

† R.P. Huntsman
S.E. Brain
G.S. Pearce
J. Orwin
S. Bainbridge
J.P. Hall
M.C. Teague **1T**
D.H. Cooke

2nd v NEW ZEALAND

LOST **15-42**
NZ: 3G 3PG 1DG 3T
England: 2G 1DG
Wellington, 8 Jun 1985

G.H. Davies

S.T. Smith
* P.W. Dodge
J.L.B. Salmon
M.E. Harrison **1T**

S. Barnes **2C 1DG**
N.D. Melville [1]

R.P. Huntsman
S.E. Brain
G.S. Pearce
J. Orwin [2]
S. Bainbridge
J.P. Hall **1T**
M.C. Teague
D.H. Cooke

1 Rep by R.J. Hill
2 Rep by W.A. Dooley

FACT FILE

- England played eight internationals during the season, opening with five new caps in the match against Australia. Nigel Melville led the side on his debut, the first England player to do so since Joe Mycock in 1947. England were easily beaten and 11 changes were made for the first ever game against Romania, played in January. Rob Andrew scored 18 points, a record haul for an Englishman on his debut.

FINAL TABLE

	P	W	D	L	F	A	Pts
Ireland	4	3	1	0	67	49	7
France	4	2	2	0	49	30	6
Wales	4	2	0	2	61	71	4
England	**4**	**1**	**1**	**2**	**44**	**53**	**3**
Scotland	4	0	0	4	46	64	0

1985-86

Five Nations Championship

v WALES

WON **21-18**
England: 6PG 1DG
Wales: 1G 1DG 3PG
Twickenham, 17 Jan 1986

G.H. Davies

S.T. Smith
† S.J. Halliday
J.L.B. Salmon
R. Underwood

C.R. Andrew **6PG 1DG**
* N.D. Melville

P.A.G. Rendall
S.E. Brain
G.S. Pearce
W.A. Dooley
M.J. Colclough
J.P. Hall
† G.L. Robbins
P.J. Winterbottom

v SCOTLAND

LOST **6-33**
Scotland: 3G 5PG
England: 2PG
Murrayfield, 15 Feb 1986

G.H. Davies [1]

S.T. Smith
S.J. Halliday
J.L.B. Salmon
M.E. Harrison

C.R. Andrew **2PG**
* N.D. Melville

P.A.G. Rendall
S.E. Brain
G.S. Pearce
W.A. Dooley
M.J. Colclough
J.P. Hall [2]
G.L. Robbins
P.J. Winterbottom

1 Rep by S. Barnes
2 Rep by N.C. Redman

v IRELAND

WON **25-20**
England: 3G‡ 1PG 1T
Ireland: 1G 2PG 2T
Twickenham, 1 Mar 1986

G.H. Davies **1T**

M.E. Harrison
K.G. Simms [1]
† F.J. Clough
R. Underwood

C.R. Andrew **3C 1PG**
* N.D. Melville

G.J. Chilcott
S.E. Brain
G.S. Pearce
W.A. Dooley
M.J. Colclough
P.J. Winterbottom
† D. Richards **2T**
G.W. Rees

1 Rep by J.A. Palmer
‡includes penalty try

1985-86

Five Nations Championship

v FRANCE

LOST 10-29
France: 2G‡ 3PG 2T
England: 2PG 1T
Parc des Princes, 15 Mar 1986

G.H. Davies [1]

M.E. Harrison
K.G. Simms
F.J. Clough
R. Underwood

C.R. Andrew
* N.D. Melville [2]

G.J. Chilcott
S.E. Brain
G.S. Pearce
W.A. Dooley **1T**
M.J. Colclough
P.J. Winterbottom
D. Richards
G.W. Rees

1 Rep by S. Barnes **2PG**
2 Rep by R.J. Hill
‡includes penalty try

FACT FILE

- England resurrected the Divisional Championship in the autumn of 1985 to provide the selectors with a convenient and timely guide to the form of England's leading 60 players.

FINAL TABLE

	P	W	D	L	F	A	Pts
France	4	3	0	1	98	52	6
Scotland	4	3	0	1	76	54	6
Wales	4	2	0	2	74	71	4
England	**4**	**2**	**0**	**2**	**62**	**100**	**4**
Ireland	4	0	0	4	50	83	0

England's Simon Smith (right) tries to pass the ball inside to team-mate Peter Winterbottom (left) as Scotland's John Jeffrey (centre), Roger Baird (on the floor) and David Johnston (second left) apply pressure at Murrayfield in 1986.

1986-87

Five Nations Championship

v IRELAND

LOST 0-17
Ireland: 1G 1PG 2T
England: Nil
Lansdowne Road, 7 Feb 1987

W.H.M. Rose [1]

M.E. Harrison
J.L.B. Salmon
K.G. Simms
R. Underwood

C.R. Andrew
* R.J. Hill

P.A.G. Rendall
R.G.R. Dawe
G.S. Pearce
N.C. Redman
† D.A. Cusani
J.P. Hall
P.D. Simpson
P.J. Winterbottom

1 Rep by S. Barnes

v FRANCE

LOST 15-19
England: 4PG 1DG
France: 1G 1PG 2DG 1T
Twickenham, 21 Feb 1987

W.H.M. Rose **4PG**

M.E. Harrison
J.L.B. Salmon
K.G. Simms
R. Underwood

C.R. Andrew **1DG**
* R.J. Hill

P.A.G. Rendall [1]
R.G.R. Dawe
G.S. Pearce
W.A. Dooley
S. Bainbridge
P.J. Winterbottom
J.P. Hall
G.W. Rees

1 Rep by G.J. Chilcott

v WALES

LOST 12-19
Wales: 5PG 1T
England: 4PG
Cardiff Arms Park, 7 Mar 1987

W.H.M. Rose **4PG**

M.E. Harrison
K.G. Simms
J.L.B. Salmon
R. Underwood

C.R. Andrew
* R.J. Hill

G.J. Chilcott
R.G.R. Dawe
G.S. Pearce
W.A. Dooley
S. Bainbridge
P.J. Winterbottom
J.P. Hall
G.W. Rees

v SCOTLAND

WON 21-12
England: 2G‡ 3PG
Scotland: 1G 2PG
Twickenham, 4 Apr 1987

W.H.M. Rose **1T 2C 3PG**

* M.E. Harrison **1T ‡**
S.J. Halliday
J.L.B. Salmon
R. Underwood

† P.N. Williams
R.M. Harding

P.A.G. Rendall
† B.C. Moore
G.S. Pearce
N.C. Redman
S. Bainbridge
J.P. Hall
D. Richards
G.W. Rees

‡includes penalty try

FACT FILE

- There was a dreadful episode at Cardiff where several English players were involved in foul acts which, though not seen by the referee, were wholeheartedly condemned by the RFU. Setting a fine example to the other Home Nations, the English Union omitted the chief culprits of the Cardiff escapade for the final game of the season.

FINAL TABLE

	P	W	D	L	F	A	Pts
France	4	4	0	0	82	59	8
Ireland	4	2	0	2	57	46	4
Scotland	4	2	0	2	71	76	4
Wales	4	1	0	3	54	64	2
England	**4**	**1**	**0**	**3**	**48**	**67**	**2**

1987 First Rugby World Cup

Group Matches

v AUSTRALIA

LOST 6-19
Australia: 1G 3PG 1T
England: 1G
Sydney, 23 May 1987

W.H.M. Rose [1]

* M.E. Harrison **1T**
K.G. Simms
J.L.B. Salmon
R. Underwood

P.N. Williams
R.M. Harding

P.A.G. Rendall
B.C. Moore
G.S. Pearce
W.A. Dooley
N.C. Redman
P.J. Winterbottom
D. Richards
G.W. Rees

1 Rep by † J.M. Webb **1C**

v JAPAN

WON 60-7
England: 7G 2PG 3T
Japan: 1PG 1T
Sydney, 30 May 1987

J.M. Webb **7C 2PG**

* M.E. Harrison **3T**
K.G. Simms [1] **1T**
J.L.B. Salmon **1T**
R. Underwood **2T**

P.N. Williams [2]
R.M. Harding

P.A.G. Rendall
B.C. Moore
G.J. Chilcott
N.C. Redman **1T**
S. Bainbridge
P.J. Winterbottom
D. Richards **1T**
G.W. Rees **1T**

1 Rep by F.J. Clough
2 Rep by C.R. Andrew

v UNITED STATES

WON 34-6
US: 1G
England: 3G 4PG 1T
Sydney, 3 Jun 1987

J.M. Webb **3C 4PG**

* M.E. Harrison **1T**
F.J. Clough
J.L.B. Salmon
M.D. Bailey

C.R. Andrew
R.J. Hill

G.J. Chilcott
R.G.R. Dawe
G.S. Pearce
W.A. Dooley **1T**
S. Bainbridge
P.J. Winterbottom **2T**
D. Richards
G.W. Rees

Quarter-final

v WALES

LOST 3-16
England: 1PG
Wales: 2G 1T
Brisbane, 8 Jun 1987

J.M. Webb **1PG**

* M.E. Harrison
K.G. Simms
J.L.B. Salmon
R. Underwood

P.N. Williams
R.M. Harding

P.A.G. Rendall [1]
B.C. Moore
G.S. Pearce
W.A. Dooley
N.C. Redman
P.J. Winterbottom
D. Richards
G.W. Rees

1 Rep by G.J. Chilcott

FACT FILE

- England went out to Wales at the quarter-final stage of the first Rugby World Cup finals, staged in Australia and New Zealand.
- Their 60-7 win against Japan in the pool round was their then record highest score and biggest winning margin.

England lose to Wales in the 1987 World Cup quarter-finals.

1987-88

Five Nations Championship

v FRANCE

LOST 9-10
France: 2PG 1T
England: 2PG 1DG
Parc des Princes, 16 Jan 1988

J.M. Webb 2PG

* M.E. Harrison
† W.D.C. Carling
K.G. Simms
R. Underwood

L. Cusworth 1DG
N.D. Melville

P.A.G. Rendall
B.C. Moore
† J.A. Probyn
J. Orwin
W.A. Dooley
† M.G. Skinner
D. Richards
P.J. Winterbottom

v WALES

LOST 3-11
England: 1PG
Wales: 1DG 2T
Twickenham, 6 Feb 1988

J.M. Webb 1PG

* M.E. Harrison
W.D.C. Carling
K.G. Simms
R. Underwood

L. Cusworth
N.D. Melville

P.A.G. Rendall
B.C. Moore
J.A. Probyn
J. Orwin
W.A. Dooley
M.G. Skinner
D. Richards
P.J. Winterbottom

v SCOTLAND

WON 9-6
Scotland: 2PG
England: 2PG 1DG
Murrayfield, 5 Mar 1988

J.M. Webb 2PG

R. Underwood
S.J. Halliday
W.D.C. Carling
† C. Oti

C.R. Andrew 1DG
* N.D. Melville

P.A.G. Rendall
B.C. Moore
J.A. Probyn
J. Orwin
W.A. Dooley
M.G. Skinner
D. Richards
P.J. Winterbottom [1]

1 Rep by G.W. Rees

1st v IRELAND

WON 35-3
England: 4G 1PG 2T
Ireland: 1DG
Twickenham, 19 Mar 1988

J.M. Webb 1PG 1C

R. Underwood 2T
S.J. Halliday
W.D.C. Carling
C. Oti 3T

C.R. Andrew 3C
* N.D. Melville [1]

P.A.G. Rendall
B.C. Moore
J.A. Probyn
J. Orwin
W.A. Dooley
M.G. Skinner
D. Richards
G.W. Rees 1T

1 Rep by R.M. Harding

Millennium Match

2nd v IRELAND

WON 21-10
Ireland: 1G 1T
England: 2G 3PG
Lansdowne Road, 23 Apr 1988

J.M. Webb 3PG 2C

† J. Bentley
S.J. Halliday
W.D.C. Carling
R. Underwood 1T

C.R. Andrew
R.M. Harding 1T

P.A.G. Rendall [1]
B.C. Moore
J.A. Probyn
* J. Orwin
W.A. Dooley
M.G. Skinner
† D.W. Egerton
G.W. Rees

1 Rep by G.J. Chilcott

FACT FILE

- Geoff Cooke (manager) and Roger Uttley (coach) were the new management team for the Five Nations.
- England's 35-3 rout of Ireland in the final championship match was their then biggest margin over the Irish. It was also in that match that 'Swing Low, Sweet Chariot' was first heard from a Twickenham crowd.
- The extra match with Ireland in April was staged as part of the Dublin Millennium celebrations.

FINAL TABLE

	P	W	D	L	F	A	Pts
Wales	4	3	0	1	57	42	6
France	4	3	0	1	57	47	6
England	**4**	**2**	**0**	**2**	**56**	**30**	**4**
Scotland	4	1	0	3	67	68	2
Ireland	4	1	0	3	40	90	2

1987-88 continued

Tour Matches

1st v AUSTRALIA

LOST 16-22
Australia: 6PG 1T
England: 2PG 1G 1T
Brisbane, 29 May 1988

J.M. Webb 2PG 1C

J. Bentley 1T
B. Barley
S.J. Halliday
R. Underwood 1T

C.R. Andrew
R.M. Harding

P.A.G. Rendall
B.C. Moore
J.A. Probyn
* J. Orwin
W.A. Dooley
D.W. Egerton
D. Richards
G.W. Rees

2nd v AUSTRALIA

LOST 8-28
Australia: 3G 2PG 1T
England: 2T
Sydney, 12 Jun 1988

J.M. Webb

† B.J. Evans
B. Barley
W.D.C. Carling
R. Underwood 1T

C.R. Andrew
R.M. Harding

P.A.G. Rendall
B.C. Moore
J.A. Probyn
* J. Orwin
W.A. Dooley
G.W. Rees
D. Richards 1T
† R.A. Robinson

v FIJI

WON 25-12
Fiji: 3PG 1DG
England: 2G 3PG 1T
Suva, 16 Jun 1988

C.R. Andrew

B.J. Evans
B. Barley 1T
W.D.C. Carling
R. Underwood 2T

S. Barnes 3PG 2C
* R.M. Harding

G.S. Pearce
B.C. Moore
G.J. Chilcott
N.C. Redman
W.A. Dooley
G.W. Rees [1]
D. Richards
R.A. Robinson

1 Rep by D.W. Egerton

1988-89

Tour Match

v AUSTRALIA

WON 28-19
England: 3G 2PG 1T
Australia: 2G 1PG 1T
Twickenham, 5 Nov 1988

J.M. Webb 3C 2PG

† A.T. Harriman
* W.D.C. Carling [1]
S.J. Halliday 1T
R. Underwood 2T

C.R. Andrew
† C.D. Morris 1T

P.A.G. Rendall
B.C. Moore
J.A. Probyn
W.A. Dooley
† P.J. Ackford
R.A. Robinson
D. Richards
D.W. Egerton

1 Rep by † J.R.D. Buckton

Five Nations Championship

v SCOTLAND

DRAWN 12-12
England: 4PG
Scotland: 1G 2PG
Twickenham, 4 Feb 1989

J.M. Webb 2PG

R. Underwood
* W.D.C. Carling
S.J. Halliday
C. Oti

C.R. Andrew 2PG
C.D. Morris

P.A.G. Rendall
B.C. Moore
J.A. Probyn
W.A. Dooley
P.J. Ackford
M.C. Teague
D. Richards
R.A. Robinson

v IRELAND

WON 16-3
Ireland: 1PG
England: 1G 2PG 1T
Lansdowne Road, 18 Feb 1989

J.M. Webb

R. Underwood
* W.D.C. Carling
S.J. Halliday
C. Oti

C.R. Andrew 2PG 1C
C.D. Morris

P.A.G. Rendall
B.C. Moore 1T
J.A. Probyn [1]
W.A. Dooley
P.J. Ackford
M.C. Teague
D. Richards 1T
R.A. Robinson

1 Rep by G.J. Chilcott

1988-89 continued

Five Nations Championship

v FRANCE

WON 11-0
England: 1PG 2T
France: Nil
Twickenham, 4 Mar 1989

J.M. Webb

R. Underwood
* W.D.C. Carling 1T
S.J. Halliday
C. Oti

C.R. Andrew 1PG
C.D. Morris

P.A.G. Rendall
B.C. Moore
G.J. Chilcott
W.A. Dooley
P.J. Ackford
M.C. Teague
D. Richards
R.A. Robinson 1T

v WALES

LOST 9-12
Wales: 1G 2PG
England: 2PG 1DG
Cardiff Arms Park, 18 Mar 1989

J.M. Webb

R. Underwood
* W.D.C. Carling
S.J. Halliday
C. Oti

C.R. Andrew 2PG 1DG
C.D. Morris

P.A.G. Rendall
B.C. Moore
G.J. Chilcott
W.A. Dooley
P.J. Ackford
M.C. Teague [1]
D. Richards
R.A. Robinson

1 Rep by G.W. Rees

Friendly

v ROMANIA

WON 58-3
Romania: 1PG
England: 8G 1PG 1DG 1T
Bucharest, 13 May 1989

† S.D. Hodgkinson 1PG 8C

R. Underwood
S.J. Halliday
† J.C. Guscott 3T
C. Oti 4T

* C.R. Andrew 1DG
† S.M. Bates

P.A.G. Rendall
B.C. Moore
G.J. Chilcott [1]
W.A. Dooley
P.J. Ackford
M.C. Teague
D. Richards [2] 1T
P.J. Winterbottom

1 Rep by J.A. Probyn 1T
2 Rep by D. Richards

FACT FILE

- Will Carling became England's youngest Test captain since Peter Howard (1931) for the victory against Australia.
- Simon Hodgkinson opened his Test career with 19 points against Romania, a new England record for a player on debut.

FINAL TABLE

	P	W	D	L	F	A	Pts
France	4	3	0	1	76	47	6
England	**4**	**2**	**1**	**1**	**48**	**27**	**5**
Scotland	4	2	1	1	75	59	5
Ireland	4	1	0	3	64	92	2
Wales	4	1	0	3	44	82	2

1989-90

Tour Match

v FIJI

WON 58-23
England: 6G 2PG 4T
Fiji: 2G 1PG 2T
Twickenham, 4 Nov 1989

S.D. Hodgkinson 2PG 5C

R. Underwood 5T
* W.D.C. Carling
J.C. Guscott 1T
M.D. Bailey[1] 1T

C.R. Andrew 1C
R.J. Hill

† M.S. Linnett 1T
B.C. Moore
† A.R. Mullins
W.A. Dooley
P.J. Ackford 1T
M.G. Skinner 1T
D.W. Eggerton
P.J. Winterbottom[2]

1 Rep by S.J. Halliday
2 Rep by G.W. Rees

Five Nations Championship

v IRELAND

WON 23-0
England: 2G 1PG 2T
Ireland: Nil
Twickenham, 20 Jan 1990

S.D. Hodgkinson 1PG 2C

R. Underwood 1T
* W.D.C. Carling
J.C. Guscott 1T
M.D. Bailey

C.R. Andrew
R.J. Hill

P.A.G. Rendall
B.C. Moore
J.A. Probyn 1T
W.A. Dooley
P.J. Ackford
M.G. Skinner
D.W. Egerton 1T
P.J. Winterbottom

v FRANCE

WON 26-7
France: 1PG 1T
England: 1G 4PG 2T
Parc des Princes, 3 Feb 1990

S.D. Hodgkinson 4PG 1C

R. Underwood 1T
* W.D.C. Carling 1T
J.C. Guscott 1T
M.D. Bailey

C.R. Andrew
R.J. Hill

P.A.G. Rendall
B.C. Moore
J.A. Probyn
W.A. Dooley
P.J. Ackford
M.G. Skinner
M.C. Teague
P.J. Winterbottom

v WALES

WON 34-6
England: 3G 4PG 1T
Wales: 1G
Twickenham, 17 Feb 1990

S.D. Hodgkinson 4PG 3C

S.J. Halliday
* W.D.C. Carling 1T
J.C. Guscott
R. Underwood 2T

C.R. Andrew
R.J. Hill 1T

P.A.G. Rendall
B.C. Moore
J.A. Probyn
W.A. Dooley
P.J. Ackford
M.G. Skinner
M.C. Teague
P.J. Winterbottom

v SCOTLAND

LOST 7-13
Scotland: 3PG 1T
England: 1PG 1T
Murrayfield, 17 Mar 1990

S.D. Hodgkinson 1PG

S.J. Halliday
* W.D.C. Carling
J.C. Guscott[1] 1T
R. Underwood

C.R. Andrew
R.J. Hill

P.A.G. Rendall
B.C. Moore
J.A. Probyn
P.J. Ackford
W.A. Dooley
M.G. Skinner
M.C. Teague
P.J. Winterbottom

1 Rep by M.D. Bailey

FACT FILE

- Rory Underwood's five tries against Fiji equalled the national record set by Douglas Lambert in 1907 and his score against Ireland took him past Cyril Lowe (18 tries 1913 to 1923) as England's leading all-time try scorer.
- Jason Leonard, England's youngest international prop since Nick Drake-Lee in 1963, began his long Test career in the first of three matches against the Pumas.

FINAL TABLE

	P	W	D	L	F	A	Pts
Scotland	4	4	0	0	60	26	8
England	**4**	**3**	**0**	**1**	**90**	**26**	**6**
France	4	2	0	2	61	78	4
Ireland	4	1	0	3	36	75	2
Wales	4	0	0	4	42	84	0

1989-90

Tour Matches

1st v ARGENTINA

WON 25-12
Argentina: 4PG
England: 1G 5PG 1T
Veléz Sarsfield, BA, 28 Jul 1990

S.D. Hodgkinson 5PG 1C

† N.J. Heslop
* W.D.C. Carling
J.R.D. Buckton
C. Oti 1T

† D. Pears
R.J. Hill

† J. Leonard
B.C. Moore
J.A. Probyn
N.C. Redman
W.A. Dooley
M.G. Skinner
† D. Ryan 1T
P.J. Winterbottom

2nd v ARGENTINA

LOST 13-15
Argentina: 5PG
England: 1G 1PG 1T
Veléz Sarsfield, BA, 4 Aug 1990

S.D. Hodgkinson 1PG 1C 1T

N.J. Heslop 1T
* W.D.C. Carling
J.R.D. Buckton
C. Oti

D. Pears
R.J. Hill

J. Leonard
B.C. Moore
J.A. Probyn
N.C. Redman
W.A. Dooley [1]
M.G. Skinner
D. Ryan
P.J. Winterbottom

1 Rep by D.W. Egerton

v ARGENTINA

WON 51-0
England: 7G 3PG
Argentina: Nil
Twickenham, 3 Nov 1990

S.D. Hodgkinson 3PG 7C

N.J. Heslop
* W.D.C. Carling
J.C. Guscott 2T
R. Underwood 3T

C.R. Andrew
R.J. Hill 1T

J. Leonard
† C.J. Olver
J.A. Probyn
P.J. Ackford [1]
W.A. Dooley
J.P. Hall 1T
D. Richards
P.J. Winterbottom

1 Rep by G.W. Rees

1990-91

Five Nations Championship

v WALES

WON 25-6
Wales: 2PG
England: 7PG 1T
Cardiff Arms Park, 19 Jan 1991

S.D. Hodgkinson 7PG

N.J. Heslop
* W.D.C. Carling
J.C. Guscott
R. Underwood

C.R. Andrew
R.J. Hill

J. Leonard
B.C. Moore
J.A. Probyn
P.J. Ackford
W.A. Dooley
M.C. Teague 1T
D. Richards
P.J. Winterbottom

v SCOTLAND

WON 21-12
England: 1G 5PG
Scotland: 4PG
Twickenham, 16 Feb 1991

S.D. Hodgkinson 5PG 1C

N.J. Heslop 1T
* W.D.C. Carling
J.C. Guscott
R. Underwood

C.R. Andrew
R.J. Hill

J. Leonard
B.C. Moore
J.A. Probyn
P.J. Ackford
W.A. Dooley
M.C. Teague
D. Richards
P.J. Winterbottom

v IRELAND

WON 16-7
Ireland: 1PG 1T
England: 1G 2PG 1T
Lansdowne Road, 2 Mar 1991

S.D. Hodgkinson 2PG 1C

N.J. Heslop
* W.D.C. Carling
J.C. Guscott
R. Underwood 1T

C.R. Andrew
R.J. Hill

J. Leonard
B.C. Moore
J.A. Probyn
P.J. Ackford
W.A. Dooley
M.C. Teague 1T
D. Richards
P.J. Winterbottom

1990-91 continued

Five Nations Championship

v FRANCE

WON 21-19
England: 1G 4PG 1DG
France: 2G 1PG 1T
Twickenham, 16 Mar 1991

S.D. Hodgkinson **4PG 1C**

N.J. Heslop
* W.D.C. Carling
J.C. Guscott
R. Underwood **1T**

C.R. Andrew **1DG**
R.J. Hill

J. Leonard
B.C. Moore
J.A. Probyn
P.J. Ackford
W.A. Dooley
M.C. Teague
D. Richards
P.J. Winterbottom

Tour Matches

v FIJI

WON 28-12
Fiji: 1G 1PG 1DG
England: 2G 2PG 2DG 1T
Suva, 20 Jul 1991

J.M. Webb **2PG 2C**

R. Underwood **1T**
* W.D.C. Carling
J.C. Guscott
C. Oti

C.R. Andrew **2DG 1T**
R.J. Hill

J. Leonard
B.C. Moore
J.A. Probyn **1T**
N.C. Redman
† M.C. Bayfield
M.C. Teague [1]
D. Richards
G.W. Rees

1 Rep by M.G. Skinner

v AUSTRALIA

LOST 15-40
Australia: 4G 4PG 1T
England: 1G 3PG
Sydney Football St, 27 Jul 1991

J.M. Webb **3PG 1C**

R. Underwood
* W.D.C. Carling
J.C. Guscott **1T**
C. Oti

C.R. Andrew
R.J. Hill

J. Leonard
B.C. Moore
J.A. Probyn
P.J. Ackford
M.C. Bayfield
M.C. Teague
D. Richards
P.J. Winterbottom

FACT FILE

- England, winners of the Grand Slam for the first time since 1980, were unchanged for a Five Nations season for only the second time.
- The win in Cardiff was their first in the Welsh capital for 28 years.
- The pre-World Cup tour ended in disappointment when Australia inflicted their then biggest victory over England in a five-star, five-try performance in Sydney.

FINAL TABLE

	P	W	D	L	F	A	Pts
England	**4**	**4**	**0**	**0**	**83**	**44**	**8**
France	4	3	0	1	91	46	6
Scotland	4	2	0	2	81	73	4
Ireland	4	0	1	3	66	86	1
Wales	4	0	1	3	42	114	1

Richard Hill, watched by Wade Dooley and Jason Leonard, fires out a pass against France at Twickenham in 1991.

1991 Second Rugby World Cup

Group Matches

v NEW ZEALAND

LOST 12-18
England: 1DG 3PG
NZ: 1G 4PG
Twickenham, 3 Oct 1991

J.M. Webb 3PG

R. Underwood
* W.D.C. Carling
J.C. Guscott
C. Oti

C.R. Andrew 1DG
R.J. Hill

J. Leonard
B.C. Moore
J.A. Probyn
P.J. Ackford
W.A. Dooley
M.C. Teague
D. Richards
P.J. Winterbottom

v UNITED STATES

WON 37-9
England: 4G 3PG 1T
US: 1G 1PG
Twickenham, 11 Oct 1991

S.D. Hodgkinson 4C 3PG

N.J. Heslop 1T
* W.D.C. Carling 1T
S.J. Halliday
R. Underwood 2T

C.R. Andrew
R.J. Hill

J. Leonard
C.J. Olver
G.S. Pearce
N.C. Redman
W.A. Dooley
M.G. Skinner 1T
D. Richards
G.W. Rees

v ITALY

WON 36-6
England: 4G 4PG
Italy: 1G
Twickenham, 8 Oct 1991

J.M. Webb 1T 4C 4PG

C. Oti
* W.D.C. Carling
J.C. Guscott 2T
R. Underwood 1T

C.R. Andrew
R.J. Hill

J. Leonard
B.C. Moore
J.A. Probyn [1]
P.J. Ackford
N.C. Redman
M.C. Teague
D. Richards
P.J. Winterbottom

1 Rep by P.A.G. Rendall

Quarter-final

v FRANCE

WON 19-10
France: 2PG 1T
England: 1G 3PG 1T
Parc des Princes, 19 Oct 1991

J.M. Webb 3PG 1C

N.J. Heslop
* W.D.C. Carling 1T
J.C. Guscott
R. Underwood 1T

C.R. Andrew
R.J. Hill

J. Leonard
B.C. Moore
J.A. Probyn
P.J. Ackford
W.A. Dooley
M.G. Skinner
M.C. Teague
P.J. Winterbottom

Semi-final

v SCOTLAND

WON 9-6
Scotland: 2PG
England: 2PG 1DG
Murrayfield, 26 Oct 1991

J.M. Webb 2PG

S.J. Halliday
* W.D.C. Carling
J.C. Guscott
R. Underwood

C.R. Andrew 1DG
R.J. Hill

J. Leonard
B.C. Moore
J.A. Probyn
P.J. Ackford
W.A. Dooley
M.G. Skinner
M.C. Teague
P.J. Winterbottom

Final

v AUSTRALIA

LOST 6-12
England: 2PG
Australia: 1G 2PG
Twickenham, 2 Nov 1991

J.M. Webb 2PG

S.J. Halliday
* W.D.C. Carling
J.C. Guscott
R. Underwood

C.R. Andrew
R.J. Hill

J. Leonard
B.C. Moore
J.A. Probyn
P.J. Ackford
W.A. Dooley
M.G. Skinner
M.C. Teague
P.J. Winterbottom

1991-92

Five Nations Championship

v SCOTLAND

WON 25-7
Scotland: 1PG 1T
England: 1G 4PG 1DG 1T
Murrayfield, 18 Jan 1992

J.M. Webb **4PG 1C**

S.J. Halliday
* W.D.C. Carling
J.C. Guscott **1DG**
R. Underwood **1T**

C.R. Andrew
C.D. Morris **1T**

J. Leonard
B.C. Moore
J.A. Probyn
M.C. Bayfield
W.A. Dooley
M.G. Skinner
† T.A.K. Rodber [1]
P.J. Winterbottom

1 Rep by D. Richards

v IRELAND

WON 38-9
England: 4G 2PG 2T
Ireland: 1G 1PG
Twickenham, 1 Feb 1992

J.M. Webb **2PG 4C 2T**

S.J. Halliday **1T**
* W.D.C. Carling
J.C. Guscott **1T**
R. Underwood **1T**

C.R. Andrew
C.D. Morris **1T**

J. Leonard
B.C. Moore
J.A. Probyn
M.C. Bayfield
W.A. Dooley
M.G. Skinner
T.A.K. Rodber
P.J. Winterbottom

v FRANCE

WON 31-13
France: 1G 1PG 1T
England: 3G‡ 3PG 1T
Parc des Princes, 15 Feb 1992

J.M. Webb **3PG 3C 1T**

S.J. Halliday
* W.D.C. Carling
J.C. Guscott
R. Underwood **1T**

C.R. Andrew [1]
C.D. Morris **1T**

J. Leonard
B.C. Moore
J.A. Probyn
M.C. Bayfield
W.A. Dooley
M.G. Skinner
D. Richards
P.J. Winterbottom

1 Rep by D. Pears
‡includes penalty try

v WALES

WON 24-0
England: 3G 2PG
Wales: Nil
Twickenham, 7 Mar 1992

J.M. Webb **2PG 3C**

S.J. Halliday
* W.D.C. Carling [1] **1T**
J.C. Guscott
R. Underwood

C.R. Andrew
C.D. Morris

J. Leonard
B.C. Moore
J.A. Probyn
M.C. Bayfield
W.A. Dooley **1T**
M.G. Skinner **1T**
D. Richards
P.J. Winterbottom

1 Rep by N.J. Heslop

FACT FILE

- This season saw the first England back-to-back Grand Slam since the 1920s.
- The side set a new International Championship record for most points in a season (118), Jon Webb scored 67 points to create a new individual record in a championship, and his place-kicking against Wales enabled him to become England's leading points-scorer, eclipsing Dusty Hare's record.

FINAL TABLE

	P	W	D	L	F	A	Pts
England	**4**	**4**	**0**	**0**	**118**	**29**	**8**
France	4	2	0	2	75	62	4
Scotland	4	2	0	2	47	56	4
Wales	4	2	0	2	40	63	4
Ireland	4	0	0	4	46	116	0

1991-92 continued

Tour Matches

v CANADA

WON 26-13
England: 2PG 4T
Canada: 1G 2PG
Wembley Stadium, 17 Oct 1992

J.M.Webb 2PG

† I.Hunter 2T
* W.D.C.Carling
J.C.Guscott 1T
† T.Underwood

C.R.Andrew
C.D.Morris

J.Leonard
C.J.Olver
† V.E.Ubogu
M.C.Bayfield
W.A.Dooley
D.Ryan
D.Richards
P.J.Winterbottom 1T

v SOUTH AFRICA

WON 33-16
England: 2G 3PG 2T
SA: 1G 2PG 1DG
Twickenham, 14 Nov 1992

J.M.Webb 3PG 2C

T.Underwood [1] 1T
* W.D.C.Carling 1T
J.C.Guscott 1T
R.Underwood

C.R.Andrew
C.D.Morris 1T

J.Leonard
B.C.Moore
V.E.Ubogu
M.C.Bayfield
W.A.Dooley
M.C.Teague
† B.B.Clarke
P.J.Winterbottom

1 Rep by † P.R. de Glanville

FACT FILE

- The autumn international against Canada at Wembley was England's first home match away from Twickenham since 1923. Refurbishment of Twickenham was the reason for the switch of venue.

1992-93

Five Nations Championship

v FRANCE

WON 16-15
England: 1G 3PG
France: 1G 1PG 1T
Twickenham, 16 Jan 1993

J.M. Webb 3PG 1C

I. Hunter 1T
* W.D.C. Carling
J.C. Guscott
R. Underwood

C.R. Andrew
C.D. Morris

J. Leonard
B.C. Moore
J.A. Probyn
M.C. Bayfield
† M.O. Johnson
M.C. Teague
B.B. Clarke
P.J. Winterbottom

v WALES

LOST 9-10
Wales: 1G 1PG
England: 2PG 1DG
Cardiff Arms Park, 6 Feb 1993

J.M. Webb 2PG

I. Hunter [1]
* W.D.C. Carling
J.C. Guscott 1DG
R. Underwood

C.R. Andrew
C.D. Morris

J. Leonard
B.C. Moore
J.A. Probyn
M.C. Bayfield
W.A. Dooley
M.C. Teague
B.B. Clarke
P.J.Winterbottom

1 Rep by P.R. de Glanville

v SCOTLAND

WON 26-12
England: 1G 3PG 2T
Scotland: 3PG 1DG
Twickenham, 6 Mar 1993

J.M. Webb 3PG 1C

T. Underwood 1T
* W.D.C. Carling
J.C. Guscott 1T
R. Underwood 1T

S. Barnes
C.D. Morris

J. Leonard
B.C. Moore
J.A. Probyn
M.C. Bayfield
W.A. Dooley
M.C. Teague
B.B. Clarke
P.J. Winterbottom

1992-93 continued

Five Nations Championship

v IRELAND

LOST 3-17
Ireland: 2PG 2DG 1T
England: 1PG
Lansdowne Road, 20 Mar 1993

J.M. Webb 1PG

T. Underwood
* W.D.C. Carling
J.C. Guscott
R. Underwood

S. Barnes
C.D. Morris

J. Leonard
B.C. Moore
J.A. Probyn
M.C. Bayfield
W.A. Dooley
M.C. Teague
B.B. Clarke
P.J. Winterbottom

FACT FILE

- Defeat at Cardiff ended a run of nine championship victories – one win short of the record set by the England team of the 1920s.
- Against Scotland, Tony and Rory Underwood became only the second pair of brothers to score tries for England in the same match. Percy and Frank Stout had done so against Wales in 1898.

FINAL TABLE

	P	W	D	L	F	A	Pts
France	4	3	0	1	73	35	6
Scotland	4	2	0	2	50	40	4
England	**4**	**2**	**0**	**2**	**54**	**54**	**4**
Ireland	4	2	0	2	45	53	4
Wales	4	1	0	3	34	74	2

1993-94

Tour Match

v NEW ZEALAND

WON 15-9
England: 4PG 1DG
NZ: 3PG
Twickenham, 27 Nov 1993

† J.E.B. Callard 4PG

T. Underwood
* W.D.C. Carling
P.R. de Glanville
R. Underwood

C.R. Andrew 1DG
† K.P.P. Bracken

J. Leonard
B.C. Moore
V.E. Ubogu
M.O. Johnson
N.C. Redman
T.A.K. Rodber
D. Richards
B.B. Clarke

Five Nations Championship

v SCOTLAND

WON 15-14
Scotland: 2PG 1DG 1T
England: 5PG
Murrayfield, 5 Feb 1994

J.E.B. Callard 5PG

T. Underwood
* W.D.C. Carling
P.R. de Glanville
R. Underwood

C.R. Andrew
K.P.P. Bracken

J. Leonard
B.C. Moore
V.E. Ubogu
M.O. Johnson
M.C. Bayfield
J.P. Hall
B.B. Clarke
† N.A. Back

v IRELAND

LOST 12-13
England: 4PG
Ireland: 1G 2PG
Twickenham, 19 Feb 1994

J.E.B. Callard 4PG

T. Underwood
* W.D.C. Carling
P.R. de Glanville
R. Underwood

C.R. Andrew
K.P.P. Bracken

J. Leonard
B.C. Moore
V.E. Ubogu
M.O. Johnson
M.C. Bayfield
T.A.K. Rodber
† S.O. Ojomoh
N.A. Back

1993-94 continued

Five Nations Championship

v FRANCE

WON 18-14
France: 3PG 1T
England: 5PG 1DG
Parc des Princes, 5 Mar 1994

D. Pears

I. Hunter
* W.D.C. Carling
P.R. de Glanville
R. Underwood

C.R. Andrew 5PG 1DG
C.D. Morris

J. Leonard
B.C. Moore
V.E. Ubogu
M.O. Johnson
N.C. Redman
T.A.K. Rodber
S.O. Ojomoh
B.B. Clarke

v WALES

WON 15-8
England: 1G 1PG 1T
Wales: 1PG 1T
Twickenham, 19 Mar 1994

I. Hunter

T. Underwood
* W.D.C. Carling
P.R. de Glanville
R. Underwood 1T

C.R. Andrew [1] 1PG 1C
C.D. Morris

J. Leonard
B.C. Moore
V.E. Ubogu
M.O. Johnson
N.C. Redman
T.A.K. Rodber 1T
D. Richards
B.B. Clarke

1 Rep by † M.J. Catt

FACT FILE

- Geoff Cooke resigned at the end of a season that included a fourth England win against the All Blacks.
- Wales took the championship ahead of England on points-difference.

FINAL TABLE

	P	W	D	L	F	A	Pts
Wales	4	3	0	1	78	51	6
England	**4**	**3**	**0**	**1**	**60**	**49**	**6**
France	4	2	0	2	84	69	4
Ireland	4	1	1	2	49	70	3
Scotland	4	0	1	3	38	70	1

Tour Matches

1st v SOUTH AFRICA

WON 32-15
SA: 5PG
England: 2G 5PG 1DG
Pretoria, 4 Jun 1994

† P.A. Hull

T. Underwood
* W.D.C. Carling
P.R. de Glanville
R. Underwood

C.R. Andrew 5PG 1DG 2C 1T
C.D. Morris

J. Leonard
B.C. Moore
V.E. Ubogu
M.C. Bayfield
N.C. Redman
T.A.K. Rodber
D. Richards [1]
B.B. Clarke 1T

1 Rep by S.O. Ojomoh

2nd v SOUTH AFRICA

LOST 9-27
SA: 1G 5PG 1T
England: 3PG
Cape Town, 11 Jun 1994

P.A. Hull

T. Underwood
* W.D.C. Carling
P.R. de Glanville
R. Underwood

C.R. Andrew 3PG
C.D. Morris

J. Leonard
B.C. Moore
V.E. Ubogu
M.C. Bayfield
N.C. Redman
T.A.K. Rodber
B.B. Clarke
S.O. Ojomoh

1993-94 continued

Tour Matches

v ROMANIA

WON 54-3
England: 6G‡ 4PG
Romania: 1PG
Twickenham, 12 Nov 1994

P.A. Hull

T. Underwood **2T**
* W.D.C. Carling **1T**
J.C. Guscott
R. Underwood **1T**

C.R. Andrew **4PG 6C**
C.D. Morris

J. Leonard
B.C. Moore
V.E. Ubogu
M.O. Johnson
M.C. Bayfield
T.A.K. Rodber **1T**
B.B. Clarke
S.O. Ojomoh

‡includes penalty try

v CANADA

WON 60-19
England: 6G 6PG
Canada: 2G 1T
Twickenham, 10 Dec 1994

P.A. Hull 1

T. Underwood 2 **1T**
* W.D.C. Carling
J.C. Guscott
R. Underwood **2T**

C.R. Andrew **6PG 6C**
K.P.P. Bracken **1T**

J. Leonard
B.C. Moore
V.E. Ubogu
M.O. Johnson
M.C. Bayfield
T.A.K. Rodber
D. Richards
B.B. Clarke

1 Rep by M.J. Catt **2T**
2 Rep by P.R. de Glanville

FACT FILE

- Rob Andrew's full-house in Pretoria – try, conversions, penalties and a drop goal – fired England to a convincing victory against the Springboks in the first match under Jack Rowell's management.
- In the autumn Tests he landed 22 place-kicks from 23 attempts and equalled the world record for a Test match with 30 points against Canada.

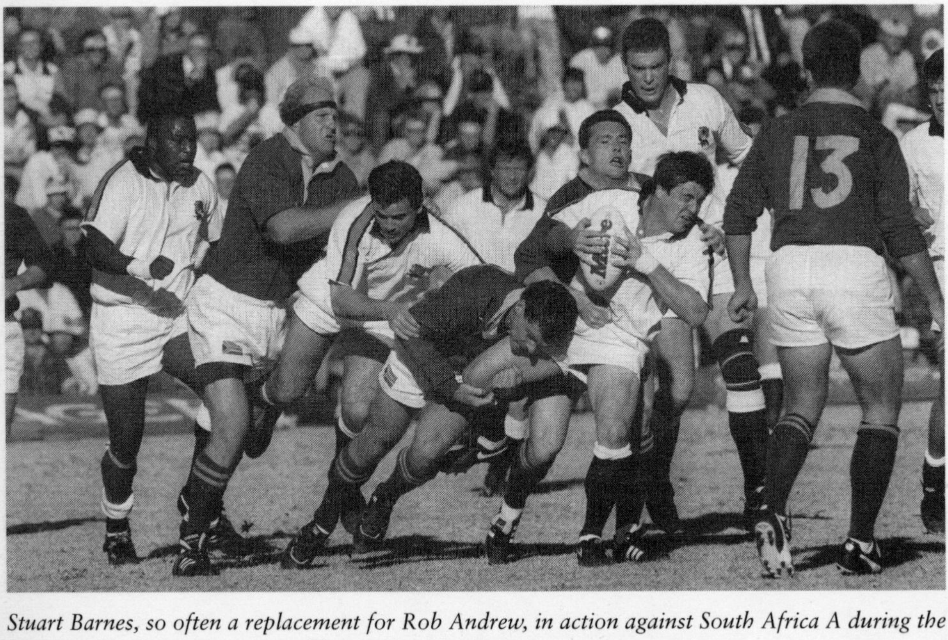

Stuart Barnes, so often a replacement for Rob Andrew, in action against South Africa A during the 1994 tour. Unfortunately, he was still unable to make the Test team.

1994-95

Five Nations Championship

v IRELAND

WON 20-8
Ireland: 1PG 1T
England: 1G 1PG 2T
Lansdowne Road, 21 Jan 1995

M.J. Catt

T. Underwood 1T
* W.D.C. Carling 1T
J.C. Guscott
R. Underwood

C.R. Andrew 1PG 1C
K.P.P. Bracken

J. Leonard
B.C. Moore
V.E. Ubogu
M.O. Johnson
M.C. Bayfield
T.A.K. Rodber
D. Richards
B.B. Clarke 1T

v FRANCE

WON 31-10
England: 2G 4PG 1T
France: 1G 1PG
Twickenham, 4 Feb 1995

M.J. Catt

T. Underwood 2T
* W.D.C. Carling
J.C. Guscott 1T
R. Underwood

C.R. Andrew 4PG 2C
K.P.P. Bracken

J. Leonard
B.C. Moore
V.E. Ubogu
M.O. Johnson
M.C. Bayfield
T.A.K. Rodber
D. Richards
B.B. Clarke

v WALES

WON 23-9
Wales: 3PG
England: 1G 2PG 2T
Cardiff Arms Park, 18 Feb 1995

M.J. Catt

T. Underwood
* W.D.C. Carling
J.C. Guscott
R. Underwood 2T

C.R. Andrew 2PG 1C
K.P.P. Bracken

J. Leonard
B.C. Moore
V.E. Ubogu 1T
M.O. Johnson
M.C. Bayfield
T.A.K. Rodber
D. Richards
B.B. Clarke

v SCOTLAND

WON 24-12
England: 7PG 1DG
Scotland: 2PG 2DG
Twickenham, 18 Mar 1995

M.J. Catt

T. Underwood
* W.D.C. Carling
J.C. Guscott
R. Underwood

C.R. Andrew 7PG 1DG
K.P.P. Bracken [a]

J. Leonard [b]
B.C. Moore
V.E. Ubogu
M.O. Johnson
M.C. Bayfield
T.A.K. Rodber
D. Richards [1]
B.B. Clarke

a Rep by C.D. Morris
1 Rep by S.O. Ojomoh
b Rep by † G.C. Rowntree

FACT FILE

- England prepared for the World Cup by securing their 11th Grand Slam and 18th Triple Crown – one more than the record set by the Welsh.
- Rob Andrew's 24 points to beat Scotland equalled the International Championship record for most points by a player in a match.

FINAL TABLE

	P	W	D	L	F	A	Pts
England	**4**	**4**	**0**	**0**	**98**	**39**	**8**
Scotland	4	3	0	1	87	71	6
France	4	2	0	2	77	70	4
Ireland	4	1	0	3	44	83	2
Wales	4	0	0	4	43	86	0

1995 Third Rugby World Cup

Group Matches

v ARGENTINA

WON **24-18**
England: 6PG 2DG
Argentina: 1G 2PG 1T
Durban, 27 May 1995

M.J. Catt

T. Underwood
* W.D.C. Carling [1]
J.C. Guscott
R. Underwood

C.R. Andrew **6PG 2DG**
C.D. Morris

J. Leonard
B.C. Moore
V.E. Ubogu
M.O. Johnson
M.C. Bayfield
T.A.K. Rodber
S.O. Ojomoh [a]
B.B. Clarke

1 Rep by P.R. de Glanville
a Rep by N.A. Back

v ITALY

WON **27-20**
England: 1G 5PG 1T
Italy: 2G 2PG
Durban, 31 May 1995

M.J. Catt

T. Underwood **1T**
P.R. de Glanville
J.C. Guscott
R. Underwood **1T**

* C.R. Andrew **5PG 1C**
K.P.P. Bracken

G.C. Rowntree
B.C. Moore
J. Leonard
M.O. Johnson
M.C. Bayfield
T.A.K. Rodber
B.B. Clarke
N.A. Back

v WESTERN SAMOA

WON **44-22**
England: 3G‡ 5PG 1DG 1T
WS: 2G 1PG 1T
Durban, 4 Jun 1995

J.E.B. Callard **5PG 3C**

I. Hunter
* W.D.C. Carling [3]
P.R. de Glanville
R. Underwood **2T**

M.J. Catt **1DG**
C.D. Morris

G.C. Rowntree [1]
R.G.R. Dawe
V.E. Ubogu
M.O. Johnson
† R.J. West
S.O. Ojomoh
D. Richards [4]
N.A. Back [2] **1T**

1 Rep by † J.A. Mallett
2 Rep by T.A.K. Rodber [a]
3 Rep by † D.P. Hopley
4 Rep by B.C. Moore
a Rep by K.P.P. Bracken
‡includes penalty try

Quarter-final

v AUSTRALIA

WON **25-22**
England: 1G 5PG 1DG
Australia: 1G 5PG
Cape Town, 11 Jun 1995

M.J. Catt

T. Underwood **1T**
* W.D.C. Carling
J.C. Guscott
R. Underwood

C.R. Andrew **5PG 1DG 1C**
C.D. Morris

J. Leonard
B.C. Moore
V.E. Ubogu
M.O. Johnson
M.C. Bayfield
T.A.K. Rodber
D. Richards [a]
B.B. Clarke

a Rep by S.O. Ojomoh

Semi-final

v NEW ZEALAND

LOST **29-45**
England: 3G 1PG 1T
NZ: 3G 1PG 2DG 3T
Cape Town, 18 Jun 1995

M.J. Catt

T. Underwood
* W.D.C. Carling **2T**
J.C. Guscott
R. Underwood **2T**

C.R. Andrew **1PG 3C**
C.D. Morris

J. Leonard
B.C. Moore
V.E. Ubogu
M.O. Johnson
M.C. Bayfield
T.A.K. Rodber
D. Richards
B.B. Clarke

Third/Fourth Place Play-off

v FRANCE

LOST **9-19**
England: 3PG
France: 3PG 2T
Pretoria, 22 Jun 1995

M.J. Catt

I. Hunter
* W.D.C. Carling
J.C. Guscott
R. Underwood

C.R. Andrew **3PG**
C.D. Morris

J. Leonard
B.C. Moore
V.E. Ubogu
M.O. Johnson
M.C. Bayfield
T.A.K. Rodber
S.O. Ojomoh
B.B. Clarke

1995-96

Tour Matches

v SOUTH AFRICA

LOST 14-24
England: 3PG 1T
SA: 3PG 3T
Twickenham, 18 Nov 1995

J.E.B. Callard 3PG

D.P. Hopley
* W.D.C. Carling [2]
J.C. Guscott
R. Underwood

M.J. Catt
K.P.P. Bracken

J. Leonard
† M.P. Regan
V.E. Ubogu
M.O. Johnson
M.C. Bayfield
T.A.K. Rodber [1]
B.B. Clarke
R.A. Robinson

1 Rep by † L.B.N. Dallaglio
2 Rep by P.R. de Glanville 1T

v WESTERN SAMOA

WON 27-9
England: 1G 5PG 1T
WS: 3PG
Twickenham, 16 Dec 1995

M.J. Catt

D.P. Hopley
* W.D.C. Carling
J.C. Guscott
R. Underwood 1T

† P.J. Grayson 5PG 1C
† M.J.S. Dawson

G.C. Rowntree
M.P. Regan
J. Leonard
M.O. Johnson
M.C. Bayfield
T.A.K. Rodber
B.B. Clarke
L.B.N. Dallaglio 1T

FACT FILE

- South Africa recorded their highest score and biggest winning margin in a Twickenham Test against England.
- Paul Grayson and Matt Dawson (Northampton) became the first club halves to make their England debuts together since Tim Taylor and George Wood (Leicester) in 1914.

Five Nations Championship

v FRANCE

LOST 12-15
France: 3PG 2DG
England: 2PG 2DG
Parc des Princes, 20 Jan 1996

M.J. Catt

† J.M. Sleightholme
* W.D.C. Carling
J.C. Guscott
R. Underwood

P.J. Grayson 2PG 2DG
M.J.S. Dawson

G.C. Rowntree
M.P. Regan
J. Leonard
M.O. Johnson
M.C. Bayfield
S.O. Ojomoh
B.B. Clarke [a]
L.B.N. Dallaglio

a Rep by D. Richards

v WALES

WON 21-15
England: 1G 3PG 1T
Wales: 1G 1PG 1T
Twickenham, 3 Feb 1996

M.J. Catt

J.M. Sleightholme
* W.D.C. Carling [1]
J.C. Guscott 1T
R. Underwood 1T

P.J. Grayson 3PG 1C
M.J.S. Dawson

G.C. Rowntree
M.P. Regan
J. Leonard
M.O. Johnson
M.C. Bayfield
T.A.K. Rodber
B.B. Clarke
L.B.N. Dallaglio

1 Rep by P.R. de Glanville

v SCOTLAND

WON 18-9
Scotland: 3PG
England: 6PG
Murrayfield, 2 Mar 1996

M.J. Catt

J.M. Sleightholme
* W.D.C. Carling
J.C. Guscott
R. Underwood

P.J. Grayson 6PG
M.J.S. Dawson

G.C. Rowntree
M.P. Regan
J. Leonard
M.O. Johnson
† G.S. Archer
B.B. Clarke
D. Richards [1]
L.B.N. Dallaglio

1 Rep by T.A.K. Rodber

1995-96 continued

Five Nations Championship

v IRELAND

WON 28-15
England: 1G 6PG 1DG
Ireland: 4PG 1DG
Twickenham, 16 Mar 1996

M.J. Catt

J.M. Sleightholme 1T
* W.D.C. Carling [1]
J.C. Guscott
R. Underwood

P.J. Grayson 6PG 1DG 1C
M.J.S. Dawson

G.C. Rowntree
M.P. Regan
J. Leonard
M.O. Johnson
G.S. Archer
B.B. Clarke
D. Richards
L.B.N. Dallaglio [a]

a Rep by T.A.K. Rodber
1 Rep by P.R. de Glanville

FACT FILE

- Rory Underwood scored the 49th and final try of his England career in the match with Wales. He remains England's leading try scorer in Tests.
- Jason Leonard led England for the only time and scored the only try of his record Test career in the match against Argentina.

FINAL TABLE

	P	W	D	L	F	A	Pts
England	**4**	**3**	**0**	**1**	**79**	**54**	**6**
Scotland	4	3	0	1	60	56	6
France	4	2	0	2	89	57	4
Wales	4	1	0	3	62	82	2
Ireland	4	1	0	3	65	106	2

1996-97

Friendlies

v ITALY

WON 54-21
England: 5G 3PG 2T
Italy: 3G
Twickenham, 23 Nov 1996

† T.R.G. Stimpson

J.M. Sleightholme 1T
W.D.C. Carling
* P.R. de Glanville
† A.A. Adebayo

M.J. Catt 3PG 5C
† A.C.T. Gomarsall [3] 2T

G.C. Rowntree
M.P. Regan [2]
J. Leonard [1]
M.O. Johnson 1T
† S.D. Shaw
T.A.K. Rodber 1T
† C.M.A. Sheasby 1T
L.B.N. Dallaglio 1T

1 Rep by † R.J.K. Hardwick
2 Rep by † P.B.T. Greening
3 Rep by K.P.P. Bracken

v ARGENTINA

WON 20-18
England: 5PG 1T
Argentina: 6PG
Twickenham, 14 Dec 1996

† N.D. Beal

J.M. Sleightholme
W.D.C. Carling
J.C. Guscott
T. Underwood

M.J. Catt 5PG
A.C.T. Gomarsall

G.C. Rowntree
M.P. Regan
* J. Leonard 1T
M.O. Johnson
S.D. Shaw
T.A.K. Rodber
C.M.A. Sheasby [1]
L.B.N. Dallaglio

1 Rep by B.B. Clarke

1996-97 continued

Five Nations Championship

v SCOTLAND

WON 41-13
England: 3G‡ 5PG 1T
Scotland: 1G 2PG
Twickenham, 1 Feb 1997

T.R.G. Stimpson

J.M. Sleightholme
W.D.C. Carling 1T
* P.R. de Glanville 1T
T. Underwood

P.J. Grayson 5PG 3C
A.C.T. Gomarsall 1T

G.C. Rowntree
M.P. Regan
J. Leonard
M.O. Johnson
S.D. Shaw
L.B.N. Dallaglio
T.A.K. Rodber
† R.A. Hill

‡includes penalty try

v IRELAND

WON 46-6
Ireland: 2PG
England: 2G 4PG 4T
Lansdowne Road, 15 Feb 1997

T.R.G. Stimpson

J.M. Sleightholme 2T
W.D.C. Carling 2
* P.R. de Glanville
T. Underwood 2T

P.J. Grayson 4PG 2C
A.C.T. Gomarsall 1 1T

G.C. Rowntree
M.P. Regan
J. Leonard
M.O. Johnson
S.D. Shaw
L.B.N. Dallaglio
T.A.K. Rodber
R.A. Hill 1T

1 Rep by † A.S. Healey
2 Rep by J.C. Guscott

v FRANCE

LOST 20-23
England: 4PG 1DG 1T
France: 2G 2PG 1DG
Twickenham, 1 Mar 1997

T.R.G. Stimpson

J.M. Sleightholme
W.D.C. Carling
* P.R. de Glanville
T. Underwood

P.J. Grayson 4PG 1DG
A.C.T. Gomarsall

G.C. Rowntree
M.P. Regan
J. Leonard
M.O. Johnson
S.D. Shaw
L.B.N. Dallaglio 1T
T.A.K. Rodber
R.A. Hill

v WALES

WON 34-13
Wales: 1G 2PG
England: 4G 2PG
Cardiff Arms Park, 15 Mar 1997

T.R.G. Stimpson 1T

J.M. Sleightholme 2
W.D.C. Carling
* P.R. de Glanville 1T
T. Underwood 1T

M.J. Catt 4 2PG 4C
A.S. Healey

G.C. Rowntree 5
M.P. Regan 1
J. Leonard
M.O. Johnson
S.D. Shaw
B.B. Clarke 3
T.A.K. Rodber
R.A. Hill 1T

1 Rep by P.B.T. Greening
2 Rep by J.C. Guscott
3 Rep by C.M.A. Sheasby
4 Rep by C.R. Andrew
5 Rep by † D.J. Garforth

FACT FILE

- England surrendered a 20-6 lead to lose 20-23 against France.
- Will Carling and Rob Andrew, two key members of the successful sides of the 1990s, retired from Test rugby after a Cardiff match that was the last ever international staged in the old Arms Park.

FINAL TABLE

	P	W	D	L	F	A	Pts
France	4	4	0	0	129	77	8
England	**4**	**3**	**0**	**1**	**141**	**55**	**6**
Wales	4	1	0	3	94	106	2
Scotland	4	1	0	3	90	132	2
Ireland	4	1	0	3	57	141	2

1996-97 continued

Tour Matches

1st v ARGENTINA

WON 46-20
Argentina: 1G 1DG 2T
England: 5G 2PG 1T
Buenos Aires, 31 May 1997

† J. Mallinder

J.M. Sleightholme
* P.R. de Glanville
† N.J.J. Greenstock 1T
A.A. Adebayo 2T

M.J. Catt 2PG 5C 1T
K.P.P. Bracken

† K.P. Yates
P.B.T. Greening [1]
D.J. Garforth
† M. Haag
N.C. Redman
† M.E. Corry [2]
† A.J. Diprose 1T
B.B. Clarke 1T

1 Rep by † R. Cockerill
2 Rep by C.M.A. Sheasby

2nd v ARGENTINA

LOST 13-33
Argentina: 2G 3PG 2T
England: 1PG 2T
Buenos Aires, 7 Jun 1997

J. Mallinder [2]

J.M. Sleightholme
* P.R. de Glanville
N.J.J. Greenstock
A.A. Adebayo [3]

† M.S. Mapletoft 1PG
K.P.P. Bracken

K.P. Yates
R. Cockerill
D.J. Garforth
M. Haag
† D.J. Grewcock 1T
M.E. Corry [1]
A.J. Diprose
B.B. Clarke

1 Rep by C.M.A. Sheasby
2 Rep by † A.D. King 1T
3 Rep by A.C.T. Gomarsall

1st v AUSTRALIA

LOST 6-25
Australia: 1G 1PG 3T
England: 1PG 1DG
Sydney F.S., 12 Jul 1997

T.R.G. Stimpson 1PG

J. Bentley
N.J.J. Greenstock
* P.R. de Glanville
N.D. Beal

M.J. Catt 1DG
M.J.S. Dawson [1]

G.C. Rowntree
M.P. Regan
D.J. Garforth
N.C. Redman
S.D. Shaw
L.B.N. Dallaglio
T.A.K. Rodber
R.A. Hill [2]

1 Rep by A.S. Healey
2 Rep by B.B. Clarke

1997-98

Tour Matches

2nd v AUSTRALIA

DRAWN 15-15
England: 5PG
Australia: 1G 1PG 1T
Twickenham, 15 Nov 1997

† M.B. Perry

† D.L. Rees
† W.J.H. Greenwood
P.R. de Glanville [a]
A.A. Adebayo [2]

M.J. Catt 5PG
K.P.P. Bracken

J. Leonard
† A.E. Long [b/1]
† W.R. Green
M.O. Johnson
G.S. Archer
* L.B.N. Dallaglio
A.J. Diprose
R.A. Hill

a Rep by P.J. Grayson
b/1 Rep by R. Cockerill
2 Rep by A.S. Healey

1st v NEW ZEALAND

LOST 8-25
England: 1PG 1T
NZ: 2G 2PG 1T
Old Trafford, 22 Nov 1997

M.B. Perry

D.L. Rees
W.J.H. Greenwood
P.R. de Glanville 1T
A.A. Adebayo [2]

M.J. Catt 1PG
K.P.P. Bracken

J. Leonard
R. Cockerill
D.J. Garforth
M.O. Johnson
G.S. Archer
* L.B.N. Dallaglio
A.J. Diprose [1]
R.A. Hill

1 Rep by N.A. Back
2 Rep by A.S. Healey

v SOUTH AFRICA

LOST 11-29
England: 2PG 1T
SA: 3G 1PG 1T
Twickenham, 29 Nov 1997

M.B. Perry

J. Bentley [3]
W.J.H. Greenwood
N.J.J. Greenstock 1T
D.L. Rees

M.J. Catt [1] 2PG
M.J.S. Dawson

J. Leonard
R. Cockerill
D.J. Garforth
D.J. Grewcock [4]
G.S. Archer
* L.B.N. Dallaglio
R.A. Hill [2]
N.A. Back

1 Rep by P.J. Grayson
2 Rep by C.M.A. Sheasby
3 Rep by A.S. Healey
4 Rep by S.D. Shaw

1997-98 continued

Tour Match

2nd v NEW ZEALAND

DRAWN 26-26
England: 1G 3PG 2T
NZ: 2G 4PG
Twickenham, 6 Dec 1997

M.B. Perry

D.L. Rees[a] 1T
W.J.H. Greenwood
P.R. de Glanville[1]
A.S. Healey

P.J. Grayson 3PG 1C
K.P.P. Bracken[2]

J. Leonard
R. Cockerill[3]
D.J. Garforth
M.O. Johnson
G.S. Archer
* L.B.N. Dallaglio 1T
R.A. Hill 1T
N.A. Back[b]

a/1 Rep by T.R.G. Stimpson
b Rep by C.M.A. Sheasby
2 Rep by M.J.S. Dawson
3 Rep by M.P. Regan

Five Nations Championship

v FRANCE

LOST 17-24
France: 1G 2PG 2DG 1T
England: 4PG 1T
Stade de France, 7 Feb 1998

M.J. Catt

D.L. Rees
W.J.H. Greenwood
J.C. Guscott
A.S. Healey

P.J. Grayson 4PG
K.P.P. Bracken

J. Leonard
M.P. Regan[1]
D.J. Garforth
M.O. Johnson
G.S. Archer
* L.B.N. Dallaglio
R.A. Hill
N.A. Back 1T

1 Rep by † D.E. West

v WALES

WON 60-26
England: 7G 2PG 1T
Wales: 3G 1T
Twickenham, 21 Feb 1998

M.B. Perry

D.L. Rees 2T
W.J.H. Greenwood[5] 1T
J.C. Guscott
A.S. Healey 1T

P.J. Grayson[4] 2PG 7C
K.P.P. Bracken[6] 1T

J. Leonard
R. Cockerill
† P.J. Vickery[2]
M.O. Johnson[1]
G.S. Archer
* L.B.N. Dallaglio 1T
R.A. Hill[3]
N.A. Back 1T

1 Rep by D.J. Grewcock
2 Rep by D.J. Garforth
3 Rep by A.J. Diprose
4 Rep by M.J. Catt
5 Rep by P.R. de Glanville
6 Rep by M.J.S. Dawson 1T

v SCOTLAND

WON 34-20
Scotland: 2G 2PG
England: 4G‡ 1PG 1DG
Murrayfield, 22 Mar 1998

M.B. Perry

A.S. Healey[2] 1T
W.J.H. Greenwood
J.C. Guscott
A.A. Adebayo

P.J. Grayson 1PG 4C 1DG 1T
M.J.S. Dawson 1T

J. Leonard
R. Cockerill[4]
D.J. Garforth
M.O. Johnson[3]
G.S. Archer
* L.B.N. Dallaglio
D. Ryan[1]
N.A. Back

‡includes penalty try
1 Rep by A.J. Diprose
2 Rep by P.R. de Glanville
3 Rep by D.J. Grewcock
4 Rep by D.E. West

v IRELAND

WON 35-17
England: 3G 3PG 1T
Ireland: 2G 1PG
Twickenham, 4 Apr 1998

M.B. Perry 1T

M.J. Catt[3] 1T
W.J.H. Greenwood[2]
J.C. Guscott
A.S. Healey

P.J. Grayson 3PG 3C
M.J.S. Dawson

J. Leonard
R. Cockerill 1T
D.J. Garforth
M.O. Johnson
G.S. Archer[1]
* L.B.N. Dallaglio
A.J. Diprose
N.A. Back

1 Rep by D.J. Grewcock
2 Rep by P.R. de Glanville 1T
3 Rep by † J.P. Wilkinson

FACT FILE

- Clive Woodward succeeded Jack Rowell as England manager.
- The 60-26 win over Wales set a new record for the highest score in a championship match.
- The match at Murrayfield was England's first on a Sunday in the championship.
- Paul Grayson bagged a full set of scoring actions, the first English player to do so in a championship match.

FINAL TABLE

	P	W	D	L	F	A	Pts
France	4	4	0	0	144	49	8
England	**4**	**3**	**0**	**1**	**146**	**87**	**6**
Wales	4	2	0	2	75	145	4
Scotland	4	1	0	3	66	120	2
Ireland	4	0	0	4	70	100	0

1997-98 continued

Tour Matches

1st v AUSTRALIA

LOST 0-76
Australia: 6G 3PG 5T
England: Nil
Brisbane, 6 Jun 1998

T.R.G. Stimpson [1]

† S.P. Brown
M.B. Perry
† S.C.W. Ravenscroft [b]
A.S. Healey

J.P. Wilkinson
† S. Benton

G.C. Rowntree
R. Cockerill
P.J. Vickery
G.S. Archer
D.J. Grewcock
† B. Sturnham
* A.J. Diprose
† R.J. Pool-Jones [a]

1 Rep by † D.E. Chapman
a Rep by B.B. Clarke
b Rep by † S. Potter

1st v NEW ZEALAND

LOST 22-64
NZ: 5G 3PG 4T
England: 2G 1PG 1T
Dunedin, 20 Jun 1998

M.B. Perry

T.R.G. Stimpson 1PG 2C
N.D. Beal
† O.J. Lewsey
A.S. Healey

J.P. Wilkinson [1]
* M.J.S. Dawson 1T

G.C. Rowntree [a]
R. Cockerill [2] 1T
P.J. Vickery [3]
G.S. Archer [4]
D.J. Grewcock
B.B. Clarke
S.O. Ojomoh [b]
† P.H. Sanderson

a/3 Rep by W.R. Green
b Rep by B. Sturnham
1 Rep by † T.D. Beim 1T
2 Rep by P.B.T. Greening
4 Rep by † D. Sims

2nd v NEW ZEALAND

LOST 10-40
NZ: 5G 1T
England: 1G 1PG
Auckland, 27 Jun 1998

M.B. Perry

T. Beim [1]
N.D. Beal
† J.J.N. Baxendell
A.S. Healey [2]

O.J. Lewsey
* M.J.S. Dawson 1PG 1C 1T

G.C. Rowntree
R. Cockerill [3]
P.J. Vickery
† R.J. Fidler
D. Sims
B.B. Clarke
A.J. Diprose
P.H. Sanderson [a]

1 Rep by T.R.G. Stimpson
2 Rep by S.C.W. Ravenscroft
3 Rep by P.B.T. Greening
a Rep by B. Sturnham

1st v SOUTH AFRICA

LOST 0-18
SA: 1G 2PG 1T
England: Nil
Cape Town, 4 Jul 1998

M.B. Perry

S.P. Brown
N.D. Beal
J.J.N. Baxendell
† P.C. Sampson [1]

O.J. Lewsey
* M.J.S. Dawson

G.C. Rowntree
R. Cockerill
P.J. Vickery
R.J. Fidler
D. Sims
B.B. Clarke
A.J. Diprose
P.H. Sanderson

1 Rep by T.R.G. Stimpson

FACT FILE

- The most disastrous four matches of all time began with a 76-0 defeat by Australia, England's biggest reverse ever.
- Danny Grewcock became only the second England player sent off in a Test when he received his marching orders in Dunedin.
- Josh Lewsey's Test debut in Dunedin was his first first-class match as a centre.

1998-99

World Cup Qualifying Matches

v NETHERLANDS

WON 110-0
England: 15G‡ 1T
Netherlands: Nil
Huddersfield, 14 Nov 1998

M.B. Perry [4]

† D.D. Luger 1T
W.J.H. Greenwood 1T
J.C. Guscott 4T
A.S. Healey 1T

P.J. Grayson 15C
M.J.S. Dawson 1T

J. Leonard
R. Cockerill 1T
D.J. Garforth [3]
* M.O. Johnson
G.S. Archer [1]
B.B. Clarke [2]
M.E. Corry 1T
N.A. Back 4T

‡includes penalty try
1 Rep by T.A.K. Rodber
2 Rep by R.A. Hill
3 Rep by G.C. Rowntree
4 Rep by N.D. Beal 1T

v ITALY

WON 23-15
England: 2G 3PG
Italy: 4PG 1DG
Huddersfield, 22 Nov 1998

M.B. Perry

A.S. Healey
W.J.H. Greenwood 1T
J.C. Guscott
D.D. Luger 1T

P.J. Grayson 3PG 2C
M.J.S. Dawson

J. Leonard
R. Cockerill
D.J. Garforth [3]
* M.O. Johnson
G.S. Archer [1]
B.B. Clarke [2]
M.E. Corry
N.A. Back

1 Rep by T.A.K. Rodber
2 Rep by R.A. Hill
3 Rep by G.C. Rowntree

Tour Matches

2nd v AUSTRALIA

LOST 11-12
England: 2PG 1T
Australia: 4PG
Twickenham, 28 Nov 1998

M.B. Perry

T. Underwood
P.R. de Glanville
J.C. Guscott 1T
A.S. Healey

P.J. Grayson [1]
M.J.S. Dawson

J. Leonard
R. Cockerill
D.J. Garforth
M.O. Johnson
T.A.K. Rodber
* L.B.N. Dallaglio
R.A. Hill
N.A. Back

1 Rep by M.J. Catt 2PG

2nd v SOUTH AFRICA

WON 13-7
England: 1G 2PG
SA: 1G
Twickenham, 5 Dec 1998

N.D. Beal

T. Underwood [1]
P.R. de Glanville [3]
J.C. Guscott 1T
D.D. Luger

M.J. Catt [a]
M.J.S. Dawson 2PG 1C

J. Leonard
R. Cockerill
D.J. Garforth
M.O. Johnson
T.A.K. Rodber [4]
* L.B.N. Dallaglio
R.A. Hill
N.A. Back

1 Rep by D.L. Rees [2]
2 Rep by A.S. Healey
3 Rep by A.D. King
4 Rep by D.J. Grewcock
a Rep by M.E. Corry

FACT FILE

- The 110-0 victory over The Netherlands in the first of two World Cup qualifiers at the McAlpine Stadium in Huddersfield set a new record-winning margin for England.
- In the same match Neil Back became the first England forward since George Burton (in 1881) to score four tries in a Test.

1998-99 continued

Five Nations Championship

v SCOTLAND

WON 24-21
England: 3G 1PG
Scotland: 3G
Twickenham, 20 Feb 1999

N.D. Beal 1T

D.L. Rees
J.P. Wilkinson 1PG 3C
J.C. Guscott
D.D. Luger 1T

M.J. Catt
M.J.S. Dawson [2]

J. Leonard
R. Cockerill
D.J. Garforth
M.O. Johnson [1]
T.A.K. Rodber 1T
* L.B.N. Dallaglio
R.A. Hill
N.A. Back

1 Rep by D.J. Grewcock
2 Rep by K.P.P. Bracken

v IRELAND

WON 27-15
Ireland: 5PG
England: 1G 4PG 1DG 1T
Lansdowne Road, 6 Mar 1999

M.B. Perry 1T

D.L. Rees
J.P. Wilkinson 4PG 1C
J.C. Guscott
D.D. Luger

P.J. Grayson 1DG
K.P.P. Bracken

J. Leonard
R. Cockerill [a]
D.J. Garforth
M.O. Johnson
T.A.K. Rodber 1T
R.A. Hill
* L.B.N. Dallaglio
N.A. Back

a Rep by † N. McCarthy

v FRANCE

WON 21-10
England: 7PG
France: 1G 1PG
Twickenham, 20 Mar 1999

M.B. Perry

D.L. Rees [3]
J.P. Wilkinson 7PG
J.C. Guscott
D.D. Luger

M.J. Catt
K.P.P. Bracken [1]

J. Leonard
R. Cockerill
D.J. Garforth [4]
M.O. Johnson
T.A.K. Rodber
R.A. Hill [2]
* L.B.N. Dallaglio
N.A. Back

1 Rep by M.J.S. Dawson
2 Rep by M.E. Corry
3 Rep by N.D. Beal
4 Rep by V.E. Ubogu

v WALES

LOST 31-32
Wales: 2G 6PG
England: 2G 4PG 1T
Wembley, 11 Apr 1999

M.B. Perry

D.D. Luger 1T
J.P. Wilkinson 4PG 2C
† B-J. Mather
† S.M. Hanley 1T

M.J. Catt
M.J.S. Dawson

J. Leonard
R. Cockerill
D.J. Garforth [1]
M.O. Johnson
T.A.K. Rodber
R.A. Hill 1T
* L.B.N. Dallaglio
N.A. Back

1 Rep by V.E. Ubogu

FACT FILE

- England became the first Test side to play a home and away match on the same ground. They had hosted the Canadians at Wembley in 1992 and, with Cardiff under reconstruction, were the visitors for Wales's home match at the ground in April.
- The Test against the Wallabies was staged to mark the centenary of international rugby union in Australia.

FINAL TABLE

	P	W	D	L	F	A	Pts
Scotland	4	3	0	1	120	79	6
England	**4**	**3**	**0**	**1**	**103**	**78**	**6**
Wales	4	2	0	2	109	126	4
Ireland	4	1	0	3	66	90	2
France	4	1	0	3	75	100	2

1998-99 continued

Friendly

v AUSTRALIA

LOST 15-22
Australia: 1G 3T
England: 1G 1PG 1T
Sydney, 26 Jun 1999

M.B. Perry[a] 2T

D.L. Rees
M.J. Catt[6]
J.C. Guscott
D.D. Luger

J.P. Wilkinson 1PG 1C
K.P.P. Bracken[1]

J. Leonard
R. Cockerill[2]
D.J. Garforth[4]
* M.O. Johnson
T.A.K. Rodber[3]
R.A. Hill
M.E. Corry[5]
N.A. Back

1 Rep by M.J.S. Dawson
2 Rep by P.B.T. Greening
3 Rep by D.J. Grewcock
4 Rep by V.E. Ubogu
5 Rep by B.B. Clarke
6 Rep by P.R. de Glanville
a Rep by N.D. Beal

World Cup Warm-up Matches

v UNITED STATES

WON 106-8
England: 13G‡ 3T
US: 1PG 1T
Twickenham, 21 Aug 1999

M.B. Perry[3] 2T

A.S. Healey
P.R. de Glanville 1T
J.C. Guscott 4T
D.D. Luger 2T

J.P. Wilkinson 13C
M.J.S. Dawson 1T

G.C. Rowntree[1]
P.B.T. Greening[5] 1T
P.J. Vickery[2]
* M.O. Johnson 1T
D.J. Grewcock[4]
R.A. Hill 1T
L.B.N. Dallaglio
N.A. Back 2T

‡includes penalty try
1 Rep by † T.J. Woodman
2 Rep by W.R. Green
3 Rep by T.R.G. Stimpson
4 Rep by T.A.K. Rodber
5 Rep by N. McCarthy

v CANADA

WON 36-11
England: 4G 1PG 1T
Canada: 2PG 1T
Twickenham, 28 Aug 1999

M.B. Perry[5] 1T

A.S. Healey[4]
W.J.H. Greenwood 2T
J.C. Guscott[6]
D.D. Luger 1T

J.P. Wilkinson 1PG 4C
M.J.S. Dawson 1T

G.C. Rowntree[1]
P.B.T. Greening[2]
P.J. Vickery[3]
* M.O. Johnson[a]
D.J. Grewcock
R.A. Hill
L.B.N. Dallaglio
N.A. Back

a Rep by M.E. Corry
1 Rep by J. Leonard
2 Rep by R. Cockerill
3 Rep by D.J. Garforth
4 Rep by N.D. Beal
5 Rep by T.R.G. Stimpson
6 Rep by M.J. Catt

Paul Grayson watches as Jeremy Guscott tries to get away from an Irish tackler, March 1999.

1999 Fourth Rugby World Cup

Group Matches

v ITALY

WON **67-7**
England: 6G 5PG 2T
Italy: 1G
Twickenham, 2 Oct 1999

M.B. Perry[6] 1T

A.S. Healey
W.J.H. Greenwood[1]
P.R. de Glanville 1T
D.D. Luger 1T

J.P. Wilkinson 5PG 6C 1T
M.J.S. Dawson 1T

J. Leonard[3]
R. Cockerill[2]
P.J. Vickery[4]
* M.O. Johnson
D.J. Grewcock[5]
R.A. Hill 1T
L.B.N. Dallaglio
N.A. Back 1T

1 Rep by J.C. Guscott
2 Rep by P.B.T. Greening
3 Rep by G.C. Rowntree
4 Rep by D.J. Garforth
5 Rep by M.E. Corry 1T
6 Rep by N.D. Beal

v NEW ZEALAND

LOST **16-30**
England: 1G 3PG
NZ: 3G 3PG
Twickenham, 9 Oct 1999

M.B. Perry

A.S. Healey
P.R. de Glanville 1T
J.C. Guscott
D.D. Luger

J.P. Wilkinson[4] 3PG 1C
M.J.S. Dawson

J. Leonard
R. Cockerill[3]
P.J. Vickery[1]
* M.O. Johnson
D.J. Grewcock[2]
R.A. Hill[a b]
L.B.N. Dallaglio
N.A. Back[5]

1 Rep by D.J. Garforth
2 Rep by T.A.K. Rodber
3 Rep by P.B.T. Greening
4 Rep by P.J. Grayson
a b/5 Rep by M.E. Corry

v TONGA

WON **101-10**
England: 12G 4PG 1T
Tonga: 1G 1PG
Twickenham, 15 Oct 1999

M.B. Perry 1T

A.S. Healey 2T
W.J.H. Greenwood[3] 2T
J.C. Guscott 2T
D.D. Luger 2T

P.J. Grayson 4PG 12C
M.J.S. Dawson[1] 1T

G.C. Rowntree
P.B.T. Greening 2T
P.J. Vickery
* M.O. Johnson[2]
G.S. Archer
† J.P.R. Worsley
L.B.N. Dallaglio[4]
R.A. Hill 1T

1 Rep by N.D. Beal
2 Rep by D.J. Grewcock
3 Rep by M.J. Catt
4 Rep by R. Cockerill

Quarter-final Play-off

v FIJI

WON **45-24**
England: 2G 7PG 2T
Fiji: 3G 1PG
Twickenham, 20 Oct 1999

M.B. Perry[7]

N.D. Beal 1T
W.J.H. Greenwood
M.J. Catt
D.D. Luger[2] 1T

J.P. Wilkinson[5] 7PG 1C
A.S. Healey[3]

J. Leonard[1]
P.B.T. Greening[6] 1T
D.J. Garforth
* M.O. Johnson
G.S. Archer[4]
J.P.R. Worsley[a]
L.B.N. Dallaglio
N.A. Back 1T

1 Rep by G.C. Rowntree
2 Rep by P.R. de Glanville
3 Rep by M.J.S. Dawson 1C
4 Rep by T.A.K. Rodber
5 Rep by P.J. Grayson
6 Rep by R. Cockerill
a/7 Rep by R.A. Hill

Quarter-final

v SOUTH AFRICA

LOST **21-44**
SA: 2G 5PG 5DG
England: 7PG
Stade de France, 24 Oct 1999

M.B. Perry

N.D. Beal[1]
W.J.H. Greenwood
P.R. de Glanville[3]
D.D. Luger

P.J. Grayson[2] 6PG
M.J.S. Dawson[4]

J. Leonard
P.B.T. Greening
P.J. Vickery
* M.O. Johnson
D.J. Grewcock
R.A. Hill
L.B.N. Dallaglio
N.A. Back

1 Rep by A.S. Healey
2 Rep by J.P. Wilkinson 1PG
3 Rep by M.J. Catt
4 Rep by M.E. Corry

FACT FILE

- The defeat of Tonga in the World Cup pool match was the start of a world record run of home-ground victories for England.
- England were knocked out in Paris in the quarter-finals by South Africa – 15 of the winners' points came from five dropped goals by Jannie de Beer, a world record for a Test match.

1999-2000

Six Nations Championship

v IRELAND

WON 50-18
England: 4G 4PG 2T
Ireland: 1G 2PG 1T
Twickenham, 5 Feb 2000

M.B. Perry [1]

A.S. Healey 2T
† M.J. Tindall 1T
M.J. Catt
† B.C. Cohen 2T

J.P. Wilkinson 4PG 4C
* M.J.S. Dawson

J. Leonard [2]
P.B.T. Greening
P.J. Vickery
G.S. Archer
S.D. Shaw [3]
R.A. Hill
L.B.N. Dallaglio
N.A. Back 1T

1 Rep by † I.R. Balshaw
2 Rep by T.J. Woodman
3 Rep by M.E. Corry

v FRANCE

WON 15-9
France: 3PG
England: 5PG
Stade de France, 19 Feb 2000

M.B. Perry [1]

A.S. Healey
M.J. Tindall
M.J. Catt
B.C. Cohen

J.P. Wilkinson 5PG
* M.J.S. Dawson

J. Leonard
P.B.T. Greening
P.J. Vickery
G.S. Archer
S.D. Shaw
R.A. Hill [2]
L.B.N. Dallaglio
N.A. Back

1 Rep by I.R. Balshaw
2 Rep by M.E. Corry

v WALES

WON 46-12
England: 3G 5PG 2T
Wales: 3PG 1DG
Twickenham, 4 Mar 2000

M.B. Perry

A.S. Healey
M.J. Tindall
M.J. Catt
B.C. Cohen 1T

J.P. Wilkinson 5PG 3C
* M.J.S. Dawson

J. Leonard
P.B.T. Greening 1T
P.J. Vickery
G.S. Archer
S.D. Shaw [1]
R.A. Hill 1T
L.B.N. Dallaglio 1T
N.A. Back 1T

1 Rep by M.E. Corry

v ITALY

WON 59-12
Italy: 1G 1T
England: 5G‡ 2PG 1DG 3T
Stadio Flaminio, 18 Mar 2000

M.B. Perry

A.S. Healey 3T
M.J. Tindall [1]
M.J. Catt
B.C. Cohen 2T

J.P. Wilkinson [4] 2PG 4C
* M.J.S. Dawson [5] 2T

J. Leonard [2]
P.B.T. Greening [6]
D.J. Garforth
G.S. Archer [7]
S.D. Shaw
R.A. Hill [3]
L.B.N. Dallaglio
N.A. Back 1DG

‡includes penalty try
1 Rep by I.R. Balshaw
2 Rep by T.J. Woodman
3 Rep by J.P.R. Worsley
4 Rep by A.D. King 1C
5 Rep by A.C.T. Gomarsall
6 Rep by N. McCarthy
7 Rep by M.E. Corry

v SCOTLAND

LOST 13-19
Scotland: 1G 4PG
England: 1G 2PG
Murrayfield, 2 Apr 2000

M.B. Perry

A.S. Healey
M.J. Tindall
M.J. Catt
B.C. Cohen [1]

J.P. Wilkinson 2PG 1C
* M.J.S. Dawson

J. Leonard
P.B.T. Greening
P.J. Vickery
G.S. Archer [2]
S.D. Shaw
R.A. Hill [3]
L.B.N. Dallaglio 1T
N.A. Back

1 Rep by I.R. Balshaw
2 Rep by M.E. Corry
3 Rep by J.P.R. Worsley

FACT FILE

- The International Championship featured six nations with Italy invited to take part for the first time.
- In Rome, Neil Back became the first England forward in 129 years of Test rugby to drop a goal.

FINAL TABLE

	P	W	D	L	F	A	Pts
England	**5**	**4**	**0**	**1**	**183**	**70**	**8**
France	5	3	0	2	140	92	6
Ireland	5	3	0	2	168	133	6
Wales	5	3	0	2	111	135	6
Scotland	5	1	0	4	95	145	2
Italy	5	1	0	4	106	228	2

1999-2000 continued

Tour Matches

1st v SOUTH AFRICA

LOST 13-18
SA: 6PG
England: 1G 2PG
Pretoria, 17 Jun 2000

M.B. Perry

T.R.G. Stimpson **2PG 1C**
M.J. Tindall
M.J. Catt[2]
D.D. Luger **1T**

A.S. Healey
K.P.P. Bracken

J. Leonard
P.B.T. Greening
† J.M. White[b]
* M.O. Johnson[1]
D.J. Grewcock[3]
R.A. Hill[a]
L.B.N. Dallaglio
N.A. Back

1 Rep by S.D. Shaw
2 Rep by † L.D. Lloyd
3 Rep by J.P.R. Worsley
a Rep by M.P. Regan
b Rep by † D.L. Flatman

2nd v SOUTH AFRICA

WON 27-22
SA: 1G 5PG
England: 8PG 1DG
Bloemfontein, 24 Jun 2000

M.B. Perry

A.S. Healey
M.J. Tindall[3]
M.J. Catt
B.C. Cohen

J.P. Wilkinson **8PG 1DG**
K.P.P. Bracken

J. Leonard
P.B.T. Greening
J.M. White[4]
* M.O. Johnson
D.J. Grewcock[1]
R.A. Hill[a/2]
L.B.N. Dallaglio
N.A. Back

1 Rep by S.D. Shaw
2 Rep by J.P.R. Worsley
3 Rep by L.D. Lloyd
a/4 Rep by D.L. Flatman

FACT FILE

- Jonny Wilkinson became the first England player to kick eight penalty goals in a Test with his winning contribution in Bloemfontein.

2000-01

Tour Matches

v AUSTRALIA

WON 22-19
England: 1G 4PG 1DG
Australia: 1G 4PG
Twickenham, 18 Nov 2000

M.B. Perry

A.S. Healey[1]
M.J. Tindall
M.J. Catt
D.D. Luger **1T**

J.P. Wilkinson **4PG 1DG 1C**
K.P.P. Bracken[2]

J. Leonard
P.B.T. Greening[3]
P.J. Vickery[a]
* M.O. Johnson
D.J. Grewcock
R.A. Hill
L.B.N. Dallaglio
N.A. Back

1 Rep by I.R. Balshaw
2 Rep by M.J.S. Dawson
3 Rep by M.P. Regan
a Rep by D.L. Flatman

v ARGENTINA

WON 19-0
England: 1G 3PG 1DG
Argentina: Nil
Twickenham, 25 Nov 2000

I.R. Balshaw

B.C. Cohen **1T**
M.J. Tindall[3]
M.J. Catt
D.D. Luger

J.P. Wilkinson **3PG 1DG 1C**
M.J.S. Dawson

J. Leonard[2]
M.P. Regan[5]
J.M. White[1]
* M.O. Johnson
D.J. Grewcock
R.A. Hill[4]
L.B.N. Dallaglio
N.A. Back

1 Rep by P.J. Vickery[a]
a/2 Rep by D.L. Flatman
3 Rep by W.J.H. Greenwood
4 Rep by M.E. Corry
5 Rep by D.E. West

3rd v SOUTH AFRICA

WON 25-17
England: 1G 6PG
SA: 4PG 1T
Twickenham, 2 Dec 2000

M.B. Perry

B.C. Cohen
M.J. Tindall
W.J.H. Greenwood[3] **1T**
D.D. Luger[1]

J.P. Wilkinson **6PG 1C**
M.J.S. Dawson

J. Leonard
P.B.T. Greening[c]
J.M. White[2]
* M.O. Johnson
D.J. Grewcock
R.A. Hill[b]
L.B.N. Dallaglio
N.A. Back[a]

1 Rep by I.R. Balshaw
2 Rep by P.J. Vickery
3 Rep by A.S. Healey
a Rep by M.E. Corry
b/c Rep by M.P. Regan

2000-01 continued

Six Nations Championship

v WALES

WON 44-15
Wales: 1G 1PG 1T
England: 4G 2PG 2T
Cardiff Arms Park, 3 Feb 2001

I.R. Balshaw [2]

B.C. Cohen 1T
W.J.H. Greenwood 3T
M.J. Catt [5]
D.D. Luger [1]

J.P. Wilkinson 2PG 4C
M.J.S. Dawson 2T

J. Leonard [3]
D.E. West
P.J. Vickery
* M.O. Johnson
D.J. Grewcock
R.A. Hill
L.B.N. Dallaglio [4]
N.A. Back

1 Rep by A.S. Healey
2 Rep by M.B. Perry
3 Rep by T.J. Woodman
4 Rep by M.E. Corry
5 Rep by M.J. Tindall

v ITALY

WON 80-23
England: 9G 4PG 1T
Italy: 2G 3PG
Cardiff Arms Park, 17 Feb 2001

I.R. Balshaw 2T

A.S. Healey 2T
W.J.H. Greenwood 1T
M.J. Catt
B.C. Cohen [1] 1T

J.P. Wilkinson 4PG 9C 1T
M.J.S. Dawson [4]

J. Leonard [5]
D.E. West [2]
P.J. Vickery
* M.O. Johnson
D.J. Grewcock [6]
R.A. Hill
L.B.N. Dallaglio 1T
N.A. Back [3]

1 Rep by † J. Robinson
2 Rep by M.P. Regan 1T
3 Rep by J.P.R. Worsley 1T
4 Rep by K.P.P. Bracken
5 Rep by T.J. Woodman
6 Rep by M.E. Corry

v SCOTLAND

WON 43-3
England: 5G 1PG 1T
Scotland: 1PG
Twickenham, 3 Mar 2001

I.R. Balshaw 2T

A.S. Healey
W.J.H. Greenwood 1T
M.J. Catt [2]
B.C. Cohen

J.P. Wilkinson 1PG 5C
M.J.S. Dawson [4]

J. Leonard
D.E. West [1]
P.J. Vickery
* M.O. Johnson
D.J. Grewcock
R.A. Hill 1T
L.B.N. Dallaglio 2T
N.A. Back [3]

1 Rep by M.P. Regan
2 Rep by J. Robinson
3 Rep by J.P.R. Worsley
4 Rep by K.P.P. Bracken

v FRANCE

WON 48-19
England: 6G 2PG
France: 1G 3PG 1DG
Twickenham, 7 Apr 2001

I.R. Balshaw [3] 1T

A.S. Healey
W.J.H. Greenwood 1T
M.J. Catt 1T
B.C. Cohen [1]

J.P. Wilkinson 2PG 6C
M.J.S. Dawson [4]

J. Leonard [c]
P.B.T. Greening [a] 1T
J.M. White
* M.O. Johnson
† S.W. Borthwick [b]
R.A. Hill [2] 1T
L.B.N. Dallaglio
N.A. Back

1 Rep by J. Robinson
2 Rep by J.P.R. Worsley
3 Rep by M.B. Perry 1T
4 Rep by K.P.P. Bracken
a Rep by D.E. West
b Rep by M.E. Corry
c Rep by D.L. Flatman

FACT FILE

- An outbreak of foot-and-mouth disease prevented the Six Nations from being completed. England did not play their scheduled match in Dublin until the start of the next season.
- The 80-23 win against Italy set a new record score and winning margin for an International Championship match, as did Jonny Wilkinson's individual haul of 35 points.

2000-01 continued

Tour Matches

1st v CANADA

WON 22-10
Canada: 1G 1PG
England: 1G 3T
Markham, 2 Jun 2001

O.J. Lewsey 2T

P.C. Sampson
L.D. Lloyd
† J. Noon
† M. Stephenson [a]

† D.J.H. Walder 1C
* K.P.P. Bracken 1T

G.C. Rowntree
D.E. West 1T
J.M. White
S.W. Borthwick [1]
† B.J. Kay
M.E. Corry
J.P.R. Worsley [2]
† L.W. Moody

1 Rep by S.D. Shaw
2 Rep by P.H. Sanderson
a Rep by T.R.G. Stimpson

2nd v CANADA

WON 59-20
Canada: 2G 2PG
England: 5G‡ 3PG 3T
Burnaby, 9 Jun 2001

O.J. Lewsey

P.C. Sampson [2]
L.D. Lloyd
J. Noon [6] 1T
M. Stephenson

D.J.H. Walder 3PG 5C 2T
* K.P.P. Bracken [1]

G.C. Rowntree [4]
D.E. West [7]
J.M. White
S.D. Shaw 2T
B.J. Kay [3]
† S. White-Cooper [a]
J.P.R. Worsley [5] 1T
L.W. Moody

‡inc penalty try
1 Rep by M.B. Wood 1T
2 Rep by T.R.G. Stimpson
3 Rep by S.W. Borthwick
a/4 Rep by D.L. Flatman
5 Rep by P.H. Sanderson
6 Rep by A.D. King
7 Rep by M.P. Regan

v UNITED STATES

WON 48-19
USA: 2G 1T
England: 4G 4T
San Francisco, 16 Jun 2001

O.J. Lewsey 2T

L.D. Lloyd 2T
† F.H.H. Waters [8]
J. Noon [1]
M. Stephenson

D.J.H. Walder [6] 4C
* K.P.P. Bracken [7]

G.C. Rowntree [4]
D.E. West [3] 1T
J.M. White
S.D. Shaw
S.W. Borthwick [5]
S. White-Cooper [b]
J.P.R. Worsley [2] 1T
L.W. Moody [a] 1T

1 Rep by † O. Barkley
a/2 Rep by P.H. Sanderson 1T
3 Rep by A.E. Long
b/4 Rep by D.L. Flatman
5 Rep by † T. Palmer
6 Rep by † T. Voyce
7 Rep by M.B. Wood
8 Rep by J. Noon

A tense moment during England's 21-15 defeat of world champions Australia at Twickenham in 2001.

2001-02

Six Nations Championship

v IRELAND

LOST 14-20
Ireland: 5PG 1T
England: 3PG 1T
Lansdowne Road, 20 Oct 2001

I.R. Balshaw

D.D. Luger [3]
W.J.H. Greenwood
M.J. Catt
J. Robinson

J.P. Wilkinson **3PG**
* M.J.S. Dawson [1]

J. Leonard
P.B.T. Greening [2]
J.M. White [5]
S.D. Shaw
D.J. Grewcock
M.E. Corry [4]
R.A. Hill
N.A. Back

1 Rep by K.P.P. Bracken
2 Rep by D.E. West
3 Rep by A.S. Healey **1T**
4 Rep by L.W. Moody
5 Rep by G.C. Rowntree

FACT FILE

- England were without their Lions (touring Australia) for the three-Test North American tour.
- They finished the International Championship in Dublin in October setting a new record points aggregate for the tournament with 229, of which 89 (also a new record) had come from Jonny Wilkinson.

FINAL TABLE

	P	W	D	L	F	A	Pts
England	**5**	**4**	**0**	**1**	**229**	**80**	**8**
Ireland	5	4	0	1	129	89	8
Scotland	5	2	1	2	92	116	5
Wales	5	2	1	2	125	166	5
France	5	2	0	3	115	138	4
Italy	5	0	0	5	106	207	0

Tour Match

v AUSTRALIA

WON 21-15
England: 5PG 2DG
Australia: 1G 1PG 1T
Twickenham, 10 Nov 2001

J. Robinson

A.S. Healey
W.J.H. Greenwood
M.J. Catt
D.D. Luger

J.P. Wilkinson **5PG 2DG**
K.P.P. Bracken

G.C. Rowntree
D.E. West
P.J. Vickery
B.J. Kay
D.J. Grewcock
R.A. Hill
J.P.R. Worsley
* N.A. Back

Tour Match

v SOUTH AFRICA

WON 29-9
England: 7PG 1DG 1T
SA: 3PG
Twickenham, 24 Nov 2001

J. Robinson

A.S. Healey
W.J.H. Greenwood
M.J. Catt [2] **1DG**
D.D. Luger **1T**

J.P. Wilkinson **7PG**
K.P.P. Bracken

G.C. Rowntree
D.E. West
P.J. Vickery
* M.O. Johnson [3]
D.J. Grewcock
R.A. Hill [1]
J.P.R. Worsley
N.A. Back [a]

1 Rep by L.W. Moody
2 Rep by M.J. Tindall
a/3 Rep by B.J. Kay

Friendly

v ROMANIA

WON 134-0
England: 14G 2PG 6T
Romania: Nil
Twickenham, 17 Nov 2001

J. Robinson **4T**

B.C. Cohen **3T**
W.J.H. Greenwood [4]
M.J. Tindall **2T**
D.D. Luger **3T**

† C. Hodgson **2PG 14C 2T**
A.S. Healey [1] **1T**

G.C. Rowntree [3]
M.P. Regan **1T**
J. Leonard
B.J. Kay [5]
S.W. Borthwick
L.W. Moody **2T**
J.P.R. Worsley **1T**
* N.A. Back [2]

1 Rep by K.P.P. Bracken
2 Rep by † A. Sanderson **1T**
3 Rep by J.M. White
4 Rep by M.J. Catt
5 Rep by D.J. Grewcock

FACT FILE

- Charlie Hodgson set an English record, scoring 44 points (on debut) against Romania as the side ran up a new record score.

2001-02 continued

Six Nations Championship

v SCOTLAND

WON 29-3
Scotland: 1PG
England: 3G 1PG 1T
Murrayfield, 2 Feb 2002

J. Robinson 2T

A.S. Healey
W.J.H. Greenwood
M.J. Tindall[3] 1T
B.C. Cohen 1T

J.P. Wilkinson[5] 1PG 2C
K.P.P. Bracken[1]

G.C. Rowntree
† S. Thompson
J.M. White[4]
* M.O. Johnson
B.J. Kay[2]
R.A. Hill
J.P.R. Worsley
N.A. Back

1 Rep by † N. Duncombe
2 Rep by D.J. Grewcock
3 Rep by I.R. Balshaw
4 Rep by J. Leonard
5 Rep by C. Hodgson 1C

v IRELAND

WON 45-11
England: 6G 1PG
Ireland: 2PG 1T
Twickenham, 16 Feb 2002

J. Robinson

A.S. Healey[3]
W.J.H. Greenwood 2T
M.J. Tindall
B.C. Cohen 1T

J.P. Wilkinson[5] 1PG 6C 1T
K.P.P. Bracken[6]

G.C. Rowntree[1]
S. Thompson
P.J. Vickery
* M.O. Johnson[2]
B.J. Kay 1T
R.A. Hill[4]
J.P.R. Worsley 1T
N.A. Back

1 Rep by J. Leonard
2 Rep by D.J. Grewcock
3 Rep by I.R. Balshaw
4 Rep by L.W. Moody
5 Rep by C. Hodgson
6 Rep by N. Duncombe

v FRANCE

LOST 15-20
France: 2G 2PG
England: 1G 1PG 1T
Stade de France, 2 Mar 2002

J. Robinson 1T

A.S. Healey
W.J.H. Greenwood
M.J. Tindall[1]
B.C. Cohen 1T

J.P. Wilkinson[5] 1PG 1C
K.P.P. Bracken

G.C. Rowntree[4]
S. Thompson[6]
P.J. Vickery
* M.O. Johnson
B.J. Kay[3]
R.A. Hill
J.P.R. Worsley[2]
N.A. Back[a]

1 Rep by † H. Paul
a/2 Rep by M.E. Corry
3 Rep by D.J. Grewcock
4 Rep by J. Leonard
5 Rep by D.D. Luger
6 Rep by D.E. West

v WALES

WON 50-10
England: 5G 4PG 1DG
Wales: 1G 1PG
Twickenham, 23 Mar 2002

A.S. Healey

D.D. Luger 2T
W.J.H. Greenwood 1T
M.J. Tindall[2]
B.C. Cohen

J.P. Wilkinson 4PG 1DG 5C 1T
K.P.P. Bracken[1]

G.C. Rowntree
S. Thompson[3]
J.M. White
D.J. Grewcock
B.J. Kay[a]
L.W. Moody[b]
R.A. Hill[4]
* N.A. Back

1 Rep by M.J.S. Dawson
2 Rep by T.R.G. Stimpson 1T
3 Rep by D.E. West
a/4 Rep by J.P.R. Worsley
b Rep by M.E. Corry

v ITALY

WON 45-9
Italy: 3PG
England: 6G 1PG
Stadio Flaminio, 7 Apr 2002

J. Robinson 1T

D.D. Luger
W.J.H. Greenwood 2T
M.J. Tindall[7]
B.C. Cohen[5] 1T

J.P. Wilkinson 1PG 5C
K.P.P. Bracken[4]

G.C. Rowntree[2]
S. Thompson[6]
J.M. White
D.J. Grewcock[a/1]
B.J. Kay
L.W. Moody
R.A. Hill
* N.A. Back[3]

a/1 Rep by M.O. Johnson
2 Rep by J. Leonard
3 Rep by L.B.N. Dallaglio 1T
4 Rep by M.J.S. Dawson 1C
5 Rep by A.S. Healey 1T
6 Rep by D.E. West
7 Rep by C. Hodgson

FACT FILE

- Jason Leonard equalled Rory Underwood's record of most International Championship match appearances when he came off the bench together with three other England captains – Martin Johnson, Lawrence Dallaglio and Matt Dawson – against Italy.

FINAL TABLE

	P	W	D	L	F	A	Pts
France	5	5	0	0	156	75	10
England	**5**	**4**	**0**	**1**	**184**	**53**	**8**
Ireland	5	3	0	2	145	138	6
Scotland	5	2	0	3	91	128	4
Wales	5	1	0	4	119	188	2
Italy	5	0	0	5	70	183	0

2001-02 continued

Tour Matches

v ARGENTINA

WON 26-18
Argentina: 6PG
England: 2G 4PG
Buenos Aires, 22 Jun 2002

† M.J. Horak

T.R.G. Stimpson **1PG**
† G. Appleford
† B. Johnston
† P. Christophers **1T**

C. Hodgson **3PG 2C**
A.C.T. Gomarsall

D.L. Flatman
S. Thompson
* P.J. Vickery
† A. Codling
B.J. Kay **1T**
A. Sanderson
J.P.R. Worsley
L.W. Moody

v NEW ZEALAND

WON 31-28
England: 2G 3PG 1DG 1T
NZ: 4G
Twickenham, 9 Nov 2002

J. Robinson

† J. Simpson-Daniel [4]
W.J.H. Greenwood [1]
M.J. Tindall
B.C. Cohen **1T**

J.P. Wilkinson **3PG 1DG 2C 1T**
M.J.S. Dawson

T.J. Woodman
S. Thompson
P.J. Vickery
* M.O. Johnson
D.J. Grewcock [2]
L.W. Moody **1T**
L.B.N. Dallaglio [3]
R.A. Hill [a]

1 Rep by B. Johnston
2 Rep by B.J. Kay
a/3 Rep by N.A. Back
4 Rep by A.S. Healey

v AUSTRALIA

WON 32-31
England: 2G 6PG
Australia: 2G 4PG 1T
Twickenham, 16 Nov 2002

J. Robinson

J. Simpson-Daniel
W.J.H. Greenwood
M.J. Tindall [1]
B.C. Cohen **2T**

J.P. Wilkinson **6PG 2C**
M.J.S. Dawson

J. Leonard
S. Thompson
P.J. Vickery
* M.O. Johnson
B.J. Kay
L.W. Moody
R.A. Hill [a]
N.A. Back

1 Rep by A.S. Healey
a Rep by L.B.N. Dallaglio

v SOUTH AFRICA

WON 53-3
England: 6G‡ 2PG 1T
SA: 1PG
Twickenham, 23 Nov 2002

J. Robinson

B.C. Cohen **1T**
W.J.H. Greenwood [5] **2T**
M.J. Tindall
P. Christophers **1T‡**

J.P. Wilkinson [2] **2PG 1C**
M.J.S. Dawson [3] **1C**

J. Leonard
S. Thompson
P.J. Vickery
* M.O. Johnson
B.J. Kay [4]
L.W. Moody [1]
R.A. Hill **1T**
N.A. Back **1T**

‡includes penalty try
1 Rep by L.B.N. Dallaglio **1T**
2 Rep by A.S. Healey
3 Rep by A.C.T. Gomarsall **2C**
4 Rep by D.J. Grewcock
5 Rep by T.R.G. Stimpson **2C**

FACT FILE

- Phil Vickery became the first Gloucester player to lead England when he skippered the side for the one-off summer Test against Argentina.
- South Africa crashed to their biggest Test defeat ever when beaten 53-3 at Twickenham.

2002-03

Six Nations Championship

v FRANCE

WON 25-17
England: 1G 5PG 1DG
France: 1G 2T
Twickenham, 15 Feb 2003

J. Robinson **1T**

D.D. Luger
W.J.H. Greenwood
C. Hodgson
B.C. Cohen

J.P. Wilkinson **1C 5PG 1DG**
A.C.T. Gomarsall

J. Leonard [1]
S. Thompson
J.M. White
* M.O. Johnson
B.J. Kay [3]
L.W. Moody [2]
R.A. Hill
N.A. Back

1 Rep by G.C. Rowntree [a]
2 Rep by L.B.N. Dallaglio
3 Rep by D.J. Grewcock
a Rep by M.P. Regan

v WALES

WON 26-9
Wales: 3PG
England: 2G 2PG 2DG
Cardiff Arms Park, 22 Feb 2003

J. Robinson [1]

D.D. Luger [5]
W.J.H. Greenwood **1T**
C. Hodgson
B.C. Cohen

J.P. Wilkinson [4] **2C 2PG 2DG**
K.P.P. Bracken

G.C. Rowntree
S. Thompson
† R. Morris
* M.O. Johnson
B.J. Kay [3]
R.A. Hill [a]
L.B.N. Dallaglio
N.A. Back [2]

1 Rep by P. Christophers
2 Rep by J.P.R. Worsley **1T**
3 Rep by D.J. Grewcock
a/4 Rep by J. Simpson-Daniel
5 Rep by A.C.T. Gomarsall

v ITALY

WON 40-5
England: 5G 1T
Italy: 1T
Twickenham, 9 Mar 2003

O.J. Lewsey [7] **2T**

J. Simpson-Daniel **1T**
W.J.H. Greenwood
M.J. Tindall **1T**
D.D. Luger **1T**

* J.P. Wilkinson [1] **4C**
M.J.S. Dawson **1C**

G.C. Rowntree
S. Thompson [5] **1T**
R. Morris [4]
D.J. Grewcock
B.J. Kay [3]
J.P.R. Worsley
L.B.N. Dallaglio [a]
R.A. Hill [6]

1 Rep by C. Hodgson [2]
2 Rep by † O.J. Smith
3 Rep by S.D. Shaw
4 Rep by † M.A. Worsley
5 Rep by M.P. Regan
a/6 Rep by A. Sanderson
7 Rep by K.P.P. Bracken

v SCOTLAND

WON 40-9
England: 4G 4PG
Scotland: 3PG
Twickenham, 22 Mar 2003

O.J. Lewsey **1T**

J. Robinson **2T**
W.J.H. Greenwood
M.J. Tindall [1]
B.C. Cohen **1T**

J.P. Wilkinson [3] **3C 4PG**
M.J.S. Dawson

G.C. Rowntree [4]
S. Thompson
J. Leonard
* M.O. Johnson
B.J. Kay [2]
R.A. Hill
L.B.N. Dallaglio [5]
N.A. Back

1 Rep by D.D. Luger
2 Rep by D.J. Grewcock
3 Rep by P.J. Grayson **1C**
4 Rep by T.J. Woodman
5 Rep by J.P.R. Worsley

v IRELAND

WON 42-6
Ireland: 1PG 1DG
England: 4G 1PG 2DG 1T
Lansdowne Road, 30 Mar 2003

O.J. Lewsey

J. Robinson
W.J.H. Greenwood **2T**
M.J. Tindall [2] **1T**
B.C. Cohen

J.P. Wilkinson [e] **3C 1PG 2DG**
M.J.S. Dawson [b]

G.C. Rowntree [c/1]
S. Thompson
J. Leonard
* M.O. Johnson
B.J. Kay [d]
R.A. Hill [a]
L.B.N. Dallaglio **1T**
N.A. Back

c/1 Rep by T.J. Woodman
2 Rep by D.D. Luger **1T**
a Rep by J.P.R. Worsley
b Rep by K.P.P. Bracken
d Rep by D.J. Grewcock
e Rep by P.J. Grayson **1C**

FACT FILE

- England bagged their first Grand Slam for eight years and their first under Clive Woodward. Jason Leonard won his 100th cap in the opening match against France.

FINAL TABLE

	P	W	D	L	F	A	Pts
England	**5**	**5**	**0**	**0**	**173**	**46**	**10**
Ireland	5	4	0	1	119	97	8
France	5	3	0	2	153	75	6
Scotland	5	2	0	3	81	161	4
Italy	5	1	0	4	100	185	2
Wales	5	0	0	5	82	144	0

2002-03 continued

Tour Matches

v NEW ZEALAND

WON 15-13
NZ: 1G 2PG
England: 4PG 1DG
Wellington, 14 June 2003

O.J. Lewsey[3]

J. Robinson
W.J.H. Greenwood
M.J. Tindall
B.C. Cohen

J.P. Wilkinson **4PG 1DG**
K.P.P. Bracken

G.C. Rowntree
S. Thompson
J. Leonard[1]
* M.O. Johnson
B.J. Kay
R.A. Hill[2]
L.B.N. Dallaglio
N.A. Back

1 Rep by P.J. Vickery
2 Rep by J.P.R. Worsley
3 Rep by D.D. Luger

v AUSTRALIA

WON 25-14
Australia: 3PG 1T
England: 2G 2PG 1T
Melbourne, 21 June 2003

J. Robinson

O.J. Lewsey
W.J.H. Greenwood **1T**
M.J. Tindall **1T**
B.C. Cohen **1T**

J.P. Wilkinson **2C 2PG**
K.P.P. Bracken[2]

T.J. Woodman
S. Thompson
P.J. Vickery
* M.O. Johnson
B.J. Kay[a]
R.A. Hill[1]
L.B.N. Dallaglio
N.A. Back

1 Rep by J.P.R. Worsley
2 Rep by M.J.S. Dawson
a Rep by S.W. Borthwick

FACT FILE

- England extended their victorious Test run to 12 matches with their win against New Zealand, a new national record.
- And the 12-match unbeaten record of Temple Gurdon's sides of the 1880s fell with England's first Test success against Australia on Aussie soil.

England celebrate Will Greenwood's pushover try in the Grand Slam decider at Lansdowne Road in 2003.

International Appearances (up to 31 July 2003)

Note: Years given for International Championship matches are for second half of season; e.g. 1932 means season 1931-32. Years for all other matches refer to the actual year of the match. Abbreviations used are as follows: A – Australia; Arg – Argentina; Bb – Barbarians; C – Canada; F – France; Fj – Fiji; I – Ireland; It – Italy; Iv – Ivory Coast; J – Japan; M – Maoris; Nm – Namibia; NZ – New Zealand; P – President's XV; Pt – Portugal; R – Romania; S – Scotland; SA – South Africa; Sm – Samoa; Sp – Spain; Tg – Tonga; U – Uruguay; US – United States; W – Wales; WS – Western Samoa; Z – Zimbabwe. (R) – Replacement or substitute; (t) – temporary replacement; [ ] – Rugby World Cup appearances. When a series has taken place, figures are used to denote the particular matches in which players have featured. Thus NZ 1, 3 would indicate that a player has appeared in the First and Third Tests of the relevant series against New Zealand.

A

Aarvold, C.D. (Cambridge U, W Hartlepool, Headingley, Blackheath) 1928 *A, W, I, F, S*, 1929 *W, I, F*, 1931 *W, S, F*, 1932 *SA, W, I, S*, 1933 *W*

Ackford, P.J. (Harlequins) 1988 *A*, 1989 *S, I, F, W, R, Fj*, 1990 *I, F, W, S, Arg* 3, 1991 *W, S, I, F, A*, [*NZ, It, F, S, A*]

Adams, A.A. (London Hospital) 1910 *F*

Adams, F.R. (Richmond) 1875 *I, S*, 1876 *S*, 1877 *I*, 1878 *S*, 1879 *S, I*

Adebayo, A.A. (Bath) 1996, *It*, 1997 *Arg* 1,2, *A* 2, *NZ* 1, 1998 *S*

Adey, G.J. (Leicester) 1976 *I, F*

Adkins, S.J. (Coventry) 1950 *I, F, S*, 1953 *W, I, F, S*

Agar, A.E. (Harlequins) 1952 *SA, W, S, I, F*, 1953 *W, I*

Alcock, A. (Guy's Hospital) 1906 *SA*

Alderson, F.H.R. (Hartlepool R) 1891 *W, I, S*, 1892 *W, S*, 1893 *W*

Alexander, H. (Richmond) 1900 *I, S*, 1901 *W, I, S*, 1902 *W, I*

Alexander, W. (Northern) 1927 *F*

Allison, D.F. (Coventry) 1956 *W, I, S, F*, 1957 *W*, 1958 *W, S*

Allport, A. (Blackheath) 1892 *W*, 1893 *I*, 1894 *W, I, S*

Anderson, S. (Rockcliff) 1899 *I*

Anderson, W.F. (Orrell) 1973 *NZ* 1

Anderton, C. (Manchester FW) 1889 *M*

Andrew, C.R. (Cambridge U, Nottingham, Wasps, Toulouse, Newcastle) 1985 *R, F, S, I, W*, 1986 *W, S, I, F*, 1987 *I, F, W*, [*J (R), US*], 1988 *S, I* 1,2, *A* 1,2, *Fj, A*, 1989 *S, I, F, W, R, Fj*, 1990 *I, F, W, S, Arg* 3, 1991 *W, S, I, F, Fj, A*, [*NZ, It, US, F, S, A*], 1992 *S, I, F, W, C, SA*, 1993 *F, W, NZ*, 1994 *S, I, F, W, SA* 1,2, *R, C*, 1995 *I, F, W, S*, [*Arg, It, A, NZ, F*], 1997 *W (R)*

Appleford, G. (London Irish) 2002 *Arg*

Archer, G.S. (Bristol, Army, Newcastle) 1996 *S, I*, 1997 *A* 2, *NZ* 1, *SA, NZ* 2, 1998 *F, W, S, I, A* 1, *NZ* 1, *H, It*, 1999 *Tg, Fj*, 2000 *I, F, W, It, S*

Archer, H. (Bridgwater A) 1909 *W, F, I*

Armstrong, R. (Northern) 1925 *W*

Arthur, T.G. (Wasps) 1966 *W, I*

Ashby, R.C. (Wasps) 1966 *I, F*, 1967 *A*

Ashcroft, A. (Waterloo) 1956 *W, I, S, F*, 1957 *W, I, F, S*, 1958 *W, A, I, F, S*, 1959 *I, F, S*

Ashcroft, A.H. (Birkenhead Park) 1909 *A*

Ashford, W. (Richmond) 1897 *W, I*, 1898 *S, W*

Ashworth, A. (Oldham) 1892 *I*

Askew, J.G. (Cambridge U) 1930 *W, I, F*

Aslett, A.R. (Richmond) 1926 *W, I, F, S*, 1929 *S, F*

Assinder, E.W. (O Edwardians) 1909 *A, W*

Aston, R.L. (Blackheath) 1890 *S, I*

Auty, J.R. (Headingley) 1935 *S*

B

Back, N.A. (Leicester) 1994 *S, I*, 1995 [*Arg (t), It, WS*], 1997 *NZ 1(R), SA, NZ* 2, 1998 *F, W, S, I, H, It, A* 2, *SA* 2, 1999 *S, I, F, W, A, US, C*, [*It, NZ, Fj, SA*], 2000 *I, F, W, It, S, SA* 1,2, *A, Arg, SA* 3, 2001 *W, It, S, F, I, A, R, SA*, 2002 *S, I, F, W, It, NZ(t + R), A, SA*, 2003 *F* 1, *W* 1, *S, I, NZ, A*

Bailey, M.D. (Cambridge U, Wasps) 1984 *SA* 1,2, 1987 [*US*], 1989 *Fj*, 1990 *I, F, S (R)*

Bainbridge, S. (Gosforth, Fylde) 1982 *F, W*, 1983 *F, W, S, I, NZ*, 1984 *S, I, F, W*, 1985 *NZ* 1,2, 1987 *F, W, S*, [*J, US*]

Baker, D.G.S. (OMTs) 1955 *W, I, F, S*

Baker, E.M. (Moseley) 1895 *W, I, S*, 1896 *W, I, S*, 1897 *W*

Baker, H.C. (Clifton) 1887 *W*

Balshaw, I.R. (Bath) 2000 *I (R), F (R), It (R), S (R), A (R), Arg, SA 3(R)*, 2001 *W, It, S, F, I*, 2002 *S (R), I (R)*

Bance, J.F. (Bedford) 1954 *S*

Barkley, O. (Bath) 2001 *US (R)*

Barley, B. (Wakefield) 1984 *I, F, W, A*, 1988 *A* 1,2, *Fj*

Barnes, S. (Bristol, Bath) 1984 *A*, 1985 *R (R), NZ* 1,2, 1986 *S (R), F (R), 1987 I (R), 1988 Fj*, 1993 *S, I*

Barr, R.J. (Leicester) 1932 *SA, W, I*

Barrett, E.I.M. (Lennox) 1903 *S*

Barrington, T.J.M. (Bristol) 1931 *W, I*

Barrington-Ward, L.E. (Edinburgh U) 1910 *W, I, F, S*

Barron, J.H. (Bingley) 1896 *S*, 1897 *W, I*

Bartlett, J.T. (Waterloo) 1951 *W*

Bartlett, R.M. (Harlequins) 1957 *W, I, F, S*, 1958 *I, F, S*

Barton, J. (Coventry) 1967 *I, F, W*, 1972 *F*

Batchelor, T.B. (Oxford U) 1907 *F*

Bates, S.M. (Wasps) 1989 *R*

Bateson, A.H. (Otley) 1930 *W, I, F, S*

Bateson, H.D. (Liverpool) 1879 *I*

Batson, T. (Blackheath) 1872 *S*, 1874 *S*, 1875 *I*

Batten, J.M. (Cambridge U) 1874 *S*

Baume, J.L. (Northern) 1950 *S*

Baxendell, J.J.N. (Sale) 1998 *NZ* 2, *SA* 1

Baxter, J. (Birkenhead Park) 1900 *W, I, S*

Bayfield, M.C. (Northampton) 1991 *Fj, A*, 1992 *S, I, F, W, C, SA*, 1993 *F, W, S, I*, 1994 *S, I, SA* 1,2, *R, C*, 1995 *I, F, W, S*, [*Arg, It, A, NZ, F*], *SA, WS*, 1996 *F, W*

Bazley, R.C. (Waterloo) 1952 *I, F*, 1953 *W, I, F, S*, 1955 *W, I, F, S*

Beal, N.D. (Northampton) 1996 *Arg*, 1997 *A* 1, 1998 *NZ* 1,2, *SA* 1, *H (R), SA* 2, 1999 *S, F (R), A (t), C (R)*, [*It (R), Tg (R), Fj, SA*]

Beaumont, W.B. (Fylde) 1975 I, *A* 1*(R)*,2, 1976 *A, W, S, I, F*, 1977 *S, I, F, W*, 1978 *F, W, S, I, NZ*, 1979 *S, I, F, W, NZ*, 1980 *I, F, W, S*, 1981 *W, S, I, F, Arg* 1,2, 1982 *A, S*

Bedford, H. (Morley) 1889 *M*, 1890 *S, I*

Bedford, L.L. (Headingley) 1931 *W, I*

Beer, I.D.S. (Harlequins) 1955 *F, S*

Beese, M.C. (Liverpool) 1972 *W, I, F*

Beim, T.D. (Sale) 1998 *NZ 1(R)*,2

Bell, F.J. (Northern) 1900 *W*

Bell, H. (New Brighton) 1884 *I*

Bell, J.L. (Darlington) 1878 *I*

Bell, P.J. (Blackheath) 1968 *W, I, F, S*

Bell, R.W. (Northern) 1900 *W, I, S*

Bendon, G.J. (Wasps) 1959 *W, I, F, S*

Bennett, N.O. (St Mary's Hospital, Waterloo) 1947 *W, S, F*, 1948 *A, W, I, S*

Bennett, W.N. (Bedford, London Welsh) 1975 *S, A*1, 1976 *S (R), 1979 S, I, F, W*

Bennetts, B.B. (Penzance) 1909 *A, W*

Bentley, J. (Sale, Newcastle) 1988 *I* 2, *A* 1, 1997 *A* 1, *SA*

Bentley, J.E. (Gipsies) 1871 *S*, 1872 *S*

Benton, S. (Gloucester) 1998 *A* 1

Berridge, M.J. (Northampton) 1949 *W, I*

Berry, H. (Gloucester) 1910 *W, I, F, S*

Berry, J. (Tyldesley) 1891 *W, I, S*

Berry, J.T.W. (Leicester) 1939 *W, I, S*

Beswick, E. (Swinton) 1882 *I, S*

Biggs, J.M. (UCH) 1878 *S*, 1879 *I*

Birkett, J.G.G. (Harlequins) 1906 *S, F, SA*, 1907 *F, W, S*, 1908 *F, W,I , S*, 1910 *W, I, S*, 1911 *W, F, I , S*, 1912 *W, I , S, F*

Birkett L. (Clapham R) 1875 *S*, 1877 *I, S*

Birkett, R.H. (Clapham R) 1871 *S*, 1875 *S*, 1876 *S*, 1877 *I*

Bishop, C.C. (Blackheath) 1927 *F*

Black, B.H. (Blackheath) 1930 *W, I, F, S*, 1931 *W, I, S, F*, 1932 *S*, 1933 *W*

Blacklock, J.H. (Aspatria) 1898 *I*, 1899 *I*

Blakeway, P.J. (Gloucester) 1980 *I, F, W, S*, 1981 *W, S, I, F*, 1982 *I, F, W*, 1984 *I, F, W, SA* 1, 1985 *R, F, S, I*

Blakiston, A.F. (Northampton) 1920 *S*, 1921 *W, I, S, F*, 1922 *W*, 1923 *S, F*, 1924 *W, I, F, S*, 1925 *NZ, W, I, S, F*

Blatherwick, T. (Manchester) 1878 *I*

Body, J.A. (Gipsies) 1872 *S*, 1873 *S*

Bolton, C.A. (United Services) 1909 *F*

Bolton, R. (Harlequins) 1933 *W*, 1936 *S*, 1937 *S*, 1938 *W, I*

Bolton, W.N. (Blackheath) 1882 *I, S*, 1883 *W, I, S*, 1884 *W, I, S*, 1885 *I*, 1887 *I, S*

Bonaventura, M.S. (Blackheath) 1931 *W*

Bond, A.M. (Sale) 1978 *NZ*, 1979 *S, I, NZ*, 1980 *I*, 1982 *I*

Bonham-Carter, E. (Oxford U) 1891 *S*

Bonsor, F. (Bradford) 1886 *W, I, S*, 1887 *W, S*, 1889 *M*

Boobbyer, B. (Rosslyn Park) 1950 *W, I, F, S*, 1951 *W, F*, 1952 *S, I, F*

Booth, L.A. (Headingley) 1933 *W, I, S*, 1934 *S*, 1935 *W, I, S*

Borthwick, S.W. (Bath) 2001 *F, C* 1,2*(R), US, R*, 2003 *A (t)*

Botting, I.J. (Oxford U) 1950 *W, I*

Boughton, H.J. (Gloucester) 1935 *W, I, S*

Boyle, C.W. (Oxford U) 1873 *S*

Boyle, S.B. (Gloucester) 1983 *W, S, I*

Boylen, F. (Hartlepool R) 1908 *F, W, I, S*

Bracken, K.P.P. (Bristol, Saracens) 1993 *NZ*, 1994 *S, I, C*, 1995 *I, F, W, S, [It, WS (t)], SA*, 1996 *It (R), 1997 Arg* 1,2, *A* 2, *NZ* 1,2, 1998 *F, W*, 1999 *S(R), I, F, A*, 2000 *SA* 1,2, *A*, 2001 *It (R), S (R), F (R), C* 1,2, *US, I (R), A, R (R), SA*, 2002 *S, I, F, W, It*, 2003 *W* 1, *It(R), I(t), NZ, A*

Bradby, M.S. (United Services) 1922 *I, F*

Bradley, R. (W Hartlepool) 1903 *W*

Bradshaw, H. (Bramley) 1892 *S*, 1893 *W, I, S*, 1894 *W, I, S*

Brain, S.E. (Coventry) 1984 *SA* 2, *A (R), 1985 R, F, S, I, W, NZ* 1,2, 1986 *W, S, I, F*

Braithwaite, J. (Leicester) 1905 *NZ*

Braithwaite-Exley, B. (Headingley) 1949 *W*

Brettargh, A.T. (Liverpool OB) 1900 *W*, 1903 *I, S*, 1904 *W, I, S*, 1905 *I, S*

Brewer, J. (Gipsies) 1876 *I*

Briggs, A. (Bradford) 1892 *W, I, S*

Brinn, A. (Gloucester) 1972 *W, I, S*

Broadley, T. (Bingley) 1893 *W, S*, 1894 *W, I, S*, 1896 *S*

Bromet, W.E. (Richmond) 1891 *W, I*, 1892 *W, I, S*, 1893 *W, I, S*, 1895 *W, I, S*, 1896 *I*

Brook, P.W.P. (Harlequins) 1930 *S*, 1931 *F*, 1936 *S*

Brooke, T.J. (Richmond) 1968 *F, S*

Brooks, F.G. (Bedford) 1906 *SA*

Brooks, M.J. (Oxford U) 1874 *S*

Brophy, T.J. (Liverpool) 1964 *I, F, S*, 1965 *W, I*, 1966 *W, I, F*

Brough, J.W. (Silloth) 1925 *NZ, W*

Brougham, H. (Harlequins) 1912 *W, I, S, F*

Brown, A.A. (Exeter) 1938 *S*

Brown, L.G. (Oxford U, Blackheath) 1911 *W, F, I, S*, 1913 *SA, W, F, I, S*, 1914 *W, I, S, F*, 1921 *W, I, S, F*, 1922 *W*

Brown S.P. (Richmond) 1998 *A* 1, *SA* 1

Brown, T.W. (Bristol) 1928 *S*, 1929 *W, I, S, F*, 1932 *S*, 1933 *W, I, S*

Brunton, J. (N Durham) 1914 *W, I, S*

Brutton, E.B. (Cambridge U) 1886 *S*

Bryden, C.C. (Clapham R) 1876 *I*, 1877 *S*

Bryden, H.A. (Clapham R) 1874 *S*

Buckingham, R.A. (Leicester) 1927 *F*

Bucknall, A.L. (Richmond) 1969 *SA*, 1970 *I, W, S, F*, 1971 *W, I, F, S (2[1C])*

Buckton, J.R.D. (Saracens) 1988 *A (R), 1990 Arg* 1,2

Budd, A. (Blackheath) 1878 *I*, 1879 *S, I*, 1881 *W, S*

Budworth, R.T.D. (Blackheath) 1890 *W*, 1891 *W, S*

Bull, A.G. (Northampton) 1914 *W*

Bullough, E. (Wigan) 1892 *W, I, S*

Bulpitt, M.P. (Blackheath) 1970 *S*

Bulteel, A.J. (Manchester) 1876 *I*

Bunting, W.L. (Moseley) 1897 *I, S*, 1898 *I, S, W*, 1899 *S*, 1900 *S*, 1901 *I, S*

Burland, D.W. (Bristol) 1931 *W, I, F*, 1932 *I, S*, 1933 *W, I, S*

Burns, B.H. (Blackheath) 1871 *S*

Burton, G.W. (Blackheath) 1879 *S, I*, 1880 *S*, 1881 *I, W, S*

Burton, H.C. (Richmond) 1926 *W*

Burton, M.A. (Gloucester) 1972 *W, I, F, S, SA*, 1974 *F, W*, 1975 *S*, A 1,2, 1976 *A, W, S, I, F*, 1978 *F, W*

Bush, J.A. (Clifton) 1872 *S*, 1873 *S*, 1875 *S*, 1876 *I, S*

Butcher, C.J.S. (Harlequins) 1984 *SA* 1,2, *A*

Butcher, W.V. (Streatham) 1903 *S*, 1904 *W, I, S*, 1905 *W, I, S*

Butler, A.G. (Harlequins) 1937 *W, I*

Butler, P.E. (Gloucester) 1975 *A* 1, 1976 *F*

Butterfield, J. (Northampton) 1953 *F, S*, 1954 *W, NZ, I, S, F*, 1955 *W, I, F, S*, 1956 *W, I, S, F*, 1957 *W, I, F, S*, 1958 *W, A, I, F, S*, 1959 *W, I, F, S*

Byrne, F.A. (Moseley) 1897 *W*

Byrne, J.F. (Moseley) 1894 *W, I, S*, 1895 *I, S*, 1896 *I*, 1897 *W, I, S*, 1898 *I, S, W*, 1899 *I*

C

Cain, J.J. (Waterloo) 1950 *W*

Callard, J.E.B. (Bath) 1993 *NZ*, 1994 *S, I*, 1995 *[WS], SA*

Campbell, D.A. (Cambridge U) 1937 *W, I*

Candler, P.L. (St Bart's Hospital) 1935 *W*, 1936 *NZ, W, I, S*, 1937 *W, I, S*, 1938 *W, S*

Cannell, L.B. (Oxford U, St Mary's Hospital) 1948 *F*, 1949 *W, I, F, S*, 1950 *W, I, F, S*, 1952 *SA, W*, 1953 *W, I, F*, 1956 *I, S, F*, 1957 *W, I*

Caplan, D.W.N. (Headingley) 1978 *S, I*

Cardus, R.M. (Roundhay) 1979 *F, W*

Carey, G.M. (Blackheath) 1895 *W, I, S*, 1896 *W, I*

Carleton, J. (Orrell) 1979 *NZ*, 1980 *I, F, W, S*, 1981 *W, S, I, F, Arg* 1,2, 1982 *A, S, I, F, W*, 1983 *F, W, S, I, NZ*, 1984 *S, I, F, W, A*

Carling, W.D.C. (Durham U, Harlequins) 1988 *F, W, S, I* 1,2, *A2, Fj,* A, 1989 *S, I, F, W, Fj,* 1990 *I, F, W, S, Arg* 1,2,3, 1991 *W, S, I, F, Fj, A,* [*NZ, It, US, F, S, A*], 1992 *S, I, F, W, C, SA,* 1993 *F, W, S, I, NZ,* 1994 *S, I, F, W, SA* 1,2, *R, C,* 1995 *I, F, W, S,* [*Arg, WS, A, NZ, F*], *SA, WS,* 1996 *F, W, S, I, It, Arg,* 1997 *S, I, F, W*

Carpenter, A.D. (Gloucester) 1932 *SA*

Carr, R.S.L. (Manchester) 1939 *W, I, S*

Cartwright, V.H. (Nottingham) 1903 *W, I, S,* 1904 *W, S,* 1905 *W, I, S, NZ,* 1906 *W, I, S, F, SA*

Catcheside, H.C. (Percy Park) 1924 *W, I, F, S,* 1926 *W, I,* 1927 *I, S*

Catt, M.J. (Bath) 1994 *W (R), C (R), 1995 I, F, W, S,* [*Arg, It, WS, A, NZ, F*], *SA, WS,* 1996 *F, W, S, I, It, Arg,* 1997 *W, Arg* 1, *A* 1,2, *NZ* 1, *SA,* 1998 *F, W (R), I, A 2(R), SA* 2, 1999 *S, F, W, A, C (R), [Tg (R), Fj, SA (R)], 2000 I, F, W, It, S, SA* 1,2, *A, Arg,* 2001 *W, It, S, F, I, A, R (R), SA*

Cattell, R.H.B. (Blackheath) 1895 *W, I, S,* 1896 *W, I, S,* 1900 *W*

Cave, J.W. (Richmond) 1889 *M*

Cave, W.T.C. (Blackheath) 1905 *W*

Challis, R. (Bristol) 1957 *I, F, S*

Chambers, E.L. (Bedford) 1908 *F,* 1910 *W, I*

Chantrill, B.S. (Bristol) 1924 *W, I, F, S*

Chapman, C.E. (Cambridge U) 1884 *W*

Chapman D.E. (Richmond) 1998 *A* 1*(R)*

Chapman, F.E. (Hartlepool) 1910 *W, I, F, S,* 1912 *W,* 1914 *W, I*

Cheesman, W.I. (OMTs) 1913 *SA, W, F, I*

Cheston, E.C. (Richmond) 1873 *S,* 1874 *S,* 1875 *I, S,* 1876 *S*

Chilcott, G.J. (Bath) 1984 *A,* 1986 *I, F,* 1987 *F (R), W,* [*J, US, W (R)*]*, 1988 I 2(R), Fj, 1989 I (R), F, W, R*

Christophers, P. (Bristol) 2002 *Arg, SA,* 2003 *W* 1 *(R)*

Christopherson, P. (Blackheath) 1891 *W, S*

Clark, C.W.H. (Liverpool) 1876 *I*

Clarke, A.J. (Coventry) 1935 *W, I, S,* 1936 *NZ, W, I*

Clarke, B.B. (Bath, Richmond) 1992 *SA,* 1993 *F, W, S, I, NZ,* 1994 *S, F, W, SA* 1,2, *R, C,* 1995 *I, F, W, S,* [*Arg, It, A, NZ, F*], *SA, WS,* 1996 *F, W, S, I, Arg (R), 1997 W, Arg* 1,2, *A* 1*(R),* 1998 *A* 1*(t), NZ* 1,2, *SA* 1, *H, It,* 1999 *A (R)*

Clarke, S.J.S. (Cambridge U, Blackheath) 1963 *W, I, F, S, NZ* 1,2, *A,* 1964 *NZ, W, I,* 1965 *I, F, S*

Clayton, J.H. (Liverpool) 1871 *S*

Clements, J.W. (O Cranleighans) 1959 *I, F, S*

Cleveland, C.R. (Blackheath) 1887 *W, S*

Clibborn, W.G. (Richmond) 1886 *W, I, S,* 1887 *W, I, S*

Clough, F.J. (Cambridge U, Orrell) 1986 *I, F,* 1987 [*J (R), US*]

Coates, C.H. (Yorkshire W) 1880 *S,* 1881 *S,* 1882 *S*

Coates, V.H.M. (Bath) 1913 *SA, W, F, I, S*

Cobby, W. (Hull) 1900 *W*

Cockerham, A. (Bradford Olicana) 1900 *W*

Cockerill, R. (Leicester) 1997 *Arg* 1*(R)*,2, *A* 2(t+R), *NZ* 1, *SA, NZ* 2, 1998 *W, S, I, A* 1, *NZ* 1,2, *SA* 1, *H, It, A* 2, *SA* 2, 1999 *S, I, F, W, A, C (R), [It, NZ, Tg (R), Fj (R)]*

Codling, A. (Harlequins) 2002 *Arg*

Cohen, B.C. (Northampton) 2000 *I, F, W, It, S, SA* 2, *Arg, SA* 3, 2001 *W, It, S, F, R,* 2002 *S, I, F, W, It, NZ, A, SA,* 2003 *F* 1, *W* 1, *S, I, NZ, A*

Colclough, M.J. (Angoulême, Wasps, Swansea) 1978 *S, I,* 1979 *NZ,* 1980 *F, W, S,* 1981 *W, S, I, F,* 1982 *A, S, I, F, W,* 1983 *F, NZ,* 1984 *S, I, F, W,* 1986 *W, S, I, F*

Coley, E. (Northampton) 1929 *F,* 1932 *W*

Collins, P.J. (Camborne) 1952 *S, I, F*

Collins, W.E. (O Cheltonians) 1874 *S,* 1875 *I, S,* 1876 *I, S*

Considine, S.G.U. (Bath) 1925 *F*

Conway, G.S. (Cambridge U, Rugby, Manchester) 1920 *F, I, S,* 1921 *F,* 1922 *W, I, F, S,* 1923 *W, I, S, F,* 1924 *W, I, F, S,* 1925 *NZ,* 1927 *W*

Cook, J.G. (Bedford) 1937 *S*

Cook, P.W. (Richmond) 1965 *I, F*

Cooke, D.A. (Harlequins) 1976 *W, S, I, F*

Cooke, D.H. (Harlequins) 1981 *W, S, I, F,* 1984 *I,* 1985 *R, F, S, I, W, NZ* 1,2

Cooke, P. (Richmond) 1939 *W, I*

Coop, T. (Leigh) 1892 *S*

Cooper, J.G. (Moseley) 1909 *A, W*

Cooper, M.J. (Moseley) 1973 *F, S, NZ 2(R),* 1975 *F, W,* 1976 *A, W,* 1977 *S, I, F, W*

Coopper, S.F. (Blackheath) 1900 *W,* 1902 *W, I,* 1905 *W, I, S,* 1907 *W*

Corbett, L.J. (Bristol) 1921 *F,* 1923 *W, I,* 1924 *W, I, F, S,* 1925 *NZ, W, I, S, F,* 1927 *W, I, S, F*

Corless, B.J. (Coventry, Moseley) 1976 *A, I (R), 1977 S, I, F, W,* 1978 *F, W, S, I*

Corry, M.E. (Bristol, Leicester) 1997 *Arg* 1,2, 1998 *H, It, SA* 2*(t),* 1999 *F(R), A, C (t), [It (R), NZ (t+R), SA (R)], 2000 I (R), F (R), W (R), It (R), S (R), Arg (R), SA 3(t),* 2001 *W (R), It (R), F (t), C* 1, *I,* 2002 *F (t+R), W (t)*

Cotton, F.E. (Loughborough Colls, Coventry, Sale) 1971 *S (2[1C]), P,* 1973 *W, I, F, S, NZ* 2, *A,* 1974 *S, I,* 1975 *I, F, W,* 1976 *A, W, S, I, F,* 1977 *S, I, F, W,* 1978 *S, I,* 1979 *NZ,* 1980 *I, F, W, S,* 1981 *W*

Coulman, M.J. (Moseley) 1967 *A, I, F, S, W,* 1968 *W, I, F, S*

Coulson, T.J. (Coventry) 1927 *W,* 1928 *A, W*

Court, E.D. (Blackheath) 1885 *W*

Coverdale, H. (Blackheath) 1910 *F,* 1912 *I, F,* 1920 *W*

Cove-Smith, R. (OMTs) 1921 *S, F,* 1922 *I, F, S,* 1923 *W, I, S, F,* 1924 *W, I, S, F,* 1925 *NZ, W, I, S, F,* 1927 *W, I, S, F,* 1928 *A, W, I, F, S,* 1929 *W, I*

Cowling, R.J. (Leicester) 1977 *S, I, F, W,* 1978 *F, NZ,* 1979 *S, I*

Cowman, A.R. (Loughborough Colls, Coventry) 1971 *S (2[1C]), P,* 1973 *W, I*

Cox, N.S. (Sunderland) 1901 *S*

Cranmer, P. (Richmond, Moseley) 1934 *W, I, S,* 1935 *W, I, S,* 1936 *NZ, W, I, S,* 1937 *W, I, S,* 1938 *W, I, S*

Creed, R.N. (Coventry) 1971 *P*

Cridlan, A.G. (Blackheath) 1935 *W, I, S*

Crompton, C.A. (Blackheath) 1871 *S*

Crosse, C.W. (Oxford U) 1874 *S,* 1875 *I*

Cumberlege, B.S. (Blackheath) 1920 *W, I, S,* 1921 *W, I, S, F,* 1922 *W*

Cumming, D.C. (Blackheath) 1925 *S, F*

Cunliffe, F.L. (RMA) 1874 *S*

Currey, F.I. (Marlborough N) 1872 *S*

Currie, J.D. (Oxford U, Harlequins, Bristol) 1956 *W, I, S, F,* 1957 *W, I, F, S,* 1958 *W, A, I, F, S,* 1959 *W, I, F, S,* 1960 *W, I, F, S,* 1961 *SA,* 1962 *W, I, F*

Cusani, D.A. (Orrell) 1987 *I*

Cusworth, L. (Leicester) 1979 *NZ,* 1982 *F, W,* 1983 *F, W, NZ,* 1984 *S, I, F, W,* 1988 *F, W*

D

D'Aguilar, F.B.G. (Royal Engineers) 1872 *S*

Dallaglio, L.B.N. (Wasps) 1995 *SA (R), WS,* 1996 *F, W, S, I, It, Arg,* 1997 *S, I, F,* 1997 *A* 1,2, *NZ* 1, *SA, NZ* 2, 1998 *F, W, S, I, A* 2, *SA* 2, 1999 *S, I, F, W, US, C,* [*It, NZ, Tg, Fj, SA*], 2000 *I, F, W, It, S, SA* 1,2, *A, Arg, SA* 3, 2001 *W, It, S, F,* 2002 *It (R), NZ, A (t), SA (R),* 2003 *F* 1 *(R), W* 1, *It, S, I, NZ, A*

Dalton, T.J. (Coventry) 1969 *S(R)*

Danby, T. (Harlequins) 1949 *W*

Daniell, J. (Richmond) 1899 *W,* 1900 *I, S,* 1902 *I, S,* 1904 *I, S*

Darby, A.J.L. (Birkenhead Park) 1899 *I*

Davenport, A. (Ravenscourt Park) 1871 *S*

Davey, J. (Redruth) 1908 *S,* 1909 *W*

Davey, R.F. (Teignmouth) 1931 *W*

Davidson, Jas. (Aspatria) 1897 *S*, 1898 *S, W*, 1899 *I, S*

Davidson, Jos. (Aspatria) 1899 *W, S*

Davies, G.H. (Cambridge U, Coventry, Wasps) 1981 *S, I, F, Arg* 1,2, 1982 *A, S, I*, 1983 *F, W, S*, 1984 *S, SA* 1,2, 1985 *R (R), NZ* 1,2, 1986 *W, S, I, F*

Davies, P.H. (Sale) 1927 *I*

Davies, V.G. (Harlequins) 1922 *W*, 1925 *NZ*

Davies, W.J.A. (United Services, RN) 1913 *SA, W, F, I, S*, 1914 *I, S, F*, 1920 *F, I, S*, 1921 *W, I, S, F*, 1922 *I, F, S*, 1923 *W, I, S, F*

Davies, W.P.C. (Harlequins) 1953 *S*, 1954 *NZ, I*, 1955 *W, I, F, S*, 1956 *W*, 1957 *F, S*, 1958 *W*

Davis, A.M. (Torquay Ath, Harlequins) 1963 *W, I, S, NZ* 1,2, 1964 *NZ, W, I, F, S*, 1966 *W*, 1967 *A*, 1969 *SA*, 1970 *I, W, S*

Dawe, R.G.R. (Bath) 1987 *I, F, W*, [*US*], 1995 [*WS*]

Dawson, E.F. (RIEC) 1878 *I*

Dawson, M.J.S. (Northampton) 1995 *WS*, 1996 *F, W, S, I*, 1997 *A* 1, *SA, NZ 2(R)*, 1998 *W (R), S, I, NZ* 1,2, *SA* 1, *H, It, A* 2, *SA* 2, 1999 *S, F(R), W, A(R), US, C*, [*It, NZ, Tg, Fj (R), SA*], 2000 *I, F, W, It, S, A (R), Arg, SA* 3, 2001 *W, It, S, F, I*, 2002 *W (R), It (R), NZ, A, SA*, 2003 *It, S, I, A (R)*

Day, H.L.V. (Leicester) 1920 *W*, 1922 *W, F*, 1926 *S*

Dean, G.J. (Harlequins) 1931 *I*

Dee, J.M. (Hartlepool R) 1962 *S*, 1963 *NZ* 1

Devitt, Sir T.G. (Blackheath) 1926 *I, F*, 1928 *A, W*

Dewhurst, J.H. (Richmond) 1887 *W, I, S*, 1890 *W*

De Glanville, P.R. (Bath) 1992 *SA (R), 1993 W (R), NZ*, 1994 *S, I, F, W, SA* 1,2, *C (R), 1995 [Arg (R), It, WS*], *SA (R), 1996 W (R), I (R), It*, 1997 *S, I, F, W, Arg* 1,2, *A* 1,2, *NZ* 1,2, 1998 *W (R), S (R), I (R), A* 2, *SA* 2, 1999 *A (R), US*, [*It, NZ, Fj (R), SA*]

De Winton, R.F.C. (Marlborough N) 1893 *W*

Dibble, R. (Bridgwater A) 1906 *S, F, SA*, 1908 *F, W, I, S*, 1909 *A, W, F, I, S*, 1910 *S*, 1911 *W, F, S*, 1912 *W, I, S*

Dicks, J. (Northampton) 1934 *W, I, S*, 1935 *W, I, S*, 1936 *S*, 1937 *I*

Dillon, E.W. (Blackheath) 1904 *W, I, S*, 1905 *W*

Dingle, A.J. (Hartlepool R) 1913 *I*, 1914 *S, F*

Diprose, A.J. (Saracens) 1997 *Arg* 1,2, *A* 2, *NZ* 1, 1998 *W (R), S (R), I, A* 1, *NZ* 2, *SA* 1

Dixon, P.J. (Harlequins, Gosforth) 1971 *P*, 1972 *W, I, F, S*, 1973 *I, F, S*, 1974 *S, I, F, W*, 1975 *I*, 1976 *F*, 1977 *S, I, F, W*, 1978 *F, S, I, NZ*

Dobbs, G.E.B. (Devonport A) 1906 *W, I*

Doble, S.A. (Moseley) 1972 *SA*, 1973 *NZ* 1, *W*

Dobson, D.D. (Newton Abbot) 1902 *W, I, S*, 1903 *W, I, S*

Dobson, T.H. (Bradford) 1895 *S*

Dodge, P.W. (Leicester) 1978 *W, S, I, NZ*, 1979 *S, I, F, W*, 1980 *W, S*, 1981 *W, S, I, F, Arg* 1,2, 1982 *A, S, F, W*, 1983 *F, W, S, I, NZ*, 1985 *R, F, S, I, W, NZ* 1,2

Donnelly, M.P. (Oxford U) 1947 *I*

Dooley, W.A. (Preston Grasshoppers, Fylde) 1985 *R, F, S, I, W, NZ 2(R)*, 1986 *W, S, I, F*, 1987 *F, W*, [*A, US, W*], 1988 *F, W, S, I* 1,2, *A* 1,2, *Fj*, A, 1989 *S, I, F, W, R, Fj*, 1990 *I, F, W, S, Arg* 1,2,3, 1991 *W, S, I, F*, [*NZ, US, F, S, A*], 1992 *S, I, F, W, C, SA*, 1993 *W, S, I*

Dovey, B.A. (Rosslyn Park) 1963 *W, I*

Down, P.J. (Bristol) 1909 *A*

Dowson, A.O. (Moseley) 1899 *S*

Drake-Lee, N.J. (Cambridge U, Leicester) 1963 *W, I, F, S*, 1964 *NZ, W, I*, 1965 *W*

Duckett, H. (Bradford) 1893 *I, S*

Duckham, D.J. (Coventry) 1969 *I, F, S, W, SA*, 1970 *I, W, S, F*, 1971 *W, I, F, S (2[1C])*, *P*, 1972 *W, I, F, S*, 1973 *NZ* 1, *W, I, F, S, NZ* 2, *A*, 1974 *S, I, F, W*, 1975 *I, F, W*, 1976 *A, W, S*

Dudgeon, H.W. (Richmond) 1897 *S*, 1898 *I, S, W*, 1899 *W, I, S*

Dugdale, J.M. (Ravenscourt Park) 1871 *S*

Dun, A.F. (Wasps) 1984 *W*

Duncan, R.F.H. (Guy's Hospital) 1922 *I, F, S*

Duncombe, N. (Harlequins) 2002 *S (R), I (R)*

Dunkley, P.E. (Harlequins) 1931 *I, S*, 1936 *NZ, W, I, S*

Duthie, J. (W Hartlepool) 1903 *W*

Dyson, J.W. (Huddersfield) 1890 *S*, 1892 *S*, 1893 *I, S*

E

Ebdon, P.J. (Wellington) 1897 *W, I*

Eddison, J.H. (Headingley) 1912 *W, I, S, F*

Edgar, C.S. (Birkenhead Park) 1901 *S*

Edwards, R. (Newport) 1921 *W, I, S, F*, 1922 *W, F*, 1923 *W*, 1924 *W, F, S*, 1925 *NZ*

Egerton, D.W. (Bath) 1988 *I* 2, *A* 1, *Fj (R), A*, 1989 *Fj*, 1990 *I, Arg 2(R)*

Elliot, C.H. (Sunderland) 1886 *W*

Elliot, E.W. (Sunderland) 1901 *W, I, S*, 1904 *W*

Elliot, W. (United Services, RN) 1932 *I, S*, 1933 *W, I, S*, 1934 *W, I*

Elliott, A.E. (St Thomas's Hospital) 1894 *S*

Ellis, J. (Wakefield) 1939 *S*

Ellis, S.S. (Queen's House) 1880 *I*

Emmott, C. (Bradford) 1892 *W*

Enthoven, H.J. (Richmond) 1878 *I*

Estcourt, N.S.D. (Blackheath) 1955 *S*

Evans, B.J. (Leicester) 1988 *A* 2, *Fj*

Evans, E. (Sale) 1948 *A*, 1950 *W*, 1951 *I, F, S*, 1952 *SA, W, S, I, F*, 1953 *I, F, S*, 1954 *W, NZ, I, F*, 1956 *W, I, S, F*, 1957 *W, I, F, S*, 1958 *W, A, I, F, S*

Evans, G.W. (Coventry) 1972 *S*, 1973 *W (R), F, S, NZ* 2, 1974 *S, I, F, W*

Evans, N.L. (RNEC) 1932 *W, I, S*, 1933 *W, I*

Evanson, A.M. (Richmond) 1883 *W, I, S*, 1884 *S*

Evanson, W.A.D. (Richmond) 1875 *S*, 1877 *S*, 1878 *S*, 1879 *S, I*

Evershed, F. (Blackheath) 1889 *M*, 1890 *W, S, I*, 1892 *W, I, S*, 1893 *W, I, S*

Eyres, W.C.T. (Richmond) 1927 *I*

F

Fagan, A.R.St.L. (Richmond) 1887 *I*

Fairbrother, K.E. (Coventry) 1969 *I, F, S, W, SA*, 1970 *I, W, S, F*, 1971 *W, I, F*

Faithfull, C.K.T. (Harlequins) 1924 *I*, 1926 *F, S*

Fallas, H. (Wakefield T) 1884 *I*

Fegan, J.H.C. (Blackheath) 1895 *W, I, S*

Fernandes, C.W.L. (Leeds) 1881 *I, W, S*

Fidler, J.H. (Gloucester) 1981 *Arg* 1,2, 1984 *SA* 1,2

Fidler, R.J. (Gloucester) 1998 *NZ* 2, *SA* 1

Field, E. (Middlesex W) 1893 *W, I*

Fielding, K.J. (Moseley, Loughborough Colls) 1969 *I, F, S, SA*, 1970 *I, F*, 1972 *W, I, F, S*

Finch, R.T. (Cambridge U) 1880 *S*

Finlan, J.F. (Moseley) 1967 *I, F, S, W, NZ*, 1968 *W, I*, 1969 *I, F, S, W*, 1970 *F*, 1973 *NZ* 1

Finlinson, H.W. (Blackheath) 1895 *W, I, S*

Finney, S. (RIE Coll) 1872 *S*, 1873 *S*

Firth, F. (Halifax) 1894 *W, I, S*

Flatman, D.L. (Saracens) 2000 *SA* 1*(t)*,2(t+R), *A (t), Arg (t+R), 2001 F (t), C* 2(t+R), *US (t+R), 2002 Arg*

Fletcher, N.C. (OMTs) 1901 *W, I, S*, 1903 *S*

Fletcher, T. (Seaton) 1897 *W*

Fletcher, W.R.B. (Marlborough N) 1873 *S*, 1875 *S*

Fookes, E.F. (Sowerby Bridge) 1896 *W, I, S*, 1897 *W, I, S*, 1898 *I, W*, 1899 *I, S*
Ford, P.J. (Gloucester) 1964 *W, I, F, S*
Forrest, J.W. (United Services, RN) 1930 *W, I, F, S*, 1931 *W, I, S, F*, 1934 *I, S*
Forrest, R. (Wellington) 1899 *W*, 1900 *S*, 1902 *I, S*, 1903 *I, S*
Foulds, R.T. (Waterloo) 1929 *W, I*
Fowler, F.D. (Manchester) 1878 *S*, 1879 *S*
Fowler, H. (Oxford U) 1878 *S*, 1881 *W, S*
Fowler, R.H. (Leeds) 1877 *I*
Fox, F.H. (Wellington) 1890 *W, S*
Francis, T.E.S. (Cambridge U) 1926 *W, I, F, S*
Frankcom, G.P. (Cambridge U, Bedford) 1965 *W, I, F, S*
Fraser, E.C. (Blackheath) 1875 *I*
Fraser, G. (Richmond) 1902 *W, I, S*, 1903 *W, I*
Freakes, H.D. (Oxford U) 1938 *W*, 1939 *W, I*
Freeman, H. (Marlborough N) 1872 *S*, 1873 *S*, 1874 *S*
French, R.J. (St Helens) 1961 *W, I, F, S*
Fry, H.A. (Liverpool) 1934 *W, I, S*
Fry, T.W. (Queen's House) 1880 *I, S*, 1881 *W*
Fuller, H.G. (Cambridge U) 1882 *I, S*, 1883 *W, I, S*, 1884 *W*

G

Gadney, B.C. (Leicester, Headingley) 1932 *I, S*, 1933 *I, S*, 1934 *W, I, S*, 1935 *S*, 1936 *NZ, W, I, S*, 1937 *S*, 1938 *W*
Gamlin, H.T. (Blackheath) 1899 *W, S*, 1900 *W, I, S*, 1901 *S*, 1902 *W, I, S*, 1903 *W, I, S*, 1904 *W, I, S*
Gardner, E.R. (Devonport Services) 1921 *W, I, S*, 1922 *W, I, F*, 1923 *W, I, S, F*
Gardner, H.P. (Richmond) 1878 *I*
Garforth, D.J. (Leicester) 1997 *W (R), Arg* 1,2, *A* 1, *NZ* 1, *SA, NZ* 2, 1998 *F, W (R), S, I, H, It, A* 2, *SA* 2, 1999 *S, I, F, W, A, C (R), [It (R), NZ (R), Fj]*, 2000 *It*
Garnett, H.W.T. (Bradford) 1877 *S*
Gavins, M.N. (Leicester) 1961 *W*
Gay, D.J. (Bath) 1968 *W, I, F, S*
Gent, D.R. (Gloucester) 1905 *NZ*, 1906 *W, I*, 1910 *W, I*
Genth, J.S.M. (Manchester) 1874 *S*, 1875 *S*
George, J.T. (Falmouth) 1947 *S, F*, 1949 *I*
Gerrard, R.A. (Bath) 1932 *SA, W, I, S*, 1933 *W, I, S*, 1934 *W, I, S*, 1936 *NZ, W, I, S*
Gibbs, G.A. (Bristol) 1947 *F*, 1948 *I*
Gibbs, J.C. (Harlequins) 1925 *NZ, W*, 1926 *F*, 1927 *W, I, S, F*
Gibbs, N. (Harlequins) 1954 *S, F*
Giblin, L.F. (Blackheath) 1896 *W, I*, 1897 *S*
Gibson, A.S. (Manchester) 1871 *S*
Gibson, C.O.P. (Northern) 1901 *W*
Gibson, G.R. (Northern) 1899 *W*, 1901 *S*
Gibson, T.A. (Northern) 1905 *W, S*
Gilbert, F.G. (Devonport Services) 1923 *W, I*
Gilbert, R. (Devonport A) 1908 *W, I, S*
Giles, J.L. (Coventry) 1935 *W, I*, 1937 *W, I*, 1938 *I, S*
Gittings, W.J. (Coventry) 1967 *NZ*
Glover, P.B. (Bath) 1967 *A*, 1971 *F, P*
Godfray, R.E. (Richmond) 1905 *NZ*
Godwin, H.O. (Coventry) 1959 *F, S*, 1963 *S, NZ* 1,2, *A*, 1964 *NZ, I, F, S*, 1967 *NZ*
Gomarsall, A.C.T. (Wasps, Bedford) 1996 *It, Arg*, 1997 *S, I, F, Arg 2(R)* 2000 *It (R)*, *2002 Arg, SA(R)*, 2003 *F* 1, *W* 1*(R)*
Gordon-Smith, G.W. (Blackheath) 1900 *W, I, S*
Gotley, A.L.H. (Oxford U) 1910 *F, S*, 1911 *W, F, I, S*
Graham, D. (Aspatria) 1901 *W*
Graham, H.J. (Wimbledon H) 1875 *I, S*, 1876 *I, S*
Graham, J.D.G. (Wimbledon H) 1876 *I*
Gray, A. (Otley) 1947 *W, I, S*
Grayson, P.J. (Northampton) 1995 *WS*, 1996 *F, W, S, I*, 1997 *S, I, F, A 2(t), SA (R), NZ* 2, 1998 *F, W, S, I, H, It, A* 2, 1999 *I, [NZ (R), Tg, Fj (R), SA]*, 2003 *S(R), I(t)*
Green, J. (Skipton) 1905 *I*, 1906 *S, F, SA*, 1907 *F, W, I, S*
Green, J.F. (West Kent) 1871 *S*
Green, W.R. (Wasps) 1997 *A* 2, 1998 *NZ* 1(t+R), 1999 *US (R)*
Greening, P.B.T. (Gloucester, Wasps) 1996 *It (R), 1997 W (R), Arg* 1 1998 *NZ 1(R),2(R)*, 1999 *A (R), US, C, [It (R), NZ (R), Tg, Fj, SA]*, 2000 *I, F, W, It, S, SA* 1,2, *A, SA* 3, 2001 *F, I*
Greenstock, N.J.J. (Wasps) 1997 *Arg* 1,2, *A* 1, *SA*
Greenwell, J.H. (Rockcliff) 1893 *W, I*
Greenwood, J.E. (Cambridge U, Leicester) 1912 *F*, 1913 *SA, W, F, I, S*, 1914 *W, S, F*, 1920 *W, F, I, S*
Greenwood, J.R.H. (Waterloo) 1966 *I, F, S*, 1967 *A*, 1969 *I*
Greenwood, W.J.H. (Leicester, Harlequins) 1997 *A* 2, *NZ* 1, *SA, NZ* 2, 1998 *F, W, S, I, H, It*, 1999 *C, [It, Tg, Fj, SA]*, 2000 *Arg (R), SA* 3, 2001 *W, It, S, F, I, A, R, SA*, 2002 *S, I, F, W, It, NZ, A, SA*, 2003 *F* 1, *W* 1, *It, S, I, NZ, A*
Greg, W. (Manchester) 1876 *I, S*
Gregory, G.G. (Bristol) 1931 *I, S, F*, 1932 *SA, W, I, S*, 1933 *W, I, S*, 1934 *W, I, S*
Gregory, J.A. (Blackheath) 1949 *W*
Grewcock, D.J. (Coventry, Saracens, Bath) 1997 *Arg* 2, *SA*, 1998 *W (R), S (R), I (R), A* 1, *NZ* 1, *SA 2(R)*, 1999 *S (R), A (R), US, C, [It, NZ, Tg (R), SA]*, 2000 *SA* 1,2, *A, Arg, SA* 3, 2001 *W, It, S, I, A, R (R), SA*, 2002 *S (R), I (R), F (R), W, It, NZ, SA (R)*, 2003 *F 1 (R), W 1 (R), It, S (R), I (t)*
Grylls, W.M. (Redruth) 1905 *I*
Guest, R.H. (Waterloo) 1939 *W, I, S*, 1947 *W, I, S, F*, 1948 *A, W, I, S*, 1949 *F, S*
Guillemard, A.G. (West Kent) 1871 *S*, 1872 *S*
Gummer, C.H.A. (Plymouth A) 1929 *F*
Gunner, C.R. (Marlborough N) 1876 *I*
Gurdon, C. (Richmond) 1880 *I, S*, 1881 *I, W, S*, 1882 *I, S*, 1883 *S*, 1884 *W, S*, 1885 *I*, 1886 *W, I, S*
Gurdon, E.T. (Richmond) 1878 *S*, 1879 *I*, 1880 *S*, 1881 *I, W, S*, 1882 S, 1883 *W, I, S*, 1884 *W, I, S*, 1885 *W, I*, 1886 *S*
Guscott, J.C. (Bath) 1989 *R, Fj*, 1990 *I, F, W, S, Arg* 3, 1991 *W, S, I, F, Fj, A, [NZ, It, F, S, A]*, 1992 *S, I, F, W, C, SA*, 1993 *F, W, S, I*, 1994 *R, C*, 1995 *I, F, W, S, [Arg, It, A, NZ, F], SA, WS*, 1996 *F, W, S, I, Arg*, 1997 *I (R), W (R), 1998 F, W, S, I, H, It, A* 2, *SA* 2, 1999 *S, I, F, A, US, C, [It (R), NZ, Tg]*

H

Haag, M. (Bath) 1997 *Arg* 1,2
Haigh, L. (Manchester) 1910 *W, I, S*, 1911 *W, F, I, S*
Hale, P.M. (Moseley) 1969 *SA*, 1970 *I, W*
Hall, C. (Gloucester) 1901 *I, S*
Hall, J. (N Durham) 1894 *W, I, S*
Hall, J.P. (Bath) 1984 *S (R), I, F, SA* 1,2, *A*, 1985 *R, F, S, I, W, NZ* 1,2, 1986 *W, S*, 1987 *I, F, W, S*, 1990 *Arg* 3, 1994 *S*
Hall, N.M. (Richmond) 1947 *W, I, S, F*, 1949 *W, I*, 1952 *SA, W, S, I, F*, 1953 *W, I, F, S*, 1955 *W, I*
Halliday, S.J. (Bath, Harlequins) 1986 *W, S*, 1987 *S*, 1988 *S, I* 1,2, *A* 1, *A*, 1989 *S, I, F, W, R, Fj (R), 1990 W, S*, 1991 *[US, S, A]*, 1992 *S, I, F, W*
Hamersley, A.St.G. (Marlborough N) 1871 *S*, 1872 *S*, 1873 *S*, 1874 *S*
Hamilton-Hill, E.A. (Harlequins) 1936 *NZ, W, I*
Hamilton-Wickes, R.H. (Cambridge U) 1924 *I*, 1925 *NZ, W, I, S, F*, 1926 *W, I, S*, 1927 *W*
Hammett, E.D.G. (Newport) 1920 *W, F, S*, 1921 *W, I, S, F*, 1922 *W*
Hammond, C.E.L. (Harlequins) 1905 *S, NZ*, 1906 *W, I, S, F*, 1908 *W, I*
Hancock, A.W. (Northampton) 1965 *F, S*, 1966 *F*

Hancock, G.E. (Birkenhead Park) 1939 *W, I, S*
Hancock, J.H. (Newport) 1955 *W, I*
Hancock, P.F. (Blackheath) 1886 *W, I*, 1890 *W*
Hancock, P.S. (Richmond) 1904 *W, I, S*
Handford, F.G. (Manchester) 1909 *W, F, I, S*
Hands, R.H.M. (Blackheath) 1910 *F, S*
Hanley, J. (Plymouth A) 1927 *W, S, F*, 1928 *W, I, F, S*
Hanley, S.M. (Sale) 1999 *W*
Hannaford, R.C. (Bristol) 1971 *W, I, F*
Hanvey, R.J. (Aspatria) 1926 *W, I, F, S*
Harding, E.H. (Devonport Services) 1931 *I*
Harding, R.M. (Bristol) 1985 *R, F, S*, 1987 *S*, [*A, J, W*], 1988 *I* 1*(R)*,2, *A* 1,2, *Fj*
Harding, V.S.J. (Saracens) 1961 *F, S*, 1962 *W, I, F, S*
Hardwick, P.F. (Percy Park) 1902 *I, S*, 1903 *W, I, S*, 1904 *W, I, S*
Hardwick, R.J.K. (Coventry) 1996 *It (R)*
Hardy, E.M.P. (Blackheath) 1951 *I, F, S*
Hare, W.H. (Nottingham, Leicester) 1974 *W*, 1978 *F, NZ*, 1979 *NZ*, 1980 *I, F, W, S*, 1981 *W, S, Arg* 1,2, 1982 *F, W*, 1983 *F, W, S, I, NZ*, 1984 *S, I, F, W, SA* 1,2
Harper, C.H. (Exeter) 1899 *W*
Harriman, A.T. (Harlequins) 1988 *A*
Harris, S.W. (Blackheath) 1920 *I, S*
Harris, T.W. (Northampton) 1929 *S*, 1932 *I*
Harrison, A.C. (Hartlepool R) 1931 *I, S*
Harrison, A.L. (United Services, RN) 1914 *I, F*
Harrison, G. (Hull) 1877 *I, S*, 1879 *S, I*, 1880 *S*, 1885 *W, I*
Harrison, H.C. (United Services, RN) 1909 *S*, 1914 *I, S, F*
Harrison, M.E. (Wakefield) 1985 *NZ* 1,2, 1986 *S, I, F*, 1987 *I, F, W, S*, [*A, J, US, W*], 1988 *F, W*
Hartley, B.C. (Blackheath) 1901 *S*, 1902 *S*
Haslett, L.W. (Birkenhead Park) 1926 *I, F*
Hastings, G.W.D. (Gloucester) 1955 *W, I, F, S*, 1957 *W, I, F, S*, 1958 *W, A, I, F, S*
Havelock, H. (Hartlepool R) 1908 *F, W, I*
Hawcridge, J.J. (Bradford) 1885 *W, I*
Hayward, L.W. (Cheltenham) 1910 *I*
Hazell, D.St.G. (Leicester) 1955 *W, I, F, S*
Healey, A.S. (Leicester) 1997 *I (R), W, A* 1*(R)*,2*(R)*, *NZ* 1*(R)*, *SA (R)*, *NZ* 2, 1998 *F, W, S, I, A* 1, *NZ* 1,2, *H, It, A* 2, *SA* 2*(R)*, 1999 *US, C*, [*It, NZ, Tg, Fj, SA (R)*], *2000 I, F, W, It, S, SA* 1,2, *A, SA* 3*(R)*, 2001 *W (R), It, S, F, I (R), A, R, SA*, 2002 *S, I, F, W, It (R), NZ (R), A (R), SA(R)*
Hearn, R.D. (Bedford) 1966 *F, S*, 1967 *I, F, S, W*
Heath, A.H. (Oxford U) 1876 *S*
Heaton, J. (Waterloo) 1935 *W, I, S*, 1939 *W, I, S*, 1947 *I, S, F*
Henderson, A.P. (Edinburgh Wands) 1947 *W, I, S, F*, 1948 *I, S, F*, 1949 *W, I*
Henderson, R.S.F. (Blackheath) 1883 *W, S*, 1884 *W, S*, 1885 *W*
Heppell, W.G. (Devonport A) 1903 *I*
Herbert, A.J. (Wasps) 1958 *F, S*, 1959 *W, I, F, S*
Hesford, R. (Bristol) 1981 *S (R), 1982 A, S, F (R), 1983 F (R), 1985 R, F, S, I, W*
Heslop, N.J. (Orrell) 1990 *Arg* 1,2,3, 1991 *W, S, I, F*, [*US, F*], 1992 *W (R)*
Hetherington, J.G.G. (Northampton) 1958 *A, I*, 1959 *W, I, F, S*
Hewitt, E.N. (Coventry) 1951 *W, I, F*
Hewitt, W.W. (Queen's House) 1881 *I, W, S*, 1882 *I*
Hickson, J.L. (Bradford) 1887 *W, I, S*, 1890 *W, S, I*
Higgins, R. (Liverpool) 1954 *W, NZ, I, S*, 1955 *W, I, F, S*, 1957 *W, I, F, S*, 1959 *W*
Hignell, A.J. (Cambridge U, Bristol) 1975 *A* 2, 1976 *A, W, S, I*, 1977 *S, I, F, W*, 1978 *W*, 1979 *S, I, F, W*
Hill, B.A. (Blackheath) 1903 *I, S*, 1904 *W, I*, 1905 *W, NZ*, 1906 *SA*, 1907 *F, W*
Hill, R.A. (Saracens) 1997 *S, I, F, W, A* 1,2, *NZ* 1, *SA, NZ* 2, 1998 *F, W, H (R), It (R), A* 2, *SA* 2, 1999 *S, I, F, W, A, US, C*, [*It, NZ, Tg, Fj (R), SA*], 2000 *I, F, W, It, S, SA* 1,2, *A, Arg, SA* 3, 2001 *W, It, S, F, I, A, SA*, 2002 *S, I, F, W, It, NZ, A, SA*, 2003 *F* 1, *W* 1, *It, S, I, NZ, A*
Hill, R.J. (Bath) 1984 *SA* 1,2, 1985 *I (R), NZ* 2*(R)*, 1986 *F (R), 1987 I, F, W*, [*US*], 1989 *Fj*, 1990 *I, F, W, S, Arg* 1,2,3, 1991 *W, S, I, F, Fj, A*, [*NZ, It, US, F, S, A*]
Hillard, R.J. (Oxford U) 1925 *NZ*
Hiller, R. (Harlequins) 1968 *W, I, F, S*, 1969 *I, F, S, W, SA*, 1970 *I, W, S*, 1971 *I, F, S (2[1C]), P*, 1972 *W, I*
Hind, A.E. (Leicester) 1905 *NZ*, 1906 *W*
Hind, G.R. (Blackheath) 1910 *S*, 1911 *I*
Hobbs, R.F.A. (Blackheath) 1899 *S*, 1903 *W*
Hobbs, R.G.S. (Richmond) 1932 *SA, W, I, S*
Hodges, H.A. (Nottingham) 1906 *W, I*
Hodgkinson, S.D. (Nottingham) 1989 *R, Fj*, 1990 *I, F, W, S, Arg* 1,2,3, 1991 *W, S, I, F*, [*US*]
Hodgson, C. (Sale) 2001 *R*, 2002 *S (R), I (R), It (R), Arg*, 2003 *F* 1, *W* 1, *It (R)*
Hodgson, J.McD. (Northern) 1932 *SA, W, I, S*, 1934 *W, I*, 1936 *I*
Hodgson, S.A.M. (Durham City) 1960 *W, I, F, S*, 1961 *SA, W*, 1962 *W, I, F, S*, 1964 *W*
Hofmeyr, M.B. (Oxford U) 1950 *W, F, S*
Hogarth, T.B. (Hartlepool R) 1906 *F*
Holford, G. (Gloucester) 1920 *W, F*
Holland, D. (Devonport A) 1912 *W, I, S*
Holliday, T.E. (Aspatria) 1923 *S, F*, 1925 *I, S, F*, 1926 *F, S*
Holmes, C.B. (Manchester) 1947 *S*, 1948 *I, F*
Holmes, E. (Manningham) 1890 *S, I*
Holmes, W.A. (Nuneaton) 1950 *W, I, F, S*, 1951 *W, I, F, S*, 1952 *SA, S, I, F*, 1953 *W, I, F, S*
Holmes, W.B. (Cambridge U) 1949 *W, I, F, S*
Hook, W.G. (Gloucester) 1951 *S*, 1952 *SA, W*
Hooper, C.A. (Middlesex W) 1894 *W, I, S*
Hopley, D.P. (Wasps) 1995 [*WS (R)], SA, WS*
Hopley, F.J.V. (Blackheath) 1907 *F, W*, 1908 *I*
Horak, M.J. (London Irish) 2002 *Arg*
Hordern, P.C. (Gloucester) 1931 *I, S, F*, 1934 *W*
Horley, C.H. (Swinton) 1885 *I*
Hornby, A.N. (Manchester) 1877 *I, S*, 1878 *S, I*, 1880 *I*, 1881 *I, S*, 1882 *I, S*
Horrocks-Taylor, J.P. (Cambridge U, Leicester, Middlesbrough) 1958 *W, A*, 1961 *S*, 1962 *S*, 1963 *NZ* 1,2, *A*, 1964 *NZ, W*
Horsfall, E.L. (Harlequins) 1949 *W*
Horton, A.L. (Blackheath) 1965 *W, I, F, S*, 1966 *F, S*, 1967 *NZ*
Horton, J.P. (Bath) 1978 *W, S, I, NZ*, 1980 *I, F, W, S*, 1981 *W*, 1983 *S, I*, 1984 *SA* 1,2
Horton, N.E. (Moseley, Toulouse) 1969 *I, F, S, W*, 1971 *I, F, S*, 1974 *S*, 1975 *W*, 1977 *S, I, F, W*, 1978 *F, W*, 1979 *S, I, F, W*, 1980 *I*
Hosen, R.W. (Bristol, Northampton) 1963 *NZ* 1,2, *A*, 1964 *F, S*, 1967 *A, I, F, S, W*
Hosking, G.R.d'A. (Devonport Services) 1949 *W, I, F, S*, 1950 *W*
Houghton, S. (Runcorn) 1892 *I*, 1896 *W*
Howard, P.D. (O Millhillians) 1930 *W, I, F, S*, 1931 *W, I, S, F*
Hubbard, G.C. (Blackheath) 1892 *W, I*
Hubbard, J.C. (Harlequins) 1930 *S*
Hudson, A. (Gloucester) 1906 *W, I, F*, 1908 *F, W, I, S*, 1910 *F*
Hughes, G.E. (Barrow) 1896 *S*
Hull, P.A. (Bristol, RAF) 1994 *SA* 1,2, *R, C*
Hulme, F.C. (Birkenhead Park) 1903 *W, I*, 1905 *W, I*
Hunt, J.T. (Manchester) 1882 *I, S*, 1884 *W*
Hunt, R. (Manchester) 1880 *I*, 1881 *W, S*, 1882 *I*

Hunt, W.H. (Manchester) 1876 *S*, 1877 *I, S*, 1878 *I*
Hunter, I. (Northampton) 1992 *C*, 1993 *F, W*, 1994 *F, W*, 1995 [*WS, F*]
Huntsman, R.P. (Headingley) 1985 *NZ* 1,2
Hurst, A.C.B. (Wasps) 1962 *S*
Huskisson, T.F. (OMTs) 1937 *W, I, S*, 1938 *W, I*, 1939 *W, I, S*
Hutchinson, F. (Headingley) 1909 *F, I, S*
Hutchinson, J.E. (Durham City) 1906 *I*
Hutchinson, W.C. (RIE Coll) 1876 *S*, 1877 *I*
Hutchinson, W.H.H. (Hull) 1875 *I*, 1876 *I*
Huth, H. (Huddersfield) 1879 *S*
Hyde, J.P. (Northampton) 1950 *F, S*
Hynes, W.B. (United Services, RN) 1912 *F*

I

Ibbitson, E.D. (Headingley) 1909 *W, F, I, S*
Imrie, H.M. (Durham City) 1906 *NZ*, 1907 *I*
Inglis, R.E. (Blackheath) 1886 *W, I, S*
Irvin, S.H. (Devonport A) 1905 *W*
Isherwood, F.W. (Ravenscourt Park) 1872 *S*

J

Jackett, E.J. (Leicester, Falmouth) 1905 *NZ*, 1906 *W, I, S, F, SA*, 1907 *W, I, S*, 1909 *W, F, I, S*
Jackson, A.H. (Blackheath) 1878 *I*, 1880 *I*
Jackson, B.S. (Broughton Park) 1970 *S (R), F*
Jackson, P.B. (Coventry) 1956 *W, I, F*, 1957 *W, I, F, S*, 1958 *W, A, F, S*, 1959 *W, I, F, S*, 1961 *S*, 1963 *W, I, F, S*
Jackson, W.J. (Halifax) 1894 *S*
Jacob, F. (Cambridge U) 1897 *W, I, S*, 1898 *I, S, W*, 1899 *W, I*
Jacob, H.P. (Blackheath) 1924 *W, I, F, S*, 1930 *F*
Jacob, P.G. (Blackheath) 1898 *I*
Jacobs, C.R. (Northampton) 1956 *W, I, S, F*, 1957 *W, I, F, S*, 1958 *W, A, I, F, S*, 1960 *W, I, F, S*, 1961 *SA, W, I, F, S*, 1963 *NZ* 1,2, *A*, 1964 *W, I, F, S*
Jago, R.A. (Devonport A) 1906 *W, I, SA*, 1907 *W, I*
Janion, J.P.A.G. (Bedford) 1971 *W, I, F, S (2[1C]), P*, 1972 *W, S, SA*, 1973 *A*, 1975 *A* 1,2
Jarman, J.W. (Bristol) 1900 *W*
Jeavons, N.C. (Moseley) 1981 *S, I, F, Arg* 1,2, 1982 *A, S, I, F, W*, 1983 *F, W, S, I*
Jeeps, R.E.G. (Northampton) 1956 *W*, 1957 *W, I, F, S*, 1958 *W, A, I, F, S*, 1959 *I*, 1960 *W, I, F, S*, 1961 *SA, W, I, F, S*, 1962 *W, I, F, S*
Jeffery, G.L. (Blackheath) 1886 *W, I, S*, 1887 *W, I, S*
Jennins, C.R. (Waterloo) 1967 *A, I, F*
Jewitt, J. (Hartlepool R) 1902 *W*
Johns, W.A. (Gloucester) 1909 *W, F, I, S*, 1910 *W, I, F*
Johnson, M.O. (Leicester) 1993 *F, NZ*, 1994 *S, I, F, W, R, C*, 1995 *I, F, W, S*, [*Arg, It, WS, A, NZ, F*], *SA, WS*, 1996 *F, W, S, I, It, Arg*, 1997 *S, I, F, W, A* 2, *NZ* 1,2, 1998 *F, W, S, I, H, It, A* 2, *SA* 2, 1999 *S, I, F, W, A, US, C*, [*It, NZ, Tg, Fj, SA*], 2000 *SA* 1,2, *A, Arg, SA* 3, 2001 *W, It, S, F, SA*, 2002 *S, I, F, It (t+R), NZ, A, SA*, 2003 *F* 1, *W* 1, *S, I, NZ, A*
Johnston, B. (Saracens) 2002 *Arg, NZ (R)*
Johnston, W.R. (Bristol) 1910 *W, I, S*, 1912 *W, I, S, F*, 1913 *SA, W, F, I, S*, 1914 *W, I, S, F*
Jones, F.P. (New Brighton) 1893 *S*
Jones, H.A. (Barnstaple) 1950 *W, I, F*
Jorden, A.M. (Cambridge U, Blackheath, Bedford) 1970 *F*, 1973 *I, F, S*, 1974 *F*, 1975 *W, S*
Jowett, D. (Heckmondwike) 1889 *M*, 1890 *S, I*, 1891 *W, I, S*
Judd, P.E. (Coventry) 1962 *W, I, F, S*, 1963 *S, NZ* 1,2, *A*, 1964 *NZ*, 1965 *I, F, S*, 1966 *W, I, F, S*, 1967 *A, I, F, S, W, NZ*

K

Kay, B.J. (Leicester) 2001 *C* 1,2, *A, R, SA (t+R)*, 2002 *S, I, F, W, It, Arg, NZ (R), A, SA*, 2003 *F* 1, *W* 1, *It, S, I, NZ, A*
Kayll, H.E. (Sunderland) 1878 *S*
Keeling, J.H. (Guy's Hospital) 1948 *A, W*
Keen, B.W. (Newcastle U) 1968 *W, I, F, S*
Keeton, G.H. (Leicester) 1904 *W, I, S*
Kelly, G.A. (Bedford) 1947 *W, I, S*, 1948 *W*
Kelly, T.S. (London Devonians) 1906 *W, I, S, F, SA*, 1907 *F, W, I, S*, 1908 *F, I, S*
Kemble, A.T. (Liverpool) 1885 *W, I*, 1887 *I*
Kemp, D.T. (Blackheath) 1935 *W*
Kemp, T.A. (Richmond) 1937 *W, I*, 1939 *S*, 1948 *A, W*
Kendall, P.D. (Birkenhead Park) 1901 *S*, 1902 *W*, 1903 *S*
Kendall-Carpenter, J.MacG.K. (Oxford U, Bath) 1949 *I, F, S*, 1950 *W, I, F, S*, 1951 *I, F, S*, 1952 *SA, W, S, I, F*, 1953 *W, I, F, S*, 1954 *W, NZ, I, F*
Kendrew, D.A. (Leicester) 1930 *W, I*, 1933 *I, S*, 1934 *S*, 1935 *W, I*, 1936 *NZ, W, I*
Kennedy, R.D. (Camborne S of M) 1949 *I, F, S*
Kent, C.P. (Rosslyn Park) 1977 *S, I, F, W*, 1978 *F (R)*
Kent, T. (Salford) 1891 *W, I, S*, 1892 *W, I, S*
Kershaw, C.A. (United Services, RN) 1920 *W, F, I, S*, 1921 *W, I, S, F*, 1922 *W, I, F, S*, 1923 *W, I, S, F*
Kewley, E. (Liverpool) 1874 *S*, 1875 *S*, 1876 *I, S*, 1877 *I, S*, 1878 *S*
Kewney, A.L. (Leicester) 1906 *W, I, S, F*, 1909 *A, W, F, I, S*, 1911 *W, F, I, S*, 1912 *I, S*, 1913 *SA*
Key, A. (O Cranleighans) 1930 *I*, 1933 *W*
Keyworth, M. (Swansea) 1976 *A, W, S, I*
Kilner, B. (Wakefield T) 1880 *I*
Kindersley, R.S. (Exeter) 1883 *W*, 1884 *S*, 1885 *W*
King, A.D. (Wasps) 1997 *Arg* 2*(R)*, 1998 *SA* 2*(R)*, 2000 *It (R)*, 2001 *C* 2*(R)*
King, I. (Harrogate) 1954 *W, NZ, I*
King, J.A. (Headingley) 1911 *W, F, I, S*, 1912 *W, I, S*, 1913 *SA, W, F, I, S*
King, Q.E.M.A. (Army) 1921 *S*
Kingston, P. (Gloucester) 1975 *A* 1,2, 1979 *I, F, W*
Kitching, A.E. (Blackheath) 1913 *I*
Kittermaster, H.J. (Harlequins) 1925 *NZ, W, I*, 1926 *W, I, F, S*
Knight, F. (Plymouth) 1909 *A*
Knight, P.M. (Bristol) 1972 *F, S, SA*
Knowles, E. (Millom) 1896 *S*, 1897 *S*
Knowles, T.C. (Birkenhead Park) 1931 *S*
Krige, J.A. (Guy's Hospital) 1920 *W*

L

Labuschagne, N.A. (Harlequins, Guy's Hospital) 1953 *W*, 1955 *W, I, F, S*
Lagden, R.O. (Richmond) 1911 *S*
Laird, H.C.C. (Harlequins) 1927 *W, I, S*, 1928 *A, W, I, F, S*, 1929 *W, I*
Lambert, D. (Harlequins) 1907 *F*, 1908 *F, W, S*, 1911 *W, F, I*
Lampkowski, M.S. (Headingley) 1976 *A, W, S, I*
Lapage, W.N. (United Services, RN) 1908 *F, W, I, S*
Larter, P.J. (Northampton, RAF) 1967 *A, NZ*, 1968 *W, I, F, S*, 1969 *I, F, S, W, SA*, 1970 *I, W, F, S*, 1971 *W, I, F, S (2[1C]), P*, 1972 *SA*, 1973 *NZ* 1, *W*
Law, A.F. (Richmond) 1877 *S*

Law, D.E. (Birkenhead Park) 1927 *I*
Lawrence, Hon.H.A. (Richmond) 1873 *S*, 1874 *S*, 1875 *I, S*
Lawrie, P.W. (Leicester) 1910 *S*, 1911 *S*
Lawson, R.G. (Workington) 1925 *I*
Lawson, T.M. (Workington) 1928 *A, W*
Leadbetter, M.M. (Broughton Park) 1970 *F*
Leadbetter, V.H. (Edinburgh Wands) 1954 *S, F*
Leake, W.R.M. (Harlequins) 1891 *W, I, S*
Leather, G. (Liverpool) 1907 *I*
Lee, F.H. (Marlborough N) 1876 *S*, 1877 *I*
Lee, H. (Blackheath) 1907 *F*
Le Fleming, J. (Blackheath) 1887 *W*
Leonard, J. (Saracens, Harlequins) 1990 *Arg* 1,2,3, 1991 *W, S, I, F, Fj, A, [NZ, It, US, F, S, A]*, 1992 *S, I, F, W, C, SA*, 1993 *F, W, S, I, NZ*, 1994 *S, I, F, W, SA* 1,2, *R, C*, 1995 *I, F, W, S, [Arg, It, A, NZ, F], SA, WS*, 1996 *F, W, S, I, It, Arg*, 1997 *S, I, F, W, A* 2, *NZ* 1, *SA, NZ* 2, 1998 *F, W, S, I, H, It, A* 2 *SA* 2, 1999 *S, I, F, W, A, C (R), [It, NZ, Fj, SA]*, 2000 *I, F, W, It, S, SA* 1,2, *A, Arg, SA* 3, 2001 *W, It, S, F, I, R*, 2002 *S (R), I (R), F (R), It (R), A, SA*, 2003 *F* 1, *S, I, NZ*
Leslie-Jones, F.A. (Richmond) 1895 *W, I*
Lewis, A.O. (Bath) 1952 *SA, W, S, I, F*, 1953 *W, I, F, S*, 1954 *F*
Lewsey, O.J. (Wasps) 1998 *NZ* 1,2, *SA* 1, 2001 *C* 1,2, *US*, 2003 *It, S, I, NZ, A*
Leyland, R. (Waterloo) 1935 *W, I, S*
Linnett, M.S. (Moseley) 1989 *Fj*
Livesay, R.O'H. (Blackheath) 1898 *W*, 1899 *W*
Lloyd, L.D. (Leicester) 2000 *SA* 1*(R)*,2*(R)*, 2001 *C* 1,2, *US*
Lloyd, R.H. (Harlequins) 1967 *NZ*, 1968 *W, I, F, S*
Locke, H.M. (Birkenhead Park) 1923 *S, F*, 1924 *W, F, S*, 1925 *W, I, S, F*, 1927 *W, I, S*
Lockwood, R.E. (Heckmondwike) 1887 *W, I, S*, 1889 *M*, 1891 *W, I, S*, 1892 *W, I, S*, 1893 *W, I*, 1894 *W, I*
Login, S.H.M. (RN Coll) 1876 *I*
Lohden, F.C. (Blackheath) 1893 *W*
Long, A.E. (Bath) 1997 *A* 2, 2001 *US (R)*
Longland, R.J. (Northampton) 1932 *S*, 1933 *W, S*, 1934 *W, I, S*, 1935 *W, I, S*, 1936 *NZ, W, I, S*, 1937 *W, I, S*, 1938 *W, I, S*
Lowe, C.N. (Cambridge U, Blackheath) 1913 *SA, W, F, I, S*, 1914 *W, I, S, F*, 1920 *W, F, I, S*, 1921 *W, I, S, F*, 1922 *W, I, F, S*, 1923 *W, I, S, F*
Lowrie, F. (Wakefield T) 1889 *M*, 1890 *W*
Lowry, W.M. (Birkenhead Park) 1920 *F*
Lozowski, R.A.P. (Wasps) 1984 *A*
Luddington, W.G.E. (Devonport Services) 1923 *W, I, S, F*, 1924 *W, I, F, S*, 1925 *W, I, S, F*, 1926 *W*
Luger, D.D. (Harlequins, Saracens) 1998 *H, It, SA* 2, 1999 *S, I, F, W, A, US, C, [It, NZ, Tg, Fj, SA]*, 2000 *SA* 1, *A, Arg, SA* 3, 2001 *W, I, A, R, SA*, 2002 *F (R), W, It*, 2003 *F* 1, *W* 1, *It, S (R), I (R), NZ (R)*
Luscombe, F. (Gipsies) 1872 *S*, 1873 *S*, 1875 *I, S*, 1876 *I, S*
Luscombe, J.H. (Gipsies) 1871 *S*
Luxmoore, A.F.C.C. (Richmond) 1900 *S*, 1901 *W*
Luya, H.F. (Waterloo, Headingley) 1948 *W, I, S, F*, 1949 *W*
Lyon, A. (Liverpool) 1871 *S*
Lyon, G.H.d'O. (United Services, RN) 1908 *S*, 1909 *A*

M

McCanlis, M.A. (Gloucester) 1931 *W, I*
McCarthy, N. (Gloucester) 1999 *I (t), US (R), 2000 It (R)*
McFadyean, C.W. (Moseley) 1966 *I, F, S*, 1967 *A, I, F, S, W, NZ*, 1968 *W, I*
MacIlwaine, A.H. (United Services, Hull & E Riding) 1912 *W, I, S, F*, 1920 *I*
Mackie, O.G. (Wakefield T, Cambridge U) 1897 *S*, 1898 *I*
Mackinlay, J.E.H. (St George's Hospital) 1872 *S*, 1873 *S*, 1875 *I*
MacLaren, W. (Manchester) 1871 *S*
MacLennan, R.R.F. (OMTs) 1925 *I, S, F*
McLeod, N.F. (RIE Coll) 1879 *S, I*
Madge, R.J.P. (Exeter) 1948 *A, W, I, S*
Malir, F.W.S. (Otley) 1930 *W, I, S*
Mallett, J.A. (Bath) 1995 *[WS (R)]*
Mallinder, J. (Sale) 1997 *Arg* 1,2
Mangles, R.H. (Richmond) 1897 *W, I*
Manley, D.C. (Exeter) 1963 *W, I, F, S*
Mann, W.E. (United Services, Army) 1911 *W, F, I*
Mantell, N.D. (Rosslyn Park) 1975 *A* 1
Mapletoft, M.S. (Gloucester) 1997 *Arg* 2
Markendale, E.T. (Manchester R) 1880 *I*
Marques, R.W.D. (Cambridge U, Harlequins) 1956 *W, I, S, F*, 1957 *W, I, F, S*, 1958 *W, A, I, F, S*, 1959 *W, I, F, S*, 1960 *W, I, F, S*, 1961 *SA, W*
Marquis, J.C. (Birkenhead Park) 1900 *I, S*
Marriott, C.J.B. (Blackheath) 1884 *W, I, S*, 1886 *W, I, S*, 1887 *I*
Marriott, E.E. (Manchester) 1876 *I*
Marriott, V.R. (Harlequins) 1963 *NZ* 1,2, *A*, 1964 *NZ*
Marsden, G.H. (Morley) 1900 *W, I, S*
Marsh, H. (RIE Coll) 1873 *S*
Marsh, J. (Swinton) 1892 *I*
Marshall, H. (Blackheath) 1893 *W*
Marshall, M.W. (Blackheath) 1873 *S*, 1874 *S*, 1875 *I, S*, 1876 *I, S*, 1877 *I, S*, 1878 *S, I*
Marshall, R.M. (Oxford U) 1938 *I, S*, 1939 *W, I, S*
Martin, C.R. (Bath) 1985 *F, S, I, W*
Martin, N.O. (Harlequins) 1972 *F (R)*
Martindale, S.A. (Kendal) 1929 *F*
Massey, E.J. (Leicester) 1925 *W, I, S*
Mather, B-J. (Sale) 1999 *W*
Mathias, J.L. (Bristol) 1905 *W, I, S, NZ*
Matters, J.C. (RNE Coll) 1899 *S*
Matthews, J.R.C. (Harlequins) 1949 *F, S*, 1950 *I, F, S*, 1952 *SA, W, S, I, F*
Maud, P. (Blackheath) 1893 *W, I*
Maxwell, A.W. (New Brighton, Headingley) 1975 *A* 1, 1976 *A, W, S, I, F*, 1978 *F*
Maxwell-Hyslop, J.E. (Oxford U) 1922 *I, F, S*
Maynard, A.F. (Cambridge U) 1914 *W, I, S*
Meikle, G.W.C. (Waterloo) 1934 *W, I, S*
Meikle, S.S.C. (Waterloo) 1929 *S*
Mellish, F.W. (Blackheath) 1920 *W, F, I, S*, 1921 *W, I*
Melville, N.D. (Wasps) 1984 *A*, 1985 *I, W, NZ* 1,2, 1986 *W, S, I, F*, 1988 *F, W, S, I* 1
Merriam, L.P.B. (Blackheath) 1920 *W, F*
Michell, A.T. (Oxford U) 1875 *I, S*, 1876 *I*
Middleton, B.B. (Birkenhead Park) 1882 *I*, 1883 *I*
Middleton, J.A. (Richmond) 1922 *S*
Miles, J.H. (Leicester) 1903 *W*
Millett, H. (Richmond) 1920 *F*
Mills, F.W. (Marlborough N) 1872 *S*, 1873 *S*
Mills, S.G.F. (Gloucester) 1981 *Arg* 1,2, 1983 *W*, 1984 *SA* 1, *A*
Mills, W.A. (Devonport A) 1906 *W, I, S, F, SA*, 1907 *F, W, I, S*, 1908 *F, W*
Milman, D.L.K. (Bedford) 1937 *W*, 1938 *W, I, S*
Milton, C.H. (Camborne S of M) 1906 *I*
Milton, J.G. (Camborne S of M) 1904 *W, I, S*, 1905 *S*, 1907 *I*
Milton, W.H. (Marlborough N) 1874 *S*, 1875 *I*
Mitchell, F. (Blackheath) 1895 *W, I, S*, 1896 *W, I, S*

Mitchell, W.G. (Richmond) 1890 *W, S, I*, 1891 *W, I, S*, 1893 *S*
Mobbs, E.R. (Northampton) 1909 *A, W, F, I, S*, 1910 *I, F*
Moberley, W.O. (Ravenscourt Park) 1872 *S*
Moody, L.W. (Leicester) 2001 *C* 1,2, *US, I (R), R, SA (R)*, 2002 *I (R), W, It, Arg, NZ, A, SA*, 2003 *F* 1
Moore, B.C. (Nottingham, Harlequins) 1987 *S*, [*A, J, W*], 1988 *F, W, S, I* 1,2, *A* 1, 2, *Fj, A*, 1989 *S, I, F, W, R, Fj*, 1990 *I, F, W, S, Arg* 1,2, 1991 *W, S, I, F, Fj, A*, [*NZ, It, F, S, A*], 1992 *S, I, F, W, SA*, 1993 *F, W, S, I, NZ*, 1994 *S, I, F, W, SA* 1,2, *R, C*, 1995 *I, F, W, S*, [*Arg, It, WS (R), A, NZ, F*]
Moore, E.J. (Blackheath) 1883 *I, S*
Moore, N.J.N.H. (Bristol) 1904 *W, I, S*
Moore, P.B.C. (Blackheath) 1951 *W*
Moore, W.K.T. (Leicester) 1947 *W, I*, 1949 *F, S*, 1950 *I, F, S*
Mordell, R.J. (Rosslyn Park) 1978 *W*
Morfitt, S. (W Hartlepool) 1894 *W, I, S*, 1896 *W, I, S*
Morgan, J.R. (Hawick) 1920 *W*
Morgan, W.G.D. (Medicals, Newcastle) 1960 *W, I, F, S*, 1961 *SA, W, I, F, S*
Morley, A.J. (Bristol) 1972 *SA*, 1973 *NZ* 1, *W, I*, 1975 *S, A* 1,2
Morris, A.D.W. (United Services, RN) 1909 *A, W, F*
Morris, C.D. (Liverpool St Helens, Orrell) 1988 *A*, 1989 *S, I, F, W*, 1992 *S, I, F, W, C, SA*, 1993 *F, W, S, I*, 1994 *F, W, SA* 1,2, *R*, 1995 *S (t)*, [*Arg, WS, A, NZ, F*]
Morris, R. (Northampton) 2003 *W* 1, *It*
Morrison, P.H. (Cambridge U) 1890 *W, S, I*, 1891 *I*
Morse, S. (Marlborough N) 1873 *S*, 1874 *S*, 1875 *S*
Mortimer, W. (Marlborough N) 1899 *W*
Morton, H.J.S. (Blackheath) 1909 *I, S*, 1910 *W, I*
Moss, F. (Broughton) 1885 *W, I*, 1886 *W*
Mullins, A.R. (Harlequins) 1989 *Fj*
Mycock, J. (Sale) 1947 *W, I, S, F*, 1948 *A*
Myers, E. (Bradford) 1920 *I, S*, 1921 *W, I*, 1922 *W, I, F, S*, 1923 *W, I, S, F*, 1924 *W, I, F, S*, 1925 *S, F*
Myers, H. (Keighley) 1898 *I*

N

Nanson, W.M.B. (Carlisle) 1907 *F, W*
Nash, E.H. (Richmond) 1875 *I*
Neale, B.A. (Rosslyn Park) 1951 *I, F, S*
Neale, M.E. (Blackheath) 1912 *F*
Neame, S. (O Cheltonians) 1879 *S, I*, 1880 *I, S*
Neary, A. (Broughton Park) 1971 *W, I, F, S (2[1C])*, *P*, 1972 *W, I, F, S, SA*, 1973 *NZ* 1, *W, I, F, S, NZ* 2, *A*, 1974 *S, I, F, W*, 1975 *I, F, W, S, A* 1, 1976 *A, W, S, I, F*, 1977 *I*, 1978 *F (R)*, 1979 *S, I, F, W, NZ*, 1980 *I, F, W, S*
Nelmes, B.G. (Cardiff) 1975 *A* 1,2, 1978 *W, S, I, NZ*
Newbold, C.J. (Blackheath) 1904 *W, I, S*, 1905 *W, I, S*
Newman, S.C. (Oxford U) 1947 *F*, 1948 *A, W*
Newton, A.W. (Blackheath) 1907 *S*
Newton, P.A. (Blackheath) 1882 *S*
Newton-Thompson, J.O. (Oxford U) 1947 *S, F*
Nichol, W. (Brighouse R) 1892 *W, S*
Nicholas, P.L. (Exeter) 1902 *W*
Nicholson, B.E. (Harlequins) 1938 *W, I*
Nicholson, E.S. (Leicester) 1935 *W, I, S*, 1936 *NZ, W*
Nicholson, E.T. (Birkenhead Park) 1900 *W, I*
Nicholson, T. (Rockcliff) 1893 *I*
Ninnes, B.F. (Coventry) 1971 *W*
Noon, J. (Newcastle) 2001 *C* 1,2, *US*
Norman, D.J. (Leicester) 1932 *SA, W*
North, E.H.G. (Blackheath) 1891 *W, I, S*
Northmore, S. (Millom) 1897 *I*
Novak, M.J. (Harlequins) 1970 *W, S, F*
Novis, A.L. (Blackheath) 1929 *S, F*, 1930 *W, I, F*, 1933 *I, S*

O

Oakeley, F.E. (United Services, RN) 1913 *S*, 1914 *I, S, F*
Oakes, R.F. (Hartlepool R) 1897 *W, I, S*, 1898 *I, S, W*, 1899 *W, S*
Oakley, L.F.L. (Bedford) 1951 *W*
Obolensky, A. (Oxford U) 1936 *NZ, W, I, S*
Ojomoh, S.O. (Bath, Gloucester) 1994 *I, F, SA* 1*(R)*,2, *R*, 1995 *S (R)*, *[Arg, WS, A (t), F*], 1996 *F*, 1998 *NZ* 1
Old, A.G.B. (Middlesbrough, Leicester, Sheffield) 1972 *W, I, F, S, SA*, 1973 *NZ* 2, *A*, 1974 *S, I, F, W*, 1975 *I, A* 2, 1976 *S, I*, 1978 *F*
Oldham, W.L. (Coventry) 1908 *S*, 1909 *A*
Olver, C.J. (Northampton) 1990 *Arg* 3, 1991 [*US*], 1992 *C*
O'Neill, A. (Teignmouth, Torquay A) 1901 *W, I, S*
Openshaw, W.E. (Manchester) 1879 *I*
Orwin, J. (Gloucester, RAF, Bedford) 1985 *R, F, S, I, W, NZ* 1,2, 1988 *F, W, S, I* 1,2, *A* 1,2
Osborne, R.R. (Manchester) 1871 *S*
Osborne, S.H. (Oxford U) 1905 *S*
Oti, C. (Cambridge U, Nottingham, Wasps) 1988 *S, I* 1, 1989 *S, I, F, W, R*, 1990 *Arg* 1,2, 1991 *Fj, A*, [*NZ, It*]
Oughtred, B. (Hartlepool R) 1901 *S*, 1902 *W, I, S*, 1903 *W, I*
Owen, J.E. (Coventry) 1963 *W, I, F, S, A*, 1964 *NZ*, 1965 *W, I, F, S*, 1966 *I, F, S*, 1967 *NZ*
Owen-Smith, H.G.O. (St Mary's Hospital) 1934 *W, I, S*, 1936 *NZ, W, I, S*, 1937 *W, I, S*

P

Page, J.J. (Bedford, Northampton) 1971 *W, I, F, S*, 1975 *S*
Pallant, J.N. (Notts) 1967 *I, F, S*
Palmer, A.C. (London Hospital) 1909 *I, S*
Palmer, F.H. (Richmond) 1905 *W*
Palmer, G.V. (Richmond) 1928 *I, F, S*
Palmer, J.A. (Bath) 1984 *SA* 1,2, 1986 *I (R)*
Palmer, T. (Leeds) 2001 *US (R)*
Pargetter, T.A. (Coventry) 1962 *S*, 1963 *F, NZ* 1
Parker, G.W. (Gloucester) 1938 *I, S*
Parker, Hon.S. (Liverpool) 1874 *S*, 1875 *S*
Parsons, E.I. (RAF) 1939 *S*
Parsons, M.J. (Northampton) 1968 *W, I, F, S*
Patterson, W.M. (Sale) 1961 *SA, S*
Pattisson, R.M. (Blackheath) 1883 *I, S*
Paul, H. (Gloucester) 2002 *F (R)*
Paul, J.E. (RIE Coll) 1875 *S*
Payne, A.T. (Bristol) 1935 *I, S*
Payne, C.M. (Harlequins) 1964 *I, F, S*, 1965 *I, F, S*, 1966 *W, I, F, S*
Payne, J.H. (Broughton) 1882 *S*, 1883 *W, I, S*, 1884 *I*, 1885 *W, I*
Pearce, G.S. (Northampton) 1979 *S, I, F, W*, 1981 *Arg* 1,2, 1982 *A, S*, 1983 *F, W, S, I, NZ*, 1984 *S, SA* 2, *A*, 1985 *R, F, S, I, W, NZ* 1,2, 1986 *W, S, I, F*, 1987 *I, F, W, S*, [*A, US, W*], 1988 *Fj*, 1991 [*US*]
Pears, D. (Harlequins) 1990 *Arg* 1,2, 1992 *F (R)*, *1994 F*
Pearson, A.W. (Blackheath) 1875 *I, S*, 1876 *I, S*, 1877 *S*, 1878 *S, I*
Peart, T.G.A.H. (Hartlepool R) 1964 *F, S*
Pease, F.E. (Hartlepool R) 1887 *I*
Penny, S.H. (Leicester) 1909 *A*
Penny, W.J. (United Hospitals) 1878 *I*, 1879 *S, I*
Percival, L.J. (Rugby) 1891 *I*, 1892 *I*, 1893 *S*

Periton, H.G. (Waterloo) 1925 *W*, 1926 *W, I, F, S*, 1927 *W, I, S, F*, 1928 *A, I, F, S*, 1929 *W, I, S, F*, 1930 *W, I, F, S*

Perrott, E.S. (O Cheltonians) 1875 *I*

Perry, D.G. (Bedford) 1963 *F, S, NZ* 1,2, *A* 1964 *NZ, W, I*, 1965 *W, I, F, S*, 1966 *W, I, F*

Perry, M.B. (Bath) 1997 *A* 2, *NZ* 1, *SA, NZ* 2, 1998 *W, S, I, A* 1, *NZ* 1,2, *SA* 1, *H, It, A* 2, 1999 *I, F, W, A US, C*, [*It, NZ, Tg, Fj, SA*], 2000 *I, F, W, It, S, SA* 1,2, *A, SA* 3, 2001 *W (R), F (R)*

Perry, S.V. (Cambridge U, Waterloo) 1947 *W, I*, 1948 *A, W, I, S, F*

Peters, J. (Plymouth) 1906 *S, F*, 1907 *I, S*, 1908 *W*

Phillips, C. (Birkenhead Park) 1880 *S*, 1881 *I, S*

Phillips, M.S. (Fylde) 1958 *A, I, F, S*, 1959 *W, I, F, S*, 1960 *W, I, F, S*, 1961 *W*, 1963 *W, I, F, S, NZ* 1,2, *A*, 1964 *NZ, W, I, F, S*

Pickering, A.S. (Harrogate) 1907 *I*

Pickering, R.D.A. (Bradford) 1967 *I, F, S, W*, 1968 *F, S*

Pickles, R.C.W. (Bristol) 1922 *I, F*

Pierce, R. (Liverpool) 1898 *I*, 1903 *S*

Pilkington, W.N. (Cambridge U) 1898 *S*

Pillman, C.H. (Blackheath) 1910 *W, I, F, S*, 1911 *W, F, I, S*, 1912 *W, F*, 1913 *SA, W, F, I, S*, 1914 *W, I, S*

Pillman, R.L. (Blackheath) 1914 *F*

Pinch, J. (Lancaster) 1896 *W, I*, 1897 *S*

Pinching, W.W. (Guy's Hospital) 1872 *S*

Pitman, I.J. (Oxford U) 1922 *S*

Plummer, K.C. (Bristol) 1969 *W*, 1976 *S, I, F*

Pool-Jones, R.J. (Stade Francais) 1998 *A* 1

Poole, F.O. (Oxford U) 1895 *W, I, S*

Poole, R.W. (Hartlepool R) 1896 *S*

Pope, E.B. (Blackheath) 1931 *W, S, F*

Portus, G.V. (Blackheath) 1908 *F, I*

Potter, S. (Leicester) 1998 *A* 1*(t)*

Poulton, R.W. (later Poulton-Palmer) (Oxford U, Harlequins, Liverpool) 1909 *F, I, S*, 1910 *W*, 1911 *S*, 1912 *W, I, S*, 1913 *SA, W, F, I, S*, 1914 *W, I, S, F*

Powell, D.L. (Northampton) 1966 *W, I*, 1969 *I, F, S, W*, 1971 *W, I, F, S (2[1C])*

Pratten, W.E. (Blackheath) 1927 *S, F*

Preece, I. (Coventry) 1948 *I, S, F*, 1949 *F, S*, 1950 *W, I, F, S*, 1951 *W, I, F*

Preece, P.S. (Coventry) 1972 *SA*, 1973 *NZ* 1, *W, I, F, S, NZ* 2, 1975 *I, F, W, A* 2, 1976 *W (R)*

Preedy, M. (Gloucester) 1984 *SA* 1

Prentice, F.D. (Leicester) 1928 *I, F, S*

Prescott, R.E. (Harlequins) 1937 *W, I*, 1938 *I*, 1939 *W, I, S*

Preston, N.J. (Richmond) 1979 *NZ*, 1980 *I, F*

Price, H.L. (Harlequins) 1922 *I, S*, 1923 *W, I*

Price, J. (Coventry) 1961 *I*

Price, P.L.A. (RIE Coll) 1877 *I, S*, 1878 *S*

Price, T.W. (Cheltenham) 1948 *S, F*, 1949 *W, I, F, S*

Probyn, J.A. (Wasps, Askeans) 1988 *F, W, S, I* 1,2, *A* 1, 2, *A*, 1989 *S, I, R (R), 1990 I, F, W, S, Arg* 1,2,3, 1991 *W, S, I, F, Fj, A*, [*NZ, It, F, S, A*], 1992 *S, I, F, W*, 1993 *F, W, S, I*

Prout, D.H. (Northampton) 1968 *W, I*

Pullin, J.V. (Bristol) 1966 *W*, 1968 *W, I, F, S*, 1969 *I, F, S, W, SA*, 1970 *I, W, S, F*, 1971 *W, I, F, S (2[1C]), P*, 1972 *W, I, F, S, SA*, 1973 *NZ* 1, *W, I, F, S, NZ* 2, *A*, 1974 *S, I, F, W*, 1975 *I, W (R), S, A* 1,2, 1976 *F*

Purdy, S.J. (Rugby) 1962 *S*

Pyke, J. (St Helens Recreation) 1892 *W*

Pym, J.A. (Blackheath) 1912 *W, I, S, F*

Q

Quinn, J.P. (New Brighton) 1954 *W, NZ, I, S, F*

R

Rafter, M. (Bristol) 1977 *S, F, W*, 1978 *F, W, S, I, NZ*, 1979 *S, I, F, W, NZ*, 1980 *W(R), 1981 W, Arg* 1,2

Ralston, C.W. (Richmond) 1971 *S (C), P*, 1972 *W, I, F, S, SA*, 1973 *NZ* 1, *W, I, F, S, NZ* 2, *A*, 1974 *S, I, F, W*, 1975 *I, F, W, S*

Ramsden, H.E. (Bingley) 1898 *W, S*

Ranson, J.M. (Rosslyn Park) 1963 *NZ* 1,2, *A*, 1964 *W, I, F, S*

Raphael, J.E. (OMTs) 1902 *W, I, S*, 1905 *W, S, NZ*, 1906 *W, S, F*

Ravenscroft, J. (Birkenhead Park) 1881 *I*

Ravenscroft, S.C.W. (Saracens) 1998 *A* 1, *NZ* 2*(R)*

Rawlinson, W.C.W. (Blackheath) 1876 *S*

Redfern, S. (Leicester) 1984 *I (R)*

Redman, N.C. (Bath) 1984 *A*, 1986 *S (R), 1987 I, S*, [*A, J, W*], 1988 *Fj*, 1990 *Arg* 1,2, 1991 *Fj*, [*It, US*], 1993 *NZ*, 1994 *F, W, SA* 1,2, 1997 *Arg* 1, *A* 1

Redmond, G.F. (Cambridge U) 1970 *F*

Redwood, B.W. (Bristol) 1968 *W, I*

Rees, D.L. (Sale) 1997 *A* 2, *NZ* 1, *SA, NZ* 2, 1998 *F, W, SA* 2*(R)*, 1999 *S, I, F, A*

Rees, G.W. (Nottingham) 1984 *SA* 2*(R), A*, 1986 *I, F*, 1987 *F, W, S*, [*A, J, US, W*], 1988 *S (R), I* 1,2, *A* 1,2, *Fj*, 1989 *W (R), R (R), Fj (R), 1990 Arg* 3*(R)*, 1991 *Fj*, [*US*]

Reeve, J.S.R. (Harlequins) 1929 *F*, 1930 *W, I, F, S*, 1931 *W, I, S*

Regan, M. (Liverpool) 1953 *W, I, F, S*, 1954 *W, NZ, I, S, F*, 1956 *I, S, F*

Regan, M.P. (Bristol, Bath, Leeds) 1995 *SA, WS*, 1996 *F, W, S, I, It, Arg*, 1997 *S, I, F, W, A* 1, *NZ* 2*(R)*, 1998 *F*, 2000 SA 1*(t), A (R), Arg, SA* 3*(t)*, 2001 *It (R), S (R), C* 2*(R), R*, 2003 *F* 1*(t), It (R)*

Rendall, P.A.G. (Wasps, Askeans) 1984 *W, SA* 2, 1986 *W, S*, 1987 *I, F, S*, [*A, J, W*], 1988 *F, W, S, I* 1,2, *A* 1,2, *A*, 1989 *S, I, F, W, R*, 1990 *I, F, W, S*, 1991 [*It (R)]*

Rew, H. (Blackheath) 1929 *S, F*, 1930 *F, S*, 1931 *W, S, F*, 1934 *W, I, S*

Reynolds, F.J. (O Cranleighans) 1937 *S*, 1938 *I, S*

Reynolds, S. (Richmond) 1900 *W, I, S*, 1901 *I*

Rhodes, J. (Castleford) 1896 *W, I, S*

Richards, D. (Leicester) 1986 *I, F*, 1987 *S*, [*A, J, US, W*], 1988 *F, W, S, I* 1, *A* 1,2, *Fj, A*, 1989 *S, I, F, W, R*, 1990 *Arg* 3, 1991 *W, S, I, F, Fj, A*, [*NZ, It, US*], 1992 *S (R), F, W, C*, 1993 *NZ*, 1994 *W, SA* 1, *C*, 1995 *I, F, W, S*, [*WS, A, NZ*], 1996 *F (t), S, I*

Richards, E.E. (Plymouth A) 1929 *S, F*

Richards, J. (Bradford) 1891 *W, I, S*

Richards, S.B. (Richmond) 1965 *W, I, F, S*, 1967 *A, I, F, S, W*

Richardson, J.V. (Birkenhead Park) 1928 *A, W, I, F, S*

Richardson, W.R. (Manchester) 1881 *I*

Rickards, C.H. (Gipsies) 1873 *S*

Rimmer, G. (Waterloo) 1949 *W, I*, 1950 *W*, 1951 *W, I, F*, 1952 *SA, W*, 1954 *W, NZ, I, S*

Rimmer, L.I. (Bath) 1961 *SA, W, I, F, S*

Ripley, A.G. (Rosslyn Park) 1972 *W, I, F, S, SA*, 1973 *NZ* 1, *W, I, F, S, NZ* 2, *A*, 1974 *S, I, F, W*, 1975 *I, F, S, A* 1,2, 1976 *A, W, S*

Risman, A.B.W. (Loughborough Coll) 1959 *W, I, F, S*, 1961 *SA, W, I, F*

Ritson, J.A.S. (Northern) 1910 *F, S*, 1912 *F*, 1913 *SA, W, F, I, S*

Rittson-Thomas, G.C. (Oxford U) 1951 *W, I, F*

Robbins, G.L. (Coventry) 1986 *W, S*

Robbins, P.G.D. (Oxford U, Moseley, Coventry) 1956 *W, I, S, F*, 1957 *W, I, F, S*, 1958 *W, A, I, S*, 1960 *W, I, F, S*, 1961 *SA, W*, 1962 *S*

Roberts, A.D. (Northern) 1911 *W, F, I, S*, 1912 *I, S, F*, 1914 *I*

Roberts, E.W. (RNE Coll) 1901 *W, I,* 1905 *NZ,* 1906 *W, I,* 1907 *S*
Roberts, G.D. (Harlequins) 1907 *S,* 1908 *F, W*
Roberts, J. (Sale) 1960 *W, I, F, S,* 1961 *SA, W, I, F, S,* 1962 *W, I, F, S,* 1963 *W, I, F, S,* 1964 *NZ*
Roberts, R.S. (Coventry) 1932 *I*
Roberts, S. (Swinton) 1887 *W, I*
Roberts, V.G. (Penryn, Harlequins) 1947 *F,* 1949 *W, I, F, S,* 1950 *I, F, S,* 1951 *W, I, F, S,* 1956 *W, I, S, F*
Robertshaw, A.R. (Bradford) 1886 *W, I, S,* 1887 *W, S*
Robinson, A. (Blackheath) 1889 *M,* 1890 *W, S, I*
Robinson, E.T. (Coventry) 1954 *S,* 1961 *I, F, S*
Robinson, G.C. (Percy Park) 1897 *I, S,* 1898 *I,* 1899 *W,* 1900 *I, S,* 1901 *I, S*
Robinson, J. (Sale) 2001 *It (R), S (R), F (R), I, A, R, SA,* 2002 *S, I, F, It, NZ, A, SA,* 2003 *F* 1, *W* 1, *S, I, NZ, A*
Robinson, J.J. (Headingley) 1893 *S,* 1902 *W, I, S*
Robinson, R.A. (Bath) 1988 *A* 2, *Fj, A,* 1989 *S, I, F, W,* 1995 *SA*
Robson, A. (Northern) 1924 *W, I, F, S,* 1926 *W*
Robson, M. (Oxford U) 1930 *W, I, F, S*
Rodber, T.A.K. (Army, Northampton) 1992 *S, I,* 1993 *NZ,* 1994 *I, F, W, SA* 1,2, *R, C,* 1995 *I, F, W, S,* [*Arg, It, WS (R), A, NZ, F*], *SA, WS,* 1996 *W, S (R), I (t), It, Arg,* 1997 *S, I, F, W, A* 1, 1998 *H (R), It (R), A* 2, *SA* 2, 1999 *S, I, F, W, A, US (R),* [*NZ (R), Fj (R)*]
Rogers, D.P. (Bedford) 1961 *I, F, S,* 1962 *W, I, F,* 1963 *W, I, F, S, NZ* 1,2, *A,* 1964 *NZ, W, I, F, S,* 1965 *W, I, F, S,* 1966 *W, I, F, S,* 1967 *A, S, W, NZ,* 1969 *I, F, S, W*
Rogers, J.H. (Moseley) 1890 *W, S, I,* 1891 *S*
Rogers, W.L.Y. (Blackheath) 1905 *W, I*
Rollitt, D.M. (Bristol) 1967 *I, F, S, W,* 1969 *I, F, S, W,* 1975 *S, A* 1,2
Roncoroni, A.D.S. (West Herts, Richmond) 1933 *W, I, S*
Rose, W.M.H. (Cambridge U, Coventry, Harlequins) 1981 *I, F,* 1982 *A, S, I,* 1987 *I, F, W, S,* [*A*]
Rossborough, P.A. (Coventry) 1971 *W,* 1973 *NZ* 2, *A,* 1974 *S, I,* 1975 *I, F*
Rosser, D.W.A. (Wasps) 1965 *W, I, F, S,* 1966 *W*
Rotherham, Alan (Richmond) 1883 *W, S,* 1884 *W, S,* 1885 *W, I,* 1886 *W, I, S,* 1887 *W, I, S*
Rotherham, Arthur (Richmond) 1898 *S, W,* 1899 *W, I, S*
Roughley, D. (Liverpool) 1973 *A,* 1974 *S, I*
Rowell, R.E. (Leicester) 1964 *W,* 1965 *W*
Rowley, A.J. (Coventry) 1932 *SA*
Rowley, H.C. (Manchester) 1879 *S, I,* 1880 *I, S,* 1881 *I, W, S,* 1882 *I, S*
Rowntree, G.C. (Leicester) 1995 *S (t),* [*It, WS*], *WS,* 1996 *F, W, S, I, It, Arg,* 1997 *S, I, F, W, A* 1, 1998 *A* 1, *NZ* 1, 2, *SA* 1, *H (R), It (R), 1999 US, C,* [*It (R), Tg, Fj (R)*], *2001 C* 1,2, *US, I (R), A, R, SA,* 2002 *S, I, F, W, It,* 2003 *F* 1 *(R), W* 1, *It, S, I, NZ*
Royds, P.M.R. (Blackheath) 1898 *S, W,* 1899 *W*
Royle, A.V. (Broughton R) 1889 *M*
Rudd, E.L. (Liverpool) 1965 *W, I, S,* 1966 *W, I, S*
Russell, R.F. (Leicester) 1905 *NZ*
Rutherford, D. (Percy Park, Gloucester) 1960 *W, I, F, S,* 1961 *SA,* 1965 *W, I, F, S,* 1966 *W, I, F, S,* 1967 *NZ*
Ryalls, H.J. (New Brighton) 1885 *W, I*
Ryan, D. (Wasps, Newcastle) 1990 *Arg* 1,2, 1992 *C,* 1998 *S*
Ryan, P.H. (Richmond) 1955 *W, I*

S

Sadler, E.H. (Army) 1933 *I, S*
Sagar, J.W. (Cambridge U) 1901 *W, I*
Salmon, J.L.B. (Harlequins) 1985 *NZ* 1,2, 1986 *W, S,* 1987 *I, F, W, S,* [*A, J, US, W*]
Sample, C.H. (Cambridge U) 1884 *I,* 1885 *I,* 1886 *S*
Sampson, P.C. (Wasps) 1998 *SA* 1, 2001 *C* 1,2
Sanders, D.L. (Harlequins) 1954 *W, NZ, I, S, F,* 1956 *W, I, S, F*
Sanders, F.W. (Plymouth A) 1923 *I, S, F*
Sanderson, A. (Sale) 2001 *R (R),* 2002 *Arg,* 2003 *It(t + R)*
Sanderson, P.H. (Sale, Harlequins) 1998 *NZ* 1,2, *SA* 1, 2001 *C* 1*(R)*,2*(R), US (t+R)*
Sandford, J.R.P. (Marlborough N) 1906 *I*
Sangwin, R.D. (Hull and E Riding) 1964 *NZ, W*
Sargent, G.A.F. (Gloucester) 1981 *I (R)*
Savage, K.F. (Northampton) 1966 *W, I, F, S,* 1967 *A, I, F, S, W, NZ,* 1968 *W, F, S*
Sawyer, C.M. (Broughton) 1880 *S,* 1881 *I*
Saxby, L.E. (Gloucester) 1932 *SA, W*
Schofield, J.W. (Manchester) 1880 *I*
Scholfield, J.A. (Preston Grasshoppers) 1911 *W*
Schwarz, R.O. (Richmond) 1899 *S,* 1901 *W, I*
Scorfield, E.S. (Percy Park) 1910 *F*
Scott, C.T. (Blackheath) 1900 *W, I,* 1901 *W, I*
Scott, E.K. (St Mary's Hospital, Redruth) 1947 *W,* 1948 *A, W, I, S*
Scott, F.S. (Bristol) 1907 *W*
Scott, H. (Manchester) 1955 *F*
Scott, J.P. (Rosslyn Park, Cardiff) 1978 *F, W, S, I, NZ,* 1979 *S (R), I, F, W, NZ,* 1980 *I, F, W, S,* 1981 *W, S, I, F, Arg* 1,2, 1982 *I, F, W,* 1983 *F, W, S, I, NZ,* 1984 *S, I, F, W, SA* 1,2
Scott, J.S.M. (Oxford U) 1958 *F*
Scott, M.T. (Cambridge U) 1887 *I,* 1890 *S, I*
Scott, W.M. (Cambridge U) 1889 *M*
Seddon, R.L. (Broughton R) 1887 *W, I, S*
Sellar, K.A. (United Services, RN) 1927 *W, I, S,* 1928 *A, W, I, F*
Sever, H.S. (Sale) 1936 *NZ, W, I, S,* 1937 *W, I, S,* 1938 *W, I, S*
Shackleton, I.R. (Cambridge U) 1969 *SA,* 1970 *I, W, S*
Sharp, R.A.W. (Oxford U, Wasps, Redruth) 1960 *W, I, F, S,* 1961 *I, F,* 1962 *W, I, F,* 1963 *W, I, F, S,* 1967 *A*
Shaw, C.H. (Moseley) 1906 *S, SA,* 1907 *F, W, I, S*
Shaw, F. (Cleckheaton) 1898 *I*
Shaw, J.F. (RNE Coll) 1898 *S, W*
Shaw, S.D. (Bristol, Wasps) 1996 *It, Arg,* 1997 *S, I, F, W, A* 1, *SA (R), 2000 I, F, W, It, S, SA* 1*(R)*,2*(R)*, 2001 *C* 1*(R)*, 2, *US, I,* 2003 *It (R)*
Sheasby, C.M.A. (Wasps) 1996 *It, Arg,* 1997 *W (R), Arg* 1*(R)*,2*(R), SA (R), NZ* 2*(t)*
Sheppard, A. (Bristol) 1981 *W (R), 1985 W*
Sherrard, C.W. (Blackheath) 1871 *S,* 1872 *S*
Sherriff, G.A. (Saracens) 1966 *S,* 1967 *A, NZ*
Shewring, H.E. (Bristol) 1905 *I, NZ,* 1906 *W, S, F, SA,* 1907 *F, W, I, S*
Shooter, J.H. (Morley) 1899 *I, S,* 1900 *I, S*
Shuttleworth, D.W. (Headingley) 1951 *S,* 1953 *S*
Sibree, H.J.H. (Harlequins) 1908 *F,* 1909 *I, S*
Silk, N. (Harlequins) 1965 *W, I, F, S*
Simms, K.G. (Cambridge U, Liverpool, Wasps) 1985 *R, F, S, I, W,* 1986 *I, F,* 1987 *I, F, W,* [*A, J, W*], 1988 *F, W*
Simpson, C.P. (Harlequins) 1965 *W*
Simpson, P.D. (Bath) 1983 *NZ,* 1984 *S,* 1987 *I*
Simpson, T. (Rockcliff) 1902 *S,* 1903 *W, I, S,* 1904 *I, S,* 1905 *I, S,* 1906 *S, SA,* 1909 *F*
Simpson-Daniel, J. (Gloucester) 2002 *NZ, A,* 2003 *W* 1*(t + R), It*
Sims, D. (Gloucester) 1998 *NZ* 1*(R)*,2, *SA* 1
Skinner, M.G. (Harlequins) 1988 *F, W, S, I* 1,2, 1989 *Fj,* 1990 *I, F, W, S, Arg* 1,2, 1991 *Fj (R),* [*US, F, S, A*], 1992 *S, I, F, W*
Sladen, G.M. (United Services, RN) 1929 *W, I, S*

Sleightholme, J.M. (Bath) 1996 *F, W, S, I, It, Arg*, 1997 *S, I, F, W, Arg* 1,2
Slemen, M.A.C. (Liverpool) 1976 *I, F*, 1977 *S, I, F, W*, 1978 *F, W, S, I, NZ*, 1979 *S, I, F, W, NZ*, 1980 *I, F, W, S*, 1981 *W, S, I, F*, 1982 *A, S, I, F, W*, 1983 *NZ*, 1984 *S*
Slocock, L.A.N. (Liverpool) 1907 *F, W, I, S*, 1908 *F, W, I, S*
Slow, C.F. (Leicester) 1934 *S*
Small, H.D. (Oxford U) 1950 *W, I, F, S*
Smallwood, A.M. (Leicester) 1920 *F, I*, 1921 *W, I, S, F*, 1922 *I, S*, 1923 *W, I, S, F*, 1925 *I, S*
Smart, C.E. (Newport) 1979 *F, W, NZ*, 1981 *S, I, F, Arg* 1,2, 1982 *A, S, I, F, W*, 1983 *F, W, S, I*
Smart, S.E.J. (Gloucester) 1913 *SA, W, F, I, S*, 1914 *W, I, S, F*, 1920 *W, I, S*
Smeddle, R.W. (Cambridge U) 1929 *W, I, S*, 1931 *F*
Smith, C.C. (Gloucester) 1901 *W*
Smith, D.F. (Richmond) 1910 *W, I*
Smith, J.V. (Cambridge U, Rosslyn Park) 1950 *W, I, F, S*
Smith, K. (Roundhay) 1974 *F, W*, 1975 *W, S*
Smith, M.J.K. (Oxford U) 1956 *W*
Smith, O.J. (Leicester) 2003 *It (R)*
Smith, S.J. (Sale) 1973 *I, F, S, A*, 1974 *I, F*, 1975 *W (R), 1976 F*, 1977 *F (R), 1979 NZ*, 1980 *I, F, W, S*, 1981 *W, S, I, F, Arg* 1,2, 1982 *A, S, I, F, W*, 1983 *F, W, S*
Smith, S.R. (Richmond) 1959 *W, F, S*, 1964 *F, S*
Smith, S.T. (Wasps) 1985 *R, F, S, I, W, NZ* 1,2, 1986 *W, S*
Smith, T.H. (Northampton) 1951 *W*
Soane, F. (Bath) 1893 *S*, 1894 *W, I, S*
Sobey, W.H. (O Millhillians) 1930 *W, F, S*, 1932 *SA, W*
Solomon, B. (Redruth) 1910 *W*
Sparks, R.H.W. (Plymouth A) 1928 *I, F, S*, 1929 *W, I, S*, 1931 *I, S, F*
Speed, H. (Castleford) 1894 *W, I, S*, 1896 *S*
Spence, F.W. (Birkenhead Park) 1890 *I*
Spencer, J. (Harlequins) 1966 *W*
Spencer, J.S. (Cambridge U, Headingley) 1969 *I, F, S, W, SA*, 1970 *I, W, S, F*, 1971 *W, I, S (2[1C]), P*
Spong, R.S. (O Millhillians) 1929 *F*, 1930 *W, I, F, S*, 1931 *F*, 1932 *SA, W*
Spooner, R.H. (Liverpool) 1903 *W*
Springman, H.H. (Liverpool) 1879 *S*, 1887 *S*
Spurling, A. (Blackheath) 1882 *I*
Spurling, N. (Blackheath) 1886 *I, S*, 1887 *W*
Squires, P.J. (Harrogate) 1973 *F, S, NZ* 2, *A*, 1974 *S, I, F, W*, 1975 *I, F, W, S, A* 1,2, 1976 *A, W*, 1977 *S, I, F, W*, 1978 *F, W, S, I, NZ*, 1979 *S, I, F, W*
Stafford R.C. (Bedford) 1912 *W, I, S, F*
Stafford, W.F.H. (RE) 1874 *S*
Stanbury, E. (Plymouth A) 1926 *W, I, S*, 1927 *W, I, S, F*, 1928 *A, W, I, F, S*, 1929 *W, I, S, F*
Standing, G. (Blackheath) 1883 *W, I*
Stanger-Leathes, C.F. (Northern) 1905 *I*
Stark, K.J. (O Alleynians) 1927 *W, I, S, F*, 1928 *A, W, I, F, S*
Starks, A. (Castleford) 1896 *W, I*
Starmer-Smith, N.C. (Harlequins) 1969 *SA*, 1970 *I, W, S, F*, 1971 *S (C), P*
Start, S.P. (United Services, RN) 1907 *S*
Steeds, J.H. (Saracens) 1949 *F, S*, 1950 *I, F, S*
Steele-Bodger, M.R. (Cambridge U) 1947 *W, I, S, F*, 1948 *A, W, I, S, F*
Steinthal, F.E. (Ilkley) 1913 *W, F*
Stephenson, M. (Newcastle) 2001 *C* 1,2, *US*
Stevens, C.B. (Penzance-Newlyn, Harlequins) 1969 *SA*, 1970 *I, W, S*, 1971 *P*, 1972 *W, I, F, S, SA*, 1973 *NZ* 1, *W, I, F, S, NZ* 2, *A*, 1974 *S, I, F, W*, 1975 *I, F, W, S*
Still, E.R. (Oxford U, Ravenscourt P) 1873 *S*
Stimpson, T.R.G. (Newcastle, Leicester) 1996 *It*, 1997 *S, I, F, W, A* 1, *NZ* 2*(t+R)*, 1998 *A* 1, *NZ* 1,2*(R), SA* 1*(R)*, 1999 *US (R), C (R), 2000 SA* 1, 2001 *C* 1*(t)*,2*(R)*, 2002 *W (R), Arg, SA (R)*
Stirling, R.V. (Leicester, RAF, Wasps) 1951 *W, I, F, S*, 1952 *SA, W, S, I, F*, 1953 *W, I, F, S*, 1954 *W, NZ, I, S, F*
Stoddart, A.E. (Blackheath) 1885 *W, I*, 1886 *W, I, S*, 1889 *M*, 1890 *W, I*, 1893 *W, S*
Stoddart, W.B. (Liverpool) 1897 *W, I, S*
Stokes, F. (Blackheath) 1871 *S*, 1872 *S*, 1873 *S*
Stokes, L. (Blackheath) 1875 *I*, 1876 *S*, 1877 *I, S*, 1878 *S*, 1879 *S, I*, 1880 *I, S*, 1881 *I, W, S*
Stone, F.le S. (Blackheath) 1914 *F*
Stoop, A.D. (Harlequins) 1905 *S*, 1906 *S, F, SA*, 1907 *F, W*, 1910 *W, I, S*, 1911 *W, F, I, S*, 1912 *W, S*
Stoop, F.M. (Harlequins) 1910 *S*, 1911 *F, I*, 1913 *SA*
Stout, F.M. (Richmond) 1897 *W, I*, 1898 *I, S, W*, 1899 *I, S*, 1903 *S*, 1904 *W, I, S*, 1905 *W, I, S*
Stout, P.W. (Richmond) 1898 *S, W*, 1899 *W, I, S*
Stringer, N.C. (Wasps) 1982 *A (R), 1983 NZ (R), 1984 SA* 1*(R), A*, 1985 *R*
Strong, E.L. (Oxford U) 1884 *W, I, S*
Sturnham B. (Saracens) 1998 *A* 1, *NZ* 1*(t)*,2*(t)*
Summerscales, G.E. (Durham City) 1905 *NZ*
Sutcliffe, J.W. (Heckmondwike) 1889 *M*
Swarbrick, D.W. (Oxford U) 1947 *W, I, F*, 1948 *A, W*, 1949 *I*
Swayne, D.H. (Oxford U) 1931 *W*
Swayne, J.W.R. (Bridgwater) 1929 *W*
Swift, A.H. (Swansea) 1981 *Arg* 1,2, 1983 *F, W, S*, 1984 *SA* 2
Syddall, J.P. (Waterloo) 1982 *I*, 1984 *A*
Sykes, A.R.V. (Blackheath) 1914 *F*
Sykes, F.D. (Northampton) 1955 *F, S*, 1963 *NZ* 2, *A*
Sykes, P.W. (Wasps) 1948 *F*, 1952 *S, I, F*, 1953 *W, I, F*
Syrett, R.E. (Wasps) 1958 *W, A, I, F*, 1960 *W, I, F, S*, 1962 *W, I, F*

T

Tallent, J.A. (Cambridge U, Blackheath) 1931 *S, F*, 1932 *SA, W*, 1935 *I*
Tanner, C.C. (Cambridge U, Gloucester) 1930 *S*, 1932 *SA, W, I, S*
Tarr, F.N. (Leicester) 1909 *A, W, F*, 1913 *S*
Tatham, W.M. (Oxford U) 1882 *S*, 1883 *W, I, S*, 1884 *W, I, S*
Taylor, A.S. (Blackheath) 1883 *W, I*, 1886 *W, I*
Taylor, E.W. (Rockcliff) 1892 *I*, 1893 *I*, 1894 *W, I, S*, 1895 *W, I, S*, 1896 *W, I*, 1897 *W, I, S*, 1899 *I*
Taylor, F. (Leicester) 1920 *F, I*
Taylor, F.M. (Leicester) 1914 *W*
Taylor, H.H. (Blackheath) 1879 *S*, 1880 *S*, 1881 *I, W*, 1882 *S*
Taylor, J.T. (W Hartlepool) 1897 *I*, 1899 *I*, 1900 *I*, 1901 *W, I*, 1902 *W, I, S*, 1903 *W, I*, 1905 *S*
Taylor, P.J. (Northampton) 1955 *W, I*, 1962 *W, I, F, S*
Taylor, R.B. (Northampton) 1966 *W*, 1967 *I, F, S, W, NZ*, 1969 *F, S, W, SA*, 1970 *I, W, S, F*, 1971 *S (2[1C])*
Taylor, W.J. (Blackheath) 1928 *A, W, I, F, S*
Teague, M.C. (Gloucester, Moseley) 1985 *F (R), NZ* 1, 2, 1989 *S, I, F, W, R*, 1990 *F, W, S*, 1991 *W, S, I, F, Fj, A*, [*NZ, It, F, S, A*], 1992 *SA*, 1993 *F, W, S, I*
Teden, D.E. (Richmond) 1939 *W, I, S*
Teggin, A. (Broughton R) 1884 *I*, 1885 *W*, 1886 *I, S*, 1887 *I, S*
Tetley, T.S. (Bradford) 1876 *S*
Thomas, C. (Barnstaple) 1895 *W, I, S*, 1899 *I*
Thompson, P.H. (Headingley, Waterloo) 1956 *W, I, S, F*, 1957 *W, I, F, S*, 1958 *W, A, I, F, S*, 1959 *W, I, F, S*

Thompson, S. (Northampton) 2002 *S, I, F, W, It, Arg, NZ, A, SA,* 2003 *F* 1, *W* 1, *It, S, I, NZ, A*

Thomson, G.T. (Halifax) 1878 *S,* 1882 *I, S,* 1883 *W, I, S,* 1884 *I, S,* 1885 *I*

Thomson, W.B. (Blackheath) 1892 *W,* 1895 *W, I, S*

Thorne, J.D. (Bristol) 1963 *W, I, F*

Tindall, M.J. (Bath) 2000 *I, F, W, It, S, SA* 1,2, *A Arg, SA* 3, 2001 *W (R), R, SA (R), 2002 S, I, F, W, It, NZ, A, SA,* 2003 *It, S, I, NZ, A*

Tindall, V.R. (Liverpool U) 1951 *W, I, F, S*

Tobin, F. (Liverpool) 1871 *S*

Todd, A.F. (Blackheath) 1900 *I, S*

Todd, R. (Manchester) 1877 *S*

Toft, H.B. (Waterloo) 1936 *S,* 1937 *W, I, S,* 1938 *W, I, S,* 1939 *W, I, S*

Toothill, J.T. (Bradford) 1890 *S, I,* 1891 *W, I,* 1892 *W, I, S,* 1893 *W, I, S,* 1894 *W, I*

Tosswill, L.R. (Exeter) 1902 *W, I, S*

Touzel, C.J.C. (Liverpool) 1877 *I, S*

Towell, A.C. (Bedford) 1948 *F,* 1951 *S*

Travers, B.H. (Harlequins) 1947 *W, I,* 1948 *A, W,* 1949 *F, S*

Treadwell, W.T. (Wasps) 1966 *I, F, S*

Trick, D.M. (Bath) 1983 *I,* 1984 *SA* 1

Tristram, H.B. (Oxford U) 1883 *S,* 1884 *W, S,* 1885 *W,* 1887 *S*

Troop, C.L. (Aldershot S) 1933 *I, S*

Tucker, J.S. (Bristol) 1922 *W,* 1925 *NZ, W, I, S, F,* 1926 *W, I, F, S,* 1927 *W, I, S, F,* 1928 *A, W, I, F, S,* 1929 *W, I, F,* 1930 *W, I, F, S,* 1931 *W*

Tucker, W.E. (Blackheath) 1894 *W, I,* 1895 *W, I, S*

Tucker, W.E. (Blackheath) 1926 *I,* 1930 *W, I*

Turner, D.P. (Richmond) 1871 *S,* 1872 *S,* 1873 *S,* 1874 *S,* 1875 *I, S*

Turner, E.B. (St George's Hospital) 1876 *I,* 1877 *I,* 1878 *I*

Turner, G.R. (St George's Hospital) 1876 *S*

Turner, H.J.C. (Manchester) 1871 *S*

Turner, M.F. (Blackheath) 1948 *S, F*

Turquand-Young, D. (Richmond) 1928 *A, W,* 1929 *I, S, F*

Twynam, H.T. (Richmond) 1879 *I,* 1880 *I,* 1881 *W,* 1882 *I,* 1883 *I,* 1884 *W, I, S*

U

Ubogu, V.E. (Bath) 1992 *C, SA,* 1993 *NZ,* 1994 *S, I, F, W, SA* 1,2, *R, C,* 1995 *I, F, W, S,* [*Arg, WS, A, NZ, F*], *SA,* 1999 *F (R), W (R), A (R)*

Underwood, A.M. (Exeter) 1962 *W, I, F, S,* 1964 *I*

Underwood, R. (Leicester, RAF) 1984 *I, F, W, A,* 1985 *R, F, S, I, W,* 1986 *W, I, F,* 1987 *I, F, W, S,* [*A, J, W*], 1988 *F, W, S, I* 1,2, *A* 1,2, *Fj, A,* 1989 *S, I, F, W, R, Fj,* 1990 *I, F, W, S, Arg* 3, 1991 *W, S, I, F, Fj, A,* [*NZ, It, US, F, S, A*], 1992 *S, I, F, W, SA,* 1993 *F, W, S, I, NZ,* 1994 *S, I, F, W, SA* 1,2, *R, C,* 1995 *I, F, W, S,* [*Arg, It, WS, A, NZ, F*], *SA, WS,* 1996 *F, W, S, I*

Underwood, T. (Leicester, Newcastle) 1992 *C, SA,* 1993 *S, I, NZ,* 1994 *S, I, W, SA* 1,2, *R, C,* 1995 *I, F, W, S,* [*Arg, It, A, NZ*], 1996 *Arg,* 1997 *S, I, F, W,* 1998 *A* 2, *SA* 2

Unwin, E.J. (Rosslyn Park, Army) 1937 *S,* 1938 *W, I, S*

Unwin, G.T. (Blackheath) 1898 *S*

Uren, R. (Waterloo) 1948 *I, S, F,* 1950 *I*

Uttley, R.M. (Gosforth) 1973 *I, F, S, NZ* 2, *A,* 1974 *I, F, W,* 1975 *F, W, S, A* 1,2, 1977 *S, I, F, W,* 1978 *NZ* 1979 *S,* 1980 *I, F, W, S*

V

Valentine J. (Swinton) 1890 *W,* 1896 *W, I, S*

Vanderspar, C.H.R. (Richmond) 1873 *S*

Van Ryneveld, C.B. (Oxford U) 1949 *W, I, F, S*

Varley, H. (Liversedge) 1892 *S*

Vassall, H. (Blackheath) 1881 *W, S,* 1882 *I, S,* 1883 *W*

Vassall, H.H. (Blackheath) 1908 *I*

Vaughan, D.B. (Headingley) 1948 *A, W, I, S,* 1949 *I, F, S,* 1950 *W*

Vaughan-Jones, A. (Army) 1932 *I, S,* 1933 *W*

Verelst, C.L. (Liverpool) 1876 I, 1878 *I*

Vernon, G.F. (Blackheath) 1878 *S, I,* 1880 *I, S,* 1881 *I*

Vickery, G. (Aberavon) 1905 *I*

Vickery, P.J. (Gloucester) 1998 *W, A* 1, *NZ* 1,2, *SA* 1, 1999 *US, C,* [*It, NZ, Tg, SA*], 2000 *I, F, W, S, A, Arg (R), SA* 3*(R),* 2001 *W, It, S, A, SA,* 2002 *I, F, Arg, NZ, A, SA,* 2003 *NZ (R), A*

Vivyan, E.J. (Devonport A) 1901 *W,* 1904 *W, I, S*

Voyce, A.T. (Gloucester) 1920 *I, S,* 1921 *W, I, S, F,* 1922 *W, I, F, S,* 1923 *W, I, S, F,* 1924 *W, I, F, S,* 1925 *NZ, W, I, S, F,* 1926 *W, I, F, S*

Voyce, T. (Bath) 2001 *US (R)*

W

Wackett, J.A.S. (Rosslyn Park) 1959 *W, I*

Wade, C.G. (Richmond) 1883 *W, I, S,* 1884 *W, S,* 1885 *W,* 1886 *W, I*

Wade, M.R. (Cambridge U) 1962 *W, I, F*

Wakefield, W.W. (Harlequins) 1920 *W, F, I, S,* 1921 *W, I, S, F,* 1922 *W, I, F, S,* 1923 *W, I, S, F,* 1924 *W, I, F, S,* 1925 *NZ, W, I, S, F,* 1926 *W, I, F, S,* 1927 *S, F*

Walder, D.J.H. (Newcastle) 2001 *C* 1,2, *US*

Walker, G.A. (Blackheath) 1939 *W, I*

Walker, H.W. (Coventry) 1947 *W, I, S, F,* 1948 *A, W, I, S, F*

Walker, R. (Manchester) 1874 *S,* 1875 *I,* 1876 *S,* 1879 *S,* 1880 *S*

Wallens, J.N.S. (Waterloo) 1927 *F*

Walton, E.J. (Castleford) 1901 *W, I,* 1902 *I, S*

Walton, W. (Castleford) 1894 *S*

Ward, G. (Leicester) 1913 *W, F, S,* 1914 *W, I, S*

Ward, H. (Bradford) 1895 *W*

Ward, J.I. (Richmond) 1881 *I,* 1882 *I*

Ward, J.W. (Castleford) 1896 *W, I, S*

Wardlow, C.S. (Northampton) 1969 *SA (R), 1971 W, I, F, S (2[1C])*

Warfield, P.J. (Rosslyn Park, Durham U) 1973 *NZ* 1, *W, I,* 1975 *I, F, S*

Warr, A.L. (Oxford U) 1934 *W, I*

Waters, F.H.H. (Wasps) 2001 *US*

Watkins, J.A. (Gloucester) 1972 *SA,* 1973 *NZ* 1, *W, NZ* 2, *A,* 1975 *F, W*

Watkins, J K (United Services, RN) 1939 *W, I, S*

Watson, F.B. (United Services, RN) 1908 *S,* 1909 *S*

Watson, J.H.D. (Blackheath) 1914 *W, S, F*

Watt, D.E.J. (Bristol) 1967 *I, F, S, W*

Webb, C.S.H. (Devonport Services, RN) 1932 *SA, W, I, S,* 1933 *W, I, S,* 1935 *S,* 1936 *NZ, W, I, S*

Webb, J.M. (Bristol, Bath) 1987 [*A (R), J, US, W*], 1988 *F, W, S, I* 1,2, *A* 1,2, *A,* 1989 *S, I, F, W,* 1991 *Fj, A,* [*NZ, It, F, S, A*], 1992 *S, I, F, W, C, SA,* 1993 *F, W, S, I*

Webb, J.W.G. (Northampton) 1926 *F, S,* 1929 *S*

Webb, R.E. (Coventry) 1967 *S, W, NZ,* 1968 *I, F, S,* 1969 *I, F, S, W,* 1972 *I, F*

Webb, St.L.H. (Bedford) 1959 *W, I, F, S*

Webster, J.G. (Moseley) 1972 *W, I, SA,* 1973 *NZ* 1, *W, NZ* 2, 1974 *S, W,* 1975 *I, F, W*

Wedge, T.G. (St Ives) 1907 *F,* 1909 *W*

Weighill, R.H.G. (RAF, Harlequins) 1947 *S, F,* 1948 *S, F*

Wells, C.M. (Cambridge U, Harlequins) 1893 *S,* 1894 *W, S,* 1896 *S,* 1897 *W, S*

West, B.R. (Loughborough Colls, Northampton) 1968 *W, I, F, S*, 1969 *SA*, 1970 *I, W, S*

West, D.E. (Leicester) 1998 *F (R), S (R)*, 2000 *Arg (R)*, 2001 *W, It, S, F (t), C* 1,2, *US, I (R), A, SA*, 2002 *F (R), W (R), It (R)*

West, R. (Gloucester) 1995 [*WS*]

Weston, H.T.F. (Northampton) 1901 *S*

Weston, L.E. (W of Scotland) 1972 *F, S*

Weston, M.P. (Richmond, Durham City) 1960 *W, I, F, S*, 1961 *SA, W, I, F, S*, 1962 *W, I, F*, 1963 *W, I, F, S, NZ* 1,2, *A*, 1964 *NZ, W, I, F, S*, 1965 *F, S*, 1966 *S*, 1968 *F, S*

Weston, W.H. (Northampton) 1933 *I, S*, 1934 *I, S*, 1935 *W, I, S*, 1936 *NZ, W, S*, 1937 *W, I, S*, 1938 *W, I, S*

Wheatley, A.A. (Coventry) 1937 *W, I, S*, 1938 *W, S*

Wheatley, H.F. (Coventry) 1936 *I*, 1937 *S*, 1938 *W, S*, 1939 *W, I, S*

Wheeler, P.J. (Leicester) 1975 *F, W*, 1976 *A, W, S, I*, 1977 *S, I, F, W*, 1978 *F, W, S, I, NZ*, 1979 *S, I, F, W, NZ*, 1980 *I, F, W, S*, 1981 *W, S, I, F*, 1982 *A, S, I, F, W*, 1983 *F, S, I, NZ*, 1984 *S, I, F, W*

White, C. (Gosforth) 1983 *NZ*, 1984 *S, I, F*

White, D.F. (Northampton) 1947 *W, I, S*, 1948 *I, F*, 1951 *S*, 1952 *SA, W, S, I, F*, 1953 *W, I, S*

White, J. (Saracens, Bristol) 2000 *SA* 1,2, *Arg, SA* 3, 2001 *F, C* 1,2, *US, I, R (R)*, 2002 *S, W, It*, 2003 *F* 1 *(R)*

White-Cooper, S. (Harlequins) 2001 *C* 2, *US*

Whiteley, E.C.P. (O Alleynians) 1931 *S, F*

Whiteley, W. (Bramley) 1896 *W*

Whitely, H. (Northern) 1929 *W*

Wightman, B.J. (Moseley, Coventry) 1959 *W*, 1963 *W, I, NZ* 2, *A*

Wigglesworth, H.J. (Thornes) 1884 *I*

Wilkins, D.T. (United Services, RN, Roundhay) 1951 *W, I, F, S*, 1952 *SA, W, S, I, F*, 1953 *W, I, F, S*

Wilkinson, E. (Bradford) 1886 *W, I, S*, 1887 *W, S*

Wilkinson, H. (Halifax) 1929 *W, I, S*, 1930 *F*

Wilkinson, H.J. (Halifax) 1889 *M*

Wilkinson, J.P. (Newcastle) 1998 *I (R), A* 1, *NZ* 1, 1999 *S, I, F, W, A, US, C*, [*It, NZ, Fj, SA (R)*], 2000 *I, F, W, It, S, SA* 2, *A, Arg, SA* 3, 2001 *W, It, S, F, I, A, SA*, 2002 *S, I, F, W, It, NZ, A, SA*, 2003 *F* 1, *W* 1, *It, S, I, NZ, A*

Wilkinson, P. (Law Club) 1872 *S*

Wilkinson, R.M. (Bedford) 1975 *A* 2, 1976 *A, W, S, I, F*

Willcocks, T.J. (Plymouth) 1902 *W*

Willcox, J.G. (Oxford U, Harlequins) 1961 *I, F, S*, 1962 *W, I, F, S*, 1963 *W, I, F, S*, 1964 *NZ, W, I, F, S*

William-Powlett, P.B.R.W. (United Services, RN) 1922 *S*

Williams, C.G. (Gloucester, RAF) 1976 *F*

Williams, C.S. (Manchester) 1910 *F*

Williams, J.E. (O Millhillians, Sale) 1954 *F*, 1955 *W, I, F, S*, 1956 *I, S, F*, 1965 *W*

Williams, J.M. (Penzance-Newlyn) 1951 *I, S*

Williams, P.N. (Orrell) 1987 *S*, [*A, J, W*]

Williams, S.G. (Devonport A) 1902 *W, I, S*, 1903 *I, S*, 1907 *I, S*

Williams, S.H. (Newport) 1911 *W, F, I, S*

Williamson, R.H. (Oxford U) 1908 *W, I, S*, 1909 *A, F*

Wilson, A.J. (Camborne S of M) 1909 *I*

Wilson, C.E. (Blackheath) 1898 *I*

Wilson, C.P. (Cambridge U, Marlborough N) 1881 *W*

Wilson, D.S. (Met Police, Harlequins) 1953 *F*, 1954 *W, NZ, I, S, F*, 1955 *F, S*

Wilson, G.S. (Tyldesley) 1929 *W, I*

Wilson, K.J. (Gloucester) 1963 *F*

Wilson, R.P. (Liverpool OB) 1891 *W, I, S*

Wilson, W.C. (Richmond) 1907 *I, S*

Winn, C.E. (Rosslyn Park) 1952 *SA, W, S, I, F*, 1954 *W, S, F*

Winterbottom, P.J. (Headingley, Harlequins) 1982 *A, S, I, F, W*, 1983 *F, W, S, I, NZ*, 1984 *S, F, W, SA* 1,2, 1986 *W, S, I, F*, 1987 *I, F, W*, [*A, J, US, W*], 1988 *F, W, S*, 1989 *R, Fj*, 1990 *I, F, W, S, Arg* 1,2,3, 1991 *W, S, I, F, A*, [*NZ, It, F, S, A*], 1992 *S, I, F, W, C, SA*, 1993 *F, W, S, I*

Wintle, T.C. (Northampton) 1966 *S*, 1969 *I, F, S, W*

Wodehouse, N.A. (United Services, RN) 1910 *F*, 1911 *W, F, I, S*, 1912 *W, I, S, F*, 1913 *SA, W, F, I, S*

Wood, A. (Halifax) 1884 *I*

Wood, A.E. (Gloucester, Cheltenham) 1908 *F, W, I*

Wood, G.W. (Leicester) 1914 *W*

Wood, M.B. (Wasps) 2000 *C* 2*(R), US (R)*

Wood, R. (Liversedge) 1894 *I*

Wood, R.D. (Liverpool OB) 1901 *I*, 1903 *W, I*

Woodgate, E.E. (Paignton) 1952 *W*

Woodhead, E. (Huddersfield) 1880 *I*

Woodman, T.J. (Gloucester) 1999 *US (R)*, 2000 *I (R), It (R)*, 2001 *W (R), It (R)*, 2002 *NZ*, 2003 *S (R), I(t + R), A*

Woodruff, C.G. (Harlequins) 1951 *W, I, F, S*

Woods, S.M.J. (Cambridge U, Wellington) 1890 *W, S, I*, 1891 *W, I, S*, 1892 *I, S*, 1893 *W, I*, 1895 *W, I, S*

Woods, T. (Bridgwater) 1908 *S*

Woods, T. (United Services, RN) 1920 *S*, 1921 *W, I, S, F*

Woodward, C.R. (Leicester) 1980 *I (R), F, W, S*, 1981 *W, S, I, F, Arg* 1,2, 1982 *A, S, I, F, W*, 1983 *I, NZ*, 1984 *S, I, F, W*

Woodward, J.E. (Wasps) 1952 *SA, W, S*, 1953 *W, I, F, S*, 1954 *W, NZ, I, S, F*, 1955 *W, I*, 1956 *S*

Wooldridge, C.S. (Oxford U, Blackheath) 1883 *W, I, S*, 1884 *W, I, S*, 1885 *I*

Wordsworth, A.J. (Cambridge U) 1975 *A* 1*(R)*

Worsley, J.P.R. (Wasps) 1999 [*Tg, Fj*], 2000 *It (R), S (R), SA* 1*(R)*,2*(R)*, 2001 *It (R), S (R), F (R), C* 1,2, *US, A, R, SA*, 2002 *S, I, F, W (t+R), Arg*, 2003 *W* 1*(R), It, S(R), I(t), NZ (R), A (R)*

Worsley, M.A. (London Irish) 2003 *It(R)*

Worton, J.R.B. (Harlequins, Army) 1926 *W*, 1927 *W*

Wrench, D.F.B. (Harlequins) 1964 *F, S*

Wright, C.C.G. (Cambridge U, Blackheath) 1909 *I, S*

Wright, F.T. (Edinburgh Acady, Manchester) 1881 *S*

Wright, I.D. (Northampton) 1971 *W, I, F, S (R)*

Wright. J.C. (Met Police) 1934 *W*

Wright, J.F. (Bradford) 1890 *W*

Wright, T.P. (Blackheath) 1960 *W, I, F, S*, 1961 *SA, W, I, F, S*, 1962 *W, I, F, S*

Wright, W.H.G. (Plymouth) 1920 *W, F*

Wyatt, D.M. (Bedford) 1976 *S (R)*

Y

Yarranton, P.G. (RAF, Wasps) 1954 *W, NZ, I*, 1955 *F, S*

Yates, K.P. (Bath) 1997 *Arg* 1,2

Yiend, W. (Hartlepool R, Gloucester) 1889 *M*, 1892 *W, I, S*, 1893 *I, S*

Young, A.T. (Cambridge U, Blackheath, Army) 1924 *W, I, F, S*, 1925 *NZ, F*, 1926 *I, F, S*, 1927 *I, S, F*, 1928 *A, W, I, F, S*, 1929 *I*

Young, J.R.C. (Oxford U, Harlequins) 1958 *I*, 1960 *W, I, F, S*, 1961 *SA, W, I, F*

Young, M. (Gosforth) 1977 *S, I, F, W*, 1978 *F, W, S, I, NZ*, 1979 *S*

Young, P.D. (Dublin Wands) 1954 *W, NZ, I, S, F*, 1955 *W, I, F, S*

Youngs, N.G. (Leicester) 1983 *I, NZ*, 1984 *S, I, F, W*

OTHER TITLES IN THE SERIES

The Essential History of...

Football		
Arsenal	Rab MacWilliam/Kevin Connolly	*0 7553 1267 8*
Blackburn Rovers	Mike Jackman	*0 7553 1022 5*
Celtic	Graham McColl/George Sheridan	*0 7553 1141 8*
Charlton Athletic	Paul Clayton	*0 7553 1020 9*
England	Andrew Mourant/Jack Rollin	*0 7553 1142 6*
Everton	Mark Platt	*0 7553 1274 0**
Leeds United	Andrew Mourant	*0 7553 1170 1**
Leicester City	Tony Matthews	*0 7553 1023 3*
Liverpool	Alex Murphy/Eric Doig	*0 7553 1268 6*
Manchester City	Ian Penney	*0 7553 1168 X**
Manchester United	Ivan Ponting/Cliff Butler	*0 7553 1269 4*
Middlesbrough	Richard Jones	*0 7553 1143 4*
Newcastle United	Paul Joannou/Bill Swann/Steve Corke	*0 7553 1270 8*
Rangers	Stephen Halliday	*0 7553 1145 0*
West Bromwich Albion	Gavin McOwan	*0 7553 1146 9*
West Ham United	Kirk Blows/Tony Hogg	*0 7553 1169 8**
Rugby Union		
Scotland	Nick Oswald/John Griffiths	*0 7553 1272 4*
Wales	Steve Lewis/John Griffiths	*0 7553 1273 2*

* *Trade paperback editions*

Please contact your local WHSmith store for details about ordering any of these titles.